THE ECLIPSES OF JOHN'S BOOK OF REVELATION

THE ECLIPSES OF JOHN'S BOOK OF REVELATION

MATKO UTROBIČIĆ

RESOURCE *Publications* • Eugene, Oregon

THE ECLIPSES OF JOHN'S BOOK OF REVELATION

Copyright © 2024 Matko Utrobičić. All rights reserved. Except for brief quotations in critical publications or reviews, no part of this book may be reproduced in any manner without prior written permission from the publisher. Write: Permissions, Wipf and Stock Publishers, 199 W. 8th Ave., Suite 3, Eugene, OR 97401.

Resource Publications
An Imprint of Wipf and Stock Publishers
199 W. 8th Ave., Suite 3
Eugene, OR 97401

www.wipfandstock.com

PAPERBACK ISBN: 978-1-6667-8122-9
HARDCOVER ISBN: 978-1-6667-8123-6
EBOOK ISBN: 978-1-6667-8124-3
VERSION NUMBER 04/11/24

All Scripture quotations, unless otherwise indicated, are taken from the Holy Bible, New International Version®, NIV®. Copyright © 1973, 1978, 1984 by Biblica, Inc.™ Used by permission of Zondervan. All rights reserved worldwide. www.zondervan.com The "NIV" and "New International Version" are trademarks registered in the United States Patent and Trademark Office by Biblica, Inc.™

Scripture quotations taken from the (NASB®) New American Standard Bible®, Copyright © 1960, 1971, 1977, 1995, 2020 by The Lockman Foundation. Used by permission. All rights reserved. lockman.org

The heavens declare the glory of God.

Ps 19:1

Contents

List of Illustrations and Tables | x

Abbreviations | xii

INTRODUCTION | 1
    The Problem and the Method | 1

THE REVELATION IN THE LITERATURE | 4
    Sources | 4
        Justin Martyr | 4
        Irenaeus | 5
        Papias | 7
        Hippolytus | 8
        Tertullian | 9
        Epiphanius | 11
        Futurism and Preterism | 12
    Linguistic Analysis | 15
        Dionysius's Comments on the Revelation | 15
        Modern Linguistic Analysis | 21
    Recent Interpretations | 23
    Main Features of Space and Time | 26
        Alexandria | 27
        Greece | 30
        Christianity | 32
        Essenes and Therapeuts | 33
        Ebionites | 34
        Anti-heresiarchs | 36
        Gnostics | 36
        Ophites, Naassenes, Peratae, and Sethians | 37

Monoimus | 38
　　Cainites | 38
　　Epiphanus | 39
　　Carpocrates | 39
　　Cerinthus | 40
　　Marcion | 40
　　Basilides | 41
　　Valentinus | 41
　　Marcus | 44
　　Bardaesan | 45
　　Apocryphal Literature | 46
　　Nag Hammadi Library | 50

　Connections Betwen the Revelation and Other Religious Systems | 51

TEXT ANALYSIS | 62

　The Number of the Beast | 62
　　A Name—A Mystery | 64

　Iconography | 69

　The Son of Man | 76
　　Berosus | 82

　Composition | 87
　　The Seven Seals | 88
　　Zand-i Vohuman Yasht | 91
　　The Seals and the Trumpets | 95
　　Astrology | 96
　　The Fifth Seal and the Fifth Trumpet | 99
　　The Sixth Seal and the Sixth Trumpet | 100
　　Composition | 108

　Historical Background | 110
　　Armenia | 113
　　Number of Man's Name | 119
　　Armageddon | 120

DATING | 131

　Apocalypse is the Unity of Heavenly and Earthly Events | 131
　　Astronomy | 131
　　Babylon | 134

Alexandria | 138
　　　John's Observations | 143
　First Event | 145
　　　Famine | 150
　　　Invasion | 154
　Second Event | 155
　Third Event | 175
　　　Ascension of Isaiah | 181
　Fourth Event | 183
　　　Fire of Rome | 188
　A Message to the Churches | 192
　　　A Message to the Churches | 193
　　　Balaam | 199
　　　Jezebel | 201
　　　Nicolaites | 203

JOHN'S THEOLOGY | 207

　Exegesis | 207
　　　The New Jerusalem | 215
　　　Pistis Sophia | 221
　Synthesis | 223
　The Way of the Soul | 226
　John | 228
　　　Philo | 231
　　　The Symbolism of the Revelation | 234

SUMMARY | 237

Bibliogrpaphy | 245

Index | 261

List of Illustrations and Tables

Figure 1. Cosmology of the Revelation

Figure 2. Composition of the Revelation at the cosmological level

Figure 3. Composition of the Revelation at the historic level

Figure 4. John's schedule of events

Figure 5. Apollo (Castor) above the eclipse on 31 May AD 48

Figure 6. Position of the planets on the ecliptic on 23 May AD 60 (Cartes du Ciel)

Figure 6a. Position of the planets on the ecliptic on 23 May AD 60 (Cartes du Ciel)

Figure 7. Transit of Venus at its maximum at dawn on 23 May AD 60 (Cartes du Ciel)

Figure 8. Planet position on the ecliptic on 23 May AD 60

Figure 9. Planets arrangement on the ecliptic on 23 May AD 60

Figure 10. Algol at the zenith at moonrise (Cartes du Ciel)

Figure 11. Planet alignment on the ecliptic on 5 November AD 63 (Cartes du Ciel)

Figure 12. Moon and Venus occultation on 5 November AD 63

Table 1. Table of the name number of the Sun (Agrippa. *Of Occult Philosophy*, II)

Table 2. Position of the star Castor (Apollo) on 31 May AD 48

Table 3. Solar eclipses near the star Castor (Apollo) from the beginning of the first century till the middle second century

Table 4. Relative positions of the Moon, the Sun, and Venus in the sky on 31 May AD 48 at 10h33m

LIST OF ILLUSTRATIONS AND TABLES

Table 5. Phases of the transit of Venus on 23 May AD 60

Table 6. Relative positions of the Sun and Venus in the sky on 23 May AD 60

Table 7. Relative positions of the Moon, Regulus and Algol on 23 May AD 60

Table 8. Moon and Regulus rising time and Algol climax on 23 May AD 60 at 9h29m

Table 9. Sequence of the planets risings, culminations, and settings on 4/5 November AD 63

Table 10. Comparison of meanings of the same events in the Revelation by the levels

Abbreviations

1 En—1 Enoch

1 John—1 John (Epistle)

1 Kgs—1 Kings

2 Kgs—2 Kings

2 Pet—2 Peter

Acts—Acts of the Apostles

Col—Colossians

Dan—Daniel

Gen—Genesis

Isa—Isaiah

Jer—Jeremiah

John—John (Gospel)

Luke—Luke

Mark—Mark

Matt—Matthew

Mic—Micah

Neh—Nehemiah

Num—Numbers

PG—Patrologia Graeca

Ps—Psalms

Rev—Revelation

Introduction

THE PROBLEM AND THE METHOD

The Revelation is the only apocalyptic book of the New Testament, the canonical text ending the New Testament, a book entirely oriented to the future as an announcement of the *parousia*, the second coming of Christ. It is also among the most controversial and books most difficult to understand, on which numberless papers, books, and interpretations have been written by the best scholars, both Biblical-liturgical and scientific. The various methods applied in the attempts to understand its contents have almost exhausted all the possibilities, and recent researchers are getting closer and closer to the final conclusion that its contents are surrealistic and incomprehensible and its function to be repetition and succession of symbols aimed to arousing religious emotions and moods through announcing mystic events and, this way, helping in constituting a new Christian community, rather than announcing a true prophecy on what "is to happen soon." The book of Revelation is also known as the John's Revelation or the John's Apocalypse (*Apokálypsis Ioánnou*), later on its common title to become the Apocalypse of the Theologians (*Apokálypsis toú Theológou*). In some manuscripts, the title adds John's name. The title comes from the first words of the book: "The Revelation of Jesus Christ" (Rev 1:1 NASB). The Son of Man brings to John God's message on what is soon to happen, which he writes to the churches in Asia Minor, prophesying great calamities, the battle of Armageddon, and restoration of peace after Christ's second coming, which is to last one thousand years, closing Satan until the final judgment against him.

Even Eusebius, in the early fourth century, in his *Church History* included the Revelation in the Antilegomena, the list of books of unclear contents or in the interpretation of which there are disputes and controversies in the first church.

> Among the disputed writings [*ton antilegoménon*], which are nevertheless recognized by many, are extant the so-called epistle

of James and that of Jude, also the second epistle of Peter, and those that are called the second and third of John, whether they belong to the evangelist or to another person of the same name.

Among the rejected writings must be reckoned also the Acts of Paul, and the so-called Shepherd, and the Apocalypse of Peter, and in addition to these the extant epistle of Barnabas, and the so-called Teachings of the Apostles; and besides, as I said, the Apocalypse of John, if it seem proper, which some, as I said, reject, but which others class with the accepted books. And among these some have placed also the Gospel according to the Hebrews, with which those of the Hebrews that have accepted Christ are especially delighted. And all these may be reckoned among the disputed books [*ton antilegoménon*].[1]

The first to mention the Revelation was Justin Martyr in his *Dialogue with Trypho, a Jew*, followed by Irenaeus in *Against Heresies* and Tertullian in *Apology*.

According to Irenaeus and Dionysius the Revelation was very popular and widely accepted in the first Christian community but was accompanied with misunderstanding and doubts from the very beginning. The first to state that the Revelation is neither apostolic nor prophetic book, and that it neither knows nor teaches on Christ, was Martin Luther. Gregory of Nyssa, a fourth century bishop, and others disagreed about including the Revelation in the New Testament canon. The Christians of Syria refused it because of its the close links with Montanism, only to have accepted it later on. However, this is the only biblical book not used in the Eastern Orthodox Church liturgy.

The author introduces himself as John and says he was on the island of Patmos, where he saw the vision he is now passing onto the churches in Asia Minor: those in Ephesus, Smyrna, Pergamum, Thyatira, Sardis, Philadelphia, and Laodicea. The tradition has it that John, the author of the Revelation, the Epistles, and the Gospel, was expelled to the island at the time of Domitian, where he saw the events he described in his book, which he wrote once he returned from Patmos to Ephesus, sometime at the time of Nerva in the years 95–96.

The theories on the common authorship brings forth the matter of similarity between the Revelation and the Gospel: both texts are soteriological and state Christ as the Word of God, although their contexts are completely different. Explaining the differences is attempted by plain description of the events (Rev 1:11; 10:4; 14:3; 19:9; 21:5), but also by the oath and the warning that nothing is to be changed: "I warn everyone who hears

---

1. Eusebius, *Church History*, bk. 3, ch. 25.

the words of the prophecy of this book: If anyone adds anything to them, God will add to him the plagues described in this book. And if anyone takes words away from this book of prophecy, God will take away from him his share in the tree of life and in the holy city, which are described in this book" (Rev 22:18–19).

Christian authors hesitate about the apostolic authorship of the Revelation. Justin Martyr, Irenaeus, and Tertullian in the second century deem John to be the author, this being continued in the third century by Clement of Alexandria and Origen, and later on by Lactantius and Methodius. Dionysius rejects this assertion, Eusebius deems the Revelation to be disputable, Jerome diminishes its importance, whereas it completely disappears in the Syrian *peshitta* version of the New Testament.

A large number of modern scholars deem the authors of the Revelation, the Epistles and the Gospel to be three different persons, proving this firstly by linguistic evidence.

J. Massyngberde Ford relates the Revelation to John the Baptist,[2] the Syrian tradition and Tertullian date it to the time of Nero, from Irenaeus on to the time of Domitian (although the intensity of the persecutions that he initiated is questionable), and Epiphanius of Salamis to the time of Claudius (PG 41:909–10).

---

2. Ford, *Revelation*.

The Revelation in the Literature

SOURCES

The problem of dating the Revelation in accordance with the texts from the times immediately after its appearance comes down to the comments by Tertullian and Irenaeus. While Irenaeus is explicit, stating the time of creation to be the time of Domitian, Tertullian states no precise time, but by mentioning in a sentence the martyrdom of Peter, Paul, and John, he suggests the same source and story, obviously of an old date and appearing in apocryphal texts, mentioning his writing on joint martyrdom of the three apostles in a wider context of the story that explicitly dates the Revelation and the John's exile to Patmos to the time of Nero.

The date stated by Irenaeus is accepted by Hippolytus,[1] Victorinus of Poetovio in *The Comments on the Revelation*, Eusebius of Caesarea in *Chronicle* and *Church History*, and Jerome in *On Illustrious Men*. Victorinus places Nero in the center of the events (DICLVX),[2] whereas Eusebius in his late work *The Proof of the Gospel* quotes Tertullian's and not Irenaeus's date. Epiphanius in *Panarion* dates it to the time of Claudius. Some authors deny the text its apostolic authorship, even the Christian contents, deeming it a heretic work.

Justin Martyr

Justin Martyr was born around the year 100 in Flavia Neapolis. Around 130 he accepted Christianity and defended it in Asia Minor and Rome, to have suffered martyrdom around the year 165.[3]

---

1. Jerome, *On Illustrious Men*, §61 comments on Hippolytus.
2. Nero Redivivus—Victorinus mentions the legend that Nero will return and take revenge on his enemies. The transposition of the number 666 (in the Roman numeral system DCLXVI) gives DICLVX.
3. Martyrdom after the *Chronicon Paschale*.

With Justin starts the post-apostolic era, and he is deemed to be the founder of theological literature. He wrote two books, *Refutation* and *Dialog with Trypho, a Jew*. He mentions John by name, stating he is an apostle: "And further, there was a certain man with us, whose name was John, one of the apostles of Christ, who prophesied, by a revelation that was made to him, that those who believed in our Christ would dwell a thousand years in Jerusalem; and that thereafter the general, and, in short, the eternal resurrection and judgment of all men would likewise take place. Just as our Lord also said, 'They shall neither marry nor be given in marriage, but shall be equal to the angels, the children of the God of the resurrection.'"[4]

According to Justin, John prophesied that those who believed in Christ would dwell a thousand years in Jerusalem, and that soon the general resurrection and the judgment day would take place. Justin's *Dialogue with Trypho, a Jew* has lots of idealized autobiographical information and states that he talked to Trypho while walking at Xist, probably a part of Ephesus. At the very beginning of the dialogue, Trypho introduces himself as a Jew who escaped from Israel during war, here meaning the Bar Kokhba revolt of 132–135, which would be a *terminus post quem*: "Then he told me openly his first and last name: 'Trypho,' says he, 'I am called; and I am a Hebrew of the circumcision, and having escaped from the war lately carried on there, and I am spending my days in Greece, and chiefly at Corinth.'"[5]

Irenaeus

Little is known about the life of Irenaeus, and even here there are contradictions. He was born in Asia Minor or in a neighboring province. As a young man he listened Polycarp, and during the exile initiated by Marcus Aurelius he was a bishop in Lyon. In the period of peace that followed after the persecutions he wrote texts against the gnostics and other heresies that spread over Gallia as well at the time. The time of his death is not certain. Most probably he died at the very end of the second or in the early third centuries, having ended his mission in martyrdom. His work is of an extraordinary importance because it gives evidence on the heroic time of the early church and the apostolic time that he was linked with through John's student Polycarp. He wrote a discussion in five volumes titled *Against Heresies*, where he opposes heresies in various early Christian communities. Another book of his is *The Proofs of Apostolic Preaching*. Other writings have been preserved in fragments only: *The Subject of Knowledge*, *On Monarchy*, and *On Ogdoad*

---

4. Justin Martyr, "Dialogue of Justin," ch. 81.
5. Justin Martyr, "Dialogue of Justin," ch. 1.

(against Valentinus), and a number of letters.[6] In *Against Heresies*, around the year 180, Irenaeus directly dates the Revelation at the end of the reign of Domitian (95–96). According to Irenaeus, John saw the events described in the Revelation at the time of Domitian, on the island of Patmos, where he was expelled because of Christ and the faith, written after the amnesty in the Nerva's time (96–97), as also said by John himself.[7] Irenaeus also claims that after leaving the exile, John also wrote the Gospel and the Epistles. In his claims Irenaeus relies on the tradition, especially on what he heard from those who had listened to the apostles—Polycarp and Papias. In this claim it is evident that John was sentenced to working in mines at Patmos when he was very old, whereafter he continued living in Ephesus and leading the church there, this also giving him enough time and energy to write. According to Irenaeus, John died four years later (in 100 or 101).

Irenaeus thinks, following analogies with Daniel, that in the Revelation, John foresees the war against the Lamb (Israel), that would be followed by nine kings serving Rome, of which eight will overpower the rest and devastate Babylon.[8] In the dispute about the beast's number, Irenaeus states that its number is proven in the oldest copies of the Revelation and testified by the people who saw John in life and who carried his witnessing. The beast's number shows its apostasy from the God in the beginning, now and at the end. Irenaeus warns of the incorrect stating of the Beast's number, in some texts being misstated as 656. Irenaeus confirms that the correct number is 666. Irenaeus finds the reason of the misunderstanding either in bad intentions or in mistakes made by the copyists, warning of the consequences of possible mistakes in guessing the name, because the antichrist can appear also under other names. For Irenaeus it is more acceptable and safer to wait for the prophesy to come true, in order to avoid a mistake, rather than to guess the antichrist's name, because he can change the name anyhow, and many names have the mentioned number. As an example he states three names that have the number 666 (Euanthas, Lateinos, Teitan).[9]

Obviously, the Revelation was popular and read at the Irenaeus's time, just as stated by Dionysius later on. Irenaeus saw several copies of the text, appeared in different variants, and he is obviously talking of the stratigraphy of copies that circled among the Christians in Asia Minor that existed

---

6. "St. Irenaeus."

7. "I, John, your brother and companion in the suffering and kingdom and patient endurance that are our in Jesus, was on the island of Patmos because of the word of God and the testimony of Jesus" (Rev 1:9).

8. Irenaeus, "Against Heresies: Book I," ch. 26.

9. Irenaeus, "Against Heresies: Book I," ch. 30.

already in his time. Expecting the second coming after the waste at the end of the time was very much spread.

Papias

Papias, as Irenaeus says, "listened to John and befriended Polycarp."[10] Although Papias himself states that he did not witness what the apostles were talking about, but that he received the truth of the faith from those who were with the apostles, among which he mentions John and John the Presbyter:

> But I shall not hesitate also to put down for you along with my interpretations whatsoever things I have at any time learned carefully from the elders and carefully remembered, guaranteeing their truth. For I did not, like the multitude, take pleasure in those that speak much, but in those that teach the truth; not in those that relate strange commandments, but in those that deliver the commandments given by the Lord to faith, and springing from the truth itself. If, then, any one came, who had been a follower of the elders, I questioned him in regard to the words of the elders, what Andrew or what Peter said, or what was said by Philip, or by Thomas, or by James, or by John, or by Matthew, or by any other of the disciples of the Lord, and what things Aristion and the presbyter John, the disciples of the Lord, say. For I did not think that what was to be gotten from the books would profit me as much as what came from the living and abiding voice.[11]

Although he himself wrote five books that have disappeared or are preserved in fragments, partly in Eusebius,[12] which describes him as a person of humble mind, Papias still shows mistrust of written word, giving advantage to what he had the opportunity to hear directly, that he as an authentic witness is certainly entitled to.[13]

---

10. "Still preserved is the testimony of this in the writing of Papias, who listened to John and was a friend of Polycarpus, in his fourth book of the five that he wrote." Irenaeus, "Against Heresies: Book V," ch. 33.

11. Eusebius, *Church History*, bk. 3, ch. 39.

12. Eusebius, *Church History*, bk. 3, ch. 29.

13. "St. Papias."

Hippolytus

Hippolytus of Portus (170-235) was a great writer of the early period, mentioned by Focius as a direct disciple of Irenaeus. He was a bishop of Rome, a martyr, and the first antipope in history, suspected for Montanistic heresy, but later on accepted in the church.[14] The controversies about him have been solved only by the finding of his *Refutation of All Heresies (Philosophumena)*. This work, except for some fragments preserved by other authors, was lost, only to be found almost entirely in the mid-nineteenth century in Armenia. Eight books have been preserved, whereas the second and the third are lost. Besides *Refutation of All Heresies*, found are fragments of his texts, collected in two books titled *Fragments*. In the first book of *Fragments*, Hippolytus briefly referred to the Revelation, much more in the second book. In the fourth book of *Refutation of All Heresies*, he widely elaborates the millenarianistic teaching that, obviously, has its traces in the Revelation as well. The millenarianism starts from the teaching that one God's day equals one thousand earth years, that is, that the time since the creation of the world is the recapitulation of the creation. That God created the world in six days, to have rested on the seventh, that is an analogy to the six thousand years since the creation, where after the kingdom of God will be established on earth to last a thousand years. The argument for this assertion is in astronomy, because in a period of sixty years all the planets will make whole numbers of their revolutions: Saturn 2, Jupiter 5, Venus 72, the Moon 720, etc. that, multiplied by one hundred, gives the period of six thousand years, when the stars will return to their initial positions, where they were when the world was created.[15] The time of birth of the Savior is 5500 years after the creation, and after lapsing six thousand years, the kingdom of God will occur to last one thousand years. The new Jerusalem will be on earth, not in the heavens. The millenarianism was strongly rooted in the minds of the people of the époque, as long as till Lactantius and the fourth century, being also Papias and Irenaeus that were infected with it.

---

14. Hippolytus, "On Christ and Antichrist," ch. 36: "For he sees, when in the isle Patmos, a revelation of awful mysteries, which he recounts freely, and makes known to others." Even Jerome mentions the Hippolytus's book on the Revelation in his *On Illustrious Men*, 61.

15. Cureton, *Spicilegium Syriacum*, 40.

Tertullian

Unlike Irenaeus, Tertullian states that John was sentenced to death in Rome and thrown in a vessel of hot oil. When he came out of the vessel unhurt, he was exiled to Patmos. Tertullian mentions the martyrdoms of Peter, Paul, and John in Rome in the same sentence, but does not say explicitly that all the three events happened at the same time: "How happy is the church, on which apostles poured forth all their doctrine along with their blood! Where Peter endures a passion like his Lord's! Where Paul wins his crown in a death like John's, where the Apostle John was first plunged, unhurt, into boiling oil, and thence remitted to his island-exile!"[16]

This very early dating of the story of the John's martyrdom is supported by the text in Polycarp's (Pseudo-Polycarp's) fragments preserved by Victor of Capua, the author of the *Codex Fuldensis* in the sixth century, where he mentions that John was immersed in a vessel with hot oil.[17]

Among the apocryphal works of the Peshitta group, in the Acts of the Apostles, there are two integral texts on the life and history of John the Apostle. One is from the fourth century and is kept in Oxford, the other from the sixth century and kept in Moscow. The Oxford copy repeats the Tertullian's story, but explicitly stating that John was exiled to Patmos in the Nero's time:

> Then they left and arrived to Rome around midnight, while the sinful Nero was sleeping, and the Lord sent to him an angel who appeared to him in flames with sword, and woke him up. And when he opened his eyes and saw him above himself, he cried and said: "Please, what have I got with you," and the angel replied to him, "Give back the man you took from Ephesus and exiled. If you do not do that this sword will have stab your sinful heart before the sunrise." Then the Angel hit him and robbed him of his speech, and he roared like a dog. And his servants came when they heard his howling and asked him: "What is happening, King the master?!" He showed and they brought to him ink and a sheet of paper, and he wrote: "Immediately—if possible today—release John, the son of Zebedee, the Galilean, who I took from Ephesus, to return there." And he also wrote and sent quickly word to Ephesus that anyone in prison is free to go and their will be honored.[18]

---

16. Tertullian, "Prescription against Heretics," ch. 36. Peter and Paul died in Rome as martyrs in the years 64 or 67.

17. Polycarp, "Fragments from Victor of Capua," §2.

18. Wright, *Apocryphal Acts of Apostles*, vol. II, The History of John.

This early dating is supported by the tradition of the church in Syria, according to which the Syrian version of the book of Revelation is titled *The Revelation Received by John the Evangelist from God at the Island of Patmos Where He Was Imprisoned by Caesar Nero*. The Syrian version of the Revelation is not clearly dated, and its authenticity is doubtful, especially because it was not used in the Syrian church liturgy. The *Peshitta* version of the Bible is among the oldest compositions, made as early as in the first and the very beginning of the second centuries. The Revelation was integrated neither then nor later. It was mentioned for the first time by Ephrem of Nisibis (?–378), when he commentated on almost the entire New Testament. The title of the Syrian Revelation shows the tradition that existed in the Ephrem's time, and that can be assumed to be much older. In his comments on this book, Andrew of Cappadocia (around 500) assumed Nero's date.

Victorinus of Poetovio follows the Irenaeus's dating: "And here there are seven kings, five of whom have fallen, one is, the seventh has not yet come, and when he does come he will remain only a little while" (Rev 17:10).[19] The time when the Revelation was written must be understood, because that was the time of the emperor Domitian, and before him had been Titus, his brother, Vespasian, Otho, Vitellius, and Galba. These five have fallen. Remaining is the one in whose time the Revelation was written—Domitian, this implying that the last who "has not yet come" is Nerva, "and when he does come he will remain only a little while," because he did not fulfill the two year period of time. Immediately after this he adds: "The Beast you saw is one of seven," because before these kings ruled Nero.[20] Victorinus does not mind placing Nero in the center of the events when dating the Revelation in the Domitian's time.

Eusebius in *Chronicle* (*Chronicon*) and *Church History* follows Irenaeus, stating the same arguments: "Domitian, having shown great cruelty toward many, and having unjustly put to death no small number of well-born and notable men at Rome, and having without cause exiled and confiscated the property of a great many other illustrious men, finally became a successor of Nero in his hatred and enmity toward God. He was in fact the second

---

19. Victorinus, "Commentary on the Apocalypse," ch. 10. "He says this, because when John said these things he was in the island of Patmos, condemned to the labour of the mines by Caesar Domitian. There, therefore, he saw the Apocalypse; and when grown old, he thought that he should at length receive his quittance by suffering, Domitian being killed, all his judgments were discharged. And John being dismissed from the mines, thus subsequently delivered the same Apocalypse which he had received from God. This, therefore, is what He says: Thou must again prophesy to all nations, because thou seest the crowds of Antichrist rise up; and against them other crowds shall stand, and they shall fall by the sword on the one side and on the other."

20. Victorinus, "Commentary on the Apocalypse," ch. 17.

that stirred up a persecution against us, although his father Vespasian had undertaken nothing prejudicial to us."[21] Whereas in his *The Proof of the Gospel* he accepts Tertullian's statement and mentions the martyrdoms of Peter, Paul, and John in a single sentence. "Afterwards James, the Lord's brother, whom of old the people of Jerusalem called 'the Just' for his extraordinary virtue, being asked by the chief priests, and teachers of the Jews what he taught about Christ, and answering that He was the Son of God, was also stoned by them. Peter was crucified head downwards at Rome, Paul beheaded, and John exiled to an island. Yet though they suffered thus, not one of the others gave up his intention, but they made their prayer to God that they themselves might suffer a like fate for their religion, and continued to bear witness to Jesus and His marvellous works with yet more boldness."[22]

Epiphanius

Clement of Alexandria comments the Revelation in accordance with Eusebius's *Church History*,[23] whereas Epiphanius dates it to Claudius's time, which is considered unreliable and exaggerated. Arethas of Caesarea, the bishop of Constantinople (around 850–944), dates the Revelation to the time of Nero and before the destruction of the temple:

> And He who gave this revelation to the Evangelist, declares, that these men shall not share the destruction inflicted by the Romans. For the ruin brought by the Romans had not yet fallen upon the Jews, when this Evangelist received these prophecies: and he did not receive them at Jerusalem, but in Ionia near Ephesus. For after the suffering of the Lord he remained only fourteen years at Jerusalem, during which time the tabernacle of the mother of the Lord, which had conceived this Divine offspring, was preserved in this temporal life, after the suffering and resurrection of her incorruptible Son. For he continued with her as with a mother committed to him by the Lord. For after her death it is reported that he no longer chose to remain in Judaea, but passed over to Ephesus, where, as we have said, this present Apocalypse also was composed; which is a revelation of future things, inasmuch as forty years after the ascension of the Lord this tribulation came upon the Jews.[24]

---

21. Eusebius, *Church History*, bk. 18, ch. 8.
22. Eusebius, *Proof of the Gospel*, 134.
23. Eusebius, *Church History*, bk. 4, ch. 14.
24. Elliott, *Horae Apocalipticae*, 1:39.

The great Post-Nicene writer Jerome mentions the book *On the Revelation* written at Marcus Aurelius's time by the bishop of Sardi—Melito.[25] Of Greek texts here are also the texts by Ecumenius and Arethas. Besides Greek texts, there are Victorinus's long and short texts (*Commentary on the Apocalypse*), the texts by Primas, Bede, and others, belonging to the Latin circle, and Syrian commentaries of which the most important are those by Bar Salib and Joachim, abbot of Flora.

Among the external proofs there are no decisive elements by which one could decide about dating in the times of Nero or Domitian, because their statements are taken from various sources and do not make authentic testimonies. Among the elements supporting Domitian's date is the interpretation of the letters to the churches in Asia Minor, meaning these had to be developed and organized at the time so that John could have called them to fulfill their obligations that he mentioned. On the other side, objectively the most powerful argument is the statement in the Revelation that John saw the events "in the time of the sixth king," this indicating that the Revelation is a sort of chronicle, wherefore this information can be harmonized with Nero who was the sixth king/Roman emperor counting after Julius Caesar, which is hard to harmonize with Domitian (see Victorinus).

For the time being this question is to be left open, and it is certain that the answers are not to be sought externally but in the very text, meaning that in dealing with the date when the Revelation was written, the very book itself is to be interpreted and John's prophecy is to be clarified. As believed by the first church, according to Matthew and Luke, Christ's second coming is expected during the lifetime of the generation to which Jesus spoke, so the judgment is expected around forty years after the resurrection or around the year 70, when the eclipses of the Sun and the Moon and earthquakes will announce the coming as a lightning flashing from east to west. Matthew and Mark call for vigilance because the coming will happen unexpectedly and will be followed by appearances of false prophets. In his Second Epistle, Peter says that the word of the prophecy has been confirmed and that it is to be "paid attention to until the Day dawns and the Morning Star rises in your hearts" (2 Pet 1:19).

Futurism and Preterism

In the interpretations of John's prophecy there are two contrasting opinions. While some deem the Revelation to be a book completely oriented to the future and describing events of the end times, calling the believers to

---

25. Jerome, *On Illustrious Men*, §24.

readiness, others deem this to be a prophecy that was fulfilled long time ago and that everything that John prophesied in metaphors actually happened sometime in the past.

Each of these two opinions has its subdivision. The preterists are divided to full and partial preterists, the former deeming the prophecies to have been fulfilled during the generation that Christ spoke to, according to Luke (Luke 21:1–37) and Matthew (Matt 24:2), which can be taken as forty years after the passion, or according to Matthew (Matt 24:2) as the announcement of the destruction of the temple in the year 70, which is a sign of war and destruction preceding the coming, or by the end of the second century at latest. The others, the partial preterists, deem that John described the long historic process and the historic development of the church.

The issue of interpretation and predictability of events opens the question to whether the time of the events of the end times, preceding the final end of the world and the beginning of the God's kingdom, either in the heavens or on the earth, is defined or not, that is, whether the events have already happened. The interpretation mostly goes in the direction of treating this text as a true prophecy, the fulfillment of which is not exactly time defined—this also being the standing of the Catholic Church. This opinion is amillenarianistic and deems that the time of fulfillment of John's prophecy depends on God's providence. Opposite of this is the millenarianistic standing that starts from the thesis that one day of God's creation equals a period of time of one thousand earth years, and that at the end of six thousand years after creation, the time of peace and prosperity begins. This understanding is based on direct interpretation of Peter's Second Epistle: "But do not forget this one thing, my friends: With the Lord a day is like a thousand years, and a thousand years are like a day" (2 Pet 3:8), although later on he calls for patience because "the Lord is not slow in keeping his promise, as some understand slowness. He is patient with you, not wanting anyone to perish, but everyone to come to repentance" (2 Pet 3:9).

What the world will be like after the second coming is illustrated by a fragment from Papias's writing inspired by the Revelation:

> As the elders who saw John the disciple of the Lord remembered that they had heard from him how the Lord taught in regard to those times, and said: "The days will come in which vines shall grow, having each ten thousand branches, and in each branch ten thousand twigs, and in each true twig ten thousand shoots, and in every one of the shoots ten thousand clusters, and on every one of the clusters ten thousand grapes, and every grape when pressed will give five-and-twenty metretes of wine. And when any one of the saints shall lay hold of a cluster, another shall cry

out, 'I am a better cluster, take me; bless the Lord through me.' In like manner, [he said] that a grain of wheat would produce ten thousand ears, and that every ear would have ten thousand grains, and every grain would yield ten pounds of clear, pure, fine flour; and that apples, and seeds, and grass would produce in similar proportions; and that all animals, feeding then only on the productions of the earth, would become peaceable and harmonious, and be in perfect subjection to man." Testimony is borne to these things in writing by Papias, an ancient man, who was a hearer of John and a friend of Polycarp, in the fourth of his books; for five books were composed by him. And he added, saying, "Now these things are credible to believers. And Judas the traitor, says he, not believing, and asking, 'How shall such growths be accomplished by the Lord.' The Lord said, 'They shall see who shall come to them.' These, then, are the times mentioned by the prophet Isaiah: 'And the wolf shall lie down with the lamb.'"[26]

Interpretations of the divine revelation in the modern church practice come down to the assertion formed at the First Vatican Council of 1870, where presented were standings that the human mind cannot fully perceive mysteries, but that God can intervene by addressing man either directly or through an intermediary (prophet). This is a brief interpretation of the standing published in the conclusions of the First Vatican Council titled *De fide catholica*. In the text *Lamentabili* of 1907, published is that the truths represented by the church are revealed from the heavens. In the last centuries the church proclaimed unacceptable various teachings, including the teaching of Anton Günther who deemed the Revelation to be a proclamation for each particular time, wherefore it changes as human knowledge develops, the "modernist" teaching challenging the possibility of communication with the God, and the "pragmatic" teaching deeming revelations in general to be fillings in the gaps of human knowledge based on analogies. These and various other standings motivated the decision of the church published in *De fide catholica* (chapter 2, canon 2) calling for anathema on all who dare claiming that divine mysteries do not exist and that teaching on faith can be explained rationally.

---

26. Papias, "Fragments," ch. 4.

LINGUISTIC ANALYSIS

The church tradition does not support exclusively the Domitian's time. The above quotations lead to the conclusion that, basically, there are only two basic dates, followed by others: Irenaeus's and Tertullian's, and that all the authors follow the authorities of their predecessors, starting from the assumption that the Revelation was written by John the apostle and evangelist. However, the doubt about the apostolic authorship of the Revelation exists from the first times. The first to put this question and analyze it chapter by chapter was Dionysius, the bishop of Alexandria, a student of the great Origen.[27] Dionysus argued with Nepos who totally rejected the Revelation, and who on this wrote the work *Refutation of the Allegorists*, claiming that it was no prophecy and that its very title was fake, and that the author was not John but Cerinthus, a heretic who loved pleasures of the flesh. This is the content of the Cerinthus's teaching: "The kingdom of Christ will be an earthly one. And as he was himself devoted to the pleasures of the body and altogether sensual in his nature, he dreamed that that kingdom would consist in those things which he desired, namely, in the delights of the belly and of sexual passion, that is to say, in eating and drinking and marrying, and in festivals and sacrifices and the slaying of victims, under the guise of which he thought he could indulge his appetites with a better grace."[28] On this Eusebius wrote in his *Church History*: "Some before us have set aside and rejected the book altogether, criticizing it chapter by chapter, and pronouncing it without sense or argument, and maintaining that the title is fraudulent. For they say that it is not the work of John, nor is it a revelation, because it is covered thickly and densely by a veil of obscurity. And they affirm that none of the apostles, and none of the saints, nor any one in the Church is its author, but that Cerinthus, who founded the sect which was called after him the Cerinthian, desiring reputable authority for his fiction, prefixed the name."[29]

Dionysius's Comments on the Revelation

Dionysius does not reject the Revelation: "But I could not venture to reject the book, as many brethren hold it in high esteem. But I suppose that it is beyond my comprehension, and that there is a certain concealed and more

---

27. Dionysius lived from 200 to 265. On Dionysius from Eusebius: Church History, bks. 6, 7; Preparation for the Gospel, bk. 14.
28. Eusebius, *Church History*, bk. 3, ch. 28.
29. Eusebius, *Church History*, bk. 7, ch. 25.

wonderful meaning in every part. For if I do not understand I suspect that a deeper sense lies beneath the words. I do not measure and judge them by my own reason, but leaving the more to faith I regard them as too high for me to grasp. And I do not reject what I cannot comprehend, but rather wonder because I do not understand it."[30]

Dionysius replies that he cannot reject this book as many brothers have very high opinion on it. In it he sees some secret and exceptional things, although he cannot understand them. By comparing the Gospel and the Epistles to the Revelation, Dionysus concludes that the Revelation was probably written by someone called John, he himself stating so, but that this is not John the son of Zebedee. He finds a possible author in John who came to Pergamum in Pamphylia with Paul of Paphos, to return to Jerusalem from there, or someone who lived in Asia Minor.

Further on, Eusebius comments the Dionysus's analysis:

> After having examined the entire Book of Revelation, and showed that it was impossible to understand it by its literal meaning, he proceeds as follows:
>
> "Having finished the entire prophecy, so to speak, the Prophet pronounces those blessed who shall observe it, and also himself. For he says, 'Blessed is he that keeps the words of the prophecy of this book, and I, John, who saw and heard these things.'"
>
> Therefore that he was called John, and that this book is the work of one John, I do not deny. And I agree also that it is the work of a holy and inspired man. But I cannot readily admit that he was the apostle, the son of Zebedee, the brother of James, by whom the Gospel of John and the Catholic Epistle were written.
>
> "For I judge from the character of both, and the forms of expression, and the entire execution of the book, that it is not his. For the evangelist nowhere gives his name, or proclaims himself, either in the Gospel or Epistle."
>
> Further on he adds: "But John never speaks as if referring to himself, or as if referring to another person. But the author of the Apocalypse introduces himself at the very beginning: 'The Revelation of Jesus Christ, which he gave him to show unto his servants quickly; and he sent and signified it by his angel unto his servant John, who bare witness of the word of God and of his testimony, even of all things that he saw.'"
>
> Then he writes also an epistle: "John to the seven churches which are in Asia, grace be with you, and peace." But the evangelist did not prefix his name even to the Catholic Epistle; but

---

30. Eusebius, *Church History*, bk. 7, ch. 25.

THE REVELATION IN THE LITERATURE 17

without introduction he begins with the mystery of the divine revelation itself: "That which was from the beginning, which we have heard, which we have seen with our eyes." For because of such a revelation the Lord also blessed Peter, saying, "Blessed art thou, Simon Bar-Jonah, for flesh and blood hath not revealed it unto thee, but my heavenly Father." (Matt 16:17)

But neither in the reputed Second or Third epistle of John, though they are very short, does the name John appear; but there is written the anonymous phrase, "the eider." But this author did not consider it sufficient to give his name once and to proceed with his work; but he takes it up again: "I, John, who also am your brother and companion in tribulation, and in the kingdom and in the patience of Jesus Christ, was in the isle that is called Patmos for the Word of God and the testimony of Jesus." And toward the close he speaks thus: "Blessed is he that keeps the words of the prophecy of this book, and I, John, who saw and heard these things."

"But that he who wrote these things was called John must be believed, as he says it; but who he was does not appear. For he did not say, as often in the Gospel, that he was the beloved disciple of the Lord, or the one who lay on his breast, or the brother of James, or the eyewitness and hearer of the Lord.

"For he would have spoken of these things if he had wished to show himself plainly. But he says none of them; but speaks of himself as our brother and companion, and a witness of Jesus, and blessed because he had seen and heard the revelations.

"But I am of the opinion that there were many with the same name as the apostle John, who, on account of their love for him, and because they admired and emulated him, and desired to be loved by the Lord as he was, took to themselves the same surname, as many of the children of the faithful are called Paul or Peter."

[But in the Acts of the Apostles] "there is also another John, surnamed Mark, whom Barnabas and Paul took with them; of whom also it is said, 'And they had also John as their attendant.' (Acts 13:5) But that it is he who wrote this, I would not say. For it not written that he went with them into Asia, but, 'Now when Paul and his company set sail from Paphos, they came to Perga in Pamphylia and John departing from them returned to Jerusalem'" (Acts 13:13).

"But I think that he was some other one of those in Asia; as they say that there are two graves in Ephesus, each bearing the name of John.

"And from the ideas, and from the words and their arrangement, it may be reasonably conjectured that this one is different from that one.

"For the Gospel and Epistle agree with each other and begin in the same manner. The one says, 'In the beginning was the Word' (John 1:14); the other, 'That which was from the beginning.' The one: 'And the Word was made flesh and dwelt among us, and we beheld his glory, the glory as of the only begotten of the Father'; the other says the same things slightly altered: 'Which we have heard, which we have seen with our eyes; which we have looked upon and our hands have handled of the Word of life, and the life was manifested'" (1 John 1:1, 4:2, 2–3).

"For he introduces these things at the beginning, maintaining them, as is evident from what follows, in opposition to those who said that the Lord had not come in the flesh. Wherefore also he carefully adds, 'And we have seen and bear witness, and declare unto you the eternal life which was with the Father and was manifested unto us. That which we have seen and heard declare we unto you also.'

"He holds to this and does not digress from his subject, but discusses everything under the same heads and names some of which we will briefly mention.

"Any one who examines carefully [Gospel, First Epistle] will find the phrases, 'the life,' 'the light,' 'turning from darkness,' frequently occurring in both; also continually, 'truth,' 'grace,' 'joy,' 'the flesh and blood of the Lord,' 'the judgment,' 'the forgiveness of sins,' 'the love of God toward us,' the 'commandment that we love one another,' that we should 'keep all the commandments'; the 'conviction of the world, of the Devil, of Antichrist,' the 'promise of the Holy Spirit,' the 'adoption of God,' the 'faith continually required of us,' 'the Father and the Son,' occur everywhere. In fact, it is plainly to be seen that one and the same character marks the Gospel and the Epistle throughout.

"But the Apocalypse is different from these writings and foreign to them; not touching, nor in the least bordering upon them; almost, so to speak, without even a syllable in common with them.

"Nay more, the Epistle, for I pass by the Gospel, does not mention nor does it contain any intimation of the Apocalypse, nor does the Apocalypse of the Epistle. But Paul, in his epistles, gives some indication of his revelations, though he has not written them out by themselves.

"Moreover, it can also be shown that the, diction of the Gospel and Epistle differs from that of the Apocalypse.

"For they were written not only without error as regards the Greek language, but also with elegance in their expression, in their reasonings, and in their entire structure. They are far indeed from betraying any barbarism or solecism, or any vulgarism whatever. For the writer had, as it seems, both the requisites of discourse, that is, the gift of knowledge and the gift of expression, as the Lord had bestowed them both upon him.

"I do not deny that the other writer saw a revelation and received knowledge and prophecy. I perceive, however, that his dialect and language are not accurate Greek, but that he uses barbarous idioms, and, in some places, solecisms. It is unnecessary to point these out here, for I would not have any one think that I have said these things in a spirit of ridicule, for I have said what I have only with the purpose of showing dearly the difference between the writings."[31]

Dionysius wrote two books *On Promises*, where he discusses the theological disputes brought into the Church by millenarianism. The above quotes relate to the Revelation that is being used as an argument in favor of the millenniarists under the circumstances commented and described by Dionysus in the first book:

> As [Nepos] taught that he could establish his private opinion [i.e., the millenarianism] by the Revelation of John, he wrote a book on this subject, entitled Refutation of Allegorists.
>
> Dionysius opposes this in his books on the Promises. In the first he gives his own opinion of the dogma; and in the second he treats of the Revelation of John, and mentioning Nepos at the beginning, writes of him in this manner:
>
> "But since they bring forward a certain work of Nepos, on which they rely confidently, as if it proved beyond dispute that there will be a reign of Christ upon earth, I confess that in many other respects I approve and love Nepos, for his faith and industry and diligence in the Scriptures, and for his extensive psalmody, with which many of the brethren are still delighted; and I hold him in the more reverence because he has gone to rest before us. But the truth should be loved and honored most of all. And while we should praise and approve ungrudgingly what is said aright, we ought to examine and correct what does not seem to have been written soundly.
>
> "Were he present to state his opinion orally, mere unwritten discussion, persuading and reconciling those who are opposed by question and answer, would be sufficient. But as some

---

31. Eusebius, *Church History*, bk. 7, ch. 25.

think his work very plausible, and as certain teachers regard the law and prophets as of no consequence, and do not follow the Gospels, and treat lightly the apostolic epistles, while they make promises as to the teaching of this work as if it were some great hidden mystery, and do not permit our simpler brethren to have any sublime and lofty thoughts concerning the glorious and truly divine appearing of our Lord, and our resurrection from the dead, and our being gathered together unto him, and made like him, but on the contrary lead them to hope for small and mortal things in the kingdom of God, and for things such as exist now, since this is the case, it is necessary that we should dispute with our brother Nepos as if he were present." Further on he says:

"When I was in the district of Arsinoe, where, as you know, this doctrine has prevailed for a long time, so that schisms and apostasies of entire churches have resulted, I called together the presbyters and teachers of the brethren in the villages, such brethren as wished being also present—and I exhorted them to make a public examination of this question.

"Accordingly when they brought me this book, as if it were a weapon and fortress impregnable, sitting with them from morning till evening for three successive days, I endeavored to correct what was written in it.

"And I rejoiced over the constancy, sincerity, docility, and intelligence of the brethren, as we considered in order and with moderation the questions and the difficulties and the points of agreement. And we abstained from defending in every manner and contentiously the opinions which we had once held, unless they appeared to be correct. Nor did we evade objections, but we endeavored as far as possible to hold to and confirm the things which lay before us, and if the reason given satisfied us, we were not ashamed to change our opinions and agree with others; but on the contrary, conscientiously and sincerely, and with hearts laid open before God, we accepted whatever was established by the proofs and teachings of the Holy Scriptures.

"And finally the author and mover of this teaching, who was called Coracion, in the hearing of all the brethren that were present, acknowledged and testified to us that he would no longer hold this opinion, nor discuss it, nor mention nor teach it, as he was fully convinced by the arguments against it. And some of the other brethren expressed their gratification at the conference, and at the spirit of conciliation and harmony which all had manifested."[32]

Dionysius's comments on the Revelation are of utmost importance. From the year 135 on, Christian authors uncritically attributed the Revelation to John the apostle, which caused confusion, because as much as the martyrdom of John before the year 70 was based on uncertain information preserved only in corners of Christianity, it could not be a mere legend. If the Revelation was written by John the apostle in Domitian's time, he could not have been tortured at Nero's time. Only Gregory of Nyssa[33] (*Laudatio s. Stephani et de Basilio magno, p. XLVII*) tried proving John's early martyrdom based on church calendars, by the proofs that can satisfy only those who already shared the same opinion on the common authorship of the Revelation, John's First, Second and Third Epistles, and the Gospel.

Modern Linguistic Analysis

A thorough modern linguistic analysis has been done by R. H. Charles, who asserts that the author of the Revelation is the author of neither the Gospel nor the Epistles. If John the apostle is the author of the Second and the Third Epistles, then the author of the Revelation is John the Elder. He is a Palestinian Jew who in his older age migrated to Asia Minor. He obviously used the Hebrew language as his mother tongue, never having mastered the Greek, using it in a very unique way. Of this there is a vague trace in Jerome: "This we say moreover because of the opinion mentioned above, where we record that it is declared by many that the last two epistles of John are the work not of the apostle but of the presbyter."[34]

The word *presbyter* was used in naming one who was with the apostles, and Papias most probably used it in this sense. John the Elder could have been a student of John the apostle. Charles concludes:

1. John's vision relates to the events of his time and the events resulting from these.
2. Future events should not be viewed symbolically or allegorically, but as final and concrete events.
3. The Revelation is made of several events that happened at several different places, some before and some after the destruction of Jerusalem.

32. Eusebius, *Church History*, bk. 7, ch. 24.
33. Gregory of Nyssa, *Sermones*, xlvii.
34. Jerome, *On Illustrious Men*, §18.

4. Study of John's style recognizes one author only. Several authors would have left a clear trace.
5. The book makes an integral unit and cannot be divided to several different sources, because the story is developed from the beginning to the end in a language that is unique in the entirety of Greek literature.
6. The authorship is unique, although the author sometimes introduces foreign elements that are not always assimilated in all details in the new context.
7. John's idea about the antichrist is unique and presented in several stages.
8. In the text there are certain places leading to the opinion that the basic text of the Revelation could not have been written by a Christian. These are certain Jewish and Greek elements of understanding the Redeemer of the world. The string of twelve precious stones shows the author's knowledge of the non-Christian city of gods and modern astronomy, from which he intentionally digresses.
9. The Revelation is the philosophy of history and faith. It was the apocalyptic philosophy, rather than the Greek, that was the first to understand that the entire history is unique—human, cosmologic, and spiritual.
10. The author speaks about spiritual experience, but the question remains to what extent the spiritual underlies the Revelation.
11. Grammatical analysis shows that a large number of words rejected by previous analysts make a genuine part of John's vocabulary.[35]

Charles's analysis confirms the Revelation to be an integral and preserved text, and that in interpreting it no subsequent interventions should be sought.

The millenarianistic belief is a variety of eschatology, and in the chapter 20 of the Revelation can be read same as by Justin, Irenaeus, and Victorinus. Tyconius in his *Apocalipsyn* rejects literal reading of the chapter 20, in this being followed by Jerome and Augustine in *On the City of God* (*De civitate Dei*), interpreting a millennium as the period of time between the first and the second comings of Christ.

The first to attempt interpreting the Revelation in a relatively methodical way is the Jesuit Ludovico Alcazar. Sir Isaac Newton with some commentators of lesser importance assert it was seen in the time of Nero,

---

35. Charles, *Critical and Exegetical Commentary*.

whereas other authors of significant reputation place it to the Domitian's time.³⁶ James Armstrong is in doubt: if the Revelation was written in Domitian's time, it described the events that have already happened, and if so this is not a prophecy and it is impossible to determine with certainty as when the Revelation was written. "We do not attempt researching this question because, although important, it does not appear important understanding parts of the prophecy that have already been fulfilled." Further on he says, "The Christian religion . . . was widely published before the publication of the Revelation [either in Nero's or in Domitian's times] so that the seal cannot have the purpose of the Christian propaganda; therefore it would be a prophecy after the event."³⁷

RECENT INTERPRETATIONS

The narratological concept is firstly focused on understanding the function of the Revelation as a theatrical show performed in Asia Minor. David L. Barr in his work *Transforming the Imagination: John's Apocalypse as Story* thinks that the Revelation has two layers, of which the basic, the lower one, is neither visible nor important for its function. The upper layer is a sequence of images repeated in concentric circles and, by their increasing emphasis, bringing the audience to a religious ecstasy, similar to shamanic sessions. Barr also presumes a change of the narrations following the change of the author. The narrator is not the author and, according to Barr, it is not important that he knows the basic story, he rather transfers his own experience as a prophetic revelation. The several authors, God, Jesus, the angels, the Son of Man, and, finally, John, are transferred to any one who then transfers John's message on. The same sequence of authors assumes further changes of the narration, because the audience transfers the message further to the next auditorium, itself becoming the narrator. John does not know certain things that are announced in the Revelation, but the complete impression of the show is achieved by acting and music in the dark, candle illuminated spaces of Asia Minor, any by the repetitive announcing the great and terrible events that are to happen. This theory is challenged by the exclusion of the Revelation from the liturgy at the Council of Laodicea and it not being read in churches, perhaps just because of its inappropriateness for public reading.

Equally abstract is the attempt to understand the contents and the message through the structure. Farrer's "model of sevens," continued and

---

36. Newton, *Observations upon the Prophecies*.
37. Armstrong, *Exposition of the Fulfilled Prophesies*, 12.

further developed by Yambro Collins, is the organizational principle of the entire book. The model of sevens corresponds to the days of the week of the creation and the Jewish seven-weeks feast. According to Farrer, John follows this matrix to call the Christians to preparedness, because the events that will happen soon will be followed by judgment day and the harvest of the faithful.

Seven churches, seven seals, seven trumpets, and seven cups, together with introductions, form four concentric circles, that is, according to the "concentric" concept of Schussler Fiorenza, the model after which the Revelation is created. According to Schussler Fiorenza, John does not interpret the *Old Testament*, but uses its words, images, phrases, and models to create his own theological statement. "He adapts and borrows entire sentences from the Old Testament as tools of his own composition, never to speak about the Old Testament as an authoritative text."[38]

Lambrecht sees composition in the three-part division of each sequence of the sevens: before each sequence there is (A) introduction, followed by (B) six elements of the sequence, and (C) the seventh element, introducing a new sequence of sevens.[39]

An interesting analysis of transformation and metamorphosis of the main characters in the Revelation is presented by G. Biguzzi.[40] Biguzzi deals with peculiarities of John's narrative technique and his surrealistic world to conclude that the notion of "surreal" is inadequate for this book. John's narration persistently goes against the common sense, because his Revelation is purely prophetic. He speaks about a new world that God is still to create, that is, indeed, partly already created in the messianic times, but will be fully shaped and created only in the eschatological eon.

In the study on the Old Testament quotations of S. Moyise, particularly interesting is the part where he elaborates the Ramsey's analysis of the historic background in the letters to the seven churches.[41] According to his quotations, in the letters to the seven churches, Ramsey finds a number of actual historic data, but concludes that these are not equally and consistently present and that John's intention was not to describe historic facts and true situation in these churches. Ramsey notices that the selection of the churches in Asia Minor indicates that these are the most important or the only churches in this area, which is wrong because Thyatira is relatively

---

38. The quote of Schussler Fiorenza is from Moyise, *Old Testament*, 24–44.

39. More about this: Tavo, "Structure of the Apocalypse." At the end of this study, Tavo favors Lambrecht's model.

40. Biguzzi, "Figurative and Narrative Language."

41. Moyise, *Old Testament*, 24–44.

insignificant compared to Colossae, although it is sent the longest message. The list did not include Troy and Magnesia, nor did he write to the churches that were closest to him. He does not mention Colossae, although according to Paul's Epistle to the Colossians, it is closely connected to Laodicea. He could not have omitted Colossae and Hierapolis if he looked at this area from Ephesus. The apostle Paul founded nine churches in Asia Minor, and John wrote only seven letters. The reason may be from the alleged earthquake that destroyed Colossae, Hierapolis, and Laodicea in the year 61, after which and until the Jewish-Roman War only Laodicea was rebuilt. The information presented on particular churches shows that he knew them well. Laodicea was well known for banking, wool production, and the famous school of medicine that specialized in eye diseases. Thyatira produced copper, Pergamum was the center of Roman power (although it is disputable whether that was Ephesus), and Smyrna to which he speaks, "Who is the First and the Last, who dies and comes to life again" (Rev 2:8) was destroyed in the third century BC not to have been rebuilt for three hundred years. To the church in Philadelphia he speaks, "Who is holy and true, and holds the key of David, what he shuts no-one can open" (Rev 3:7) because the local inhabitants kept the promise and because Philadelphia was situated on busy trade roads.[42]

Furthermore, Moyise states a number of conclusions on John listing the churches of Asia Minor for other reasons. To Laodicea he says: "Amen, the faithful and true witness, the ruler of God's creation" (Rev 3:14), "the firstborn of all creation" (Col 1:15). Eventually Ramsey concludes that the historic context of Laodicea cannot be read from the letters, because different towns, like Ephesus and Sardis, share the same title, mentioning the sword does not reflect the local situation, the open door of the underworld and David's keys are not necessarily the keys to the hell and the death, Smyrna cannot be related to the title "the First" and "the Last." Moreover, connecting the metal industry in Thyatira with "bronze" is just speculative. All these hypotheses are based on the assumption that to John the local situation is more important than the theological intention and the Old Testament quotes.[43] The moral dilemmas and the violence of God's judgment that demands revenge and punishment make up the subject matter of an article by Oluola K. Peters.[44]

---

42. Noah Ian has two keys in his hand, showing that he invented the door and, also, that sacred places and temples are to be locked and fortified not to become unclean. (Lynche, *Historical Treatise*).

43. Moyise, *Old Testament*, 24–44.

44. Peters, *Politics of Violence*.

Robert M. Royalty presents the thesis that the Revelation is a pamphlet written against other teachers, prophets, and members of the church in Asia Minor, against the rule of the Jewish synagogue, and finally against the Roman rule.[45] The Revelation as an apparently prophetic text subversively copies Jewish texts and mobilizes the readers around ideological and conceptual conflicts. Members of antagonistic groups within and outside John's church are those who he calls "false apostles," "so-called Jews," "Nicolaites," and "followers of Balaam."

Furthermore, D. H. Lawrence[46] and H. Bloom[47] interpret the Revelation as a gnostic text related to Sufism and Kabala,[48] whereas P. Thimmes[49] interprets its female characters from a feminist aspect.

The lack of interest for the basic plan of the Revelation in both structural and narrative concepts assumes John's extraordinary artistic potential to communicate and manipulate just empty phrases and symbols. In none of the above-mentioned methods anything would have been changed even if John had had a specific, real concept which he hides from us and retells only in symbols. His treatment could be apparently contradicting the common sense if it metaphorically described the so far unknown real perceptions. The previous theories do not negate but avoid the question as how much John's story is documented in the reality.

MAIN FEATURES OF SPACE AND TIME

The Revelation was created in a time of very intensive and dynamic social processes caused by global integration and mixing of different heterogeneous cultures and religions within the Roman Empire. The ancient Greek world, by Alexander's conquest squeezed to the areas of the central and eastern Mediterranean, opens new cognitive perspectives, spreading the Hellenistic culture to the end of the world, but also enabling approaches to other cultures. The wars caused by the division of the Alexander's state among his successors partly slowed down the processes of exchanging various cultural

---

45. Royalty, "Don't Touch This Book."

46. Lawrence, *Apocalypse and the Writings*.

47. On the ethic problem of the Apocalypse: "Anger and inexistence of love is the teaching of the Revelation of the Divine John. This is a book with no wisdom, holiness or feeling of any sort, although it is suitable that the end of the world not to be just barbarian, but barely literate. When the content is so inhuman, who would wish the rhetoric to be more convincing or depicted more vividly?" Bloom, *Revelation of St. John*, 4.

48. More on this can be found in the essay by Lee Irwin, "Omens of the Millennium."

49. Thimmes, "Women Reading Women."

experiences, fully opened in the time of the Roman rule, when in the field of religion occurred a flood of new brotherhoods, communities, and clubs of all sorts and shapes, to which the state cults and the official religion got exposed. These organizations were mostly closed and private, not only in the sense that the state did not control them, but also that they kept their businesses secret, which was the main reason of the reports on them being incomplete. Among these were not only some minor and marginal cults but also the largest ones, such as the Phrygian, Bacchus's, Isis's, or Mithraic mysteries that spread all over the empire. The Eleusinian mysteries were still protected by the state, but because of their fame they were even more closed.

It is generally thought that the most respectable Greeks, men and women, were members of the Pythagorean schools. After the death of Pythagoras, the Pythagoreans gradually accepted the Orphic purity and modesty to have moved into Orphic communities.

Around the year AD 25 Philo mentions numerous groups of people all over the world, especially in Egypt and around Alexandria, who renounced their possessions, withdrew from the world and dedicated their entire lives to researching wisdom. Among them, of course, there were members of various schools such as the Therapeuts and the Essenes, the countless schools commonly named the gnostics. Just as the Essenes can be related to Pythagorean influences, conclusions also can be made that Greece was through Pythagoras influenced by the Indian Buddhist propaganda two centuries before the direct contact of the two civilizations and Alexander's conquests. At the Pythagoras's time, Persia was in contact with India, even Darius at the end of the sixth and the beginning of the fifth centuries BC sent an expedition led by the general Scylax to the Indus, whereas Herodotus noted that Punjab became the twentieth Persian satrapy and that the Indians fought at Plataea with Xerxes. After Alexander, the maritime and caravan routes were wide open and connected his successors with India; thence in the oldest Trismegistic texts, dated to the first century AD, can be found phrases most closely connected with the Upanishads and Bhagavad Gita.

Alexandria

One of the most interesting and most dynamic points of commercial exchange and, therefore, also of religious and philosophical ones was Alexandria. The library founded at the time of the first Ptolemaics, which consisted of an intensive and passionate collection of books, made Alexandria a world intellectual center where the successors of Pythagoras's, Plato's, and Aristotle's philosophies gathered, along with rhetoricians who lived on public discussions and polemics and were surrounded by their numerous successors, fans, and idols along with numerous travelers, pilgrims, and sectarians of all cult or ethnical characteristics. From the very beginning of the Alexandrian library, collected were around four hundred thousand scrolls, or around six thousand books, that made almost the entire knowledge of the then Mediterranean. There the Euclidian geometry experts tried computing the distance from the Sun to the Earth and the Earth's circumference, forecasting solar eclipses; there Archimedes tried solving the problems of hydrostatics; there lived Callimachus and Aristophanes, the poet Theocritus, and so on.

Besides these also existed numerous different philosophical schools: Sophists, followers of Pythagoras, Socrates, Plato, and Aristotle, repeating the learned phrases of their long-time dead teachers, members of the Megarian, Pyrrhonian, and Cyrenaic schools; skeptics, Epicureans, academics, Peripatetics, and Stoics. Alexandria had no philosophic school of its own, but here merged all the possible philosophic ideas. Applied were different methods, the ecclesiastic method of synthesizing the selected, the syncretistic mixing of various heterogeneous contents, the analogue method of comparing and linking different contents, the numberless attempts to discover the global religion, to synthesize science, philosophy, and religion. The human species was at its end and what had not been achieved in the course of the all history must have been created then, at the very end. Everything that related to the man, human life, and this world was mixed; mixed were good and evil, lies and truth, and what had been discovered lied below aggregations of useless and barren knowledge, preserved in its pure form only in the words of the few who witnessed through their words and lives. The task was to separate or extract from everything gathered throughout human history that what could be useful when the time comes. Such knowledge was in possession of a few, and around them erected were protective borders through exclusivity of the clubs to which they belonged, in the hermeticism and empty space they created around themselves. Although Rome at that time subjected the world to its control, the situation in the state about religion and morality was bad. Provinces were subordinated to the emperor, but religious institutions enjoyed complete and absolute freedom.

Translating the Hebrew scripts by the Seventy at the beginning of the rule of Ptolemy Philadelphus appears not to have impressed the learned Greeks in Alexandria. The Hebrew ideas related to the Jews, and from the very beginning these hermetic and jealous believers kept the scripts for themselves. The Alexandrine rabbis kept the scripts in the centuries to come, therefore remaining the central persons of the Judaic religion, called the "light of Israel," allowing mixing of old Jewish teachings and beliefs with the teachings from Chaldea and the traditional wisdom of Egypt, perfected together in the cabalistic teachings. Such processes were met with different appreciations, approved by some, disapproved by others. So Aristobulus claimed the peripatetic philosophy to have started with Moses, while Irenaeus claimed that old religions and philosophies were repeating the devil's instructions.

Christianity in its popular form was completely immersed in the Jewish religious tradition that knew nothing about the cabalistic mysticism or any kind of philosophy, but its spreading to other peoples brought to the foreground the matter of circumcision and the national exclusivism, a perfectly unimportant matter to non-Jews. Thus appeared the first heresy at the church in Jerusalem, which essentially remained Jewish but soon turned into a close sect, even to those who Judaism considered to be a natural root of the Christianity. The new propaganda, partly among more learned non-Jews, especially the Greeks, set new requirements for spreading cognitive horizons and developing religion, which implied involving learned people into polemics with other philosophies and religions. Such liberal endeavors and freedom in interpreting the faith caused suspicion with the orthodox part of the believers, who showed mistrust even about the very moderate and careful Clement and Origen. Generally, the victory of the orthodoxy meant cursing the learned, Origen himself getting anathemized eventually.

Thus the Alexandrine school of Christianity, whose famous teachers were Clement and Origen, founded in the first half of the third century, next door to the museum from which the Christians were excluded for their lack of education, opened the children Sunday school, Didascaleion. From this school developed the Catholic theology.

In Egypt, from as early as the time of the first Ptolemies, developed was the practice of translating, the beginning of which is related to the Egyptian historian and chronologist Manetho, who engaged in polemics with his Chaldean colleague Berossus in proving the importance of the Egyptian history and civilization against the Chaldean, from whom Plutarch probably draws information on the cult of Isis. Various sources show that the teachings that are deemed traditional in Egypt have their roots in the Greek literature of Trismegistus, whose mystic and theosophical debates are used as literature in hermetic schools. This is the tradition on Thoth, or Tehut, the god of wisdom, whom the Greeks added the adjective Trismegistus—Three Times the Greatest. In the Trismegistic literature may be found various doctrines of the Christian Gnosticism, but without mentioning the historic Christ, which appear to have existed in the Egyptian tradition a thousand years before Christianity, especially in the teaching about the Logos, the Savior, and the Virgin Mary, the second birth and the final uniting with God.

Same as in Greece, in Egypt existed all forms of blending, syncretisms, and influences, not only in the external popular cults, but also in the internal tradition.

Since as early as the first half of the second millennium BC, since the time of the Hyksos, there is an intensive mixing with the Semitic tradition. Since then, Set (a name of the Semitic root) is identified with Sotis, Sirius, the patron star of Egypt, and the mysteries of Set are mixed with those of Osiris. After the expulsion of the hated Hyksos, Set was gradually replaced with Typhon, Osiris's enemy, which is not so developed directly from the cult of Set, but from the fact that the Iranian Arians used to use the word *daevos* to denote an evil being. Neither to them nor to the early Christians meant a lot that the Greeks by this name meant beings that brought good and benefit. This shows the rivalry between the races and the religions.

The contacts between Chaldea and Egypt have been proven by archaeological finds. The subsequent Persian conquest of Egypt, too, had influences in the fields of religion, especially the mystery traditions.

In Egypt priests had large knowledge, not easily published, but there was a base on which could have been built numerous varieties that preachers promoted and conveyed to the masses that followed them. Some of these spiritual preachers, completely devoted to high mysteries by the ways in which they lived, their dedication to God, and to the benefits of the fellow neighbors whom they cured and helped in their spiritual and physical healths, spreading all over Egypt in large numbers, especially in Alexandria, were called the Therapeuts. These secret societies let no traces, kept aside, and the world did not know them, but undoubtedly they made a part of the gnostic belief and a link in its chain of development.[50]

Greece

In the dawn of intellectual development, over a brief period of time, in the world appeared several exceptional names: Confucius, Lao Tse, Buddha, Zarathustra, and Pythagoras. Although this appears to be a phenomenon, and that these great men appeared without a herald, which all of their followers eagerly tried to prove, deeming them the source and founders of the philosophic and religious thought, it appears that was not exactly so. In Greece before Pythagoras there were the first heralds of philosophy, Anaximander and Tales in Asia Minor, but also long time before them there

---

50. On the Therapeuts: Philo, *About the Contemplative Life.*

had been various nameless teachers in Egypt and Chaldea. Homer and his followers composed poems to ancient heroes and, like Hesiod in his *Theogony*, they stated and knew the events belonging to the oldest barbaric Greek history yet were unable to say anything on the religion. With them those old myths were much more legible and understandable than in the old Orphic tradition that no one, except those totally uneducated, believed.

Immediately before the Xerxes's invasion, where Greece found its life threatened, they started collecting of old myths and renewal of old tradition. In a way, the consequences passed the events and the harmonization of the Greek world that was to take place during or after the external danger, spontaneously had started taking place before it.

In Greece alongside public cults and popular tradition also developed mysteries, the inner, closed systems that kept their teachings in secrecy under the threat of death. Alongside the great and widely present Orphic, Dionysian, and Eleusinian mysteries, there were numerous closed, private cults. But this tradition, actually based just on the Orphic poetry and mythological foundations, in spite of the national enthusiasm and its prophetic character, was not apt for the newly created stratum of learned Greeks who saw the paradigm of intellectual life somewhere else, especially in the old Egyptian and Chaldean heritage.

Revitalization of the tradition is a substrate that through myths and mysteries reaches Pythagoras and Plato. It is in no way coincidental that, among other contemporaries, young Pythagoras too went to Egypt to study old wisdoms, in the sequence of dire circumstances to have ended his study tour as a prisoner of war in Chaldea. The synthesis of these old experiences made to the Greeks a challenge that, free of the burden of tradition, they were able to respond, giving it a new interpretation. Pythagoras is said to have been initiated in the Egyptian, Chaldean, Orphic, and Eleusinian mysteries. At the same time, he was the founder of the Greek philosophy. He noticed that the growing intellectual potential of Greece needed a leadership. Plato continued his task, although in a slightly different way. He was more open than Pythagoras and his work was mostly public. He mostly tried clearing the philosophy of errors and misinterpretations, enabling the intellect to see the things as they are. It is wrong to think that Pythagoras formed a new and different philosophic system. He mostly settled accounts with the old teachings arrived to him inherited from various mysteries. Hence most conclusions of his discussions are negative, except by the end of his life when he wrote the positive text on *Timaeus*, partly compiled from older Pythagorean texts. Those interested in his texts note the dialectics to end in itself and in negation. Aristotle followed with his stunning method of analysis and exact observation of phenomena. In his time Greece spread far away from Plato's Hellas. Its live spirit conquered the entire East, centuries later to be transferred to the Egyptian Alexandria. The national and local cults gradually accepted the symbols taken from the Chaldeo-Egyptian tradition, worshiping the spiritual sun Logos, that in this form or another became common to all cults.

With time, Mithra, to those ignorant the visible Sun, but as Plato says, to the knowledgeable the spiritual Sun, the mediator between the light and the darkness, became the light to the entire Roman Empire.

Christianity

The historic roots of Christianity are still hidden in an impenetrable darkness. Little is known on the true background of the canon in the first half of the first century, the historic reports in the Gospels mostly being a selection from numerous different legends and traditions. Only in the second half of the second century appeared the idea of the New Testament canon, promoted mostly from Rome and by the Western ecclesiastical authors. The early ecclesiastical authors in Alexandria, including Clement, did not know the canon. Tertullian, Irenaeus, and Hippolytus, following the first apologists and with the help from the church of Rome, created foundations of Christianity and the first foundations of the faith that is today considered to be the authentic church of Christ.

In the first two centuries, instead of a single idea being developed appeared numerous sects and heresies, against which early Christianity fought to life and death. The first firm foundations of the new faith were created when the Gospels were composed, sometimes between the 70s and the end of the Hadrian's rule. Of the Gospels, of which three (synoptic) are alike, whereas the fourth, John's, differs by the idea and style, reflecting a completely different concept. Expecting the end of the world and the coming of Christ—chiliasm, millenarianism—was spread everywhere. Christianity of the time was a way of living rather than a dogma. There were no firm borders and a great freedom in preaching was allowed. The word of God was not absolute yet, it was discussed, and there was no firm connection between the churches, wherefore they themselves developed on their own.

Although the authenticity of Paul's Epistles is still being examined, perhaps they are the oldest written source from the first half of the first century. Paul ended religious exclusivity and equaled the Jews and the non-Jews, spreading Christianity among other nations in Asia Minor. The first controversy within the Christian community appeared about spreading the word among the non-Jews and circumcision. Paul's decision to carry

Christianity to the non-Jews was against the original followers of Christ's teaching. The first Christians in Christ saw a wise man, a prophet, Jonah or Solomon, he was the Messiah who was sent, but did not yet appear as the Messiah of the end times. He would become that once he appeared for the second time. Born as Jesus, he was just a prophet and would reappear as the king, all the nations would submit to the rule of the Jewish people, and for a thousand years there would be peace and prosperity on earth. The conflict between Peter and Paul continued unabated for years; Peter's and Paul's writings were diligently revised and between Paul's Epistles and the Gospels inserted was a carefully composed compilation of different legends on the acts of the apostles. Christianity in the beginning was considered a national religion promising the Jews the rule over other nations, whereas Paul's missionary acting mostly annulled this highly motivating element of the Christianity.

Essenes and Therapeuts

Based on the Christ's words in the Gospels and the situation in the early church as described in the Acts of the Apostles, many deem Christ to have been an Essene, a member of a closed religious community that inhabited the coasts of the Dead Sea for centuries before the Christian era. They believed in one God, the creator, immortality of the soul, and the judgment. By their ascetic life and preaching the love for God, man, and virtue, they earned respect of the people around them. All the community members engaged in all jobs, together they worked in the fields, traded and produced, strictly practicing celibacy. Their day begun with common prayer, with their faces turned east toward the rising Sun. After work, the common meal was prepared, which was considered a sacrament and was taken in silence. At a certain time of the day the secrets of the revelation and the heavenly events were studied. Saturday was strictly respected and, since there were no priests, the members took turns in reading the Law and in leading the common prayer. Each full member could present his interpretation of the mysteries connected with the Tetragrammaton or with the secret name of the Creative Force that consisted of four letters. At joining the community, the novices gave up their properties, and only after one year of preparations and two more as novices, they became full members of the community. Essenism is considered a form of Pharisaism, but they rejected the idea of resurrection in flesh, held as the main doctrine by the Pharisees. They were known for truthfulness and mercy for man, rejecting their sins, but accepting them as persons. Philo separates them from the Therapeuts, deeming that the

Essenes dedicated themselves to practical things and the Therapeuts rather to the contemplative life.[51]

Discovering the Dead Sea Scrolls opened new perspectives for studying the Essenes and their religious life. From the fragments discovered in eleven caves near Qumran by the Dead Sea reconstructed are eight hundred original manuscripts, the oldest preserved manuscripts. Some of them are well preserved, whereas with others it may only be guessed what they are about, but together they show how dynamic and divergent the Judaist religious thought was at the beginning of the era. The best preserved texts are Divine Throne, Book of Secrets, Thanksgiving Hymns, Fruit Bearing Tree Parable, Baptismal Liturgy, Coming of Melchizedek, Tongues of Fire, and others. From these texts can be concluded that the Essenes were not believers of a single faith, but rather the learned who were interested in all mysteries, believers who studied the Chaldean and Zarathustra's teachings, the mysteries of Trismegistus, and other religious literature. The conventional attribution of the scrolls to the Essenes does not appear fully reliable because this collection presents a wider cultural context.

Ebionites

In the very beginning of the first century appeared the first of Christ's followers, the Ebionites or the Nazarenes, who were dispersed from Syria to Mesopotamia as late as at the end of the fourth century. A collection of their teachings is in the Hebrew Gospel, that essentially differs from the Synoptic Gospels, their traces today existing in the Mandaean community in south Babylonia.

It remains in darkness who the first Essenes or Nazarenes were, especially so because in later propaganda against heresies, this sect gained certain characteristics that it had not had before, which went as far as inventing the creators of the sect, Ebion, Epiphanus, Colarbasus, and Elkesai, originally metonyms for the teacher, the Holy Four, and the Secret Force.

The Ebionites were so named because of poverty, the word "poor" later on being added the wording "by their mind" and not "by their ascetic living," although it is to be kept in mind that Christ's social teaching was among the reasons of the fast spreading of the new religion and that expected was the day when the poor will be risen above the rich. They practiced public teachings that they witnessed by their lives, and undoubtedly they had collections of written speeches.

---

51. Philo, *On the Contemplative Life*.

According to the Ebionites, Jesus was a man, born like everybody else, the human son of Joseph and Mary. Only thirty years later the Spirit came down to him and he became a prophet. They therefore preserved his heritage as a sign of future events, although they knew nothing about his divine history. Indeed, Jesus was Christ, but that could have been everyone who bore witness to the truth. Therefore they naturally rejected the Paul's new doctrine, considering him a renegade from the law and negating his being a Jew. Only later did they accept the Hebrew Gospel, about which Jerome says it is the same as the Gospel of the Nazarenes,[52] where there is nothing on the legendary birth of Jesus and Nazareth, which were added for the prophecies to come true. The Ebionites did not return to Jerusalem after the colony Aelia Capitolina was founded in AD 138, because they as Jews were not permitted to return there, wherefore the church based on their public teaching could not have been sustained there, and the new colony, since it was inhabited by non-Jews, remained Pauline in its Christian aspect.

There is a vast literature on Gnosticism. Most of it is indirect sources written by Christian anti-heresiarchs, most of them coming from the Western Christian tradition, unable to understand the subtle Eastern mysticism like their Eastern colleagues, and who were the most agile opponents of Gnosticism. Some direct manuscripts are preserved as well through Coptic transcriptions. From the first and three quarters of the second century there are no preserved polemics and rejections of heresies and the gnostics, if they existed at all before Irenaeus, who wrote in Lion in Gallia, far away from the place of the events. All other polemics and rejections of the Gnostics are based mostly on Irenaeus and his arguments and method. Only Eusebius mentions one Agrippa Castor before Irenaeus:

> Of these there has come down to us a most powerful refutation of Basilides by Agrippa Castor, one of the most renowned writers of that day, which shows the terrible imposture of the man. While exposing his mysteries he says that Basilides wrote twenty-four books upon the Gospel, and that he invented prophets for himself named Barcabbas and Barcoph, and others that had no existence, and that he gave them barbarous names in order to amaze those who marvel at such things; that he taught also that the eating of meat offered to idols and the unguarded renunciation of the faith in times of persecution were matters of indifference; and that he enjoined upon his followers, like Pythagoras, a silence of five years.[53]

---

52. Parts of the Gospel by the Nazarenes exist only in Epiphanius, Panarion, 46–48.
53. Eusebius, *Church History*, bk. 4, ch. 7.

Anti-heresiarchs

Justin Martyr wrote a book on heresy, *Syntagma Against All the Heresies* or *The Summary*, that has been lost. It appears from the rest of his writings that the memoires of the apostles that he often mentioned were not similar to the canonical gospels, but probably the gospels as they were in his time.

Clement of Alexandria, who wrote in the end of the second and the very beginning of the third century, lived in the most powerful center of gnostic activities and knew personally some of the most influential teachers of the gnostic philosophy. In his work there are no hard judgments against the gnostics, especially none of those unfounded criticisms for amorality, because most part of their teachers were considered themselves dominantly rigid ascetics. Tertullian copied Irenaeus, except for what he wrote against Marcion, where he stated new arguments and method; Hippolytus, from Port at the mouth of the Tiber, was a student of Irenaeus. He wrote *Against Heresies*; Origen wrote against Celsus.

Philastrius, the bishop of Brescia, Epiphanius, the bishop of Salamis, and Jerome wrote at the end of the fourth century and were not, except where they carried on older sources, relevant to the events and processes of the first and the second centuries.

A summary of the propaganda against heresies until the early fourth century was presented by Eusebius in his *Church History*, but his reliability has been questioned.

Finally, in inheriting and passing on the standings and ideas, the only text that remains by its originality, reliability, and authorial authenticity is Irenaeus's *Against Heresies*, in spite of being written in far Gallia, in an area where completely different relationships existed. Then how was Irenaeus able to speak objectively and truly about the network and composition of large and small flows that mutually permeated, bifurcated, and closed a network of general beliefs and expectations and particular philosophic attempts, many of them looking at soteriology as a part of ontology and witnessing by their acts and lives that salvation is possible only in spirit, through cognition and pure philosophic life, though complete dedication to one, in the premonition obvious, but in the praxis hardly achievable way?

Gnostics

Irenaeus mentions an obviously early gnostic system of three initial principles: Father and Son, the Second Man, and the Holy Spirit, who is a woman and the mother of everything alive. Below this triad was a mass made of the elements: water, darkness, depth, and chaos. Of this, the Father and the Son created the Great Light—Christ, who, in turn, together with the First Man and the Son, created the Church. From the water created was Sophia (light, heavenly spheres), who gave birth to the creator of the material world, Yaldabaoth. The material world is inexistent, it is just an illusion and image of the real, higher world. Yaldabaoth is not the true savior but an aspirant who created Adam and demanded him to worship him above everything else, as the true God. Adam immediately accepted the First Man and his Son and rejected his creator, Yaldabaoth.

Ophites, Naassenes, Peratae, and Sethians

Another branch of Gnosticism is Ophitic, that Hippolytus dedicated the fifth book of his *Refutation of All Heresies* to. Hippolytus deems the Ophites to be the first gnostics. Of their vast literature he mentioned just the book of Baruch. The Ophitic theology is based on the Syrian myth on creation, carried by Herodotus, and on the Hercules's three sons born to him by the woman-snake, one of which became the founder of the Scythians.[54]

In the book of Baruch, too, there are three principles: the Good or Omniscient Deity; the Father of the Spirit, the Creative Force; and Elohim and material spirit, that is, the woman with snake below her called Eden. Of Elohim and Eden created were twenty-four angels, twelve of Elohim and twelve of Eden. Of the animal parts of Eden created were animals, and of the human parts humans. Eden breathed life into the first man. Elohim ascended to heaven taking with him his angels; he placed them in the sky as stars and of them made the zodiac. Thus were created the earthly, Eden's, and the heavenly, Elohim's, gardens. In the earthly paradise Baruch forbade eating from the tree of knowledge.

Hippolytus mentions three schools belonging to this circle, calling them the Naassenes, the Peratae, and the Sethians. Although the name of the Naassenes derives from the Hebrew word meaning snake (*naas*), Hippolytus does not connect them with the Ophites, but with these he connects the Cainites and the Nochaites (from *nachash* = snake). They are attributed vast literature that includes the Gospel of Perfection, the Questions of Mary, On Mary's Delivery, the Gospel of Philip, the Gospel of Thomas, and the Gospel of the Egyptians. Generally, the universe is presented as a male-female human, having three aspects: bodily, spiritual, and psychic. All the three characteristics are perfectly formed only in Jesus who is, therefore, the true Son of Man.

54. Herodotus, *History of Herodotus*, bk. 4, chs. 8–10.

Furthermore, the Peratae are a gnostic school that certainly preceded Clement of Alexandria. Their base are the old cults of stars and watching the planets. Hippolytus when speaking on the futility of the astrologers' and the mathematicians' knowledge mainly comments on the Peratae, saying that their systems are allegorized astrology. The Peratae depicted the universe as a circle inscribed in a triangle. The triangle presents the first trinity, that what is uncreated, self-created, and created, which are the three aspects of vertices of a square, presenting God, the Logos, the Mind, and the Man, that is, three Gods, three Logoi, three Minds, and three Men. When the creation process started, the Savior rose with triple power, triple nature and triple body, hence from the two higher worlds appeared the lower, created world.

The mysteries symbolized by the snake make the root of every gnostic teaching. The Peratae in the Sun saw the Father, in the Moon the Son, and in the Earth the matter. The Moon is depicted as a snake turning its face towards the Sun or the Earth, in accordance with its phases.

The Docets leaned their teaching on the Christ's teaching after his death, when he appeared among the disciples and taught for eleven years in the body that some could see and touch, while to others it was invisible. Subsequently this was continued in the teachings of the best-known gnostic teachers, Basilides and Valentinus. They depict the God symbolically as a fig tree—it is the shelter for the exiled, the cloak for the naked. The fig symbolizes generations, because from its seed appears the germ, from it the seedling, then the tree, the leaf, and finally the fruit that contains seeds. Even before the world was created, its emanation existed in the form of root—eon. The Savior saves the souls from rebirth (*metensomatosis*).

Monoimus

Monoimus, mentioned only by Hippolytus and Theodoret, promotes the idea of the Heavenly Man (the universe) and the Son of that Man, the perfect man, all other men, being imperfect, reflecting this ideal model. Monoimus was almost certainly connected with the school of Valentinus.

Cainites

Of the Cainites very little is known, and this from Irenaeus and Eusebius. Basically they belonged to the Ophites, their members calling themselves simply the gnostics. They got their name from worshiping Jude and Cain, enough by itself for them to get stigmatized. The creator of everything is not God, but a weaker creation force that symbolizes the unclean pleroma, which includes the material world and heaven (Yaldabaoth). The material world is created in the second stage, after the first birth that had come from the clean, spiritual pleroma, the ideal eons. The lower force was the God of Creation. The Old Testament relates to nothing else but to submission to lower forces. Hence those refuting the old laws are more just and worthy than those obeying them—Cain and Jude than Abel, Moses than Jacob. This interpretation may have a deeper meaning, because Abel offered a bloody offering and Cain bloodless, which Jehovah did not like. The Cainites were strict ascetics but, similar to Carpocrates, claimed that the man cannot be saved unless he passed through every experience.

Epiphanus

In the fourth century a legend was composed on the young Epiphanus, who had lived two hundred fifty years earlier and who was, after Carpocrates, the best-known name of his circle. At the age of seventeen Epiphanus formed the Carpocratian thought. After his early death, Epiphanus was worshiped as a deity on the new moon day. Actually, Epiphanus's cult was a misinterpretation and redesign of the actual cult of the young Moon (*epiphany*).

Carpocrates

Carpocrates was a Platonist. He deemed the souls of the dead passed the spheres of the ruler of the material world (planets) in concentric circles, trying to release themselves from their power by passing to the highest sphere. This very complex system of karmic philosophy was continued after Carpocrates in Rome in the mid-second century by Marcellina.

The Carpocratians were a gnostic sect in Alexandria in the second century, trying to renew old Christian communities of common ownership. The Carpocratians are considered to have introduced the monadic gnoses: everything is created from the eternal Unity, and into the Unity everything will return. But the world is ruled by earthly forces, confronting the Unity. Perfect are the souls that pass all the differences and limits to the higher Unity. They defy the earthly forces and treat the external as unimportant, believing in and loving only the essential.

Cerinthus

The Cerinthians allegedly got their name after Cerinthus, who lived in the apostolic time and made a direct connection to the Ebionites with the non-Pauline tradition at the beginning of the second century. Allegedly he taught Egyptian teaching in Asia Minor and is attributed the authorship of the Revelation.

In his cosmology God is above everything. Jesus, the son of Joseph and Mary, connected himself with Christ at the baptism. All the texts attributed to them are subsequent apocrypha. The fourth Gospel, John's, was considered to have been composed against Cerinthus, but there is no proof for this.

The author of the Revelation says twice that he hates the Nicolaites and their works. Based on this, Irenaeus claims that the Nicolaites are those who eat meat dedicated to idols and make offerings, which became the label of the Cerinthus's teaching.

Marcion

Marcion's predecessor was Cerdon, who lived around the year AD 135. More is known about Marcion. He was a ship owner, bishop, and son of a bishop. He stayed in Rome between the years AD 150–160. In the beginning he belonged to the Christian community and was helping the church in Rome, but was accused of heresy and, probably, excommunicated. The little that is known about his teaching is that it spread fast, so that as already in the fifth century Theodoret converted over a thousand Marcionites. Christ preached a universal faith, the new revelation of the Good God. Christ was not a Messiah preached on by the Jews, as the Messiah was king of this world and had not yet arrived. Marcion was the first to understand Christ outside the Jewish sectarianism and, wherefore he accepted Paul's teaching, he rejected other Gospels. According to Marcion, there were three skies, on the highest of these was the Good God, on the middle one the God of the Law, whereas the lowest one was inhabited by angels above the material world (*hyle*). Adam and Eve lived in the paradise until the God of the Law told Adam, wanting him to serve only him: "Adam, I am the only God, and have no other gods before me. If you worship other gods you will die!" Adam remained faithful to the highest, the true God, whereas Eve, having seen that Adam abandoned her, spread idolatry all over the world. God sent Jesus to cure the world.

Basilides

In the early second century appeared one of the deepest and the hardest to understand gnostic schools, its foundations being known from different patristic polemics. Basilides taught in Alexandria sometimes between AD 120 and 130. He knew the Septuagint and wrote twenty-four books on the Gospels. He also mentioned several of Paul's Epistles. About himself he says he was a student of one Glaucus, an "interpreter of Paul," and mentions Matthew, to whom he pays great honors. Basilides's system is closed and complex, which cannot be presented in brief in this text.

The universe after Basilides consists of parts—eons: above the Earth is the first and the lowest sublunary sphere, visible and invisible. Above this are the Moon's foundations (the sky) through which is the ethereal world of stars, their endless inhabitants, spaces and regions, orders and hierarchies, spreading to the very end of the space and the time, to the great foundation and the end of the phenomenological universe, after which is the space of the world of ideas, spreading outside the space and the time. Its borders are everywhere and nowhere. About the man who is trying to understand these spaces of paradox can be spoken only in the terms describing the phenomenological notions, calling them region, although this is not a region but a living eon. Although it transcends life, praising it as the world of light, its light, because of its intensity, is darkness for the eyes. This is the pleroma, the world of perfection and perfect harmony. The mind bounces off it, unable to understand it. Then it is the world of silence, with no words and symbols, where the mind is mute and the spirit rests.

Valentinus

Above the entire gnostic movement stands Valentinus, a man who, for his learning and eloquence, was respected even by his enemies. On him as a person and his writings just a few fragments have survived, although he made the main path of Gnosticism. His teaching allowed a large freedom in interpretation, so much so that Eusebius said that he had never met two members of this school agreeing with each other. Although there is no firm information on Valentinus himself and his life, he acted sometimes between AD 100 and 150. The first movement leaders were Secundus and Marcus, who around the year AD 150 gave name to a large sect (the Marcosians). Valentinus was an Egyptian, educated in Alexandria. Most part of his life he spent in Egypt, the rest in Rome and in Cyprus. He wrote numerous homilies, letters, and psalms, perhaps also a gospel and the discussion titled

Sophia. According to Valentinus, the one called by the Jews God and the Father is "the image and the prophet of the true God."[55] Prophet here meaning the one who speaks and interprets. The image is Sophia's world, and the one carrying forms from higher spheres to the canvas of this world is the real and true God. He is the God of Life, whereas the image is the God of Death. All the things coming in pairs (syzygies, conjunctions, marriages) are fullness (*pleromata*), and all those coming from a single principle are images.

Valentinus's cosmology is clearly shown in a psalm fragment:

> I see in spirit that all are hung
> I know in spirit that all are borne
> Flesh hanging from soul
> Soul clinging to air
> Air hanging from upper atmosphere
> Crops rushing forth from the deep
> A babe rushing forth from the womb.[56]

Hippolytus passes a myth that is probably taken from a discourse known as Pistis Sophia, where she is depicted as a newborn child, giving his interpretation of this vision: the body is hyle or hebdomad (sublunary sphere), the soul is the demiurge of the ethereal space, the demiurge hangs on the spirit. This is the boundary dividing the pleroma from the kenoma (phenomenal universe, everything outside the eons, outside the pleroma, the world of the phenomena) or the space between these, which is Sophia. So the demiurge hangs on Sophia, Sophia on the Great Beyond or the Horos, the Horos on the pleroma, the pleroma on the Bythos, the Great Depth, or Abyss, the Father and God above all.

The eons are alive, they are a fullness of the beings, they are eternal and thereby outside the space and the time; the kenoma is emptiness, an image, created from monad and belonging to the inanimate world.

Valentinus and Heracleon and Ptolemy and the entire school of these gnostics, students of Pythagoras and Plato, set the arithmetic science to be the basic principle of their teaching.

For them the beginning of everything is the monad, uncreated, eternal, and incomprehensible. The Father, unknowable, is the creator and the cause of everything created. On his nature there are differences among them: some claim that Father is free of the female aspect, outside of syzygy and alone, whereas others claim it is impossible for creation to be just from

---

55. Droz, *Literary Journal*, 181.
56. Layton, *Gnostic Scriptures*, 306.

a single, male principle, wherefore for him to be able to be the Father, the other, they add to him the female principle, the Silence (*Sige*).[57]

In the beginning the Father was alone, uncreated, without space or time, and without anyone who would advise him. He was in himself, and from the moment he arose he wanted to create what is the best and the most beautiful in him. He himself was the love, but love without the loved one is no love. Therefore, Father, alone and as he was, he conceived and created Mind-and-Truth, the dyad that is the creator of all the eons existing in the pleroma. The Mind-and-Truth had the same powers of creating as their Father and after his ideal they created World-and-Life, and the World-and-Life further created Man-and-Church. Thus the paternity is shifted from the Mind-and-Truth to the World-and-Life, and from the World-and-Life to the Man-and-Church. Out of gratitude, the Mind-and-Truth gave to Father ten (perfect number) eons. Following them, their children, World-and-Life, wanted to thank their parents, but since their birth was not that sublime as their parents', they offered them in gratitude an imperfect number of eons—twelve. So the number of the eons was increased from eight by ten, then by twelve, or four plus five plus six pairs, thirty in total.

According to Clement of Alexandria, Valentinus was a student of Paul's student Theudas. His theological system was exceptionally complex, and many modern scholars doubt whether he was able to create it all by himself. Members of the sect believed everyone was to establish the cosmic peace for himself and that the gnosis and not the faith was the path of salvation.

In the center of the Valentinianism always stands the youngest eon, Sophia, the Wisdom, a renegade from whom nothing could have been born and who, exiled from Pleroma, created the material world. G. R. S. Mead claims that, according to Plutarch, the source of the Valentinianistic Sophia is the Egyptian myth on Isis. Anthropos does not appear as a human in the material world, but as a heavenly being, a deity impersonated in the church. Christ is the son of the fallen Sophia, drowned in the material world from which he resurrects once again. Horos separates heavenly from fallen eons, and Valentinus is believed to have written a discussion on the triple human nature, according to which humans are divided into spiritual, animal, and material (pneumatics, psychics, and hylics), which is a very old teaching, dated to the fourth century BC. Same as the Savior has his fallen aspect on the earth, and his fallen aspect is Sophia, so each gnostic on the earth has his heavenly pair before God. Irenaeus states that Valentinus's followers keep meditating on the secret unity with their heavenly pair (syzygy).

---

57. Hippolytus's account of one of the variants of the Sophia myths.

Marcus

Marcus, Valentinus's student from early times, introduced a developed numerical system. Each numerical expression contains also the sum of all numerical systems containing the letters of its name and, further on, all their letters to the infinity by hierarchy. Such symbolic presentation was called one element configuration or tunes of sound.

In the myth on the Holy Spirit, the white dove is alpha and omega (alpha + omega = 1 + 800 = 801), in Greek *peristerá*, this having the numerical equivalent 80 (p) + 5 (e) + 100 (r) + 10(i) + 200(s) + 300(t) + 5(e) + 100(r) + 1 (a) = 801. The role of the numbers goes as far as the very cosmology that consists of ten spheres, of which seven are nonconcentric spheres, the eighth that surrounds them, and the spheres of the Sun and the Moon. This shows that the seven spheres in the Marcosianian cosmology are not spheres of the planets, nor this is about astrology and astronomy, but the dodecade is presented in a zodiac circle. The seven spheres move fast, much faster than the eighth sphere—the heaven, wherefore the entire system passes through each zodiac sign, or a twelveth part of the revolution. Thus, the final limit of the spheres determines the limits of the pleroma, the "mother of thirty names," as many names as is the number of months the Moon requires to make a revolution, which the Sun makes in twelve months, which is the number of hours in a day that is divided into thirty parts, as there are subdivisions of each zodiac sign, 360 in total if multiplied by twelve, as many as there are climates on Earth, etc.

Ptolemy too, same as Marcus, was among the Valentinus's oldest students. According to some, the laws come from the God and the Father, whereas others deem the opposite, from the prosecutor and the devil, acording to Ptolemy from the Logos. Ptolemy's idea is at the beginning of the fourth Gospel. The principle is the first existence that was created by the God, and is called Mind, Son, and the only begotten (meaning born only by the Father, not the only one born or the only one of his kind). "In the beginning was the [Logos], and the [Logos] was with God, and the [Logos] was God. He was with God in the beginning" (John 1:1–2). First of all the difference is to be established between God, the principle, and the Logos: the Principle is by the Father and from the Father, and by it is the Logos. The Gnostic Heracleon wrote a discussion on the fourth Gospel, carried on by Origen and making the first comment of a canonical Christian text by a gnostic.

Bardaesan

Bardaesan is said to be the last gnostic, the last in the sense that he was the last to promote secret learning and gnostic mysteries inside Christianity. He was a friend of King Abgar who introduced his learning as the state religion for a short period of time.

> "The human soul is capable of knowing what masses do not know"—says Bardaesan—"and all they do good, and all they do wrong, and all the things that happen to them in riches and in poverty, and in sickness and in health, and in defects of the body, it is from the influence of those Stars, which are called the Seven, they befall them, and they are governed by them. But there are others who say the opposite of these things, how that this art is a lie of the Chaldeans, or that Fortune does not exist at all, but it is an empty name; and all things are placed in the hands of man, great and small; and bodily defects and faults happen and befall him by chance. But others say that whatsoever a man does, he does of his own will, by the free-will that has been given to him, and the faults and defects and the destiny, the evil things which happen to him, he receives as a punishment from God. But as for myself, in my humble opinion, it appears to me that these three sides are partly true, and partly false. They are true, because men speak after the fashion which they see, and because, also, men see how things happen to them, and mistake; because the wisdom of God is richer than their, which has established the worlds and created man, and has ordained the Governors, and has given to all things the power which is suitable for each one of them. But I say that God, and the Angels, and the Powers, and the Governors, and the Elements, and men and animals have this power; but all these orders of which I have spoken have not power given to them in everything. For he that is powerful in everything is One; but they have power in some things, and in some things they have no power, as I have said: that the goodness of God may be seen in that in which they have power, and in that in which they have no power they may know that they have a Lord. There is, therefore, Fortune, as the Chaldeans say. And that everything is not in our own Free-will, that is that Free-will is not absolute, is plainly visible in everyday experience. Fortune also plays its part, but is not absolute, and Nature also. Thus we, the men are found to be governed by

Nature equally, and by Fortune differently, and by our Free-will each as he wishes."[58]

In this almost scientifically objective tractate, Bardaesan introduces three great elements of the karmic law: free will, destiny, and nature. The free will relates to the spirit, the destiny to the soul and the nature to the body. None of these aspects are absolute, the absolute is only with God.

Ephraim says that Bardaesan taught of seven essences and objects his three errors: that he denied resurrection and deemed separation of the soul and the body to be a blessing, that he taught the theory of the divine Mary who with the Father of life gave birth to the Son of the living, and that he believed in lesser gods, eternal beings subordinated to God. From Bardaesan, preserved is the Hymn of the Soul, a beautiful legend on initiation, telling a story completely different from the Ephraim's.

In the second century there were many of such texts presenting a major part of gnostic propaganda. Early church fathers interpreted them in their way, mostly caricaturing and ridiculing them, while gnostics, mostly because of the vow of silence and the closeness of their communities and schools, did not respond. However, these texts, perhaps exaggerated from the modern point of view, at the time of a proliferation of mysticism appeared perfectly reliable and able to defend themselves. The church critics did not know how to stop the flood of such mystic texts but, at best, they redacted them and offered them to their readers in a clean form, cleaned of the poison of delusion. Censorship and redacting were not complete, and the echo of these gnostic ideas is felt in a group of apocryphal texts, mostly taking position between Gnosicism and Orthodox Christianity.

Apocryphal Literature

By everything similar to Bardaesan's Hymn of the Robe of Glory in the apocryphal Acts of Thomas or Judas is the Hymn of Wisdom.

The apocryphal Acts of John were mentioned already by Clement of Alexandria. The entire fragment relates to John's monologue where preserved is an interesting tradition of the secret life of Jesus. The entire base is very much docetic and constructed by the powers available to the "perfect man" as existing in numerous gnostic philosophers' christological and soteriological theories. After his death and resurrection, Christ returned and taught in closed Christian communities, an idea from which came numerous protean Christian traditions. He returned in the only possible

---

58. Mead, *Fragments of a Faith Forgotten*, 398–9.

way, in the spiritual body, the body that can be seen only by those allowed, that can even be touched, but not as a mere physical body. He is the voice from the heaven, the voice containing the experience of the mystery from the first hand, able to carry it and teach about it, where from comes the term docetism.

In the apocryphal Acts of John, the author sees Jesus in prayer, his head reaching the sky, and becoming as small as a thumb when replying to John's call, that is, when he returned from his meditation. This is an image speaking about the John's inner Jesus, an image connecting the ontology and the exegesis. The idea of Jesus reaching the sky is presented also in the apocryphal Acts of Andrew: "The one part of thee stretcheth up toward heaven that thou mayest signify the heavenly word (or, the word that is above) (the head of all things): and another part of thee is spread out to the right hand and the left that it may put to flight the envious and adverse power of the evil one, and gather into one the things that are scattered abroad (or, the world): And another part of thee is planted in the earth, and securely set in the depth, that thou mayest join the things that are in the earth and that are under the earth unto the heavenly things (Laud. that thou mayest draw up them that be under the earth and them that are held in the places beneath the earth, and join, &c.)."[59] This is the allegory of the cross, allegory of the passion in a divided world that is to be united in the Word (symbolic gathering of the arms of the cross), or as he continues saying: "O cross, device (contrivance) of the salvation of the Most High! O cross, trophy of the victory [of Christ] over the enemies! O cross, planted upon the earth and having thy fruit in the heavens! O name of the cross, filled with all things (lit. a thing filled with all). Well done, O cross, that hast bound down the mobility of the world (or, the circumference)! Well done, O shape of understanding that hast shaped the shapeless (earth?)! Well done, O unseen chastisement that sorely chastisest the substance of the knowledge that hath many gods, and drivest out from among mankind him that devised it! Well done, thou that didst clothe thyself with the Lord, and didst bear the thief as a fruit, and didst call the apostle to repentance, and didst not refuse to accept us!"[60]

Andrew in the final words of the prayer to the cross introduces reincarnation; Peter in the apocryphal Acts wants to imitate the passion, but with the head turned down. He justifies his intention: "And when they had hanged him up after the manner he desired, he began again to say: Ye men unto whom it belongeth to hear, hearken to that which I shall declare unto

---

59. James, "Acts of Andrew."
60. James, "Acts of Andrew." Brackets in the original.

you at this especial time as I hang here. Learn ye the mystery of all nature, and the beginning of all things, what it was. For the first man, whose race I bear in mine appearance (or, of the race of whom I bear the likeness), fell (was borne) head downwards, and showed forth a manner of birth such as was not heretofore: for it was dead, having no motion. He, then, being pulled down—who also cast his first state down upon the earth—established this whole disposition of all things, being hanged up an image of the creation (Gk. vocation) wherein he made the things of the right hand into left hand and the left hand into right hand, and changed about all the marks of their nature, so that he thought those things that were not fair to be fair, and those that were in truth evil, to be good."[61] In presenting what is right he implies that the people think that the worst solutions are the best, "concerning which the Lord saith in a mystery: Unless ye make the things of the right hand as those of the left, and those of the left as those of the right, and those that are above as those below, and those that are behind as those that are before, ye shall not have knowledge of the kingdom."[62]

From the entire gnostic opus remained three larger collections of manuscripts, known as the Bruce, the Akhmim, and the Askew Codices. The Askew Codex is written in the Upper Egyptian dialect, made is in the form of a book, not a scroll. It consists of 346 pages, most of them well preserved. Of the entire collection, just a few pages are missing. The codex is a copy translated from Greek, consisting of a discourse known as Pistis Sophia. Other parts, of roughly the same size, are titled *The Questions of Mary* and *The Events Before Him*. The Bruce Codex is brought from Upper Egypt and is kept in the Bodleian Library in Oxford. It is written on papyrus in the Greek cursive script, in the Upper Egyptian dialect. It consists of 78 pages, in the form of a book. Many pages are missing, and it is generally in a very bad condition. It contains two gnostic texts and a few fragments, including the *Book of the Great Logos*. According to the *Pistis Sophia Treatise*, Jesus will, once resurrected, come among his disciples to teach them for eleven years. His teaching will go to a certain limit that the disciples will be able to understand, and only he will be revealed all the mysteries, including the greatest mystery of all the mysteries, or the gnosis of all the gnoses, the mystery on the Father in the shape of a dove. On the fifteenth day of the month Tibi, that is, by the full moon, above the Teacher appeared a light that consisted of all the sorts of radiation (planetary conjunctions). Jesus interpreted this event to the disciples: "It came to pass then, when the Sun had risen in the east, that a great light-power came down, in which was my

61. James, "Acts of Peter."
62. James, "Acts of Peter."

Vesture, which I had left behind in the four-and-twentieth mystery, as I have said unto you. And I found a mystery in my Vesture, written in five words of those from the height: Zama, Zama, Ozza, Rachama, Ozai. O Mystery, which is without in the world, for whose sake the universe hath arisen, this is the total outgoing and the total ascent, which hath emanated all emanates and all that is therein and for whose sake all mysteries and all their regions have arisen."[63]

The central character in the gnostic literature is Sophia. In the beginning she was the thirteenth eon, in the middle between the lowest eons and the highest, the twenty-fourth eon but, according to the First Mystery, while looking up, at the world above her, she saw the light and wanted to ascent to that elevated area. She made it to the mystery of the thirteenth eon, but no more, all the time singing hymns on the light she had seen. The twelve rulers of the lower eons hated her because she knew their mysteries (syzygies or dualities) and wanted to be above them. Having gathered the powers of their light and their matter (matter is reflection of the light that was up, above her, in the higher eons), they tricked Sophia, who having looked down thought that was the real light to which she aspired. In her ignorance she descended to the lower world saying, "I am going to that region, without husband, to take the light that the eons of light created for me." From the twelfth eon, to which she descended, she was banned, all the way down to the world of the chaos, where the devil surrounded her with his light and weakened her. Sophia asked help from the light that she trusted in the beginning (*pistis*—faith). This entire story speaks about the man immersed in the chaotic material world (hyle), whose greatest enemy is the fake light (fake teaching, fake prophets, and the seducer). The twenty-four material powers created reflections of the kingdom of the light thus misleading Sophia and causing her downfall. There are forty-nine lower and higher powers, including Sophia. Sophia will free herself from the chaos through her love for the light and after thirteen repentances, when Christ comes down to the earth. Sophia still does not know who he is. Christ radiates light by himself, with no help from the First Mystery, and sends it to help Sophia. This is the fulfillment and the First Mystery itself sends the light that fully cleanses Sophia, her powers are renewed, and she is filled with new light that she received from her husband, without whom she tried reaching enlightenment by herself, making an error in that. This only starts the final battle. Sophia is not only crowned, but fully surrounded with light. Her enemies are adapting and changing their form, becoming much more dangerous. Sophia is helped by Michael and Gabriel, the Sun and the Moon.

---

63. Mead, *Pistis Sophia*, chapter 10.

Wings of the great bird shiver, the winged globe shows its cogs, and the forces are preparing for the final battle. At the first moment Sophia killed the seven-headed basilisk, destroying his body to prevent any seeds to come from it, and after that sang the victorious song. Now the First Mystery could see the lower regions opened until three times are fulfilled, that is, until the cycle of three times or eras is ended, because it is the time of the fourth era, and three more are to come. Then heaven will open and the world will enter the state of eternal peace. *The Pistis Sophia Treatise*, *The Books of the Savior*, and *The Book of the Great Logos* are very close and probably belong to the same school, that is, they are synthesized and reformulated from older materials according to a common concept sometimes from around the first quarter of the second century till the mid-third century.

In the early centuries of Christianity numerous different mysteries circulated, legends and religious romances called memoirs, acts and gospels, and sayings of the Lord or *logia*. Mostly, these were prophecies or instructions under the common motto: thus spoke the Lord. In the second century the traditional, mystic, and legendary teachings got a new interpretation. In further theological practice only a few documents survived to have become parts of the canonical orthodox teaching. Some of these non-canonical texts are variants of similar canonical teachings and are particularly interesting in studying the roots from which the compilers drew their materials. Others, again, have nothing in common with these, belonging to a completely different development direction. This interesting philosophy encountered uncompromising criticisms from the orthodox anti-heresiarchs Justin Martyr, Clement of Alexandria, Tertullian, Hippolytus, Origen, Eusebius, Epiphanius, and Theodoret, and for the centuries to come the Christian propaganda fed on the attacks against them.

Interest in the long-ago forgotten knowledge of the old hidden mystery teachers appeared already in the Renaissance, from the mid-sixteen century, with Marcossius (*De Vitis, Secretis, et Dogmatibus omnium Haereticorum*, 1569), Macarius (*Abraxas seu Apistopistus quæ est antiquaria de Gemmis basilidianis*, 1659), Siricius (*Simonis Magi Hæreticorum omnium*, 1664), Michaelis (*Dissertatio de Indiciis Philosophiæ gnosticæ*, 1667), and others.

Nag Hammadi Library

The Nag Hammadi library was discovered accidentally in the mid-twentieth century, containing Coptic translations of Greek originals. It comprises thirteen codices:

1. The Jung's Codex, comprising the Prayer of the Apostle Paul, the Apocryphon of James, the Gospel of Truth, the Treatise on the Resurrection, and the Tripartite Tractate
2. The Apocryphon of John, the Gospel of Thomas, the Gospel of Philip, the Hypostasis of the Archons, On the Origin of the World, the Exegesis of the Soul, and the Book of Thomas the Contender
3. The Apocryphon of John, the Gospel of the Egyptians, Eugnostos the Blessed, the Sophia of Jesus Christ, the Dialogue of the Savior
4. The Apocryphon of John and the Gospel of the Egyptians
5. Eugnostos the Blessed, the Apocalypse of Paul, the First and the Second Apocalypses of James, and the Apocalypse of Adam
6. The Acts of Peter and the Twelve Apostles, The Thunder, Perfect Mind, Authoritative Teaching, the Concept of Our Great Power, Plato's Republic, the Discourse of the Eight and Ninth, the Prayer of Thanksgiving, and Asclepius (the last three being hermetic discourses)
7. The Paraphrase of Shem, the Second Treatise of the Great Shem, the Gnostic Apocalypse of Peter, the Teaching of Silvanus, and the Three Steles of Seth
8. Zostrianos and the Letter of Peter to Philip
9. Melchizedek, the Thought of Norea, and the Testimony of Truth
10. Marsanes
11. The Interpretation of Knowledge; a Valentinian Exposition: On the Anointing, On the Baptism, On the Eucharist; Allogenes; and Hypsiprone
12. The Sentences of Sextus, the Gospel of Truth, and some fragments
13. Trimorphic Protennoia and On the Origin of the World

The Nag Hammadi library and the Dead Sea Scrolls with numerous recently found lost and forgotten manuscripts aroused an exceptional interest in the times of the first centuries of Christianity.

CONNECTIONS BETWEN THE REVELATION AND OTHER RELIGIOUS SYSTEMS

According to the oldest times authors, the Revelation was highly esteemed and read in the first church, so much that the church authorities objected that the believers gave it priority and placed it above the Gospels. A text this popular and highly respected, with certain editing and adjustments, could have been accepted in other religions and teachings as well, especially having in mind the dynamics of the interreligious relationships and the intensity by which new beliefs were created at the time.

There is a certain iconographic similarity between the Revelation and the two texts preserved in the oral tradition, but whose roots reach deep into the past, in the heritage of a group of believers, small and marginal by size but exceptionally significant by importance in studying the religious processes, called the Mandaeans or John's Christians. It is hard directly to relate the Revelation and these texts, but there are certain symbolic similarities suggesting that the Revelation motivated thoughts that shaped these texts.

The Mandaeans are recorded in literature of the distant past. In the end of the thirteenth century, the dominican of Toscana, Ricoldo da Montecroce (also known as Ricoldo Pennini) described the Mandaeans as simple people claiming they held the God's laws, kept in beautiful books. "Their script is somewhere between the Syrian and the Arab. They detest Abraham because of the circumcision, and above all revere John the Baptist. . . . They wash themselves day and night in order not to offend the God."[64]

This brief description by Pennini was added to by the Tuscan Gerolamo Vecchietti, who was entrusted by the Holy See to study the manuscripts written in Eastern languages, including the Mandaean. In the long ago year of 1604 he met a group of Mandaean Christians on his way from Bagdad to Basra. One of them, a refugee from Khuzestan who spoke Portuguese, gave him the basic information on his people, telling him there were around sixty thousand of them. Vecchietti noticed that their language was similar to the Syrian, although they called it the Chaldean. In Basra he met another large group of the Mandaeans whom he related to the Chaldeans, holding them to be descendants of the old Chaldean Christians, whose numbers were drastically reduced by Islamic persecutions and who, living in unfavorable conditions, culturally deteriorated, yet had preserved their legends, religious tradition, and ceremonies. The time of their decadence occurred at the end of the Abbasid dynasty and the fall of Babylon to the hands of the Mongols after the year 1258.

Besides this, there are many more allegations in Christian literature, but these remained unpublished as long as till the mid-nineteenth century, when Pennini's report was published. Some Portuguese Jesuits mention certain "St. John's Christians" or the Mandaeans around Hormuz at the time

---

64. Lupieri et al., "Mandaeans."

of the battle between the Portuguese fleet and the Turkish army in Bahrain. The connections between the Christian missionaries and the Mandaeans continued, and it appears that over the time the Mandaeans got ready to accept the church of Rome. Even before, from their own religious experience, they knew about the seven sacraments and the adequate prayers, which made the very conversion simple and logical. Everything in Mandaean history demonstrates a strong connection with the old Babylonian society in southern Mesopotamia, including the old Chaldeans. The Mandaeans who continued living in the southern Mesopotamia kept many common linguistic, religious, and cultural characteristics of their predecessors who had lived over five hundred kilometers farther north. The confusion in recognizing their cultural importance and particularity originated mostly from the decision of the Roman church to name all the Nestorians who accepted Catholic teaching the "Chaldeans," this aiming to introduce and keep a unique administrative area that included all the religious varieties, thus leaving the Mandaean religious specificity in shadow. By this generalization every Nestorian who converted to Christianity, from Cyprus to India, was referred to as a Chaldean, whereby Vatican de facto deprived the Mandaeans of their legitimate heritage.

The oldest Mandaean texts are gathered in the Hymns of Glory (*Qualasta*) containing *The Book of Souls* (*Sidra d-Nishmata*), *Glory to the King* (*Abahatan Quadmaiia*), daily prayers *Rahmia*, *To Our First Father* (*Sidra d-Nishmata*), *Prayers for Marriage*, *Blessed Sacrifice* (*Zidqua Brika*) and other texts. The rest of the texts are gathered in the *Great Book* (*Sidra Rba* or *Ginza*).

The Mandaean language is an Eastern Aramaic language, developed around the seventh century AD, similar to the language of the Babylonian Talmud, and under a constant influence of the Persian language. Its alphabet has twenty-four letters, twenty-two being standard letters, the twenty-third being a diphthong, and the twenty-fourth the repeated first letter "a." Thus, the Mandaean alphabet corresponds to the number of hours in a day. Unlike other Semitic languages, the vowels are written in their full form, same as all other letters.

The traditional way of living in the swampy area of Babylonia by the Shat-al-Arab and the rivers feeding it, in houses made of mud, was replaced by the urban way of living. There is still a significant number of them still living in Bagdad, but because of constant persecutions the majority lives in exile.

The Mandaean priests baptized in the name of John the Baptist. Under the Islam they had the status of a protected sect. Traditionally, when a Mandaean family converted to another faith, they lost their nationality.

The Mandaeans treat Sunday as a holy day, the Sunday religious ceremonies lasting the entire morning. They believe in one god, in their holy books and other religious scripts named the Great Life or the Eternal Life. The origin of the name of this religion is not certain, although it is assumed to have been derived from the word by which they called themselves—to be a *mandaiia*, deriving from *madda*—knowledge. The rituals are led by the priests called the pupils (*tarmidia*). According to another opinion, the name is derived from the name of the highest and the only god, Manda d-Hiie, the Knowledge of Life. It is certain that the Arab surroundings named them the Subbateans from the Arab word *subba*, those who baptize. The Mandaeans hold the running water to be the force that created the world. The Mandaean world rests on the shoulders of Ur, a large snakelike sea monster of the underground. In Ginza Rabba, the best known Mandaean holy book, there are at least seven different theories about the beginning of the universe. Most texts on the Mandaean language and believing have been gathered by the Catholic missionaries, but these contain numerous inaccuracies and doubts.

In their culture, highly respected are mathematics and astronomy. The alphabet coincides with the number of hours in a day, and astrology is present in daily star observations and interpretations of their messages. Very interesting is the practice of giving a child four names, the first by the priest who performed the baptismal ceremony, the second is the family name, the third is the name of the clan, and the fourth is the Arab personal name used in addressing. The first, or the astrological, also called the name of the zodiac, is determined by the zodiac that begins with Aries and ends with Pisces. From the constellation in which the child is born the priest counts as many places as was the hour of the moment of the child's birth in order to come to the constellation that will influence the child. Then the numerical value of the sign in which the child is born is added the numerical value of the mother's astrological name. Once the final numerical value is obtained, the parents chose a corresponding name from the *Book of the Zodiac*. To predict the future the priests also study stars and heavenly events. In the Mandaean community highly respected were those who, although not priests, had religious knowledge, and cultivated were mathematics and astronomy.[65]

The Cologne Manichean Codex states elements from the Mandaean tradition that were very important, if not the base in forming the new Manichean religion. The Mandaean holy books come from Adam, presenting revelation from the beginning times. Adam calls himself Balsam, the greatest

---

65. Drower, *Mandaeans*, 73–83.

angel of light who became more powerful than all the angels and creation forces. This short segment is the preserved part of Adam's Revelation, once a part of the Elcesait Scriptorium. In Ginza there are several original Adam's Revelations. Adam's endeavor to publish his revelations makes an important element of the Mandaean apostolic doctrine. It is interesting that Adam demands his revelations to be written on clean papyrus, and not on parchment, which he obviously considers to be perishable and unclean.

Some Mandaean beliefs show an exceptional similarity with old teachings. The mythic history preserved in the Mandaean tradition says that they, as the true children of Adam, used to live at Ceylon, when a plague wiped out the entire population, survived only by Ram and Rud. From them originated the entire global population that was destroyed once again when Hiwel Ziwa destroyed the world with fire. This second scourge was survived only by Shurbey and Shurhabiel. A hundred thousand years later Noah was born, three hundred years before the flood. Six thousand years later the planets, who are the children of Ruha and Ur, built Jerusalem, to be ruled by Moses. Moses was an enemy of the Mandaeans, at war with them in Egypt, until they fled from Egypt and until the sea closed over their persecutors. They took shelter in mountains, where the twelve signs of the zodiac and the seven planets could do no harm to them. Moses followed them, but could not pass through the mountains but returned to Jerusalem. There they lived until Inoshwey (Elisabeth) gave birth to John the Baptist.

In these texts there is no mention that Adam lived six thousand years earlier, as claimed by the biblical, Jewish, and Chaldean sources, but much, much longer ago. The Mandaeans believe they are the children of Adam and Eve without interruptions, because the race and the blood never mixed. They believe that their ancestors are Hibel, Shitel, and Anosh, the children of Adam and Eve. The Mandaean tradition claims that Adam lived over 445,000 years ago, and that the existing world will last 448,000 years in total. This period of time is divided into eras ruled by certain prophets or the angels of light, one after the other Ram, Shoorbai with his wives, Sam and his wife, Noreitha, and all children of the apostle Nua or Noah and his wife, Nuraitha. This world will be followed by another one, where the blessed will continue living.

Modern Mandaeans do not support this tradition, deeming it to misstate the older and more accurate tradition based on astrological movements of celestial bodies through the zodiac. Harran Gawaitha and the oral tradition, especially among the Iranian Mandaeans, divide the time of the world into seven periods ruled by the seven planets, each of them lasting 68,571 years, 5 months, 4 days, 6 hours, 31 minutes and 30 seconds. The planetary rulers take turns as follows: Sun, Venus, Mercury, Moon, Saturn,

Jupiter, and Mars. At the end of the time the Great Light (Manda d-Hiia) will appear to Nua and his wife, Nuraitha (Noah and his wife).

The myth of the Dana Nuk's (Daniel's) way into the heaven[66] shows certain similarities with the Revelation, and to understand this it should be taken in a wider form: in the past there was just one religion in the world. All Adam's sons were Mandaeans. Among them twenty-four were learned, but only one was wise, whose name was Dana Nuk, who was more elevated than the others. They came to him for advice, because he had all the holy books given by Hiwel Ziwa to Adam, and he certainly knew them from the bottom of his heart. Among the books were Ginza Gawaitha, Sidra d Yahita, Asfar Malwasha, Diwan haran Gawaitha, Diwan Awathur, Alf Trisar Shiala, Diwan Malkutha Ileytha, Qualst'a, and Iniani d-Rahmi. The twenty-four of them had different knowledges; one knew Shamish (the Sun), others Water, Bel, Nirig, etc. (the planets), but the great Dana Nuk knew them all. Every planet had a particular power over its follower, the one who loved and served it, but Dana Nuk had the knowledge of them all. He had a room where he kept the books given by Ziwa Hiwel to Adam, stacked one on top of the other. He kept the room locked at all times. Once he entered the room and found an unknown book on top of all the others. It was written in the Mandaean language, but represented another teaching (tariqah)—the Way of the Son (Moon). Dana Nuk said, "No one could have entered this room to which only I have the key. I shall burn this book." And he burned it. He went to wasteland, sat under a tree, and pondered, "How could that book have entered my room?" And then he saw the book in front of him! He took it, tore it up and threw it into the river. He returned home, unlocked the door to the room and entered, and saw the book on top of all others as before. He asked himself, "How is something like this possible?" He was confused. He discussed this with the scholars, asking, "What is the meaning of this? The book appeared above Ginza Rabba! Perhaps we should read it, perhaps we learn something, but it promotes another way?" They answered him: "If it was above all other holy books, it must be true. The planets ruled it that way! It must be true!"

Dana Nuk returned to sleep and when he woke up the book was under his head. Again he went to the scholars and told them, "I destroyed this book twice, and here it is! I found it under my head when I woke up!" Some scholars said, "It must be from God, the book is to be read!" Some of them took and read it and accepted its way, they and their wives, and were lightened up. Since then they and their children worshiped the light of the Moon. There are still those who worship the Moon and the secrets of

---

66. Drower, *Mandaeans*, 300–308.

the Jews, and their magic comes from the Moon, which they learned from that book. Yes, they and their children worship the Moon. Three weeks later another book appeared in the Dana Nuk's room above all other books and he gave this one to the scholars as well. It promoted the Way of Kiwan (Saturn) and some scholars and their relatives believed in it. In a similar way five more books appeared, making the total of seven of them, each of them promoting another way. Some scholars accepted one, others another way. The last book appeared illuminated with bright light. Dana Nuk's heart turned to that book, he read it and believed what was written in it, and he saw the perfection of the divine knowledge. When he read it, his heart rejoiced and every fear abandoned him. God gave him the book and he accepted it as his own way.[67]

The iconographic similarities of the myth on the Dana Nuk's way to the heaven and the Revelation are hardly visible at this level. The twenty-four learned Mandaeans correspond to the twenty-four Elders in the Revelation celebrating the One seated on the throne (Rev 4:4) and revealing the mysterious book similar to the books in the Mandaean text. Clearly, this story brings the myth of the creation of religions, but when compared with the text called *Millennium*, brought from the Mandaean oral tradition by Drower,[68] it has a different interpretation. The books found by Dana Nuk in a sacred and protected place announce different planetary announcements, announcements going from the Moon that appears first, to Saturn, and on to the seventh planet, accepted by Dana Nuk.

In the first sentence of the *Millennium* announces the great power of the King of Darkness at the end of the time and great wars, when the world will be poisoned with something that will put death in the air and the water. Seven great rulers will gather at one place and make peace. The spirit will appear and reveal the secret to one of them. Others will kill this one with envy, for the spirit to be revealed to another one, who was also killed by the others, and so on until of the seven rulers remained just one. The last one is Shamish, and with him the peace will come and in the world there will be just one religion. This myth, preserved till today just in oral tradition, speaks about the sequence of the seven eons ruled by the planets and whose rule ends (dies) by the appearance of the next one that comes with a new revelation for its time, and when in the combat between God and the devil the peace will be established. The myth is carried on in a derived Manichaeistic form, showing a tendency to redact and adapt from old myths, speaking

---

67. Drower, *Mandaeans*, 308–9.
68. Drower, *Mandaeans*, 308–9.

about four historic eons presided and revealed by prophets, each one for his time. The announcements are carried to them by the angel of great glow.

The Dana Nuk story goes on: later on, while he prayed in the garden, before him he saw a creature made of light. He bowed to the creature, who told him, "Those who took other books will be thrown to the earth once the resurrection comes and will neither ascend nor know the way to Avathur. But you will resurrect, because your book is the book of Shamish (Sun), and Shamish is the only one from God and the devil cannot act against him. He who reads this book will understand everything. Did you read it to others?" Dana Nuk answered, "Only I and my family have read it." Then the creature said, "I must take your soul to the world of the light, so that you can understand the truth and can, when you return, tell others what you saw."

He took him to the cottage hidden among the trees in the middle of the field, and left him there saying, "Sleep!" Dana Nuk fell asleep because he wanted to see the world of light. The creature gave him an airy form, the same as it itself had, and the Dana Nuk's soul entered in it. Adam's sons could see him no more. His body was asleep, his pulse thumped, but his soul was far away.

The creature took him to Phytill (Demiurge) and Ziwa Hiwel showed himself to him saying, "You are lucky to have come to this place." And he ordered melkies and uthras (angels) to take him and show him the underground with demons and the purgatory in Mat'aratha. Then the melkies took him to the dwellings of Sera (Sira, Moon) and Liwet (Venus), and their dwellings were beautiful. Then they took him to the place that God gave to Ruha, God's place of great charm. Then to Shamish (Sun), the places of light and indescribable glare. Then they took him high, high, until they reached paradise, the place where God dwells and more is beautiful than all the previous ones. Dana Nuk wept: "I want to stay here and never to leave." But they took him even higher, to the place where dwell the Great Four, whose names are Arham Haiy, En Haiy, Shom Haiy, and Ziwa Haiy. When he saw them in all their beauty, he cried to Ziwa Haiy, because he took him through the garden, "I can go no further. Let me rest here." Hiwel Ziwa replied, "No, you have to go on!" They stood up and arrived to the pace Melka d'Anhura, and it was vast and all made of light. Here were four stationary suns, that did not rotate like our Sun, and their power was the axis of Hiwel Ziwa. This is the place of power and strength.

Hiwel Ziwa took him even higher, until they arrived at the second heaven, also illuminated with four suns, but even larger and brighter. Dana Nuk asked, "Whose is this?" Hiwel Ziwa replied, "This is my place, but we must go higher!" They continued moving up and came to a place full of uthras, where there was a sea of light. Its waters were pure light and around it were melkies, male and female, adoring God. Dana Nuk asked Hiwel Ziwa, "I can see no children in the sea of light, where are they?" He replied, "In the belly of the sea, Yardne of light, they grow and once they are ready for prayer they will come out of these waters, because we do not multiply like you. Our seed is in the waters of the ocean of light. They eat from the paradise trees and there are no wastes and spoils from what they eat. Everything is power and light."

When Dana Nuk saw the heaven of the heavens, he was to return and tell what he saw. His travel lasted fourteen years. When he woke up he thanked Hiwel Ziwa, saying, "Pray Shamish, Liwet, and Nirigh (Sun, Venus, and Saturn) to protect me—pray all those who hold bow (planets)!"

Dana Nuk visited the world of Ruha, after having visited those of Moon and Venus. Ruha is the daughter to Hagh and his wife Magh. Hiwel Ziwa (the king of light) brought her from the world of darkness, ruled by Akrun. With him were Gaf and Gaphan, Hgh and Magh, Sagi and Sargani, male-female pairs, and, at the end, Ruha's husband, Ashdum. Their symbols are lion, scorpion, and hornet. After the mythic battle and the victory over Akrum, Hiwel Ziwa saved Ruha from the world of darkness. She was pregnant and gave birth to Phatil, the child of light and darkness that judges the souls of the dead.[69]

The story of the Dana Nuk's mythic travel to the heaven shows also structural similarity to the Revelation. His visit to the Moon and its dwelling looks like the description of the heavenly throne around which seated are twenty-four elders and four living creatures (stationary suns), whereas before them was "like a sea of glass, clear and crystal" (Rev 4:1–14). The second sphere is the dwelling of Venus, the pleroma, the Mandaean Elisabeth, the mother of the prophet John the Baptist, who gives birth in the heaven with a star above her head:

> A child was transplanted from on high, a secret was revealed in Jerusalem.
>
> The priests had a dream. An utter silence fell upon the Eulaeus, an utter silence fell upon Jerusalem (Ur-Ashlam). . . .
>
> I saw in my night visions, in my vision when I lay sown—
> I didn't sleep, rest or lie down, and sleep did not overtake me in the night.
> I didn't sleep and I didn't rest—that a star came to Enisbhai (Elizabeth),
> a ire rose, burning over elder father Zechariah,

---

69. Drower, *Mandaeans*, 269–73.

> three lamps appeared, the sun set and the lamps shined forth.
> A fire hung bout the synagogue, and smoke wreathed the Temple.
> A sound rumbled on the chariot, the Earth shook from its place.
> A shooting star burst over Judaea, a hooting star burst over Jerusalem.
> The sun appeared at night, and the moon shined forth during the day....
>
> The star came and rose over Elisabeth: the child was transplanted from the upper heights,
> and he came and was given to Elisabeth.
> The fire that burns upon elder father Zechariah: Yuhana (Johannes) is born in Jerusalem.[70]

This part is very much similar to the description of the woman giving birth clothed with the Sun (Rev 12:1–12), whereas in the third part dwells Ruha, the creator of the material world, a woman kidnapped an taken to the underground. It reminds of the woman sitting on a scarlet beast that was covered with blasphemous names and had seven heads and ten horns (Rev 17:1–18). John's travel ends at the level of the heavenly Jerusalem, corresponding to Hiwel Ziwa's dwelling. This is the center of the spheres, the fourth sphere where the paradise is. Above it are the other three spheres through which Dana Nuk continued his travel to God's dwelling. The similarity of the Revelation and the Mandaean belief is at the level of iconographic recognizing, or interpretation that has no deeper significance, except refabulation and shaping into a myth compatible with the Mandaean belief that has no role in the interpretation of the Revelation and John's message. Furthermore, the elements that the Mandaeans perhaps took from the Revelation exist in other religious systems that could have equally influenced creation and shaping of both stories.

In the Mandaean belief, same as in other gnostic texts, evident is a marked connection with astronomy, especially in the myths that are always built on the unity of opposites, presented through personalized pairs showing opposite qualities, male and female principles, light and darkness, good and evil. Gaf and Gafan, Hagh and Magh, Sagi and Sargani, Ashdum and Ruha, male-female pairs correspond to the Egyptian ogdoad (ογδοάς) Naunet and Nu, Amaunet and Amun, Kauket and Kuk, and Huh and Hauhet, eight gods of the Old Kingdom that subsequently passed to enead (nine principles), representing male or female aspect of the elements of which the

---

70. Mead, *Mandaean Book*, ch. 1.

world is created: water Naunet and Nu, air or invisible Amaunet and Amun, darkness Kauket and Kuk, and eternity or endless space Huh and Hauhet.

The Revelation apparently builds a particular theology of the elements that may support the author's main idea, and he uses elements spontaneously and noncritically, drawing on the experiences within his reach. The Valentinianism is a mature and developed theology, developed in a religious and cultural ambient in which some time earlier the Revelation had been created, same as it may make part of the ambient that may have partly inspired the Mandaeans to take over its elements in buiding their own mythology, but all of them may have much deeper and common roots.

The Valentinian ogdoad indicates these male-female principle syzygies in their spiritual and material forms, but also in the earthly-heavenly one. Syzygy is on one hand a marriage, where different elements act jointly, but as an astronomical notion it includes mutual conjunctions of two planets and also conjunctions of celestial and terrestrial events, analogous unity of male and female eons, astronomical conjunction/occultation of celestial bodies, and astrology/connection of a gnostic with his celestial pair. These elements certainly appear in the Revelation in the image of the woman sitting on the beast, images describing the first and the second beast, conjunction of the woman and the Sun, and of the Sun and the Son of Man with the churches.

Text Analysis

THE NUMBER OF THE BEAST

The Revelation starts with a prologue in which John announces the prophecy which he received from Jesus Christ and which he passes on to believers. This event occurs at the very beginning and its dramatic development takes place through a series of dramatic events he describes in metaphors, leading up to the final victory of those who hear his prophecy and are prepared. They are promised a reward for the hardships and suffering they will endure. He addresses each of the churches of Asia Minor separately, promising each of them a different reward:

1. "To him who overcomes, I will give the right to eat from the tree of life, which is in the paradise of God" (Rev 2:7).

2. "He who overcomes will not be hurt at all by the second death" (Rev 2:11).

3. "To him who overcomes, I will give some of the hidden manna. I will also give him a white stone with a new name written on it, known only to him who receives it" (Rev 2:17).

4. "To him who overcomes and does my will to the end, I will give authority over the nations—he will rule them with an iron scepter; he will dash them to pieces like pottery—just as I have received authority from my Father. I will also give him the morning star" (Rev 2:26–28).

5. "He who overcomes will, like them, be dressed in white. I will never blot out his name from the book of life, but will acknowledge his name before my Father and his angels" (Rev 3:5).

6. "Him who overcomes I will make a pillar in the temple of my God. Never again will he leave it. I will write on him the name of my God and the name of the city of my God, the new Jerusalem, which is

coming down out of heaven from my God; and I will also write on him my new name" (Rev 3:12).

7. "To him who overcomes, I will give the right to sit with me on my throne, just as I overcame and sat down with my Father on his throne" (Rev 3:21).

The Son of Man promises to "those who overcome" eternal life (1, 2, 5) a new name (3), authority over nations and the morning star (4), and the new Jerusalem (3 and 7). On the one hand, the reward is obviously eschatological, as it contains the promise of life after death, while on the other hand the authority over the nations which one will dash to pieces like pottery represents the authority over hylics, the unenlightened ones, those with whom one who overcomes death could not be associated with on the eschatological level. The new Jerusalem is the kingdom of God which those whose names are written in the Book of Life will enter. However, John himself states that this kingdom is coming down out of heaven, meaning that it is unclear whether the victorious ones will enjoy the fruits of their victory in heaven or on earth.

Such a premise should not be considered unusual, as apocalyptic philosophy introduces the new idea of the unity of human, cosmological, and spiritual history. The revelation seen by John in signs implies the transfer of content from one level to another. Thus, Peter explains why he wants to be crucified upside down: "Whence in a mystery the Lord hath said: 'If ye make not the Right like as the Left, the Left like as the Right, Above as the Below, Before as the Behind, ye shall not know God's kingdom.' This saying have I made manifest in me, my brothers; this is the way in which your eyes of flesh behold me hanging."[1]

The events simultaneously take place on all levels, representing at the same time eschatological, cosmological, and terrestrial historical events, described by John within a single image. The approach to understanding the images depicted by John therefore primarily implies discerning between the different parts of the images and assigning them to the appropriate levels.

Such an analysis assumes that the text has been preserved in its original form and that there have been no significant interventions to the text that could have disrupted or altered its meaning and context. The unique language that no one had used before in the manner used by John, building his own unique grammar and syntax, could not have been altered without visible traces, which—according to the already presented conclusions of the analysis conducted by Charles—clearly suggests that the Revelation had

---

1. Mead, *Fragments of a Faith Forgotten*, 448.

been written by a single author and that no later interventions are likely to have altered it. In addition, the text is protected by the final oath: "If anyone adds anything to them [the words of this book of prophecy], God will add to him the plagues described in this book. And if anyone takes words away from this book of prophecy, God will take away from him his share in the tree of life and in the holy city, which are described in this book" (Rev 22:18–19). The third and possibly the most secure protection is the complete incomprehensibility that created the semblance of a mysterious meaning with no central points that could be identified where one could or should intervene. Based on the early interpretations of the text that put the Revelation in a completely different context in terms of its content and authorship, it seems evident that John's true message was forgotten in the early days, not long after it had been written. Such circumstances brought a new character of the text into focus, as it increasingly began to be seen as a mystery prophesying future events, interesting among other things for its magnificent invocations, but primarily as a mystery announcing hidden truths and revelations of God.

Such a reputation of John's Revelation is owed primarily to the very author, who calls upon readers to solve riddles that he himself highlights in the text. In this way, John emphasizes the central points of his message that those who are to understand it must take special note of, suggesting that his riddles can be decoded and inviting the recipients of the message to do so. This may indicate that the text was originally intended for quite a limited audience of persons who were closely associated with John in terms of their cultural, religious, and professional background and would as such be able to understand and decipher his message. Those who deciphered the message were then entrusted with passing it on to the wider public. The author elaborates on the events, offering arguments aimed at gathering and mobilizing the recipients of the message around a particular goal. The question nevertheless remains whether this goal is an abstract promise of salvation (eternal life, hidden manna, and a white stone, righteousness and a name, a pillar/throne in the temple/new Jerusalem) or an actual new Jerusalem.

A Name—A Mystery

In addition to highlighting the potential central points within the text, John also provides a key of sorts to his metaphors, directly calling for them to be solved and indicating with a similar phrase (hidden name) the particular points within the text that conceal the identity of the main actors of his drama. In this context, one should by all means take into account the mystical function of a name as such, which does not simply denote or identify the one who carries it, as we would understand it today, but rather conveys the function of a particular subject, defining it in the deepest mystical sense. The main subjects (i.e., actors) of John's drama may be pinpointed through phrases mentioning their names:

a. "This calls for wisdom. If anyone has insight, let him calculate the number of the Beast, for it is a man's number. His number is 666" (Rev 13:18).

b. "This title [i.e. name] was written on her forehead: mystery.... 'Why are you astonished? I will explain to you the mystery of the woman and of the beast she rides, which has the seven heads and ten horns'" (Rev 17:5–7). "This calls for a mind with wisdom. The seven heads are seven hills on which the woman sits. They are also seven kings" (Rev 17:9).

c. "I saw heaven standing open and there before me was a white horse, whose rider is called Faithful and True. With justice he judges and makes war. His eyes are like blazing fire, and on his head are many crowns. He has a name written on him that no one knows but he himself" (Rev 19:11–12).

The narrative imagery involves personification, and each of the images has two levels:

$$A - B - C = A_1 - B_1 - C_1$$

One highlights a celestial (i.e., heavenly) characteristic (rider in the open heaven), while the other reflects an earthly trait (woman sitting on seven hills). The image of the woman sitting on seven hills is quite clear and can be assumed to stand for Rome—and its heavenly counterpart, of course—that sits on seven hills and used to have seven kings.

The third actor is concealed, and his identity may be established by other means. The relation may be represented in the following manner:

$$A - B - C \text{ (rider)} = A_1 - B_1 \text{ (Rome)} - C_1$$

The second and at the same time most intriguing mystery of the Revelation of John is the question of the antichrist and of his number, but this problem can't be solved in this way. Both Irenaeus and Victorinus state that the number 666 is the name number of the Sun, but that it can also be the number of other names, among which Irenaeus lists those of Euanthas, Lateinos, and Teitan. Victorinus solves this issue in a similar manner: by stating that the number of the beast is the number of its name, and that it is in fact the number of a man (Rev 13:18).

The mystery of the number 666 represents a global enigma. Victorinus gives the following interpretation:

> As they have it reckoned from the Greek characters, they thus find it among many to be *teitan* (i.e., Titan), for teitan has this number, which the Gentiles call Sol and Phoebus; and it is reckoned in Greek thus: *t* three hundred, *e* five, *i* ten, *t* three hundred, *a* one, *n* fifty—which taken together become six hundred and sixty-six. For as far as belongs to the Greek letters, they fill up this number and name; which name if you wish to turn into Latin, it is understood by the antiphrase DICLUX, which letters are reckoned in this manner: since D figures five hundred, I one, C a hundred, L fifty, V five, X ten—which by the reckoning up of the letters makes similarly six hundred and sixty-six, that is, what in Greek gives *teitan*, to wit, what in Latin is called DICLUX; by which name, expressed by antiphrases, we understand Antichrist, who, although he be cut off from the supernal light, and deprived thereof, yet transforms himself into an angel of light, daring to call himself light.

Victorinus goes on to refer to the word *antemos* found in a certain Greek codex, whose letters calculated in this way give the same number as above: *a* one, *n* fifty, *t* three hundred, *e* five, *m* forty, *o* seventy, *s* two hundred—which together makes six hundred and sixty-six.

Another word with the same numerical equivalent is found in Gothic, namely the word *genshrikos*, which Victorinus, surprisingly, also interprets according to the Greek alphabet: *g* three, *e* five, *n* fifty, *s* two hundred, *h* eight, *r* a hundred, *i* ten, *k* twenty, *o* seventy, and *s* also two hundred, which, as has been said above, make six hundred and sixty-six.[2] These attempts by Victorinus show how interested he was in the problem.

It is evident from both sources that the authors use simple methods of substituting the characters of the alphabet with their numerical equivalents in Greek, with two examples where Victorinus attempts to solve the problem in Latin by translating a numerical expression into a word, and in Gothic where he also uses the Greek gematria methodology.

Ever since the beginnings of Greek philosophy and the time of Pythagoras, numbers had been attributed additional mystical meanings. Through the course of the centuries, quite complex formulas and methods evolved from such teachings, which were later used in and became part of

---

2. Victorinus, *Commentary*, 13:18.

the Kabbalah method, but also an important element of the philosophy of Marcosians—a sect that developed on the foundations of the Pythagorean school of thought in the second century AD, a time immediately following the time when the Revelation was written, and whose fundamental ideas had by then already been around for centuries. What both Irenaeus and Victorinus refer to is simple Greek gematria, although John, who is a Jew, is more likely to have used the Hebrew or Aramaic language, pronunciation, and alphabet. The number of the name may also have been taken over from another geographical area to which the man referred to here had belonged. Both authors agree on one thing: the number 666 relates to the Sun (Sol or Phoebus).

With the Arab invasions of the early Middle Ages, traces of ancient and forgotten occult philosophies and cabalistic teachings were first introduced to Europe and continued spreading across the old continent throughout the Renaissance period. New innovations are created based on old skills, ancient knowledge is reinterpreted and adapted, leaving a clear trace of the oldest written sources. In his book series *Of Occult Philosophy*, one of the greatest magicians in history Heinrich Cornelius Agrippa von Nettesheim (1486–1535) provides an answer to the mystery of the number 666.

The first step here does not involve gematria, but rather tables of the planets, which were also used for divination, but the method of calculation was completely different, and the number of a planet's name was calculated from the number of the planet. Each planet has its own number: Saturn comes first, and the number assigned to it is three. Its name number is calculated from a square divided into nine fields, with three columns and three rows (3 x 3). Nine numbers—from one to nine—are entered in the fields, so that the sum of all numbers in each column, row and diagonal is the same (magic square). The sum of the first and last row, the first and last column and of both diagonals gives the planet's name number. A simple way to calculate the name number is this: Saturn has nine fields and the average value of the numbers from 1 to 9 is (1 + 9) / 2 = 5. Each row, column, and diagonal has three fields (5 x 3 = 15), and this number should be multiplied by 6 (two rows, two columns, and two diagonals for each planet) or, calculated by the shortcut formula $f_{(x)} = 3x(x^2+1)$.

- The number of Saturn is 3, and its name number is 90.
- The number of Jupiter is 4, and its name number is 204.
- The number of Mars is 5, and its name number is 390.
- The number of the Sun is 6, and its name number is 666.
- The number of Venus is 7, and its name number is 1050.

- The number of Mercury is 8, and its name number is 1560.
- The number of the Moon is 9, and its name number is 2214.

6	32	3	34	35	1
7	11	27	28	8	30
19	14	16	15	23	24
18	20	22	21	17	13
25	29	10	9	26	12
36	5	33	4	2	31

Table 1. Table of the name number of the Sun[3]

Thus, according to Agrippa, Irenaeus, and Victorinus, the number 666 is the name number of the Sun. The very text of the Revelation tells us that it "performed great and miraculous signs, even causing fire to come down from heaven to earth in full view of men" (Rev 13:13). As John describes two situations within a single image, we need to distinguish between separate elements of the text according to the different levels to which they belong. Only one sentence, except for the sentence (Rev 13:1) where John mentions the beast with two horns (the zodiac sign of Taurus, represented by the bull, which comes from the Earth element and in which the Sun is found at the moment of the event), very briefly states the character of the Sun, saying that it causes fire to come down from heaven. The rest of the narrative image does not refer to the Sun but to another event that is in relation/conjunction with it and to a man whose name number matches the name number of the Sun.

The mystery of the name of the beast must have been a matter of common knowledge in John's time, but the interesting and crucial question here

3. Agrippa, *Of Occult Philosophy*, bk. 2.

is this: who is the man with the name number 666 who is in conjunction with the Sun because he shares the same name number as the Sun? The beast "forced everyone, small and great, rich and poor, free and slave, to receive a mark on his right hand or on his forehead, so that no one could buy or sell unless he had the mark, which is the name of the beast or the number of his name" (Rev 13:16–17). The name of the beast or the number of its name (its monogram) is found on the money without which no one can buy or sell, meaning that the beast is a ruler who mints his own currency. Here we are able to discern the historical context of the narrative. John brings celestial events into connection with the Sun and an earthly ruler whose name number is 666. If John is describing the current events of his time, it is quite unlikely that the mystery wasn't already solved in the early times after his Revelation, since the number of rulers who were enemies of John was relatively limited and it would have been quite easy to deduce who he was referring to. Although the name number of the Sun was a matter of common knowledge at the time, the name of the ruler John is referring to seems to have been even more renowned and known to the early interpreters of the Revelation, who—from the very beginning—adjusted the number of his name according to their own language and alphabet, ignoring the name number of the Sun in the process, which resulted in various different interpretations in the early texts which Irenaeus refers to.

If John was indeed writing about his own time and speaking up against the politics and the powermongers of his own period, such a simple and easily solvable riddle could by all means have been detrimental both to himself and to all those who were in contact with him and who conveyed his message.

Here we can clearly recognize John's intention to bring celestial events into connection with historical events by referring to celestial bodies (planets) which are in conjunction with certain historical figures. Against the backdrop of John's narrative, we are able to discern a historical context that will later on be brought into connection with the name number of the mysterious antichrist ruler.

A (the Sun) – B – C (rider) = A_1 (ruler 666) – B_1 (Rome) – C_1

ICONOGRAPHY

But if the woman sitting on the beast is Rome and its heavenly counterpart, and the second beast is the Sun and the ruler with the name number of 666, who is then the mysterious rider on a white horse?

According to David Barr, John's Revelation was originally meant to be read aloud to an audience in meetings of the early Christian community. John's narration takes place at multiple narrative levels, and on each of these levels a separate plot is developed. The entire drama spirals upward to its culmination, and to understand the author's process we must first assess the voices through which the narrative is presented and the ears to which it is addressed (Who hears?). By distinguishing the various levels of narration and assessing the different plots and stories unfolded at each narrative level, we can reconstruct the persuasive force of John's story on the implied oral audience.[4]

Barr believes that a simplified overview of the narrative levels of the story is necessary to begin the analysis, arguing that—while the actual telling of the story is more complex—there are three basic levels to John's narrative: the level of the reader/hearer, the level of the revealer, and the level of the revealed. The story opens with an unattributed voice addressing the implied audience, declaring the revelation of Jesus Christ, which God gave to him to show his servants what must soon take place; he made it known by sending his angel to his servant John, who testified to the word of God and to the testimony of Jesus Christ, even to all that he saw. Blessed is the one who reads the words of this prophecy, and blessed are those who hear it and take to heart what is written in it, because the time is near!

The central question here is whose voice this is (God/Jesus?) and what its result will be (blessedness), and to whom does it speak? According to Barr, it is not the voice of anyone in the story. It refers to John in the third person, as the voice of a lector, the one who reads aloud. On the other hand, it is clearly John who is the narrator, at least to the degree that John is the implied author of the text. As the implied author, he introduces the narrative with another narrator, one who stands on a different narrative level and is different from the author. Such a narrator, often appearing omniscient, stands "above" the story and controls its unfolding. The second level of communication is seen in the letters to the churches, where John appears on the same fictional level as the characters in the story. The third level of the narrative is reflected in the relation between John who is standing on the beach on Patmos and John "in the spirit" who sees and interacts with the majestic, divine figure. In this transition, it is no longer John who appears as the narrator, but rather God/Jesus. John's direct addressing of readers/hearers as he introduces himself in the story as its author is quite minimal and the appeals he makes are very general: he addresses the servants of Jesus and they gather to hear him. The appeals made to the churches at the second level are much

---

4. Barr, "Who Says? Who Hears?"

more detailed and each is individually characterized in a message directed to its angel. Together they form a complex group containing both rich and poor, faithful and unfaithful, hardworking and sleepers, harsh and loving, and John's message here is universal and addressed to all those who wish to hear it. At the third level, John invokes the authority of a higher narrator to explain to him the events he himself does not understand.

The narrative transmission from the revealer to John/the narrator ("The revelation of Jesus Christ, which God gave him to show his servants *what must soon take place*" [Rev 1:1]) in the relation God – Jesus – servants through John differs from the line of narration that follows in the next sentence ("He made it known by sending his angel to his servant John, who testifies to everything he saw—that is, the word of God and the testimony of Jesus Christ" [Rev 1:2]), where the angel is introduced as an intermediary and the line goes from God – Jesus – angel – servant John.

On Patmos, the Son of Man addresses John ("I turned around to see the voice that was speaking to me. And when I turned, I saw seven golden lampstands, and among the lampstands was someone like a son of man" [Rev 1:12–13]), giving him the following instruction: "Write on a scroll what you see and send it to the seven churches: to Ephesus, Smyrna, Pergamum, Thyatira, Sardis, Philadelphia and Laodicea" (Rev 1:11) and specifying the audience to which his revelation is addressed.

He who sits on a throne also gives John a scroll with writing on both sides ("Then I saw in the right hand of him who sat on the throne a scroll *with writing on both sides and sealed* with seven seals") which no one can read ("And I saw a mighty angel proclaiming in a loud voice, 'Who is worthy to break the seals and open the scroll?' But no one in heaven or on earth or under the earth could open the scroll or even look inside it" [Rev 5:2–3]) until it is read by the Lion of the tribe of Judah ("See, the *Lion* of the tribe of *Judah*, the *Root* of David, has triumphed. He is able to open the scroll and its seven seals" [Rev 5:5]).

An angel gives John the scroll ("Then the voice that I had heard from heaven spoke to me once more: 'Go, take the scroll that lies open in the hand of the angel who is standing on the sea and on the land.' So I went to the angel and asked him to give me the little scroll. He said to me, 'Take it and eat it. It will turn your stomach sour, but in your mouth it will be as sweet as honey'" [Rev 10:8–9])

The line of narrators is different in each of these examples:

1. God (author) – Jesus (narrator) – servants
2. God – Jesus (author) – angel – John (narrator)

3. Son of Man – John (author) – churches of Asia Minor
4. Son of Man (author) – John (narrator) – churches of Asia Minor
5. He who sits on a throne (author) – angel – Lion of the tribe of Judah (narrator)
6. ? (author) – angel (narrator) – John

Although examples 3 and 4 follow the same line, the authorship changes. The Son of Man has a direct encounter with John who writes the revelation addressed to the churches. In example 1, John merely states the revelation to be from God and Jesus for believers, example 5 is completely out of correlation and at a higher level, while the remaining examples include John who sees the Son of Man/angel/throne in heaven, and the narrative is transmitted through the following line of narrators: God – Jesus, Son of Man/angel/throne in heaven – John – churches of Asia Minor/servants. The revelation comes from Jesus Christ; yet John doesn't encounter him, but his angel.

The Son of Man instructs John to write to "the angels of the seven churches," which—based on the interpretation "the mystery of the seven stars that you saw in my right hand and of the seven golden lampstands is this: The seven stars are the angels of the seven churches, and the seven lampstands are the seven churches" (Rev 1:20)—means "to the stars." Similarly, substituting the seven lampstands with the seven churches in "before the throne, seven lamps were blazing. These are the seven spirits of God" (Rev 4:5) would mean that there are seven churches before the throne—and thus Asia Minor itself, or, in turn, that there are seven stars before the throne in heaven. If we look at the image of the heavenly/earthly throne with twenty-four elders and four living creatures, and before it "a *Lamb*, looking as if it had been *slain*. . . . He had seven horns and *seven eyes*" (Rev 5:6), we can assume this to be the same lamb as the one with which the beast is compared in "then I saw another beast, coming out of the earth. He had two horns like a lamb, but he spoke like a dragon" (Rev 13:11). Taking the term "lamb" to mean the same in both cases, we could conclude that—if the throne is both in heaven and on earth—before the earthly throne stands Asia Minor, perhaps even Israel with two horns—kingdoms. By analogy, the beast with two horns is a state with two kingdoms such as Israel (Parthia and Media?), which implies that the throne in heaven is not a mirror image of Israel, but rather that Israel lies before it.

The attributes of the Son of Man in the first image where he instructs John on what to do are the same as those listed in the titles of the letters to the churches:

- "To the angel of the church in Ephesus write: These are the words of him who holds the seven stars in his right hand and walks among the seven golden lampstands" (Rev 2:1).
- "To the angel of the church in Smyrna write: These are the words of him who is *the First and the Last*, who died and came to life again" (Rev 2:8).
- "To the angel of the church in Pergamum write: These are the words of him who has the sharp, double-edged sword" (Rev 2:12).
- "To the angel of the church in Thyatira write: These are the words of the Son of God, whose eyes are like blazing fire and whose feet are like burnished bronze" (Rev 2:18).
- "To the angel of the church in Sardis write: These are the words of him who holds the seven spirits of God and the seven stars" (Rev 3:1).
- "To the angel of the church in Philadelphia write: These are the words of him who is holy and true, who holds the *key of David. What he opens no one can shut,* and *what he shuts no one can open*" (Rev 3:7).
- "To the angel of the church in Laodicea write: These are the words of the *Amen*, the *faithful* and true *witness*, the ruler of God's creation" (Rev 3:14).

These attributes are similar to those of the one who speaks to John on Patmos:

"I turned around to see the voice that was speaking to me. And when I turned [to Ephesus] I saw seven golden lampstands, and among the lampstands was someone like a Son of Man, dressed in a robe reaching down to his feet and with a golden sash around his chest. His head and hair were white like wool, as white as snow, [to Thyatira] and his eyes were like blazing fire. His feet were like bronze glowing in a furnace, and his voice was like the sound of rushing waters. [To Sardis] In his right hand he held seven stars, [to Pergamum] and out of his mouth came a sharp double-edged sword. His face was like the sun shining in all its brilliance. When I saw him, I fell at his feet as though dead. Then he placed his right hand on me and said [to Smyrna]: 'Do not be afraid. I am the First and the Last. I am the Living One; I was dead, and behold I am alive for ever and ever! [To Philadelphia] And I hold the keys of death and Hades" (Rev 1:12–20).

The message to Laodicea is similar to the message to Philadelphia, that reads: "These are the words of him who is holy and true, *who holds the key of David. What he opens no one can shut, and what he shuts no one can open*" and is somewhat different from the wording in the introductory description

"And I hold the keys of death and Hades." This gives us an explanation to another metaphor: the key of David is the key of death and Hades. When put into the context of the verse "The fifth angel sounded his trumpet, and I saw a star that had fallen from the sky to the earth. The star was given the key to the shaft of the Abyss" (Rev 9:1), this means that the key of David is the key of the Abyss, which appears later on in "And I saw an angel coming down out of heaven, having the key to the Abyss and holding in his hand a great chain. He seized the dragon, that ancient serpent, who is the devil, or Satan, and bound him for a thousand years" (Rev 20:1–2).

The Revelation is made known to John by Jesus Christ, who is given the word of God "to show his servants what must soon take place." However, he doesn't do this directly, but rather "by sending his angel to his servant John" (Rev 1:1) who brings the message of peace "from him who is, and who was, and who is to come, and from the seven spirits before his throne, and from Jesus Christ, who is the faithful witness, the firstborn from the dead, and the ruler of the kings of the earth" (Rev 1:4–5). The message again comes from two sources—from the one who is, and who was, and who is to come, and from Jesus Christ, the faithful witness, the firstborn from the dead, and the ruler of the kings of the earth. John repeats this in the final warning at the end of the book: "I, Jesus, have sent my angel to give you this testimony for the churches. I am the Root and the Offspring of David, and the bright Morning Star" (Rev 22:16).

The Revelation is again mentioned in the scene where John sees the throne in heaven and the living creatures around it that never stop saying, "Holy, holy, holy is the Lord God Almighty, who was, and is, and is to come" (Rev 4:8)—as not Jesus but someone else was previously addressed, the same as in the invocation "to him who sits on the throne and to the Lamb be praise and honor and glory and power, for ever and ever!" (Rev 5:13), meaning that the one sitting on the throne in this scene is not the one sitting with God in the new Jerusalem: "The throne of God and of the Lamb will be in the city, and his servants will serve him. They will see his face, and his name will be on their foreheads" (Rev 22:3–4) and who is again addressed as "I am the Alpha and the Omega, the First and the Last, the Beginning and the End" (Rev 22:13).

A new element is introduced in the line of narrators—the messenger (M):

$$A - B - C - M = A_1 - B_1 - C_1 - M_1$$

which on earth is John (either as the author or narrator), and in heaven Jesus (also either as the author or narrator).

$$\text{the Sun} - B - \text{rider} - \text{Jesus} = \text{ruler } 666 - \text{Rome} - C_1 - \text{John}$$

The two lines of narrators run parallel to and separate from each other. Jesus is the author of one story that involves the Sun – B – rider, while John is the author of the other, involving ruler 666 – Rome – C_1.

John is the counterpart of Jesus who conveys to him the secrets of heaven which he then spreads further in his community. John receives his vision—the Revelation—just once, but this image is repeated several times. He who sits on the throne is the same one who gives John the message on Patmos, and the same one as the mighty angel coming down from heaven "robed in a cloud, with a rainbow above his head; his face was like the sun, and his legs were like fiery pillars" (Rev 10:1). But John gives an additional description this time: a rainbow above his head and his legs like fiery pillars—quite similar to the first description—with one foot on the sea and the other on the land, he gave a loud shout like the roar of a lion, and swore by "him who lives for ever and ever, who created the heavens and all that is in them, the earth and all that is in it, and the sea and all that is in it, and said, 'There will be no more delay! But in the days when the seventh angel is about to sound his trumpet, the mystery of God will be accomplished, just as he announced to his servants the prophets" (Rev 10:6–7).

The same character also appears as the rider, this time with the common attributes: "I saw heaven standing open and there before me was a *white horse*, whose rider is called Faithful and True. With justice he judges and makes war. His eyes are like blazing fire, and on his head are many crowns. He has a name written on him that no one knows but he himself. He is dressed in a robe dipped in blood, and his name is the Word of God. The armies of heaven were following him, riding on white horses and dressed in fine linen, white and clean. Out of his mouth comes a sharp sword with which to strike down the nations. 'He will rule them with an iron scepter.' He treads the winepress of the fury of the wrath of God Almighty. On his robe and on his thigh he has this name written: king of kings and lord of lords" (Rev 19:11–16).

In these images, John paints double portraits that differ from one another in that one portrait (Jesus) is completely personalized, while the other (Son of Man) who has very similar attributes is not. Jesus is not the same as the one who sits on the throne, nor is he as the angel who stands both on the sea and on land with a rainbow above his head. Everything has a double meaning here. Although he introduces elements from the Old Testament, John's Christian education is rather thin and the elements of soteriology he introduces into the plot are mixed with other theological and cultural concepts. John introduces a new syncretism by connecting the two elements:

A (the Sun) – B – (C rider – M Jesus) = A_1 (ruler 666) – B_1 (Rome) – (C_1 – M_1 John)

In other words, new elements are introduced in the line of transmission of the message in which a total mirror image of the narrative is created, where the narrative is transmitted from the beginning (Alpha) to the end (Omega) and towards the final realization of John's quest (for the New Jerusalem[5]).

(C rider − M Jesus) − B − A (the Sun) = A_1 (ruler 666) − B_1 (Rome) − (M_1 John − C_1 New Jerusalem)

Both John and Jesus are messengers of the same revelation, but of different stories, and the antagonism that Royalty refers to lies in this: Jesus and the rider in heaven stand—together with John—against the ruler with the number 666 and Rome on one side and his heavenly counterpart and the Sun on the other side. It is, therefore, not difficult to surmise that this is a message of hope and faith in the success of their quest and that the true purpose of the Revelation is in fact to mobilize John's community towards a common goal—the realization of the New Jerusalem.

THE SON OF MAN

The Septuagint refers to the Son of Man as *anthropos*, a synonym for the ideal man. While making a strict distinction between God and man in Numbers, "God is not human, that he should lie, not a human being, that he should change his mind" (Num 23:19), Isaiah connects them: "Blessed is the man who does this, and the Son of Man who holds it fast" (Isa 56:2). God addresses Ezekiel more than ninety times as the Son of Man. The term is used only in reference to Ezekiel, except in one other scene where Gabriel says to Daniel: "Son of man, . . . understand that the vision concerns the time of the end," (Dan 8:17), and "in my vision at night I looked, and there before me was one like a Son of Man, coming with the clouds of heaven. He approached the Ancient of Days and was led into his presence. He was given authority, glory and sovereign power; all nations and peoples of every language worshiped him. His dominion is an everlasting dominion that will not pass away, and his kingdom is one that will never be destroyed" (Dan 7:13–14).

The person who appears as the Son of Man is associated with Israel's messianic king. In this latter sense it is mentioned in the book of Enoch, where it is used almost as a title, together with attributes such as the Just, the Chosen One, and the Messiah (1 En 61:8–9) who will preside over the last

---

5. The name of New Jerusalem is to be understood metaphorically and what it represents is to be found both in heaven and on earth.

judgement, judging the living and the dead. The book of Enoch speaks of the existence of the Son of Man: "And before the sun and the signs were created, before the stars of heaven were made, his name was called before the Lord of the spirits" (1 En 48:3).[6] The Son of Man was hidden and revealed only to chosen ones. Most often he sits on the throne of glory. The term is generally considered to have acquired its messianic meaning in Christianity through Jewish eschatology. Daniel mentions the Son of Man or someone like the Son of Man who comes on the clouds; his Son of Man is mortal, and therefore his eschatological function is not possible and was obviously added later.

Christ is referred to as the Sun of Man eighty-one times in the Gospels, but only when he speaks himself. The apostles, on the other hand, address him otherwise—such as Paul, for example, who calls him the second or the last Adam.

Early Christian authors consider this name to emphasize the human nature of Christ. The name was evidently known and accepted from the very beginnings of Christianity, as a part of religious belief and as a constant authority against heretics, the brightest adornment of every book involving the Holy Trinity.

The Son of Man appears in all central places throughout the Revelation, always carrying the same attributes as an identification mark.

- *He is the ruler of God's creation* (the Alpha and the Omega, the one who is, who was, and who is to come, the Living One, who was dead and is now alive for ever and ever; the First and the Last; the ruler of God's creation; the one who lives for ever and ever; the firstborn from the dead; the Alpha and the Omega; the Amen),
- *he is the faithful witness* (holy and true; called Faithful and True; the Amen, the faithful and true witness; the faithful witness),
- *whose name no one knows* (he has a name written on him that no one knows but he himself; his name is the Word of God),
- *and who is coming on a cloud* (and there before me was a white cloud, and seated on the cloud was one "like a Son of Man"; coming down from heaven, robed in a cloud; coming with the clouds, with a crown of gold on his head),
- *with a sickle or a sword in his hand* (a sharp sickle in his hand; out of his mouth came a sharp double-edged sword; him who has the sharp, double-edged sword),

6. Charles, "Enoch."

- *dressed in a white robe washed in blood* (someone "like a Son of Man," dressed in a robe reaching down to his feet and with a golden sash around his chest; dressed in a robe dipped in blood).
- *His head is as white as snow* (his head and hair were white like wool, as white as snow) *and his face is like shining Sun* (his face was like the sun shining in all its brilliance; his face was like the sun),
- *his eyes like fire* (his eyes are like blazing fire; whose eyes are like blazing fire; and his eyes were like blazing fire),
- *his feet like bronze* (his feet were like bronze glowing in a furnace; whose feet are like burnished bronze; his legs were like fiery pillars), *and his voice like waters* (his voice was like the sound of rushing waters).
- *He holds seven stars in his hand* (him who holds the seven stars in his right hand; and walks among the seven golden lampstands; him who holds the seven spirits of God and the seven stars; in his right hand he held seven stars) and
- *holds the key of David* (I hold the keys of death and Hades; who holds the key of David. What he opens no one can shut, and what he shuts no one can open; a star that had fallen from the sky to the earth. The star was given the key to the shaft of the abyss; coming down out of heaven, having the key to the abyss and holding in his hand a great chain).
- *He is also a ruler of all rulers* (on his head are many crowns; the ruler of the kings of the earth; Lord God Almighty).

With these attributes comes the name of the one they are associated with: someone like the Son of Man; a throne in heaven with someone sitting on it; an angel; a star that had fallen from the sky to the earth with the key to the shaft of the abyss; mighty angel; Someone like the Son of Man sitting on a cloud; a white horse, whose rider is called Faithful and True; an angel holding a key to the Abyss and in his hand a great chain; with the Son of Man, the throne, the angel, the star, the One called Faithful and True, all representing the same person.

The Son of Man as the *primum principium* is found in numerous creation myths, especially in Pythagorean and Hermetic teachings which were quite widespread in John's day and age, and that on a territory much larger than Asia Minor. Hermetic and Pythagorean cosmologies and theogonies reflect the range of varieties and hierarchies that were created in different religious systems. Essentially, before all things that exist and before every beginning there is one God, remaining immoveable in the solitude of his unity, immixed neither with himself nor with any other thing. He is the principle, the exemplar of the God who is the Father to himself, born of himself, the only Father and the only true God. For he is something greater and the first, the source of all things and the root of the primary intelligible form of existence. He is the self-ruling God who created the light, because he is father to himself and self-ruling; he is the beginning of everything and God of all gods. He is the monad from the one, before being, but the first principle of being, he is the source of all being and essence and is as such celebrated as the beginning of reason and all intelligible.

This fragment of hermetic beliefs presents the most ancient principles of all things, which Hermes places first in order, before the ethereal and empyrean gods and the celestial. But, according to another division, Hermes himself places the god Emeph as the ruler of the celestial gods, describing him as the intellect that understands himself, and converts other intellects to himself. Before this he places the indivisible One, which takes the form of an effigy and is called Eicton, and in which the first intellect and the first reason resides. This One is worshiped in silence. Besides these, other rulers are imagined to exist, which rule the creation of things apparent. Amon is the demiurgic intellect, which governs truth and wisdom, and is transferred through generations, seeking to shed light on the inapparent forces of secret reasons, and Phtha perfects all things. The Greeks, however, changed the word Phtha into Hephæstus (the demiurge). Osiris is seen as the producer of good things, and based on its other powers and attributes, it can have different names.

There is also another principle that governs all the elements in a state of generation, and rules the powers inherent to them, four of which are male, and four female (ogdoad); and this principle is the Sun. And there is yet another principle of all nature which is regarded as the ruler over generation, which role is assigned to the Moon.

According to their teachings, the heavens are divided into two parts, or into four, or twelve, or thirty-six, or the double of these, and leaders are assigned to them in greater or lesser number, with one leader superior to them all. In his second coming, Christ shall transform the heaven and earth, and stars shall yield to his will and become white.[7]

Hence, from the highest to the last, the doctrine of the Egyptians relies on principles that trace the origin of all things from One, with different gradations to the many; which (the many) are again under the supreme government of the One: and the nature of infinity is considered entirely

---

7. A quote from the *Gospel of Philip* follows the same pattern: "The Lord went into the dye works of Levi. He took seventy-two different colors and threw them into the vat. He took them out all white. And he said, 'Even so has the Son of Man come as a dyer'" (para. 41).

subservient to the nature of the final and supreme unity, which is the cause of all things. God created matter from the material of separated essence, which is the material of life itself, and which the demiurge took, fabricating from it the harmonious and imperturbable spheres, and using dregs of it for the creation of generated and perishable bodies. These are clear reflections of Pythagorean and Platonic thought that essentially include Plato's account of the creation described in the *Timaeus*.

According to the writings of Eusebius (*Preparation for the Gospel*), there were also those who denied the creation of anything before the visible world and agreed with the Egyptians who hold that there are no other gods other than those which are called the planets and the constellations of the zodiac. They say, also, that the honors paid to the ten great gods and those which are called heroes, whose names appear in the almanacks, are nothing more than means of seduction of evil, and observations of the risings and settings of the stars on which they base their prognostications of future events. Thus, they esteem the Sun to be the demiurge, and believe the legends about Osiris and Isis, and all other their mythological fables, to refer either to the stars, their appearances and occultations, and the periods of their risings, or to the increase and decrease of the moon, or to the cycles of the sun, or the diurnal and nocturnal hemispheres. Most of them, also, suppose that some inextricable link exists between our efforts and concerns and the motions of the stars, by a kind of necessity which they call destiny, as all things are connected with these gods, and depend upon them. Therefore they honor and serve them as the only beings capable of influencing destiny.[8] Eusebius writes about those who believed in astrology and practiced it. Such beliefs were widespread at the time of the Revelation. Nero had his own astrologer, and they were expelled from Italy at the time of Claudius, while Philo believed that the stars were placed in the sky not to shine, but rather to show the future, and that this was their function in the living universe over which the One God resides. According to Philo, also Abraham based his prophecies on the magic of the motions of heavenly bodies, and thus came to know God while living in Chaldea. "He who understands creation, knows God," said Abraham, who—according to the writings of Nicolaus of Damascus—knew the Creator by knowing the creation. Josephus Flavius reports that Abraham instructed the Egyptians in the science of arithmetics and astronomy, who were unacquainted with those parts of learning before Abraham came to Egypt.[9]

8. Eusebius, *Preparation for the Gospel*, bk. 3, ch. 4.
9. "Abraham sanctitate et sapientia omnium praestantissimus, primum Caldaeos, deinde Phoenices, demum Egyptios Sacerdotes, Astrologia et Divina docuerit." Turner, *Arbatel of Magic*, 2.

Much later, the *Arbatel of Magic* describes astrology as a special kind of magic that judges of the events of things to come, both natural and human, by the motions and influences of the stars upon the lower elements, observed and understood by astrologers.

In addition, according to the *Arbatel*, Hermes Trismegistus, "that divine Magician and Philosopher, who (as some say) lived long before Noah, attained to much Divine knowledge of the Creator through the study of Magick and Astrologie."[10]

Abraham was an astronomer and he carried around his neck a healing stone. After Abraham's death, God attached the stone to the wheel of the Sun, which thus obtained its crucial astrological significance.[11]

As already stated, there were different conceptions and disagreements among ancient astrologers as to which came first among the planets, as a "throne in heaven." Some believed that it was Jupiter, as the supreme deity, others held it was Saturn, as the one who announced the horoscope, while some argued it was the Sun as the most powerful among the planets, or even Mercury.

Among the more than twenty thousand clay tiles discovered by A. H. Layard in the ruins of Ashurbanipal's palace (dated 668–626 BC) and library, seven tablets were found describing the oldest Assyrian creation myth, therefore known as the Seven Tablets of Creation, or—derived from the opening lines of the piece—the Enuma Elish. The story describes the mythical battle of Bel Marduk and the beast Tiamat (the Moon). Bel Marduk killed the beast, cut it in half, and made heaven and earth and the celestial planets out of its halves (the myth coincides with the Egyptian myth of Nun). After Marduk created heaven and earth and placed the gods in their heavenly stations, the gods complained because they had no one to worship them, so Marduk decided to create man out of blood and bones. The gods sacrificed Kingu, the second husband of Tiamat, and out of his blood Ea made humans to service the gods. The Annunaki, wishing to pay tribute to Marduk, built him an altar in Babylon (the "Gate of the Gods"). The same way he placed the gods in their heavenly stations, Marduk now placed them in their stations in the temple. Afterwards, the mythical battle between god Marduk and Tiamat, the Mother of all Creation, took place.[12] The quarrel among the gods continued, and possibly even inspired the myth of Satan's apostasy and his influence on humans derived from some as yet unknown Babylonian or Assyrian source.

10. Turner, *Arbatel of Magic*, 2.
11. Rodkinson, *Babylonian Talmud*, 1:53.
12. King, *Seven Tablets of Creation*; Budge and Smith, *Babylonian Legends*.

In this Assyrian myth, the gods are combined in groupings known as triads. The fourth tablet thus mentions the triad of Anu – Bel – Ea (the sky, space under the sky including the earth, and the underground), while the fifth tablet refers to the triad of Sin – Shamash – Ishtar (the Moon – the Sun – Venus).

The ancient myth found its followers in numerous future generations of Assyrian and Persian-Babylonian scholars, in whose ideas and works its living tradition is reflected.

Berosus

At the end of the fourth century BC, Alexander opened the door for a new wave of Eastern tradition that spread from Mesopotamia, bringing with it different, new, and very attractive ideas for the territory of the Mediterranean, that were represented as revelations of true divine mysteries. The most famous among those spreading the ancient—but for the new audience unknown—teachings was Berosus, a priest of Bel, who had arrived in Greece from Babylon.

Berosus lived during and after the time of Alexander the Great. Although the exact time of his birth and death is unknown, he is known to have lived during the reign of Antiochus I Soter (280–261 BC), to whom he dedicated his history of Babylonia known as the *Babyloniaca* or, according to Josephus Flavius and Clement of Alexandria, the *Chaldaica*. Little has been preserved of his work, only fragments in Apollodorus,[13] Abydenus,[14] Josephus Flavius[15] and Alexander Polyhistor.[16]

According to Vitruvius and Pliny, he was well versed in astronomy and astrology. After leaving Babylon, he relocated to the island of Cos in Greece, where he established a school of astronomy and astrology. From there, he moved on to Athens, where he became famous for his oratory skills and marvelous predictions, for which Athens officially erected a statue of him with a gilt tongue.[17] Vitruvius attributes the invention of the semicircular sundial to him.[18] Tatian, originally from Babylonia himself, calls him the most learned historian of Western Asia. His history of Babylonia was divided into three parts. In book 1, he writes about the history of the world

13. "Berossus: From Appolodorus."
14. "Berossus: From Abydenus."
15. "Berossus: From Josephus."
16. "Berossus: From Alexander Polyhistor."
17. Pliny the Elder, *Natural History*, bk. 7, ch. 37.
18. Vitruvius, *Ten Books on Architecture*, bk. 9, ch. 8.

from its creation to the flood. In book 2, he covers the period from the flood to the second half of the eighth century BC, while book 3 relates the history of Babylon up until the time of Alexander and Antiochus. He claimed to have obtained the material for his historical accounts from old chronicles and inscriptions kept in the temple of Bel in Babylon. Many of his texts have unfortunately been lost and now exist only in fragments preserved and transmitted in the writings of Alexander Polyhistor, Abydenus, and Apollodorus. However, as many of their works have also been lost, only fragments of fragments of his accounts have survived in tertiary sources, such as the writings of Josephus Flavius, Eusebius, Syncellus, and others.

In addition to his accounts of the flood, his chronological history of Babylon remains. In the first period, up until the flood, he recounts the 432,000 years of reign of the first ten kings; the second period covers some 34,080 years, up until ca. 2500 BC, in which there were eighty-six kings, while the third generation includes eight kings in the period of the Median occupation of Babylon. The book of the fourth generation, covering the reign of eleven kings, has been lost, while the fifth generation includes the reign of forty-two Chaldaean kings up until 2000 BC. The sixth period is the period of the Semitic dynasty to which King Hammurabi belonged. Later historical accounts by Berosus, until the year 747 BC and the time of Nabonassar, are missing.

He describes the beginning of the world as a time in which there was nothing but darkness and an abyss of waters, where the most hideous creatures lived, created of a two-fold principle. Men with two wings were born, and others with four wings and two faces. Some of these had one body but two heads, male and female, and two sets of sexual organs, accordingly. Further, there were other men with the legs of goats and the horns of goats on their heads and yet others had horses' feet. Others had the lower body of a horse and human bodies for their upper body, in the form of hippocentaurs. Bulls were engendered with human heads, and dogs with four bodies, and had fish tails on their hindquarters. In short, there were animals who had the extremities of all sorts of creatures combined, and finally, there were fish, reptiles, serpents, and many other monstruous creatures which assumed each other's shape and countenance. Records of them are preserved in the temple of Bel in Babylon.

The mystical creatures from Berosus's accounts are similar to those described by John:

- "In the center, around the throne, were four living creatures, and they were covered with eyes, in front and in back. The first living creature was like a lion, the second was like an ox, the third had a face like a man, the fourth was like a flying eagle. Each of the four living creatures had six wings and was covered with eyes all around" (Rev 4:6–8).

- "Then I saw a Lamb, looking as if it had been slain, standing in the center of the throne, encircled by the four living creatures and the elders. He had seven horns and seven eyes, which are the seven spirits of God sent out into all the earth" (Rev 5:6).

- "The locusts looked like horses prepared for battle. On their heads they wore something like crowns of gold, and their faces resembled human faces. Their hair was like women's hair, and their teeth were like lions' teeth. They had breastplates like breastplates of iron, and the sound of their wings was like the thundering of many horses and chariots rushing into battle. They had tails and stings like scorpions" (Rev 9:7–10).

- "The horses and riders I saw in my vision looked like this: Their breastplates were fiery red, dark blue, and yellow as sulfur. The heads of the horses resembled the heads of lions, and out of their mouths came fire, smoke and sulfur.... The power of the horses was in their mouths and in their tails; for their tails were like snakes, having heads with which they inflict injury" (Rev 9:17–19).

- "Then another sign appeared in heaven: an enormous red dragon with seven heads and ten horns and seven crowns on his heads" (Rev 12:3).

- "And I saw a beast coming out of the sea. He had ten horns and seven heads, with ten crowns on his horns, and on each head a blasphemous name. The beast I saw resembled a leopard, but had feet like those of a bear and a mouth like that of a lion" (Rev 13:1–2).

- "Then I saw another beast, coming out of the earth. He had two horns like a lamb, but he spoke like a dragon" (Rev 13:11).

- "There I saw a woman sitting on a scarlet beast that was covered with blasphemous names and had seven heads and ten horns" (Rev 17:3).

- " . . . the beast she rides, which has the seven heads and ten horns" (Rev 17:7).

Berosus was a famous astronomer whose teachings must have been impactful and known in John's time. His texts, which are today lost, must have existed and been available, especially in the territory of Asia Minor, where his school of astronomy was located. Of particular interest are the accounts recorded by Vitruvius:

"As for the branch of astronomy which concerns the influences of the twelve signs, the five stars, the sun, and the moon upon human life, we must leave all this to the calculations of the Chaldeans, to whom belongs the art of casting nativities, which enables them to declare the past and the future by means of calculations based on the stars. These discoveries have been transmitted by the men of genius and great acuteness who sprang directly from the nation of the Chaldeans; first of all, by Berosus, who settled in the island state of Cos, and there opened a school. Afterwards Antipater pursued the subject; then there was Archinapolus, who also left rules for casting nativities, based not on the moment of birth but on that of conception."[19] Cos lies in the immediate vicinity of Patmos (Aegean Dodecanese). Berosus's successor and head of the school on Cos was called Antipatrus. As Berosus had been associated with the court of Pergamum in Attalus's time, it is likely that Antipatrus continued his affairs as well. Apart from such indications, there is no other evidence to suggest that Antipatrus and John's Antipas, his faithful witness, are the same person (Rev 2:13).

Gods beheading one another and making various creatures from blood mixed with earth's soil are present in the Revelation as well.

- "Then I saw a Lamb, looking as if it had been slain, standing in the center of the throne, encircled by the four living creatures and the elders. He had seven horns and seven eyes, which are the seven spirits of God sent out into all the earth" (Rev 5:6), and
- "Worthy is the Lamb, who was slain, to receive power and wealth and wisdom and strength and honor and glory and praise!" (Rev 5:12), but probably also
- "And I saw a beast coming out of the sea. . . . One of the heads of the beast seemed to have had a fatal wound, but the fatal wound had been healed" (Rev 13:1–3).

A fragment from the writings of Alexander Polyhistor testifies to Berosus continuing the tradition of the Enuma Elish and putting the Moon first as the ordering principle:

> The person, who presided over them, was a woman named Omoroca;[20] which in the Chaldean language is Thalatth; in Greek Thalassa, the sea; but which might equally be interpreted the Moon. All things being in this situation, Belus came, and cut the woman asunder: and of one half of her he formed the

---

19. Vitruvius, *Ten Books on Architecture*, bk. 9, ch. 6.
20. Um-Uruk, the mother of Uruk.

earth, and of the other half the heavens; and at the same time destroyed the animals within her. All this (he says) was an allegorical description of nature. For, the whole universe consisting of moisture, and animals being continually generated therein, the deity above-mentioned took off his own head: upon which the other gods mixed the blood, as it gushed out, with the earth; and from thence were formed men. On this account it is that they are rational, and partake of divine knowledge. This Belus, by whom they signify Jupiter, divided the darkness, and separated the Heavens from the Earth, and reduced universe to order. But the animals, not being able to bear the prevalence of light, died. Belus upon this, seeing a vast space unoccupied, though by nature fruitful, commanded one of the gods to take off his head, and to mix the blood with the earth; and from thence to form other men and animals, which should be capable of bearing the air. Belus formed also the stars, and the sun, and the moon, and the five planets.[21]

Omoroca is the ordering principle and the mother of all creation (the alpha and the omega). Another account of Berosus's conception of creation is found in *On First Principles* of Damascius, the last Athenian Neoplatonist: "Among the barbarians, the Babylonians dismissed the first principle and imagined two, Taute (Tiamat, Tehom), who they say is the 'mother of the gods' and Apsu, who is considered to be Tauta's husband. The fruit of their union was the only son Miomis (Mummu), descended from the first two principles, from which the next generations came into being, Dahe and Dahos (who are supposed to be Lahme and Lahmos = Laham and Luhmu). The third generation was born of the same parents, Kishar and Asor (Aushar) from whom three gods came to be: Anos (Anu), Ilinois (Elim, Bel) and Aos (Ea); and finally, the son of Aos and Damkina is Bel (Bel-Marduk)."

Although there is a distinct iconographic and substantive similarity between Berosus's conception and John's characters, there is also a distinguishing feature here: everything described in Berosus's fashion is headed for ruin, except for the Lamb and the Son of Man. They will subdue Berosus's world and heaven and earth will yield to the will of the One God. Opposite these demonic creatures stands the Son of Man, a perfect creature, whose divine origin and power, unlike Berosus's creatures, lies in the power of revelation and the word he brings.[22] The sons of God, heroes, are distinguished by their strength and skills, demons take a form that shows their divine origin, and the Son of Man has only a human form, true, without blemish,

---

21. Budge and Smith, *Babylonian Legends of the Creation*.
22. Nearly fifty times Jesus is referred to as the Son of Man.

while his divine attribute is the Word alone. His role is to subdue Berosus's demonic creatures. "You are worthy to take the scroll and to open its seals, because you were slain, and with your blood you purchased men for God from every tribe and language and people and nation. You have made them to be a kingdom and priests to serve our God, and they will reign on the earth" (Rev 5:9–10). The seven Spirits of God who stand before the throne in heaven (Rev 4:5) are the astrological powers of the planets that created the world and govern it. The Slaughtered Lamb is an episteme, the science of astronomy and astrology, that has knowledge of the celestial events and planets (the seven horns) and understands and interprets them (the seven eyes). The Lamb was not sacrificed to the episteme, but mixed its own blood with the Revelation seen and interpreted by John. Mixing blood and the Revelation signifies creation.

COMPOSITION

> "The heavens declare the glory of God."
>
> —Ps 19:1

The symbolic language abounding in metaphors and substitutions creates an allegory that is not easy to understand. The question of composition and the sequence of images that are arranged in sets of seven are reminiscent of Daniel, and the author seems to have had this text before him as he shaped his work as a divine arcana to safeguard the message from undesirable readers on the one hand, but also to leave enough clues for those to whom it was addressed to understand it. This implies that his audience had a specific enough knowledge of his writing to be able to understand his language, but also that the book was accompanied by a background story that determined the theme and context, even if it concerned only the current events of the author's time to which it referred. The mystical atmosphere that this book emanates and that accompanies it as its most impressive and prominent feature allows the assumption that the entire plot was elevated to the highest level of abstraction which was not clear even at the moment when it was written and that what remains of the entire text is nothing more than an external reference with an emphasis on tradition reflected in the beliefs of the people of John's time. The mystification is so extensive that it is only in the form and composition of the book that a certain connection with the current time and space may be established, as in the notion of the Feast of (Seven) Weeks, and that John's message could only be understood if observed generally through the structure, as attempted by Yambro Collins, Farrer, Lambrecht, Schüssler Fiorenza, and others. But it is Lambrecht who, to an extent, introduces us to the actual problem. He interprets the Revelation as a series of sevens starting with an opening set of seven, followed by a series of five sets of sevens and ending with the final, seventh set of sevens which is an introduction to a new cycle of sevens. This way, the final seven of one series of sevens represents the opening of the next one. The sets of sevens are seven churches, seven seals, seven trumpets, seven thunders, seven bowls.

The Seven Seals

Although John's story is almost illegible and difficult to understand, the composition itself is not so complicated. The book opens with a prologue in which John states from whom he had received the Revelation, and then goes on to introduce himself and describes the circumstances under which the Revelation was received. He writes to the churches, mentioning them one by one, which completes the introductory part. The second part includes the seven seals and the seven trumpets, and the third the battle of Armageddon and the description of the new Jerusalem. A further division of the text is not necessary at this point as all events in between the letters to the churches and the image of the final judgment refer to the seals and trumpets, which provide the timeline and framework into which John inserts his events.

At first glance, it can be observed that the Revelation is completely oriented toward the Revelation that John saw in signs, as he himself claims in the very first sentence of the prologue (Rev 1:1), and there is no reason to interpret this otherwise. He goes on to explain what kind of revelation it is. The Son of Man from whom he receives the Revelation resembles the Son of Man from the book of Enoch, which is again for the most part an astronomical compendium, and he, like Enoch's Son of Man, holds in his hand seven golden lampstands, adding that they are:

- "The seven stars are the angels of the seven churches, and the seven lampstands are the seven churches" (Rev 1:20),
- to the cold church at Ephesus he conveys the words of "him who holds the seven stars in his right hand" (Rev 2:1),
- to Thyatira of the one "whose eyes are like blazing fire and whose feet are like burnished bronze" (Rev 2:18), and

- to Sardis of "him who holds the seven spirits of God and the seven stars" (Rev 3:1).
- In heaven he sees "a door standing open" (Rev 4:1),
- a "mighty angel coming down from heaven" (Rev 10:1), and
- two prophets who "went up to heaven in a cloud" (Rev 11:12).
- In heaven "God's temple . . . was opened, and within his temple was seen the ark of his Covenant" (Rev 11:19),
- a "great and wondrous sign appeared" (Rev 12:1),
- the dragon and his angels were not strong enough in battle "and they lost their place in heaven" (Rev 12:8),
- and "I heard a sound from heaven like the roar of rushing waters" (Rev 14:2),
- an "angel flying in midair" (Rev 14:6),
- another "angel came out of the temple in heaven" (Rev 14:17).
- After this, "in heaven the temple, that is, the tabernacle of the Testimony, was opened" (Rev 15:5).
- Again, there is "another angel coming down from heaven" (Rev 18:1),
- and "another voice from heaven" (Rev 18:4) is heard,
- and a "roar of a great multitude in heaven shouting" (Rev 19:1),
- "heaven [was] standing open and there . . . was a white horse" (Rev 19:11),
- "birds flying in midair" (Rev 19:17) and
- "a new heaven" (Rev 21:1).

Although the ultimate message is targeted much more toward the current events of John's time, on the surface he leaves a more distinct trace in the descriptions of heavenly events, leaving us with the question whether these events are real and, if so, whether their character is such that they can be recognized, interpreted and proved, as John seems to adhere to the instructions of the much later *Arbatel* that whoever knows secrets should keep secret things secretly, and should reveal only those things that are to be revealed, and seal those things which are to be sealed; and not give holy things to dogs, nor cast pearls before swine. According to the *Arbatel*, to those who observe this law, the eyes of understanding shall be opened to understand the divine secrets which will be revealed to them to their heart's content.[23] John also secured his scroll with seven seals, which represents the most intriguing part of John's enigma (Rev 6:1–17), along with the throne in heaven (Rev 4:1–11) and the creation of the people of God (Rev 7: 1–17 and 8:1–6). These three elements build the framework of his story.

The seal, along with the written document and signature, is one of the three elements of a Jewish deed. Men can "buy fields for money, and write it in deeds, and seal them, and certify it by witnesses. 'Write it in deeds' means a simple document; 'seal' means a folding one; 'certify' means by two witnesses; 'by witnesses' means three."[24] A seal is thus a folded deed, which applies to both parties, a *symbolon*, one half of a valuable token in the hands of both parties in a legal proceeding involving property. Here it means a deed between heaven and earth (a covenant), by which the heaven and heavenly bodies are bound to act in accordance with their preordained powers and authorities since, as even the Scripture testifies, God appointed names to things and persons, and with them he also distributed certain powers and offices; so the characters and names of stars do not have any power by reason of their figure or pronunciation, but by virtue of the office which God had ordained to them. There is no power either in heaven or in earth, or in hell, which does not come from God; and without his permission, they cannot act.[25]

Within the set of seven seals and seven trumpets there is a distinct separation between the set of seven and a sub-set of four elements. The first four seals—the four riders of the apocalypse—are synchronized with the first four trumpets, and should be read as a single unit, while the last two seals are completely separate from the trumpets and there is no visible synchronization or congruence in content. The last seal is only mentioned in a rather mysterious formulation: "When he opened the seventh seal, there was silence in heaven for about half an hour" (Rev 8:1), which merely indicates the suspense and importance of the event accompanying the opening of the seventh seal, and the author simply moves on to the next set of seven trumpets. If the opening of the seals and trumpets are synchronous events, then a partial explanation of the event might be found in the following verses: "Then the angel I had seen standing on the sea and on the land raised his right hand to heaven. And he swore by him who lives for ever and ever, who created the heavens and all that is in them, the earth and all that is in it, and the sea and all that is in it, and said, 'There will be no more delay!

---

23. Turner, *Arbatel of Magic*, 7.

24. A certified contract concluded between the parties before two witnesses; Rodkinson, *Babylonian Talmud*, 7:358.

25. Turner, *Arbatel of Magic*, 8.

But in the days when the seventh angel is about to sound his trumpet, the mystery of God will be accomplished, just as he announced to his servants the prophets'" (Rev 10:5–7). With the sounding of the seventh trumpet and the opening of the seventh seal, the prophecy of the second coming and the establishment of the kingdom of God both in heaven and on earth shall be fulfilled. The time of the second coming will ensue after a period of desolation, ruin, and wars.

Zand-i Vohuman Yasht

This part involves the idea that from the beginning of creation to the end of time conditions become worse, faith corrupts and is neglected, and eventually, when the conditions are at their worst, the Savior will appear and reestablish old, genuine relationships and customs, restore faith, and by defeating demons and false prophets create new conditions and peace. John's story is not new and is, in general outlines, present in the books of the Old and New Testament, but also much more broadly in texts that are not a part of the Christian heritage. However, in building his story, John does not rely on biblical texts, but takes an old prophecy from Zand-î Vohûman Yasht literally and adapts it to his own cultural and religious context.

The Vohûman is probably the most extensive ancient prophecy which has been preserved and consists of three books. In the first book, Ohrmazd explains to Zarathustra the character of time and the fate of the world he created, a world that will go through difficult periods until morality and faith are finally reconstituted. The third book speaks about the coming of the Savior at the end of time. John literally repeats the Vohûman, merely changing the actors of events and adapting them to his own needs and beliefs.

Inquiries into the teachings of Zarathustra (*Lógia, Lógia toú Zoroástrou* or *Oracula Chaldaica sive Magica*) began a very long time ago (he is mentioned by Xanthus the Lydian, who is said to have lived before Herodotus).

It is a Persian dualistic doctrine in which Ahura-Mazda, the supreme god, is opposed by Angra Mainyu who spreads false teachings (the seducer), also known as Magism, Zoroastrianism, or fire-worship, preached by Zarathustra. In the seventh century AD, a century after the collapse of the Sassanian state, members of this faith were brought over to Islam, either by force, policy, or the attractive power of the new faith, and a smaller part moved to the west coasts of India where, among the tolerant Hindus, they continued to freely worship their old gods and perform their old rites.

During the five centuries which preceded and the seven which followed the birth of Christ, a period which gave to the world the Gospels, the Talmud, and the Qur'an, the impact of the Avesta was an invaluable, and it was most eagerly studied in the first centuries of our era, when it inspired various Christian sects and heretical teachings. According to James Darmesteter, one of the best scholars and experts in the field, in the first centuries of Christianity, the religion of Persia was more studied and less understood than it had ever been before, while the real object of studying the old religion was to form a new one.[26]

Zarathustra introduces the idea of the great cosmic cycle of twelve thousand years that is divided into periods of three thousand years. After Zarathustra's death three of his sons will come, and the last Astavat-ereta will see the end times.

In the third book of the Zand-î Vohûman Yasht, Zarathustra asks Ohrmazd about the end of the millennium, wondering what will happen then: the most evil of periods is coming, a hundred kinds, a thousand kinds, a myriad of kinds of demons (cf. "Release the four angels who are bound at the great river Euphrates . . . to kill a third of mankind. The number of the mounted troops was two hundred million ['*two myriads of myriads*']. I heard their number" [Rev 9:14–16]) with disheveled hair (cf. "On their heads they wore something like crowns of gold, and their faces resembled human faces. Their hair was like women's hair, and their teeth were like lions' teeth" [Rev 9:8]), will rush into the country of Iran from the direction of the east. The inferior race, the race of Wrath, with uplifted banners will slay all those living in the world. This race was miscreated and its origin is not known. They will lead the country into tyranny and during that time the night will be brighter, and the year, month, and day will diminish one third (cf. "The sun turned black like sackcloth made of goat hair, the whole moon turned blood red, and the stars in the sky fell to earth, as late figs drop from a fig tree when shaken by a strong wind" [Rev 6:12–13]). In the history of Iran there have never been seven towns which were desolate as they will be at the end of the millennium. The towns of Iran will be ploughed up by their horses' hoofs, and their banners will reach unto Padashkhvargar (east of the Caspian Sea). Signs will appear: the Sun and the darkness, and the Moon will become manifest in various colors with earthquakes and violent winds. Jupiter and Mercury will come under sovereignty of the vile, and when Jupiter comes up to its culminating point and casts Venus down, sovereignty will come to the prince.

---

26. Darmesteter, *Zend Avesta*, xiii.

Those of the race of Wrath and the extensive army of Shedaspih, whose names are the two-legged wolf and the leather-belted demon on the bank of the Arvand, will wage three battles, one in Sped-razhur and one in the plain of Nishanak, for which some have said that it was on the lake of the three races, some have said that it was in Maruv brilliant, and some have said in Pars. The innumerable army will hoist banners of tiger skin, and their wind banner of white cotton. They will slay so that a thousand women can afterwards see and kiss but one man.

At the end of time, Ohrmazd will send Neryosang the angel and Srosh the righteous to Kangdezh to preach their religion dressed in black marten fur and garments as of the good spirits.

And the illustrious Peshotan will advance, and the Farnbag fire, the Gushnasp fire, and the triumphant fire of Burzin-Mihr will smite the fiend of excessive strength, extirpate the idol temples, and restore the true faith.

And the wolf time will pass and the sheep period will come. Demons and witches will be destroyed. The final war of good and evil, fire and death will descend upon all, every man will have to cross over burning lava and for the righteous it will be warm as milk, and for the wicked it will be deadly.

The astrologer Jamasp says that this time will be announced by several signs: the nights will become brighter, the star Haptoiring (the Great Chariot) will leave its place and head for Khorasan.[27]

This myth is the most extensive prophecy of ancient times which has been preserved. John builds his entire story on it, placing it at the center of events, as a framework into which he fits the events he has seen, those that confirm that the final period announced by the Vohûman is precisely John's time in which, according to the signs seen by John, the Revelation will be fulfilled.

At the end of time (the seventh seal), John prophesies the final battle of judgement day (battle of Armageddon) and, after the victory of good over evil, the establishment of the new Jerusalem. The time is fixed on the timeline (seven seals) and the final events will take place after the appearance of the Savior, when the angel opens the seventh seal and the seventh trumpet is sounded. In addition to the story, John also took over the structure of the Vohûman.

In the first chapter of the Vohûman, Zarathustra asks for immortality from Ohrmazd for the first time, and he explains to him a dream he had of a root of a tree with four branches that represent eons, or periods to come, that break down and become worse, starting from the golden one to the one mixed up with iron, which is at the end of time. In his second attempt to

---

27. Modi, "Jamasp Namak," ch. 9.

obtain immortality, Ohrmazd interprets to him the second dream of seven periods, from the golden one to the one mixed with up iron. The first dream is closely associated with Daniel, while the second is almost directly copied into the Revelation:

> "And I saw a tree on which were seven branches, one golden, one of silver, one brazen, one of copper, [one of tin], one of steel, and one was mixed up with iron." Ohrmazd spoke thus: "O Zartosht the Spitaman! This is what I say beforehand, the one tree which thou sawest is the world which I, Ohrmazd, created; and those seven branches thou sawest are the seven periods which will come. And that which was golden is the reign of King Vishtasp, when I and thou converse about religion, and Vishtasp shall accept that religion and shall demolish the figures of the demons, and the demons desist from demonstration into concealed proceedings; Ahriman and the demons rush back to darkness, and care for water, fire, plants, and the earth of Spandarmad becomes apparent. And that which was of silver is the reign of Ardashir the Kayanian (Kai), whom they call Vohuman son of Spend—dad, who is he who separates the demons from men, scatters them about, and makes the religion current in the whole world. And that which was brazen is the reign of Ardashir, the arranger and restorer of the world, and that of King Shahpur, when he arranges the world which I, Ohrmazd, created; he makes happiness (bukhtakih) prevalent in the boundaries of the world, and goodness shall become manifest; and Adarbad of triumphant destiny, the restorer of the true religion, with the prepared brass, brings this religion, together with the transgressors, back to the truth. And that which was of copper is the reign of the Ashkanian king, who removes from the world the heterodoxy (javid-rastakih) which existed, and the wicked Akandgar-i Kilisyakih is utterly destroyed by this religion, and goes unseen and unknown from the world. And that which was of tin is the reign of King Vahram Gor, when he makes the sight of the spirit of pleasure manifest, and Ahriman with the wizards rushes back to darkness and gloom. And that which was of steel is the reign of King Khosraw son of Kobad, when he keeps away from this religion the accursed Mazdak, son of Bamdad, who remains opposed to the religion along with the heterodox. And that which was mixed with iron is the reign of the demons with disheveled hair of the race of Wrath, when it is the end of the tenth hundredth winter of thy millennium."[28]

---

28. West, "Zand-i Vohuman Yasht," ch. 2, paras. 14–22.

The Seals and the Trumpets

The periods of time or eons in the Vohûman represent kings and descriptions of their periods of reign, just as with John who divided these characteristics into two series within the first subset of four seals/trumpets, which should be read together for the purposes of easier understanding: $S_1T_1 - S_2T_2 - S_3T_3 - S_4T_4$.

S_1—"I watched as the Lamb opened the first of the seven seals. Then I heard one of the four living creatures say in a voice like thunder, 'Come!' I looked, and there before me was a *white horse*! Its rider held a bow, and he was given a crown, and he rode out as a conqueror bent on conquest" (Rev 6:1–2).

T_1—"Then the seven angels who had the seven trumpets prepared to sound them. The first angel sounded his trumpet, and there came hail and fire mixed with blood, and it was hurled down upon the earth. A third of the earth was burned up, a third of the trees were burned up, and all the green grass was burned up" (Rev 8:6–7).

S_2—"When the Lamb opened the second seal, I heard the second living creature say, 'Come!' Then another *horse* came out, a *fiery red* one. Its rider was given power to take peace from the earth and to make men slay each other. To him was given a large sword" (Rev 6:3–4).

T_2—"The second angel sounded his trumpet, and something like a huge mountain, all ablaze, was thrown into the sea. A third of the sea turned into blood, a third of the living creatures in the sea died, and a third of the ships were destroyed" (Rev 8:8–9)

S_3—"When the Lamb opened the third seal, I heard the third living creature say, 'Come!' I looked, and there before me was a *black horse*! Its rider was holding a pair of scales in his hand. Then I heard what sounded like a voice among the four living creatures, saying, 'A quart of wheat for a day's wages, and three quarts of barley for a day's wages, and do not damage the oil and the wine!' (Rev 6:5–6).

T_3—"The third angel sounded his trumpet, and a great star, blazing like a torch, fell from the sky on a third of the rivers and on the springs of water—the name of the star is Wormwood. A third of the waters turned bitter, and many people died from the waters that had become bitter" (Rev 8:10–11).

S_4—"When the Lamb opened the fourth seal, I heard the voice of the fourth living creature say, 'Come!' I looked, and there before me was a pale horse! Its rider was named Death, and Hades was following close behind him. They were given power over a fourth of the earth to kill by *sword, famine and plague, and by the wild beasts* of the earth" (Rev 6:7–8).

T$_4$—"The fourth angel sounded his trumpet, and a third of the sun was struck, a third of the moon, and a third of the stars, so that a third of them turned dark. A third of the day was without light, and also a third of the night. As I watched, I heard an eagle that was flying in midair call out in a loud voice: 'Woe! Woe! Woe to the inhabitants of the earth, because of the trumpet blasts about to be sounded by the other three angels!'" (Rev 8:12–13).

The first image shows a creature calling out to a rider on a white horse with a bow in his hand that can easily be identified as or assumed to be the Sun, which rules the summer and during whose reign grass and vegetation wither from drought. Roofs of Jewish houses used to have grass growing on them that symbolized rapid decay, because it quickly withered. The second rider on the fiery red horse holding a sword who takes peace from the earth is Mars, the god of war. The mountain ablaze is a metaphor of the celestial forces that impact the weather conditions and the characteristics of seasons on earth, which for autumn means the seasonal interruption of navigation on *dies navigationis navalis* when the sea becomes dangerous for navigation. The apocalyptic literature of the time abounds in mountains ablaze. The sea stands for "all waters connected" including the ocean and the rivers: the Nile and the Euphrates, the Red Sea, the Mediterranean, etc. The third rider on a black horse with a scale selling wheat and barley is Mercury, a merchant who in winter sells at high prices the groceries he bought at harvest time and gets rich. Cold north winds freeze water, causing the people to die from cold and hunger, but severe winter conservates oil and wine (Rev 6:6). The fourth rider on a pale horse, which corresponds to Zoe's world of neither light nor darkness, is Venus, the mother goddess who, like birth, is only accompanied by death and nothingness. This is a simple message meaning that everything born must die. "They [the seasons] were given power over a fourth of the earth *to kill by sword, famine and plague*, and by the *wild beasts of the earth*" (Rev 6:7–8).

Astrology

John translates the first of Zarathustra's dreams into the periods of the four seasons ruled by the planets Sun, Mars, Mercury, and Venus. They are heavenly rulers and in the first series John describes their characteristics, while in the second he depicts the characteristics of their reigns (emanations). With this, John's interpretation turns to the sky, towards astronomy and astrology. The sky (i.e., heaven) is the space where signs and revelations are shown.

In order to understand John's message, it is important to explain the roles and characteristics of individual planets. Ptolemy's *Tetrabiblos*, the most comprehensive discussion of ancient astrology, explains the methods applied by astrologers until the second century AD. The book comprises the teachings of ancient astrologers and presents a solid account for understanding astrology in a wider time span, even much before it was composed. Each of the planets have their own individual characteristics which are predetermined, but they change depending on the conjunction with the other planets they affect, according to their position in the sky and relative to the celestial background, but also depending on whether they are climbing towards the zenith or descending westwards.

The Sun is "found to produce heat and moderate dryness. His magnitude, and the changes which he so evidently makes in the seasons, render his power more plainly perceptible than that of the other heavenly bodies; since his approach to the zenith of any part of the earth creates a greater degree of heat in that part."[29]

Mercury is mostly known for his "faculty of absorbing moisture and creating dryness [which] proceeds from his situation with regard to the Sun, from which he is at no time far distant in longitude; and, on the other hand, he produces moisture, because he borders upon the Moon's sphere, which is nearest to the earth; and, being thus excited by the velocity of his motion with the Sun, he consequently operates rapid changes tending to produce alternately either quality."[30]

"Mars chiefly causes dryness, and is also strongly heating, by means of his own fiery nature, which is indicated by his color, and in consequence of his vicinity to the Sun; the sphere of which is immediately below him."[31]

Venus has the same powers and the same temperate quality as Jupiter, but has an opposite effect, "since the heat she produces by her vicinity to the Sun is not so great as the moisture which she generates by the magnitude of her light, and by appropriating to herself the moist vapors of the earth, in the same manner that the Moon does."[32]

The planetary spheres and their distances from earth correspond to the ages of human life, according to specific periods. For the first four years of life, the Moon dominates the life of a child, as a result of which its body is elastic and grows rapidly, while the liquid food, the highly variable habit of the child's condition, and its mental incompleteness correspond to the

29. Ptolemy, *Tetrabiblos*, 37.
30. Ptolemy, *Tetrabiblos*, 39.
31. Ptolemy, *Tetrabiblos*, 37.
32. Ptolemy, *Tetrabiblos*, 38.

operative influence of the Moon. The next ten-year period is the second period of childhood, in which intelligence and logic begin to take shape and the seeds of learning are instilled, through which a child's character and abilities are revealed. Venus rules the next and third age, which lasts for a period of eight years. During this time, a certain kind of madness, unrestrained impetuosity, desire, passion, and love blindness enters the soul. The middle age of life is governed by the Sun and lasts for nineteen years. It is a period when the authority of action and the desired course of life are instilled in the spirit, and property, distinction, and glory are desired. The fifth age of life is ruled by Mars, and the period of his influence lasts for fifteen years. He induces greater austerity of life, together with vexation, care, and trouble of both the mind and body. Jupiter influences the twelve years of the mature age, while Saturn regulates the final old age, from the age of seventy until the end of one's life when "the movements both of body and soul are cooled and impeded in their impulses, enjoyments, desires, and speed; for the natural decline supervenes upon life, which has become worn down with age, dispirited, weak, easily offended, and hard to please in all situations, in keeping with the sluggishness of his movements."[33] In the last—Saturnian—period of life, neither the kings of the earth, the princes, the generals, the rich, the mighty, nor any slave or free man can escape the inevitable death and judgment.[34] After Saturn's domination and death, those who have been marked by God's seal will find peace in heaven, where God's people will be created.[35]

Masculine planets are the Sun, Mars, Jupiter, and Saturn, the Moon and Venus are said to be feminine, while Mercury (hermaphrodite) is both masculine and feminine depending on its position in the sky; in the eastern part of the sky it is masculine, and when in the western part of the sky it becomes feminine. The planets are in a special relationship (conjunction) with the signs of the zodiac that dominate particular seasons. These are the so-called solid signs, which have the most distinct characteristics of seasons and are located between equinoctial signs and tropical signs that touch the places where the Sun crosses the ecliptic or where it is in maximum declination. The planets' domiciles or the zodiac signs in which they have the most powerful influence and over which they have rulership are the constellation of Taurus (a creature similar to a bull), which is the domicile to Venus, the constellation of Leo (a creature similar to a lion) as the domicile

---

33. Ptolemy, *Tetrabiblos*, 448.

34. Ptolemy, *Tetrabiblos*, 443–8.

35. The power of Kronos they perceived to be sluggish and slow and cold, and therefore attributed to him the power of time; and they figure him standing, and gray-headed, to indicate that time is growing old (Porphyry, "On Images," fr. 8).

to the Sun, Scorpio (previously eagle, now scorpio) as the domicile to Mars, and Aquarius (a creature similar to man) as the domicile to Mercury.

The heavenly sun chariot is pulled along the ecliptic by horses of various capabilities; on the outer sides of the four-horse-carriage there is on one side the fastest horse of poor endurance (racehorse), and on the other side a slow horse of great endurance (working horse). Horses alternatively take the initiative by pulling the chariot at different speeds and strength. The chariot is not able to move linearly, but its path meanders describing the ecliptic. The enduring but slow horses lead in the summer, which is why the days last longer and the sun produces great heat, while a fast horse transports the carriage across the sky in a much shorter time in winter, thus making the day shorter.

The Fifth Seal and the Fifth Trumpet

If the first four seals are planets, consequently, so are the remaining two. Trumpets describing the reigns of the first four planets here are not general descriptions of their reigns, but rather refer to historical events that occurred during the particular reigns.

S_5—The fifth seal is Jupiter, the god of law, justice, and virtue, to whom the souls of those who had been slain because of the word of God and their testimonies call out to avenge them: "When he [the Lamb] opened the fifth seal, I saw under the altar the souls of those who had been slain because of the word of God and the testimony they had maintained. They called out in a loud voice, 'How long, Sovereign Lord, holy and true, until you judge the inhabitants of the earth and avenge our blood?' Then each of them was given a white robe, and they were told to wait a little longer, until the number of their fellow servants and brothers who were to be killed as they had been was completed" (Rev 6:9–11).

Jupiter's activity is moderate, as it moves between the cold influence of Saturn and the fiery power of Mars. It both warms and brings moisture, and because of the spheres below it, which increase its heating power, it produces fertile winds.[36] This image is followed by the first "woe," which is not a general description of a planet's characteristics, but rather an event that took place during the planet's rulership/reign.

"As I watched, I heard an eagle that was flying in midair call out in a loud voice: 'Woe! Woe! Woe to the inhabitants of the earth, because of the trumpet blasts about to be sounded by the other three angels!'" (Rev 8:13) and the angel cries out "woe" three times, which John lists individually

---

36. Ptolemy, *Tetrabiblos*, 383–93.

by placing them in parentheses and thus taking them out of the context through phrases specifying that a particular woe is past and the next one is to come. The event referring to Jupiter is put within the formula "the first woe is coming" and "the first woe is past; two other woes are yet to come" (Rev 9:12):

> The fifth angel sounded his trumpet, and I saw a star that had fallen from the sky to the earth. The star was given the key to the shaft of the Abyss. When he opened the Abyss, *smoke rose from it like the smoke from a* gigantic *furnace*. The *sun and sky were darkened* by the smoke from the Abyss. And out of the smoke *locusts came down upon the earth* and were given power like that of scorpions of the earth. They were told not to harm the *grass of the earth* or *any plant or tree*, but only those people who did not have the *seal* of God on their foreheads. . . .
>
> . . . They were not given power to kill them, but only to torture them for five months. And the agony they suffered was like that of the sting of a scorpion when it strikes a man. During those days men *will seek death*, but will not find it; they will long to die, but death will elude them. The locusts looked *like horses* prepared *for battle*. On their heads they wore something like crowns of gold, and their faces resembled human faces. Their hair was like women's hair, and their *teeth* were *like lions' teeth*. They had breastplates like breastplates of iron, and the sound of their wings was like the thundering of many horses and chariots *rushing into battle*. They had tails and stings like scorpions, and in their tails they had power to torment people for five months. They had as king over them the angel of the Abyss, whose name in Hebrew is Abaddon, and in Greek, Apollyon." (Rev 8:13; 9:1–11)

This scene is an abstract and does not provide enough elements to be understood directly.

The Sixth Seal and the Sixth Trumpet

S_6—Saturn: "I watched as he opened the sixth seal. There was a great earthquake. The *sun* turned black like sackcloth made of goat hair, the whole moon turned blood *red*, and *the stars in the sky fell* to earth, *as late figs drop from a fig tree* when shaken by a strong wind. *The sky* receded like a *scroll, rolling up*, and every mountain and island was removed from its place.

"Then *the kings of the earth, the princes*, the generals, the rich, the mighty, and every slave and every free man *hid in caves* and *among the rocks* of the mountains. They called to the mountains and the rocks, 'Fall on us and hide us from the face of him who sits on the throne and from the wrath of the Lamb! For the great day of their wrath has come, and who can stand?'" (Rev 6:12–17).

The sixth seal is Saturn, which is accompanied by earthquake and darkness. The seed from the tree of life is weaker, it dominates the last years of human life. Saturn is dry and cold due to its distance from the Sun. According to Ptolemy, "Saturn produces cold and dryness, for he is most remote both from the Sun's heat and from the earth's vapors."[37]

The phrase "the first woe is past; two other woes are yet to come" opens and the phrase "the second woe has passed" closes the three paragraphs into a separate whole and gives a more complex picture than the previous one. At the end of the second and at the beginning of the third "woe" John announces the establishment of the kingdom of God, that is, the end of the sixth and the beginning of the seventh period. The transition from the sixth to the seventh eon is the moment of the second coming—John sees the signs of the second coming, which he describes right after the sixth period.

> The sixth angel sounded his trumpet, and I heard a voice coming from the horns of the golden altar that is before God. It said to the sixth angel who had the trumpet, "Release the four angels who are bound at the great river Euphrates." And the four angels who had been kept ready for this very hour and day and month and year were released to kill a third of mankind. The number of the mounted troops was two hundred million. I heard their number. The horses and riders I saw in my vision looked like this: Their breastplates were fiery red, dark blue, and yellow as sulfur. The heads of the horses resembled the heads of lions, and out of their mouths came fire, smoke and sulfur. A third of mankind was killed by the three plagues of fire, smoke and sulfur that came out of their mouth. The power of the horses was in their mouths and in their tails; for their tails were like snakes, having heads with which they inflict injury. The rest of mankind that were not killed by these plagues still did not repent of the *work of their hands*; they did not stop worshiping demons, and idols of gold, silver, bronze, stone and wood—idols that cannot see or hear or walk. Nor did they repent of their murders, their magic arts, their sexual immorality or their thefts. (Rev 9:13–21)

The first image describes an actual earthly army, while the second depicts the transfer of power from the forces of evil to the Savior.

---

37. Ptolemy, *Tetrabiblos*, 375–7.

> Then I saw another mighty angel coming down from heaven. He was robed in a cloud, with a rainbow above his head; his face was like the sun, and his legs were like fiery pillars. He was holding a little scroll, which lay open in his hand. He planted his right foot on the sea and his left foot on the land and he gave a loud shout like the roar of a lion. When he shouted, the voices of the seven thunders spoke. And when the seven thunders spoke, I was about to write; but I heard a voice from heaven say, "Seal up what the seven thunders have said and do not write it down." Then the angel I had seen standing on the sea and on the land *raised his right hand to heaven*. And *he swore by him who lives for ever and ever, who created the heavens* and all that is in them, *the earth and all that is in it, and the sea and all that is in it*, and said, "There will be no more delay! But in the days when the seventh angel is about to sound his trumpet, the mystery of God will be accomplished, just as he announced *to his servants the prophets*." Then the voice that I had heard from heaven spoke to me once more: "Go, take the scroll that lies open in the hand of the angel who is standing on the sea and on the land." So I went to the angel and asked him to give me the little scroll. He said to me, "Take it and *eat it*. It will turn your *stomach* sour, but in your *mouth* it will be *as sweet as honey*." I took the little scroll from the angel's hand and *ate it*. *It tasted as sweet as honey in my mouth*, but when I had eaten it, my stomach turned sour. Then I was told, "You must prophesy again about many peoples, nations, languages and kings." (Rev 10: 1–11)

The third image is an element of dating without which it would not be possible to determine the date of the event that is essential for John.

> I was given a reed like a measuring rod and was told, "Go and measure the temple of God and the altar, and count the worshipers there. But exclude the outer court; do not measure it, because it has been given to the Gentiles. They will trample on the holy city for 42 months. And I will give power to my two witnesses, and they will prophesy for 1,260 days, clothed in sackcloth." These are the two *olive trees* and the two *lampstands* that stand before the Lord of the earth. If anyone tries to harm them, fire comes from their mouths and devours their enemies. This is how anyone who wants to harm them must die. These men have power to shut up the sky so that it will not rain during the time they are prophesying; and they have power to turn the waters into blood and to strike the earth with every kind of plague as often as they want. Now when they have finished their

testimony, the beast that comes up from the Abyss *will attack them, and overpower* and kill them. Their bodies will lie in the street of the great city, which is figuratively called Sodom and Egypt, where also their Lord was crucified. For three and a half days men from every people, tribe, language and nation will gaze on their bodies and refuse them burial. The inhabitants of the earth will gloat over them and will celebrate by sending each other gifts, because these two prophets had tormented those who live on the earth. But after the three and a half days a *breath of life from God entered them, and they stood on their feet*, and terror struck those who saw them. Then they heard a loud voice from heaven saying to them, "Come up here." And they went up to heaven in a cloud, while their enemies looked on. At that very hour there was a severe earthquake and a tenth of the city collapsed. Seven thousand people were killed in the earthquake, and the survivors were terrified and gave glory to the God of heaven. (Rev 11:1–14)

The first six seals in turn represent: the Sun and its season (summer), Mars and its season (autumn), Mercury and it season (winter), Venus and its season (spring), Jupiter and the event that occurred during its reign (the invasion of locusts), and Saturn and the events of his time of rule (the invasion of kings from the Euphrates—East), the announcement of the authority of the One God, as a sign of the transition from the sixth to the seventh period and the mission of two prophets as an element of dating. It is conspicuous that John does not mention the seventh planet—the Moon.

According to Berosus, the Moon presides over the other planets, it is the source of creation, everything was created from it and, due to its proximity to the earth, it strongly influences climatic and other events on earth. It governs the seas and seasons, and along with Venus it gives fertility and moisture. When John mentions the four creatures sitting around the throne in heaven, he is referring in part to the four solid signs of the zodiac that rule the seasons.

"I watched as the Lamb opened the first of the seven seals. Then I heard one of the four living creatures say in a voice like thunder, 'Come!' I looked, and there before me was a white horse! Its rider held a bow" (Rev 6:1–2).

"When the Lamb opened the second seal, I heard the second living creature say, 'Come!' Then another horse came out, a fiery red one. Its rider was given power to take peace from the earth" (Rev 6:3–4).

"When the Lamb opened the third seal, I heard the third living creature say, 'Come!' I looked, and there before me was a black horse! Its rider was holding a pair of scales in his hand" (Rev 6:5).

"When the Lamb opened the fourth seal, I heard he voice of the fourth living creature say, 'Come!' I looked, and there before me was a pale horse!" (Rev 6:7-8).

"Then one of the four living creatures gave to the seven angels seven golden bowls filled with the wrath of God, who lives for ever and ever" (Rev 15:7).

Jasper and carnelian are semiprecious stones of yellowish and reddish color as that of the Moon. After the flood, God decided not to flood the earth again and put a rainbow in the sky as a sign of the covenant. This sign appears in the Revelation in the form of rainbow, resembling an emerald, which encircled the throne, while the sea of glass represents the Moon's aura, according to whose color weather conditions were predicted.[38]

> After this I looked, and there before me was a door standing open in heaven. And the voice I had first heard speaking to me like a trumpet said, "Come up here, and I will show you what must take place after this." At once I was in the Spirit, and there before me was a throne in heaven with someone sitting on it. And the one who sat there had the appearance of jasper and carnelian. A rainbow, resembling an emerald, encircled the throne. Surrounding the throne were twenty-four other thrones, and seated on them were twenty-four elders. They were dressed in white and had crowns of gold on their heads. From the throne came flashes of lightning, rumblings and peals of thunder. Before the throne, seven lamps were blazing. These are the seven spirits of God. Also, before the throne there was what looked like a sea of glass, clear as crystal. In the center, around the throne, were four living creatures, and they were covered with eyes, in front and in back. The first living creature was like a lion, the second was like an ox, the third had a face like a man, the fourth was like a flying eagle. Each of the four living creatures had six wings and was covered with eyes all around, even under his wings. Day and night they never stop saying: 'Holy, holy, holy is the Lord God Almighty, who was, and is, and is to come.' Whenever the living creatures give glory, honor and thanks to him who sits on the throne and who lives for ever and ever. (Rev 4:1-9)[39]

---

38. The crystal clear sea of glass appears in the Mandaean oral tradition in the saga of Dana Nuk's (Daniel's) journey to the upper worlds in which priests grow to prayer, 360 of them, one for each day of the year. In the Zend Avesta, such is the purgatory where frozen souls of sinners stand motionless with their hands raised until a new birth.

39. "The moon, conceived according to her brightness, they called Artemis, as it were, 'cutting the air.' And Artemis, though herself a virgin, presides over childbirth,

The roles of the actors in John's drama can now be divided as follows: (C the Moon – M Jesus) – B – A (the Sun) = A_1 (ruler 666) – B_1 (Rome) – (M_1 John – C_1 New Jerusalem).

Jesus is the heavenly messenger who conveys to John the message in signs, and the signs are associated with the Moon, the Sun, and another celestial sign (Venus clothed as the Sun, the prostitute sitting on the beast). Heavenly signs show John the events that will take place on earth, and in them the earthly new Jerusalem, Rome, and the ruler with the number of the name 666 will play the main roles.

According to the iconographic comparison, the throne in heaven is the Moon, the alpha and omega, the one who was in the beginning, who is now and who will be forever and ever; it is one of the seven (seals), but also the eighth (the principle), meaning that the beast on which the prostitute sits is the Moon.

The signs of the zodiac are divided into fixed and tropical signs. The fixed signs are Taurus (a creature similar to a bull), Leo (a creature similar to a lion), Aquarius (a creature similar to man), and Scorpio (previously eagle). The Lamb stands among the creatures and the elders, i.e., in the sky among the constellations.[40] These zodiac signs are the domiciles (houses) of the planets: Sun is domicile in Leo, Mercury in Aquarius, Mars in Scorpio, and Venus in Taurus.

In the following part of the text (Rev 7:1–16), the metaphor of the four angels holding back the winds only emphasizes the stationary nature and motionlessness of the next image depicting the creation of a new Jewish people. Unlike planets, the zodiac signs move in the sky along a fixed regular trajectory, their motion never stops, and they never return in the

---

because the power of the new moon is helpful to parturition. What Apollo is to the sun, that Athena is to the moon: for the moon is a symbol of wisdom, and so a kind of Athena. But, again, the moon is Hecate, the symbol of her varying phases and of her power dependent on the phases. Wherefore her power appears in three forms, having as symbol of the new moon the figure in the white robe and golden sandals, and torches lighted; the basket, which she bears when she has mounted high, is the symbol of the cultivation of the crops, which she makes to grow up according to the increase of her light; and again the symbol of the full moon is the goddess of the brazen sandals. Or even from the branch of olive one might infer her fiery nature, and from the poppy her productiveness, and the multitude of the souls who find an abode in her as in a city, for the poppy is an emblem of a city. She bears a bow, like Artemis, because of the sharpness of the pangs of labour" (Porphyry, "On Images," fr. 8).

40. The *Bundahishn* lists the four stars that rule the sky: Tishtar (Sirius) the east, Sataves the west, Vanand (Vega) the south, and Haptoiring (the Great Chariot) the north. Sirius is associated with Mercury, Sataves with Jupiter, Vanand with Venus, and Haptoiring with Mars. West, "Bundahishn," ch. 2.

opposite direction.[41] John here substitutes the twelve signs of the zodiac with twelve Jewish tribes.

In this context it is necessary to emphasize the implications for the consciousness of the people of that time caused by the fact that the behavior of the planets was not governed by a fixed law, but that they seemed to have their own will, and much like Homer's and Hesiod's gods made alliances against other gods and people. The realization that the eclipses of the Sun and Moon occur periodically, just like the retrograde motion of the planets and their apparent stopping in the sky, must have had extraordinary consequences, as it seemed that above the planets and all other celestial phenomena which rule the Earth there was the will of a single supreme being that governed everything.

> After this I saw four angels standing at the four corners of the earth, holding back the four winds of the earth to prevent any wind from blowing on the land or on the sea or on any tree.
>
> Then I saw another angel coming up from the east, having the seal of the living God. He called out in a loud voice to the four angels who had been given power to harm the land and the sea: "Do not harm the land or the sea or the trees until we put a seal on the foreheads of the servants of our God." Then I heard the number of those who were sealed: 144,000 from all the tribes of Israel. From the tribe of Judah 12,000 were sealed, from the tribe of Reuben 12,000, from the tribe of Gad 12,000, from the tribe of Asher 12,000, from the tribe of Naphtali 12,000, from the tribe of Manasseh 12,000, from the tribe of Simeon 12,000, from the tribe of Levi 12,000, from the tribe of Issachar 12,000, from the tribe of Zebulun 12,000, from the tribe of Joseph 12,000, from the tribe of Benjamin 12,000. (Rev 7:1–8)

The new people are God's creation. Like God, they cannot lie and cannot change their mind, and like the Son of Man (Num 23:19), who is the Creator of God's kingdom on earth, they cannot beget or have their own offspring. This is why they did not defile themselves with women.[42] "They follow the Lamb wherever he goes. They were purchased from among men and offered as firstfruits to God and the Lamb. No lie was found in their

---

41. The illogical nature of planetary motion is caused by the mutual position of the ecliptics and is inexplicable from the position of the geocentric understanding of the universe.

42. "A Hebrew makes another Hebrew, and such a person is called 'proselyte.' But a proselyte does not make another proselyte. . . . Just as they . . . and make others like themselves, while others simply exist" ("Gospel of Philip," para. 1).

mouths; they are blameless" (Rev 14:4–5).[43] Christians do not beget and are not a people.

However, the answer to the question of to what extent John's vision is associated with Mazdaean beliefs can clearly be found in this passage. The topic here is, nevertheless, not the creation of a new people, but simply the period of time that will pass from the beginning of the reign of the first planetary ruler, the Sun, to the end of Saturn's reign and the final reckoning, that is, the duration of the eon that ends with the coming of Christ. The Mazdaean era is an allegorized year divided into four seasons and lasts twelve thousand years, meaning that a month on earth lasts a thousand years with God. The Jewish tribes are associated with the zodiac belt and signs, so the twelve tribes in this case stand for the zodiac order of the year that will be repeated twelve thousand times; thus, John's era lasts 12 x 12000 = 144000 months, the same as that of Zarathustra. Logically, John does not allow angels to harm the earth until the time has come.

Consequently, John's promise of salvation is not locally Jewish but universal. A place in heaven is not only promised to the few that belong to the Jewish people, but to all the righteous among all nations when the time has come:

> After this I looked and there before me was a great multitude that no one could count, from every nation, tribe, people and language, standing before the throne and in front of the Lamb. They were wearing white robes and were holding palm branches in their hands. And they cried out in a loud voice: "Salvation belongs to our God, who sits on the throne, and to the Lamb." All the angels were standing around the throne and around the elders and the four living creatures. They fell down on their faces before the throne and worshiped God, saying: "Amen! Praise and glory and wisdom and thanks and honor and power and strength be to our God for ever and ever. Amen!" Then one of the elders asked me, "These in white robes—who are they, and where did they come from?" I answered, "Sir, you know." And he said, "These are they who have come out of the great tribulation; they have washed their robes and made them white in the blood of the Lamb. Therefore, they are before the throne of God and serve him day and night in his temple; and he who sits on

---

43. Cf.: "There is the Son of Man and there is the son of the Son of Man. The Lord is the Son of Man, and the son of the Son of Man is he who creates through the Son of Man. The Son of Man received from God the capacity to create. He also has the ability to beget. He who has received the ability to create is a creature. He who has received the ability to beget is an offspring. He who creates cannot beget. He who begets also has power to create" ("Gospel of Philip," para. 95).

the throne will spread his tent over them. Never again will they hunger; never again will they thirst. The sun will not beat upon them, nor any scorching heat.

For the Lamb at the center of the throne will be their shepherd; he will lead them to springs of living water. And God will wipe away every tear from their eyes." (Rev 7:9–17)

John's cosmology is relatively simple: the Moon is the ordering principle and rules the seasons which are represented by the four planets above which Jupiter stands, maintaining the regular shifts of seasons and celestial cycles, and above it Saturn—the time. Above the sphere of Saturn lies the starry sky, *ouranos*, which was formed by the mythical division of the upper and lower waters, Nun, Tiamat, the Moon.

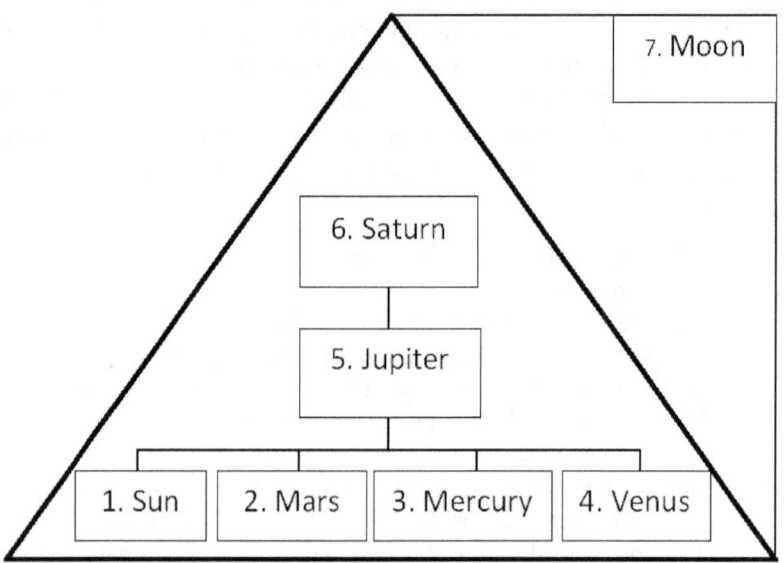

Cosmology of the Revelation

Composition

John's composition progresses linearly from the prologue in which he announces the Revelation that he received from Jesus or from Jesus through an angel, the greeting, and the opening vision in which he describes the circumstances of the revelation he received and conveys the message to the churches. He addresses each of the churches directly and greets them, referring to the source of the revelation with the same attributes as in the opening vision. In the letters, he also mentions the specific traits and attitudes of each of the churches, warning them that the time is near. The letters to churches are, however, just an introduction to the actual message conveyed in the remaining part of the text, which gives a detailed account of events and represents a common message for everyone to pass on further to those who need to hear it. In the message, John speaks of the Moon that was there at the beginning of creation and from which all things came into being, and of the reigns of the six rulers/planets who were his successors in times, which continue to get worse until the epilogue in the final period when the Savior will be born and will take on the forces of evil/rulers and establish a kingdom of justice. John inserts events that are important to him and that carry a prophecy into the reign of each ruler/seal, namely: the invasion of locusts during the fifth ruler, the army of the Euphrates during the sixth, the two prophets, the announcement of God's authority and the woman clothed with the Sun as the central part of the revelation that marks the transition from the sixth to the seventh period. This moment signifies the death of the sixth ruler and the beginning of the reign of the seventh, which, although prophesied, did not happen because "one of the heads of the beast seemed to have had a fatal wound, but the fatal wound had been healed" (Rev 13:3).

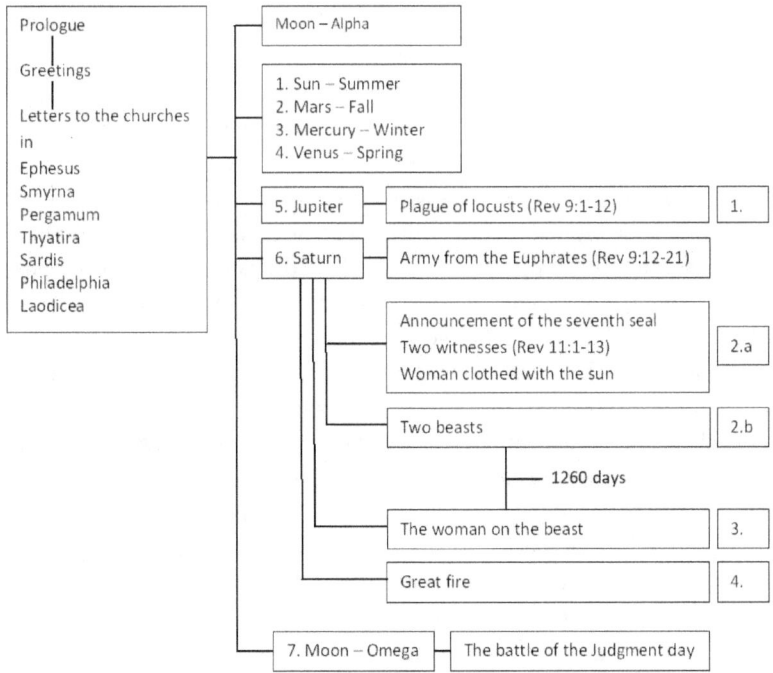

Composition of the Revelation at the cosmological level

But the prophecy will be fulfilled after all: "If anyone is to go into captivity, into captivity he will go. If anyone is to be killed with the sword, with the sword he will be killed. This calls for patient endurance and faithfulness on the part of the saints" (Rev 13:10). Exactly 1,260 days after this event, a third will take place when the woman flees into the wilderness where God has prepared a shelter for her to feed there for 1,260 days (Rev 12:6). The fourth event can be determined based on the model obtained from the previous scheme.

HISTORICAL BACKGROUND

John's image of the judgement day's events sums up Vohuman in brief lines. Despite the same theological inspiration, John emphasizes the character of the Son of Man as a triumphator coming with the clouds (Rev 1:6), rather than the dramatic events of the judgment day: "I saw heaven standing open and there before me was a white horse, whose rider is called Faithful and True. With justice he judges and makes war; his eyes are like blazing fire, and on his head are many crowns. He has a name written on him that no one knows but he himself. He is dressed in a robe dipped in blood, and his name is the Word of God. The armies of heaven were following him, riding on white horses and dressed in fine linen, white and clean. Out of his mouth comes a sharp sword with which to strike down the nations. He will rule them with an iron scepter. He treads the winepress of the fury of the wrath of God Almighty. On his robe and on his thigh, he has this name written: *king of kings and lord of lords*" (Rev 19:11–16). The time of the arrival is clearly defined: "But in the days when the seventh angel is about to sound his trumpet, the mystery of God will be accomplished, just as he announced to his servants the prophets" (Rev 10:7), and again, "The seventh angel sounded his trumpet, and there were loud voices in heaven, which said: 'The kingdom of the world has become the kingdom of our Lord and of his Christ, and he will reign for ever and ever.'" (Rev 11:15). Time is coming! In the creation/knowledge from the Zand (*Bundahishn*) the descriptions are more dramatic, underlining the catastrophe of the last days: the planets, with many demons, dashed against the celestial sphere, and they mixed the constellations; and the whole creation was as disfigured as though fire disfigured every place and smoke arose over it.[44] The Zand's creation introduces astronomy and clearly states the signs to follow. Planets moving in retrograde motion are generally a bad sign in an astrological sense, but also an important element for astrological divination. Planets that move in

---

44. West, "Bundahishn," ch. 5.

this way lose their characteristics or their action is weaker. The punishment for those who disobey God's laws is the same in both texts: at the coming of the Savior the wicked will be cast into hell, which Zand places "in the middle of the earth; there where the evil spirit pierced the earth and rushed in upon it."[45] According to Ptolemy, the middle of the Earth is located at the intersection of the lines connecting Gibraltar and the Gulf of Issus and the mountain massif extending to the east and the lines connecting the Arabian Gulf, the Aegean Sea, the Pontus, and the Maeotis (somewhere near Issus).[46]

The crime that John charges against those who will be thrown into the sea of fire is repeated several times in the text, being specifically only those who worship the image of the beast and are marked with its number: "There is no rest day or night for those who worship the beast and his image, or for anyone who receives the mark of his name" (Rev 14:10–11) and "Then I saw the beast and the kings of the earth and their armies gathered together to make war against the rider on the horse and his army. But the beast was captured, and with him the false prophet who had performed miraculous signs on his behalf. With these signs he had deluded those who received the mark of the beast and worshiped his image. The two of them were thrown alive into the fiery lake of burning sulfur. The rest of them were killed with the sword that came out of the mouth of the rider on the horse, and all the birds gorged themselves on their flesh" (Rev 19:19–21). There is a clear distinction between the armies of heaven (*farohars*) dressed with white linen and the worshipers of the beast. The event that John places at the center of the drama of Revelation is thus emphasized. This is followed by the eschatological promise, the resurrection, the new Jerusalem, and the peace of a thousand years until the final conflict of good and evil in which evil and death will be destroyed. This millenarian speculation is very general and is the only prophecy that John uttered in his book.

John also mentions the geographical names: Jerusalem, Egypt, Babylon, Sodom, and Euphrates. Jerusalem and Babylon probably in a figurative sense, apparently as well as Sodom, which ceased to exist long time ago. But when he writes about the kings of the Euphrates he means specific kings, places, and events: "The sixth angel sounded his trumpet, and I heard a voice coming from the horns of the golden altar that is before God. It said to the sixth angel who had the trumpet, 'Release the four angels who are bound at the great river Euphrates.' And the four angels who had been kept ready for this very hour and day and month and year were released to kill

---

45. West, "Bundahishn," ch. 5.

46. Ptolemy, *Tetrabiblos*, 23–31. Maeotis follows the Black Sea in its northern part. According to the legend, this is the location where Jonah was swallowed by a whale.

a third of mankind. The number of the mounted troops was two hundred million. I heard their number. The horses and riders I saw in my vision looked like this: Their breastplates were fiery red, dark blue, and yellow as sulfur. The heads of the horses resembled the heads of lions, and out of their mouths came fire, smoke and sulfur. A third of mankind was killed by the three plagues of fire, smoke and sulfur that came out of their mouths. The power of the horses was in their mouths and in their tails; for their tails were like snakes, having heads with which they inflict injury. The rest of mankind that were not killed by these plagues still did not repent of the work of their hands; they did not stop worshiping demons, and idols of gold, silver, bronze, stone and wood—idols that cannot see or hear or walk. Nor did they repent of their murders, their magic arts, their sexual immorality or their thefts" (Rev 9:13–21).

There had already been attempts to connect the kings from the East with historical figures who ruled the Mesopotamian area in the first century, but the short sketch that portrayed the first seal was connected with the Parthian king Vologases I, who won an important victory over Rome in AD 62. In this interpretation, it is unclear how Vologases could have been connected with the current events in Israel in John's time.

In the first century BC the Parthians were often at war against Rome, from Mithridates in 96, 53, 40, 36, and 12–9 BC, to be continued by Vologases I in AD 58–63 and other Parthian rulers in AD 164, 197 and 216–217, till the end of the Parthian state. Vologases's campaign was conducted against the Roman general Corbulo from AD 58–63. If the book of Revelation records the fear of the Parthian cavalry whose strength is in their tails because they shoot arrows when retreating ("They had tails and stings like scorpions, and in their tails, they had power to torment people for five months" [Rev 9:10]; "The number of the mounted troops was two hundred million. I heard their number. The horses and riders I saw in my vision looked like this: Their breastplates were fiery red, dark blue, and yellow as sulfur. The heads of the horses resembled the heads of lions, and out of their mouths came fire, smoke and sulfur" [Rev 9:16–17]) then he has a different event at his focus altogether, given that since the Roman-Parthian war which ended in peace in AD 63 until Trajan's intervention in AD 115, therefore for fifty years the relations between Rome and Parthia were stable and Rome had no reason to fear their invasion.

A historical context of the time can be identified via several short references:

1. When the fifth trumpet sounds, locusts arise from the Abyss equipped as an army prepared for battle.

2. When the sixth angel sounded his horn, four angels who are bound at the great river Euphrates were released, and its water was dried up to prepare the way for the kings from the East (Rev 15:12).
3. The armies of the kings of the world gathered at a place called Armageddon.
4. The second beast made a statue of the first beast.

If it was a real invasion of the army from the Euphrates (Parthia), it could not have happened between AD 63 and 115, because after the treaty in Rhandeia, which both warring parties, Rome and Parthia, considered as their victory, the relations between the two world powers were stable at that time, so Irenaeus's dating of the event to the time of Domitian is also questionable, when there was no military threat from Parthia and the events cannot be reconciled with his time. But if Nero's time is accepted as the time in which the Revelation was written, the events fit perfectly, especially John's term that all this happened in the time of the sixth king—Nero.

The story of the Roman-Parthian war in Revelation is briefly outlined; especially considering that John condemns his countrymen who accepted the mark of the beast and worship his statue, it means nothing else than that John is a member of a political party in conflict with the Parthians and condemns his opponents who betrayed him, the country, and the idea by accepting the rule/salary of Vologases. The plural form *kings from the East* corresponds to the historical situation (four kings) and it seems that it is precisely Vologases I, king of Parthia, his brother Pacorus, king of Media, and king of Adiabene Monobazus II who went to war with Rome together claiming the right to the royal crown in Armenia for Vologases's youngest brother Tiridates. The historical context is to be read in its entirety, allowing for a clear understanding that John wrote about completely real events and that his interest was not religion but practical politics. If this interpretation is correct and can be proven, the Revelation will be translated into a historical chronicle that does not exist in the world's cultural heritage.

Armenia

Instead of reducing the status of Armenia to a province, Augustus rather decided to keep it in a sort of vassal relation. Upon request of the Armenian noblemen, he gave the hereditary right of succession to the throne to Tigranes's royal family. However, after the elections both Parthians and Romans tried to rule over Armenia via rulers loyal to them, so that neither of these so-called rulers were able to guarantee the hereditary succession right to their family.

The historians describing the Roman war operations in the East dedicate no space to Armenian kings whose survival depended on whom they were sided with. Armenian chronicle writers ignore the very existence of such kings. From the scarce data of the time, some light has been cast on several episodes. In one moment Vonones, son of Phraates IV of Parthia, at the request of Parthian noblemen was released from captivity in Rome and came to Armenia wanting to become a candidate for their king. His western manners, acquired through his Roman education, were ill-received in Armenia. Soon enough he was overthrown by Arthaban III, king of Parthia, and Vonones escaped to Syria. In response to this, Rome sent Germanicus to stop the Parthians from conquering Armenia. The two opponent sides in Armenia agreed to give the throne to Zenon, the son of queen Pythodorida of Pontus, whose husband was a faithful Roman vassal. Zenon was raised with Eastern manners, and his love for hunting and celebrations had made him popular in Armenia. Upon his arrival to Artaxata, Germanicus put the royal crown onto his head in front of the gathered mass, which was deemed as great victory and celebrated by triumph (in AD 18). Zenon's rule was a period of peace. But after his death in AD 34, Artabanus, king of Parthia put his eldest son Arsacus to the throne. The latter immediately claimed the return of the treasure that Vonones had taken to Syria and Cilicia with him, as well his hereditary rights he had had since Alexander and Darius. Tiberius brought additional forces with him to the border, and in the next twenty-five years Armenia became site to heavy battles of the two best known global forces. The victories quickly took place among the opponents, thus subjugating the original population of the force more powerful in that moment. Amidst those fights the invasion of Iberians took place, under the command of the Roman vassal Mithridates in AD 44, who additionally plundered one part of Armenia and ruled from Artaxata several years. Parthian aspirations were once again revealed by Vologases I (his name was mentioned in a whole series of variants: Valarses, Vagharshes, Vologasos, Walagash, Balash), who put his brother Tiridates to the throne. The new king chased away the Iberian pretenders, but upon his return to Parthia for a winter sojourn, Rhadamistus of Iberia broke in, committing many crimes and violence. Provoked by many incidents, the inhabitants of the capital opposed Rhadamistus, who barely made it to Caucasus where he fled.

Roman intervention was sparked once more. In AD 58 Nero sent Domitius Corbulo to prevent Tiridates from breaking into Roman urban areas. Corbulo's legions (IV Scitica and XII Fulminata) also accessed the suburbs of Artaxata and passed the river in order to attack the Parthian army's flanks. Tiridates had already evacuated the city and Corbulo set it on fire and left it in ruins. After that he went south to take Tigranocerta. Vologases I, Parthian king of kings, took over the command himself and threatened the Romans at the Aras River. Corbulo changed his progressions and hurried to help his endangered legions, not succeeding in anything but successfully retreating to the west of the Euphrates, considered to be a Roman border by Vologases.

Rome was celebrating a nonexistent victory over the enemy when the messengers turned up, proving that the Roman army was forced out of Armenia. The emperor ordered the war to be continued, but was ready to discuss the conditions of peace. After the negotiations, Corbulo accepted Tiridates as king under the condition to accept the Armenian crown from the Roman emperor. Tiridates agreed with this and accepted the initiation ceremony.

The Romans set up camp near Artaxata, put a curule seat on the throne with Nero's image (statue) over it. From afar came Tiridates leading a magnificent parade made of military and civilian dignitaries. The Parthian and Armenian cavalry stood in front of the stage in a long line, and opposite them stood the Roman legions with their eagles and insignia. Statues of gods were placed between the rows of soldiers as in a temple. The animals were sacrificed, and then Tiridates ascended the stage, knelt before the statue, removed the diadem from his head, and placed it at the feet of the statue of Nero. The diadem was given to Corbulo, who sent it to Rome.

Tiridates had to go to Rome to be crowned by the emperor himself. Before the trip, he visited his mother and brothers in Media and Parthia. After that, he began a long journey together with his family, accompanied by three thousand Parthian and Armenian horsemen. As a Mazdaean priest, Tiridates avoided traveling by sea and traveled the whole way by land. The journey through Thrace, Illyricum, and northern Italy lasted nine months and he arrived in Rome at the end of the year AD 66.

Nero welcomed Tiridates to Naples. He sent a state carriage before him. Tiridates refused to hand over the sword, which was never allowed in the emperor's presence, but fastened to the scabbard so that it could not be drawn. Games were arranged and Tiridates had the opportunity to show off his shooting skills by killing two bulls with one arrow.

For this great occasion, Rome was magnificently decorated, decorated with flags and illuminated at night. Nero came to the forum in ceremonial dress, and Tiridates knelt before him with folded hands on his chest and addressed him: "My lord, I am a descendant of Arzacs and brother of the kings Vologases and Pacorus. I came to you because you are my god, I will worship you as Mitra, I will be everything you ask of me, because you are my destiny and happiness."

Nero answered him: "You have done well to come in person. I give you what your father did not leave and what your brother did not keep. I agree with you and make you king of Armenia, so that you know as well as they that I have power to take and give kingdoms." After that, Tiridates went up the stairs and knelt so that Nero would put the royal diadem on him. Nero kissed him and sat down on a chair a little lower than his own.

Never in the history of Rome was a reception equal to this one in terms of luxury. The Roman authorities paid the total cost of the trip and gave Tiridates five million sesterces. Peace reigned throughout the Roman Empire. Nero closed the doors of the Temple of Janus, which were never closed except in times of world peace. On his return, Tiridates brought with him a large number of excellent artists to restore Artaxata. He changed the name of the city to Neroni, and nearby he built a royal residence with colonnades and monuments of exceptional luxury.

Rome treated Armenia as a loyal ally after Nero's death and throughout Vespasian's reign, until another invasion. The Alans, together with other Caucasian tribes, first invaded Media and then in AD 72 Armenia, too. Tiridates bravely opposed them, barely avoiding captivity. The Alans retreated, taking large amounts of booty with them.

The main problem remained, of course, the question of inheritance. Tiridates died in AD 75 without an heir and Rome chose a foreigner who was not from the Arsacid family. Osroes II, Parthian king, wasted no time in deposing the new puppet and replacing him with one of his nephews. Trajan (AD 98–117), in an effort to bring glory to his reign, came in person to Armenia in AD 115 and encamped before the walls of the Karin (Erzurum). The Parthian candidate, missing the opportunity to propitiate and persuade Trajan, decided to flee, but was killed by a Roman guard. Trajan's campaign ended with the capture of Mesopotamia and after that great military venture, Trajan died of a stroke aboard a ship on his way back to Rome. After that, instead of force, Hadrian decided to apply a smarter policy and let Armenia choose its own king. The peace achieved in Nero's time lasted until AD 115, which earned Nero great popularity in Parthia where he was celebrated as a deity long after his death.

John's subject stems from this historical event. Everyone who accepted the treaty in Rhandeia and its political consequences, those who worship the statue of the beast and bear its mark, were cursed by John and sentenced to eternal torment. They have no other sin.

John describes the treaty in Rhandeia in AD 63 (Rev 13:11–18). The beast that comes out of the earth and has two horns like the Lamb (Israel) is an astrological image of the Taurus constellation, which really comes out of the earth and in which, at the moment John prophesies, is the Sun (ruler 666) that brings down fire from heaven and their earthly counterpart Parthia/Media. An important element for astrological forecasts is locating the places to which astronomical events refer. Events in Taurus refer to Asia Minor and Parthia. This beast is apparently Vologases I who does what Rome asks of him, forces the land and inhabitants to submit to Roman rule and the mortally wounded beast that has healed. Vologases does what the beast allowed him to do, erects a statue of the beast before which he bows down and accepts its authority and orders that all those who do not accept its authority be killed. Vologases puts the mark of the beast on his hands and forehead, mints money with his name on it. This is John's brief recapitulation of the history and ending of the Roman-Parthian War.

The first beast, with ten horns and seven heads and with ten crowns on its horns, to which Vologases raises a statue, is obviously Nero. Nero comes at the head of a force consisting of three great nations: the Greeks (leopard), the Gauls (bear), and the Romans (lion). The dragon (devil) gave it power over the world.

Nero was predicted by astrologers to die in AD 60 (Suetonius, Tacitus, Dio Cassius), from which he redeemed himself with bloodshed. The unfulfilled prophecy was merely postponed because "if anyone is to go into captivity, into captivity he will go. If anyone is to be killed with the sword, with the sword he will be killed. This calls for patient endurance and faithfulness on the part of the saints" (Rev 13:10). Prophecy is the mortal wound of the beast, it is the sword that hangs over its head. Nero was given to speak blasphemies and defeat the holy Armenians. The phrase "he also bowed down to the Beast, saying: 'Who is like the beast? Who can make war against him?'" meaning "Who is like Rome? Who can make war against Rome?" indicates the time when the Revelation was written. John repeats the opening phrase of the speech of Marcus Julius Agrippa who calms the Jews and tries to dissuade them from the war in AD 67 which means that the Revelation was written during Nero's lifetime, and at the very beginning of the Jewish war, i.e., AD 67-68.

Following the logic of Jesus transmitting the revelation through the Sun and the Moon, we come to Venus, who was born from sea foam[47] (comes from the sea) and who is connected to the Julian-Claudian dynasty as their progenitor, with Nero as their last member. Caesar's line ended with Nero. He was the last ruler of Caesar's name, which his successors continued

---

47. "She (Aphrodyte) comes from the sea, a watery element, and warm, and in constant movement, and foaming because of its commotion, whereby they intimate the seminal power" (Porphyry, "On Images," fr. 8).

to bear as a title. In the last years of Nero's reign, the laurel near the Villa Ad Gallinas, which Livia had planted and which was used to make wreaths for triumphs, withered. All the chickens used in the auspices died. A thunderbolt knocked the heads off all the statues in Caesar's temple and the scepter fell out of Augustus's hand.[48]

This introduces new elements into the composition: the planets are also the Roman emperors, of which Nero is obviously the sixth, i.e., the Sun is Caesar, Mars is Augustus, Mercury is Tiberius, Venus is Caligula, Jupiter is Claudius, Saturn is Nero, and the seventh is not there yet.

The protagonists can be extended to Venus: "The woman you saw is the great city that rules over the kings of the earth" (Rev 17:18).

(C Moon – M Jesus) – B Venus – A (Sun) = A1 (Vologases I) – B1 (Nero – Rome) – (M1 John – C1 Armenia).

The story of John's Revelation is the story of the occultations of the Sun, Moon, and Venus, which follow and introduce occultations in the relations of Rome, Parthia, and Armenia in real time.

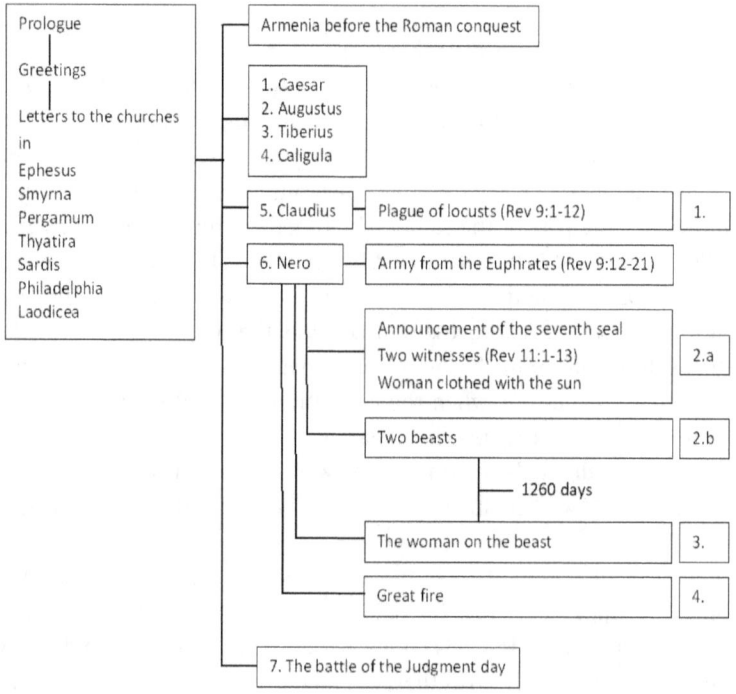

Composition of the Revelation at the historic level

48. Suetonius, *Caesars, Volume II*, 182.

Number of Man's Name

Names have a natural affinity with their objects, according to Cratylus, "because he who knows names also knows the matter of things,"[49] and numbers come out of the stars. The identification of Vologases as the man with the name number 666 is very obvious. The gematric calculation of the number of the name itself is facilitated by the fact that he mints money, and his name should appear on Vologases's money in the form according to which John calculates his number. The aggravating circumstance is that in the text that John composes according to real events, such a coincidence connecting all elements without intervention and adaptation is hardly possible, but any other association is also possible. On the other hand, such calculation is made difficult by John's poor knowledge of the Greek language and the fact that he distorts the language and the names he states. The numerical equivalent of a name depends on the pronunciation, language, and alphabet used by John, and he probably calculates the number of the name in a language other than Greek. Irenaeus's calculation of the number of the name of the beast (Euanthas, Lateinos, Teitan) was calculated by simply adding the numerical values of the Greek alphabet; Viktorin calculates the opposite—he extracts the name in Latin from the numerical expression and applies Irenaeus's method in Gothic. It is also a question of how he pronounces his name and whether he uses the Hebrew, Aramaic, Pahlavi, or Greek numerical system.[50] A lingering question is according to which method John calculates names, because there are many. Irenaeus's method is the simplest calculation method. He only adds the numerical equivalents of the Greek alphabet, and there is another method by which the number of names is calculated in reverse, so that the first letter of the alphabet is given the highest value and the last one the lowest value, therefore during adding the values are reduced to a lower level, from decades to monads, etc. Gematria is a simple process of replacing the letters of a name with their numerical equivalent.[51]

---

49. Guthrie, *Kasni Platon i Akademija*, 61.

50. The Hebrew, Greek, and Aramaic numeral systems are derived from the numerical equivalent of the letters of the alphabet, while Pahlavi has a separate numeral system similar to Arabic numerals.

51. Irenaeus's names have the following numerical expressions (name numbers):
Euanthas: $E = 5$, $U = 400$, $A = 1$, $N = 50$, $TH = 9$, $A = 1$, $S = 200$, total 666
Teitan: $T = 300$, $E = 5$, $I = 10$, $T = 300$, $A = 1$, $N = 50$, total 666
Lateinos: $L = 30$, $A = 1$, $T = 300$, $E = 5$, $I = 10$, $N = 50$, $O = 70$, $S = 200$, total 666, which confirms the method used in the first or second century AD. In Basilides's gnostic system, the highest god is called Abraxas, because his name has a numerical expression in Greek 365, which corresponds to the number of days in the year and the

In the literature, Vologeases's name appears in a number of variants: Valarses, Vagharsh, Vologosos, Walakhsh, Balash, of which the Greek pronunciation is attested on the coin. The coin bears the title king of kings and lord. The Aramaic initial appears on the coins of Vologases II (AD 77–80) as Wlgsh and Wlgshy (Valgash/Valgashi).[52]

Calling for a solution to the riddle, "this calls for wisdom. If anyone has insight, let him calculate the number of the beast, for it is man's number. His number is 666" (Rev 13:18). John brings Vologases into connection with the Sun, whose number is 666, but it is not certain that he is referring to gematria. The association that the answer should be sought in money is obvious: "He also forced everyone, small and great, rich and poor, free and slave, to receive a mark on his right hand or on his forehead, so that no one could buy or sell unless he had the mark, which is the name of the beast or the number of his name" (Rev13:16–17).[53]

Vologases is the Sun and is in conjunction with it (syzygy), therefore also with the first seal, described as a rider with a bow in his hand. An archer with a bow in his hand is almost regularly depicted on Vologases's coins: "I looked, and there before me was a white horse! Its rider held a bow, and he was given a crown, and he rode out as a conqueror bent on conquest" (Rev 6:2), which is the sign of the Sun that brings Vologases into connection with John's image and the number of the beast.

Armageddon

Armenia is John's inspiration. He writes of a mighty kingdom that existed before all "at the beginning of time." The kingdom where Adam, the first man, was buried, where Noah's ark ran aground and where the first city of Naxuana was built. John speaks of a kingdom that had power and freedom

---

number of aspects of the planetary powers.

ABRAXAS: A = 1, B = 2, R = 100, A = 1, Ks = 60, A = 1, S = 200

The Hebrew alphabet is different from the Greek, as are the numerical equivalents, including the number of the name:

A/silent 1 Aleph, B/V 2 Bet, G 3 Gimel, D 4 Daled, H 5 He, V/O/U 6 Waw, Z 7 Zayin, Ch 8 Heth, T 9 Teth, Y 10 Yodh, K/ Kh 20 or 500 Kaph, L 30 Lamed, M 40 or 600 Mem, N 50 or 700 Nun, S 60 Samekh, quiet 70 Ayin, P/F 80 or 800 Pe, Tz 90 or 900 Tsadi, Q 100 Qoph, R 200 Resh, Sh/S 300 Shin, T/S 400 Taw

52. "Chronological Listing of Parthian Rulers."

53. Vologases's name appears in the basic form in Aramaic as *wl* and Greek: *[vasileos] vasileo[n arsakou] everge[tou] dikaiou epifano[ys fil]llin[os]*; *[vasileos] vasileo[n arsakou] everget[ou] dikaiou epifanou[s fil]ellino[s]*, and in one case as *oligasoo(y) tou kyri(o)y*.

Oligasoos—70 + 30 + 10 + 3 + 1 + 200 + 70 + 70 + 200 = 654.

over the centuries from the first settlement and the great kingdom of Urartu (Nairi), after which the Armenian kingdom arose, which in the time of Mithridates II and Tigranes occupied a wide area from Asia Minor through Syria deep into Media. The kingdom represented a powerful force in the East and collapsed after long and difficult battles with the Roman legions led by the generals Lucullus and Crassus.

The name Armenia comes from the Aryan vocabulary. During more than four millennia of history, the country had gone through several phases of reconstruction and the greatest calamities that have ever hit humanity. Its rulers—good, bad or indifferent—often made large and devastating errors in their relations with other rulers and opponents, but the courage and determination of the people never failed. In some times it reached the splendor and power equal to other great eastern empires, in other times, squeezed between the brutal world military powers it fought to survive. In the era of the state of Urartu (Assyrian name) it fought against Assyria and Babylon without fearing anyone. This was followed by a decline that begins with Alexander's conquests, dependence on the Seleucids, to reach its historical peak again as an empire under Tigranes the Great, who took the title of king of kings.

Written sources on the beginnings of Armenia are fragmentary and often unreliable. The earliest chronicles were written in Greek and Syriac and were written by Agathangelos, Zenobios, and Faustus of Byzantium (Buzand). The part of the history written by Mar Apas Catina (one of the sources used by the ancient Armenian chronicler Moses Chorenensis), originally written in Chaldean, was translated into Greek by order of Alexander the Great. The invention of the Armenian script and the translation of the Bible in AD 432 represents the beginning of the golden age of Armenian literature and a large number of historians who, of course, accepted, preserved, and passed on various legends that were preserved in the national memory.

Herodotus writes that the Armenians, having crossed the Hellespont, together with some Balkan and Greek tribes, came to Asia Minor at the beginning of the twelfth century BC, destroying the kingdom of Hatti, to remain in Asia Minor for the next six hundred years.

In ancient times, this part of Western Asia, mostly mountainous, with fertile plateaus and valleys, was the scene of bloody conflicts on one side or the other. Nations and kingdoms rose and fell.

The remains from the Stone Age show that Armenia was inhabited long before the first historical sources appeared, during the time when Mesopotamia was still under water and Mount Ararat merely a lonely island. For a long time, it was thought among Christians that Noah's ark ran aground on the peaks of Mount Ararat, which is a misreading: "On the seventeenth day of the seventh month the ark came to rest on the mountains of Ararat" (Gen 8:4), because Ararat in Hebrew is not a mountain, but the area around it, the old center of Armenia, also known as Erirath, Urartu, etc. Jeremiah mentions the kingdom of Ararat, which was actually called Urartu at the time: "Raise a banner in the land! Blow the ram's horn among the nations! Prepare the nations against her. Summon the kingdoms against her—Ararat, Minni, and Ashkenaz. Appoint a captain against her; bring up horses like swarming locusts!" (Jer 51:27). The progenitor of the Armenians was the heroic Hayk (Haik) after whom the Armenians got their name. He is shown as a triumphator on a white horse with a bow, exactly as the first seal. Ararat is a volcano that has awakened many times in history and the thunder and lightning coming from the throne is probably an image of the mountain and the mysterious powers that dwell in it.

Hayk, an excellent archer, has long since become part of the legend as the forefather of the Armenians, who adopted the patronym Hay. The legend goes back to prehistoric times when the first Armenians came to the land of Urartu under his command. According to legend, he rebelled against the tyrant Bel from Babylon and went north with his family and followers. Bel, at the head of a large army, went in pursuit and caught up with him. Hayk challenged Bel to a fight and killed him with an arrow and dispersed his army and freed the land known as Hark, the homeland of the Hay people.

John's composition on the cosmological level places the Alpha Moon at the beginning of time and the Omega Moon at the end. It implies that on the historical level the description of the location in the first place is the same as the description in the last location, i.e., that the battle of the judgment day in Armageddon is in the place where the world began. In the formula: "At once I was in the Spirit, and there before me was a throne in heaven with someone sitting on it. And the one who sat there had the appearance of jasper and carnelian. A rainbow, resembling an emerald, encircled the throne" (Rev 4:2–3). John describes the Moon, but the description is also a toponym, bearing the same meaning as Armageddon. Armenians never called their famous mountain Ararat but Massis (Armenian *har(a)* = mountain and the name of the mountain Massis; Harmassis = mountain Massis and the area around it; Armageddon = Armenia).[54] The name is preserved in the names of two peaks of today's Mount Ararat. The Greater Massis is

---

54. Strabo mentions Mount Masius, which separates Sophena and Armenia from Mesopotamia and is located above Tigranocerta (Strabo, *Geography*, bk. 11, ch. 12).

5,165 meters high, and the Little Massis is 3,896 meters high.[55] The great mountain was often the site of earthquakes and thunderstorms, and in 1840 the old volcano erupted for the last time. The province of Sophene is known as Anahita's throne, the throne of the Moon—Athor Anahta (throne that is in heaven [Rev 4:2]). Anahita is identified with Artemis in the *interpretatio graeca* and she is the mother of all gods.[56]

Three large lakes, usually called seas, are Sevan, Van, and Urmia.[57] The time of the kingdom that lasts from the beginning ("I am the First and the Last, and I am alive! I was dead" [Rev 1:18]; "These are the words of him who is the First and the Last, who died and came to life again" [Rev 2:8]) ends after the greatest and most brilliant rise in the bloody historical episode. Tigranes II (95–54 BC) gained the throne by ceding to the Parthians the territory over which his predecessors had fought with the Medes and Iberians, the occupation of which was the pretext for the military expedition of Mithridates II of Parthia. A conflict broke out between him and Vardanes, king of Sophene. Tigranes attacked Vardanes, defeated him, took his lands, and extended his kingdom from the valley of Kur to Melitine and Cappadocia. Mithridates VI of Pontus, intending to annex Cappadocia, entered into an alliance with Tigranes by marrying one of his daughters. The danger of an invasion of Cappadocia made its king, Ariobarzanes, urgently seek the help of Rome, which was provided without hesitation. Sulla came to Asia Minor, restored Ariobarzanes to the throne, and forced the Armenian army to retreat across the Euphrates. The civil war in Rome in 90 BC made it possible to repeat the Armenian military operation and Ariobazanes had to flee again.

After the death of Mithridates II in 88 BC, Tigranes occupied the lands that had been taken from him as far as Atropatene, Corduene, and Adiabene and part of Mesopotamia, thereby including the territory of Urartu, taking the title "king of kings," which he carved on money. Thus, the supremacy that once belonged to Persia and Parthia passed on to Armenia, reaching its peak when Tigranes was invited to Syria where he was offered the Seleucid crown.

The capital city of Artaxata, due to the expansion of the territory, became unsuitable and distant from the center of the kingdom, and Tigranes founded a new one, calling it Tigranocerta after his own name. The nobles

---

55. The inscription PH314428—*o vasilèfs Ar-madoeíron Míthras Erónti vasileí chaírein*—mentions Armadoeiron (Armenia?). More in Russell, *Zoroastrianism in Armenia*.

56. De Jong, *Traditions of the Magi*.

57. Kurkjian, *History of Armenia*, 90.

of the entire kingdom moved to the new capital, which was inhabited by people from Asia Minor and other parts of the kingdom.

The verbal peace agreement between Sulla and Mithridates VI Eupator in 83 BC was merely a truce. Murena, the governor of Asia Minor renewed hostilities without the consent of the Roman Senate. Mithridates offered peace, but in vain. Roman internal politics needed victory on the borders. Lucullus came with a powerful army and navy to Asia Minor and Mithridates, abandoned by his officers, was severely beaten and an escape to Armenia remained his only option. Since Tigranes promised and provided help to him, he started a war not only with the Romans, but with the Parthians, too.

Lucullus planned to expand operations to Armenia without declaring war. Immediately after the refusal to extradite Mithridates, the Romans went after Tigranes. After the initial disbelief that the Roman intervention would happen and losing a lot of time, Tigranes tried to organize a defense. Mirbarzanes, one of his generals, lost about three thousand horsemen in the conflict with Sextilius and the Armenian army was dispersed. Tigranes fled to the North, leaving money and women behind. In the meantime, Sextilius besieged Tigranocerta and occupied the suburbs. Tigranes still had enormous military potential. At his call, the kings of Adiabene, Atropatene, Iberia, and Albania came to his aid. Gathering an army of about one hundred thousand soldiers, Tigranes rejected advice to surround the much smaller enemy force and opted for frontal assault.

Lucullus left Murena with about six thousand horsemen to guard Tigranocerta, and, using an infantry unit of ten thousand soldiers and some cavalry, set out to meet Tigranes. Plutarch says that Tigranes, when he saw the small enemy forces, cynically remarked that there were many of them if they came as messengers, and too few if they were soldiers.

In the fall, on August 6, 69 BC, Lucullus launched an attack with two cohorts, climbing a hill that Tigranes had not taken over. From there, the Romans rushed at the cavalry, which began to retreat chaotically. In a short time, the Armenian army was defeated and fleeing, and the king lost his diadem while fleeing.

The situation of Tigranes and Mithridates was critical. All the provinces south of the Taurus were lost. The Greek mercenaries who were left to defend Tigranocerta revolted and the city was conquered and looted.

Lucullus spent the winter of 69/68 BC in Corduene, looking for allies among the small kings around Armenia. In the spring he mobilized his forces and crossed the Tigris, marching towards Artaxata. Tigranes's army took up strong positions on the hills, while the king himself commanded the cavalry, trying to cut the Roman supply routes. The battle took place in September of 68 BC. In an attempt to divert the Roman army, Tigranes moved to the other side of the river, trying to attack from behind. The Median horsemen and Iberian spearmen scattered before the Roman infantry. Tigranes attacked at the center and Mithridates attacked from behind. For a moment the situation became dangerous for the Romans, but Lucullus threw Mithridates into confusion by attacking Tigranes's guards. The armies separated without victory with many casualties.

Artaxata was far away, and the Armenian summer was drawing to a close. The Roman advance was stopped by a sudden winter and heavy snow. Lucullus gave up the conquest of Artaxata and retreated to the south.

With Lucullus retreating to Mesopotamia, Tigranes and Mithridates returned to their countries. Mithridates even fought another battle in which about seven thousand Romans were killed. In the offensive that they took immediately after these events, they took back Cappadocia and drove the Romans out of Pontus. Roman gains from this war were thus lost.

Rome could consolidate its Asian provinces only through mortal combat with Tigranes and Mithridates. After having spent winter in Cilicia, Pompey, who succeeded Lucullus in 66 BC, went against Mithridates. Mithridates tried to make an alliance with the Parthians, but Pompey overtook him in this effort and made an alliance with them himself. Mithridates was defeated in the first battle, and the Parthian king Phraates III forced Tigranes to retreat to the mountains, but due to the strong resistance of Artaxata, he gave up and returned to his homeland.

Now Pompey himself marched towards Artaxata, but when he was within reach of the city, Tigranes appeared with a retinue, asking for peace and offering a monetary reward to the Roman soldiers. Armenia paid for peace with large territorial concessions.

How John sees Armenia is shown in the image of the throne in heaven (Rev 4:1–11; 5:1–14). It is clear that it is a picture of a throne on earth that exists in historical memory and in hope. The voice of the Son of Man (Armenia) in form of a trumpet promises the restoration of the throne. John, too, sees the ancient mountain of Massis, Ararat, the throne of the Moon in the middle of Armenia. There was an arch around the mountain,[58] in

---

58. "After this, the ark rested on the top of a certain mountain in Armenia; which, when Noah understood, he opened it; and seeing a small piece of land about it, he continued quiet, and conceived some cheerful hopes of deliverance. But a few days afterward, when the water was decreased to a greater degree, he sent out a raven, as desirous to learn whether any other part of the earth were left dry by the water, and whether he might go out of the ark with safety; but the raven, finding all the land still overflowed, returned to Noah again. And after seven days he sent out a dove, to know the state of the ground; which came back to him covered with mud, and bringing an olive branch: hereby Noah learned that the earth was become clear of the flood. So after he had staid

the place where the first civilization was born, at the location of the ancient Naxuana, the first city in the world, where the proud and powerful kingdom of Urartu was located and where not so long ago the mighty Tigranes had decided the fate of the world, and on the peaks of the ancient Massis mountain there was a rainbow the arch that God made as a sign of covenant and promise in the first times that there would be no more floods. Around the throne, again in a vision, John sees twenty-four kingdoms that stood around his homeland and that paid tribute to it as the greatest and strongest power. Thunder, lightning and voices come out of the mountain. The old volcanic mountain is waking up. In front of it is the greater Lake Van, which looks like a window. The whole world, both north and south, and east and west, pay tribute to Armenia, around which six vassal kingdoms are located on each side. Holy is the Armenia that was, that is, and that will be for ever and ever, because it is worthy, because from it everything has become; she who gives the book with seven seals from the time of Adam or Noah, in which the fate of the world is written to Israel who will read it. Here the alliance of Israel and Armenia is introduced, to which countless multitudes approach: to Armenia and Israel all honor, glory, and power forever and ever.

These events are the subject of Revelation. The kingdom that practically disappeared at the time of the first triumvirate and which in political

---

seven more days, he sent the living creatures out of the ark; and both he and his family went out, when he also sacrificed to God, and feasted with his companions. However, the Armenians call this place *Apovatirion*, The Place of Descent; for the ark being saved in that place, its remains are shown there by the inhabitants to this day.

Now all the writers of barbarian histories make mention of this flood, and of this ark; among whom is Berosus the Chaldean. For when he is describing the circumstances of the flood, he goes on thus: 'It is said there is still some part of this ship in Armenia, at the mountain of the Cordyaeans; and that some people carry off pieces of the bitumen, which they take away, and use chiefly as amulets for the averting of mischiefs.' Hieronymus the Egyptian also, who wrote the Phoenician Antiquities, and Mnaseas, and a great many more, make mention of the same. Nay, Nicolaus of Damascus, in his ninety-sixth book, hath a particular relation about them; where he speaks thus: 'There is a great mountain in Armenia, over Minyas, called Baris, upon which it is reported that many who fled at the time of the Deluge were saved; and that one who was carried in an ark came on shore upon the top of it; and that the remains of the timber were a great while preserved'" (Josephus Flavius, *Antiquities*, bk. 1, 90–95).

"This *Apovatirion* or Place of Descent, is the proper rendering of the Armenian name of this very city. It is called in Ptolemy Naxuana, and by Moses Chorenensis, the Armenian historian, Idsheuan; but at the place itself Nachidsheuan, which signifies The first place of descent, and is a lasting monument of the preservation of Noah in the ark, upon the top of that mountain, at whose foot it was built, as the first city or town after the flood. See Antiq. B. XX. ch. 2. sect. 3; and Moses Chorenensis, who also says elsewhere, that another town was related by tradition to have been called Seron, or, The Place of Dispersion, on account of the dispersion of Xisuthrus's or Noah's sons, from thence first made" (Josephus Flavius, *Antiquities*, bk. 1, 90–95n1).

and military relations after those events became only a passive object of encroachment between Rome and Parthia and the place of their mutual conflicts in the Roman–Parthian War finds its chance to restore its old glory. The treaty in Rhandeia, which was concluded in the best interests of the warring parties, paid for the loss of the dream of independence and freedom.

Armenia after the treaty in Rhandeia is a great deception, a betrayal of the ideals of independence and freedom. Rome is a harlot who reigns over the kings of the earth. It sat down on Armenia, drunk with betrayal and corruption. With Tigranes's coronation, Armenia became the beast from the heavenly throne and the old Armenia, the one that was and is no longer. New Armenia accepts the Roman kings (seven heads and seven hills on which Rome sits), it is one of the seven planets that rule the times, but also the eighth—the beginning from which everything became. Ten kings will receive power, but they only think about the alliance with Rome. They will make war against Israel, but he will defeat them. The peoples ruled by Rome will rebel against it, devastate it, and burn it with fire.

John is not against Rome, but is against Parthia. It is an old Armenian rival and enemy with whom there is another deep disagreement—religion. John possesses certain information about Christianity, he knows the Old Testament, because he extracts quotes and images from it and then uses them in his story, but he reduces the role of Christ to that of a divine messenger. He introduces syncretism in which he places Armenian legends and beliefs in the bottom layer, and above them a thin layer in which Jesus appears as a messenger. The influence and penetration of Christianity in the area of Asia Minor is recorded in the Acts during Paul's apostolic activity, when he "planted" the cross in Asia Minor, but traces of Christian influence in the area of Armenia are even earlier.

Eusebius cites a letter from Abgar, king of Edessa (near Tigranocerta), to Jesus and a letter from Jesus to Abgar, which were thought to be preserved in the archives at Edessa.[59] Today there is not only the Syriac text but also its Armenian translation, two independent Greek versions, shorter than the Syriac one, and several stone inscriptions. Only two works mention these events: Eusebius's *Church History* and the *Teachings of Adai*, which are thought to originate from the apostolic period.

The story goes like this: Abgar, the king of Edessa, having fallen ill with an incurable disease, heard about the power and miracles of Jesus. He wrote him a letter begging him to come and heal him. Jesus removed it but promised to send a messenger, who would convey his power, one of the

---

59. Eusebius, *Church History*, bk. 1, ch. 13.

seventy-two. The letter of both Jesus and Abgar differ in the Eusebius and Thaddeus versions.

"Abgar Ouchama to Jesus, the Good Physician Who has appeared in the country of Jerusalem, greeting:

"I have heard of Thee, and of Thy healing; that Thou dost not use medicines or roots, but by Thy word openest (the eyes) of the blind, makest the lame to walk, cleansest the lepers, makest the deaf to hear; how by Thy word (also) Thou healest (sick) spirits and those who are tormented with lunatic demons, and how, again, Thou raisest the dead to life. And, learning the wonders that Thou doest, it was borne in upon me that (of two things, one): either Thou hast come down from heaven, or else Thou art the Son of God, who bringest all these things to pass. Wherefore I write to Thee, and pray that thou wilt come to me, who adore Thee, and heal all the ill that I suffer, according to the faith I have in Thee. I also learn that the Jews murmur against Thee, and persecute Thee, that they seek to crucify Thee, and to destroy Thee. I possess but one small city, but it is beautiful, and large enough for us two to live in peace."[60]

When Jesus had received the letter, in the house of the high priest of the Jews, He said to Hannan, the secretary, "Go thou, and say to thy master, who hath sent thee to Me: 'Happy art thou who hast believed in Me, not having seen Me, for it is written of Me that those who shall see Me shall not believe in Me, and that those who shall not see Me shall believe in Me. As to that which thou hast written, that I should come to thee, (behold) all that for which I was sent here below is finished, and I ascend again to My Father who sent Me, and when I shall have ascended to Him I will send thee one of My disciples, who shall heal all thy sufferings, and shall give (thee) health again, and shall convert all who are with thee unto life eternal. And thy city shall be blessed forever, and the enemy shall never overcome it.'"[61] According to Eusebius, it was not Hannan who wrote the answer but Jesus himself.

An interesting legend emerged from that imaginary event. The nature of Abgar's disease was widely debated with arguments that suited the author's imagination. Some say it was gout, others leprosy; the first say that it lasted seven years, the second that he was infected with the disease during his stay in Persia. The key point of this letter is that Christ promises that Edessa is going to beat its enemies. This gave the small town a popularity that lasted until the day it was conquered. Those who believed in the promise attributed the destruction of the city more to God's wrath because of the sins of the inhabitants who failed God, than to the error of Christ.

60. Eusebius, *Church History*, bk. 1, ch. 13.
61. Eusebius, *Church History*, bk. 1, ch. 13.

The facts stated in the text have no historical value. The story is composed on the basis of two sources: the first is the gospel, and the second is Tatian's *Diatessaron*, and thus the origin of the story is set in the middle of the third century.

Thaddeus's text contains a detail about Hannan who wrote according to Christ's dictation. Hannan was an archivist in Edessa and a painter of King Abgar who painted and took with him a portrait of Christ, which some say was painted by Christ himself, and which became an object of universal worship and the nucleus from which the cult of the Image of Edessa developed. From this, icons of miraculous origin called *acheiropoietoe* (not made by hands) were created.

Although Christian propaganda has widely used this story as evidence for the claim that Jesus' work was known far beyond Israel even during his lifetime, this royal, courtly correspondence has a completely different, hidden character. Abgar is the king of Edessa and his life, fate, and illness are closely related to his kingdom. Ancient astrologers predicted the destinies of states and kingdoms according to the personal horoscope of the ruler, the fate of cities according to the date of foundation or according to the date of birth of the founder or according to the date of birth of the living ruler if other data were not known. Abgar's letter is not an account of his illness, but an account of the illness of his kingdom. Edessa is at the center of the world that the devil will attack and where the Savior will be born. Jesus answers him that he is the Savior and that his time has come and that he shall perform his duty where it is necessary—in Israel. Finally, he sends him his disciple and his image (an idea without content), saying that Edessa is not the place of the battle of the doomsday, that it will be there for a long time and that he, Abgar, is not the Savior. This reflects the Gospels in which a multitude of false prophets are announced at the end of time, but it is possible that it was an echo of religious confrontations between Jewish Christians and the Mithraites, who were recorded in the area around Issus at the time of Pompey's campaigns against pirates in 67 BC.

The time of collection and reorganization of the Zend Avesta texts at the time of Vologases I, precisely at the time when John wrote the Revelation, may have activated mutual religious relations, as well as antagonisms. Tiridates was a Mazdaean priest. Although there is no trace in historical sources about the relations between Christians and Mazdaeans at that time, the events at the beginning of the fourth century and the introduction of Christianity into Armenia during the time of Gregory the Illuminator speak of a dramatic hostility: "In the great fortress of Kissaneh, a real battle took place between the army of pagan priests and the regular army. Gregory ordered that the Kissaneh idol, made of copper and twelve cubits high, to be torn down. The pagan priests fought fanatically, shouting, "We'd better die before the great Kissaneh is destroyed." In that place—says Zenobios—"there was a gate of demons whose number in Kissaneh was like in the abyss of hell . . . who shouted—even if you drive us out of here, there will never be peace for those who live there."[62]

According to Zenobios, the pagan priests in the service of Kissaneh were black and long-haired, Indian by race, and after being forced to accept Christianity, left a long curl on the heads of their young men in memory of their old cult. Such a custom prevails in certain families, but Faustus thinks that it is common to all Armenians. Christians believe that the temple of Kissaneh is at the gates of hell and Sandaramet and that Sandaramet and Kissaneh were brothers. Sandaramet is connected to Bacchus and with the lord of hell and the underworld, which would be Indo-Greek religious syncretism.[63]

---

62. Kurkjian, *History of Armenia*, 119.
63. Kurkjian, *History of Armenia*, 378.

Dating

APOCALYPSE IS THE UNITY OF HEAVENLY AND EARTHLY EVENTS

Astronomy

Today's astronomical knowledge is the result of a long scientific evolution, and what represents general knowledge today was created through centuries of intensive observation, study, and interpretation of celestial events and their precise measurement, and the old astronomers were mainly dissuaded from the ultimate understanding of the sky and its architecture by wrong scientific assumptions imposed by the most prominent scientific authorities.

A simple fact today was an unfathomable mystery not so long ago. Contrary to the knowledge of ancient astronomers, today it is a well-known fact that the Earth moves and that its movement is complex. It rotates around the poles and makes one circle during one day. It also revolves around the Sun and makes one circle in one year. The line passing through the center of the Earth and the center of the Sun defines the plane on which the Earth rotates, and that plane is called the ecliptic. If projected into space, the ecliptic passes through the zodiac belt. When it is observed from Earth, it creates the impression that the Sun passes through that belt, only to return to its initial position after one year.

The Earth's axis of rotation is not perpendicular to the ecliptic and deviates from it by 23.50. This deviation causes seasonal climate changes throughout the year. Seasonal changes are accompanied by changes in the length of day and night. Twice a year, day and night are the same length, and those days are called the spring and autumn equinoxes. When the Sun is in the maximum positive declination, then it is the summer solstice and the day lasts the longest; on the contrary, when it is in the maximum negative declination, then it is the winter solstice and the day lasts the shortest.

The Earth's axis of rotation is perpendicular to the equator. By expanding the surface of the Earth's equator into space, the celestial equator is obtained. It is inclined to the ecliptic, as is the axis of rotation by 23.50. The spring and autumnal equinoxes are the dates when the ecliptic and the celestial equator overlap.

In addition to rotation, revolution, and tilting, the Earth staggers. This movement is similar to the movement of a carousel whose axis of rotation revolves around a perpendicular. The axis of rotation tilts around a direction perpendicular to the plane of the ecliptic and its deviation is constantly 23.50. The fluctuation of the equatorial plane has the effect that the point of overlap of the equatorial plane and the ecliptic moves and that the point where the Sun is observed for the vernal and autumn equinoxes changes. The point of overlap moves slowly through the zodiac belt. This movement is very slow and one cycle lasts twenty-five thousand years. During this time, the vernal equinox point makes a full circle through the zodiac belt and returns to its starting point. Such movement is called the precession of the equinoxes. Moving the equinox point through one zodiac sign (1/12 horoscope) takes 2,150 years. Six thousand years ago, the vernal equinox was in Taurus, two thousand years ago the equinox had just entered Pisces, and today it is almost entering Aquarius. The regular changes of the seasons and the repetition of the Sun's path across the sky could be predicted by the arrival of the Sun at one of the solstice or equinox points. Determining its place in the sky and dividing its path into equal arc lengths corresponding to the distance it travels in one day is what makes the calendar. Along with the Sun's path, the Moon's path was also followed. It was observed that the Moon makes twelve cycles through the starry background during one year and another eleven days of the thirteenth cycle. Harmonizing the lunar cycle with the solar cycle was the largest problem when creating the calendar. The year (one solar cycle) was divided into twelve months (twelve lunar cycles of thirty days), and the difference that remained until the 365 number of days in the year was subsequently added. The modern calendar was created using the Julian calendar, which counted the year as 365 days and one quarter day and divided it into twelve months of thirty or thirty-one days. That division is a modified model taken from the Greek astronomer Callippus from the fourth century BC.

This short presentation is the result of recent developments in science. It took millennia to get to the Copernican and Kepler models and for the heliocentric model to become finally accepted as an indisputable scientific fact. But the path to get there was not easy; although in the history of astronomy there were correct opinions about the nature of the solar system, they were only hypotheses that could not be proved, always in the shadow of great authorities who advocated a different, geocentric model. Starting with the traditional national religious teachings of the Chaldeans, Egyptians, Jews, and through Aristotle and Ptolemy, the geocentric system remained dominant and unchallenged until the end of the Renaissance.

Astronomy is certainly the oldest natural science. It dates back to the time before the first civilizations and its roots are deep in religions and mythologies. Astrological practice (astrology, the science of the stars) developed together with it, becoming inseparably connected to it for centuries in public and private aspects until a few centuries ago.

The night sky is filled with stars. They rise together with the setting Sun and remain hidden by its light during the day. Stars differ in brightness and color. Some are extremely bright, while others are barely visible even in the clear night sky. They can be white, yellow, blue, and red. They seemingly form groups in the sky, which in the earliest times were isolated as separate units and called constellations. Constellations had their own names and characters that changed and adapted over time.

The shapes of the constellations remain constant and unchanged for millennia. In contrast to these stars that stand still in the sky, there are others that move relatively quickly and always pass through the constellations (zodiac) on the same path. These stars are celestial wanderers (planets) that move back and forth, stop in the sky, passing once above and the other time below a certain star. The movements of the planets Mercury, Venus, Mars, Jupiter, and Saturn were observed in the night sky and their positions were compared with events on earth. The first predictions were based on forecasts of natural disasters and wars, and later a personal horoscope was introduced, which was mainly related with the state leader. The Greeks connected their gods with the planets and gave them their names, later the Romans translated them into their language and their names have remained so to this day. The horoscope belt covers about nine degrees of latitude on both sides of the ecliptic. The Moon's path is entirely within that belt. Most of the constellations through which the Sun passes were given animal shapes and are therefore called the zodiac (*zodiakos kyklos*, "circle of animals" or *ta zodia*, "small animals"). The Mesopotamian form of the zodiac has survived to this day because it became the basis of the sexagesimal numerical system that best describes the ecliptic. Around 450 BC, the ecliptic was clearly formed and divided into twelve signs.

Since the beginning of astronomy/astrology, certain characteristics have been attributed to the stars. The most visible star is the Sun and it has the strongest influence. Astrologically, the Sun is seen as a lens through which the influences of the constellations above it are magnified and which affect life on earth.

Babylon

The Sumerians were the first to worship the Moon, the Sun, and Venus, although they were not the most important gods in their pantheon. Sumerian beliefs spilled over to the Akkadians, who, in accordance with their linguistic assumptions, changed the names of the Sumerian gods, inheriting their characteristics. Priests were the first rulers to communicate with the gods. The political system based on temple was introduced and hundreds of people were employed in the service of the priests. Later, with the change of the system, the kings became the leaders of the army, but they always took with them a priest advisor who was supposed to read and interpret messages from the sky, predicting the outcomes of political and military interventions, observing primarily solar and lunar eclipses.

Often the life of the first priests depended on accurate forecasts and they were under great pressure. The first forecasts depended on skill and intuition and there were no "scientific" methods to follow that would allow greater certainty in divination. However, it seems that they managed to mathematically overlook the time of solar and lunar eclipses. Over time, various more or less permanent methods were developed and careful study of the movements of the heavenly bodies led to the calendar and the twelve-month annual cycle.

Astrology similar to today's originated during the time of the Old Babylonian state. It primarily concerned the king's well-being and the well-being of the state. Events related to the movement of Venus were especially monitored. Somewhere around the thirteenth century BC, the time of the personal, natal horoscope begins, which is calculated according to the position of the Moon and its relationship to other celestial bodies. The oldest tablet on which astronomy is connected with mathematics dates from the Old Babylonian period and refers to mathematic calculations of the duration of the summer day. Centuries of sky observations are recorded on tablets called Enuma Anu Enlil (the oldest text is table 63, listing the risings and setting of Venus during twenty one years, from which it is evident that the movement of Venus was considered periodic). The Assyrian conquest brought mostly nominal changes in religion. Forecasts are still made mainly around state issues and are especially valued those who forecast good events. A safe calendar, charts of the sky, and lists of stars were made (the oldest star catalog dates from about 1200 BC). They formed eighteen constellations whose characteristics correspond mainly to the weather prevailing at the time when the Sun is in them. The Assyrians developed constellations and formed eighteen of them. Some survived later and some disappeared when the zodiac belt was formed. The role of the constellations today is mainly related to the weather that prevails when the Sun is in them. At the end of the last century BC, more horoscopes from that time were found that indicated the positions of the planets with little or no astrological forecasts.

A series of magical texts attributed to the physician and magician Hermes Trismegistus originated in Egypt.

Much later in Greece, a scientific method was developed in both astronomy and astrology. From the beginning, astrology and mythology were connected, and gradually the idea of micro and macrocosm was born. Different parts of the body are associated with the planets and signs of the zodiac.

In Greece, apart from those who accepted and developed astrology, there were also critics, such as Eudoxus, who considered astrology to be a ridiculous superstition. The same attitude was later dominant in Rome where traditionalists strongly resisted the spread of such superstition. Among the arguments against astrology was the question of how it was possible for people born on the same day to have different destinies, or how it was possible for people born on different dates to die in a battle. The first traces of the acceptance of astrology go back to the middle of the third century BC, since when it spread despite occasional persecutions.

The ancient Greeks considered astronomy a branch of mathematics at a very sophisticated level. The first three-dimensional model describing the movement of the planets was developed in the fourth century BC by Eudoxus and Callipus with the model of concentric spheres, centered on the Earth. Heraclitus assumed that the Earth rotates on its axis.

Even Anaxagoras of Clasomena (around 500–428 BC) correctly interpreted the eclipses of the Sun and the Moon and the phases of the Moon as a consequence of their movement. He believed that heaven and earth were created in the same process and that they consist of the same matter. At the same time, agnostic schools were rejecting the experimental method, such as the Eleatic school, which, according to the teachings of its founder Zeno of Elea (around 490–425 BC), believed that the senses cannot be trusted.

An extraordinary reflection on the structure of matter consisting of atoms and emptiness began with Leucippus of Miletus (born around 490 BC). Leucippus may have been Zeno's student, the first creator of the atomistic theory, which he later gave up, and his student Democritus of Abdera (around 470–380 BC) continued in his footsteps. Democritus expanded Leucippus's theory. He claimed that visible matter is made of atoms and that atoms are eternal, unchanging, and indestructible. He wrote studies on physics, astronomy, zoology, botany, and medicine. At one point he stated that the Milky Way is a cluster of stars.

A completely different direction was represented by Plato. Plato is a famous philosopher and student of Socrates who founded the Academy in Athens. His work is written in the form of a dialogue between Socrates and his interlocutors. He believed that the head of the state must be a philosopher and advocated the quadrivium. Knowledge is lost at birth and can be renewed. He considered knowledge to be a search for pure knowledge (forms, paradigms). God creates form (paradigm) from matter. A demiurge cannot create a perfect world from imperfect matter. Plato believed that everything was created from four elements: air, earth, fire, and water. He believed that the Earth was round and the center of the universe and that the planets moved in regular spheres. He introduced the theory of perception by introducing three streams of light, the light of the object, the light of the eye, and the third from the light source. He considered astronomy to be an exact mathematical science that studies the regularity of the universe and a good means of reaching the level of pure philosophical knowledge. Plato sought the truth beyond the visible world, although he believed that this truth could not be reached.[1] Plato described five regular solids: tetrahedron, cube, octahedron, dodecahedron, and icosahedron.

Eudoxus of Cnidus (around 400–347 BC) was an astronomer and mathematician who accepted Plato's idea about the rotation of the planets around the earth in regular spheres, but he also mentioned that this theory did not agree with observations. He tried to fix Plato's model by adding spheres that revolve inside a higher sphere. This model has no mechanical explanation and is only a mathematical model.

Aristotle (384–322 BC) studied at the Academy, but did not agree with Plato. He was convinced that the natural world could be understood. He divided philosophers into two groups: physiologists, who deal with the natural world, such as Thales, Anaximander, and Anaximenes, and theologians, who deal with myths and gods, such as Homer and Hesiod. Aristotle believed that there was a golden mean or mean between these extremes. He founded his own school in Athens, which was called the Lyceum or Peripatetic school, which preferred natural philosophy. His work is collected in 150 books that include *Physics*, *Metaphysics*, *On the Heavens*, and others. Aristotle discussed almost all problems. He divided living beings into chains of beings, which consisted of God, humans, mammals, animals born from eggs of perfect form (birds), animals born from eggs of imperfect form (fish), insects, plants, and inanimate nature. He called each of these groups species (*Creations of Animals* and *History of Animals*).

---

1. Guthrie, *Kasni Platon i Akademija*, bk. 5.

In *On the Heavens* Aristotle accepts Eudoxus's spheres. He believes that the Earth is round and that it is the center of the universe. He believed that the elements have properties, that they are hot, dry, wet, or cold. Two separate laws operate in the universe, one applies to the Earth and the other to the universe. Earthly motion is imperfect, rectilinear, vertical, and finite, while heavenly motion is always circular and uninterrupted. He rejected Democritus's atomistic theory. He studied earlier philosophers. He thought that all events have material (the object that changes), formal (what comes out of the object that changes), affective (the influence responsible for the change), and final (the cause of the change) aspects. Aristotle's work became the absolute truth in the twelfth and thirteenth centuries and strongly stifled the development of science for ages.

How alive the experimental spirit was in Greek science can be seen from the biography of Archimedes of Syracuse (around 287–212 BC). We mostly know about him from Plutarch's biography of the soldier Marcel. Archimedes performed a series of geometric proofs using Euclid's geometry. He is credited with the discovery of a method for calculating the volume of a sphere, which has a volume of two-thirds of the smallest cylinder that encloses it. He established that Ludolphian number is at 3 and 1/7 and formulated the so-called Archimedes's law of the lever and the principle of buoyancy, where he asserted that buoyancy is equal to the weight of the displaced liquid.

Using the postulates of the same Euclidean geometry, Apollonius of Pergamum (around 262–190 BC) on a theoretical level came up with the idea that the planets revolve around the Sun. He is believed to have introduced the system of epicycles and eccentric spheres used by Hipparchus. He also wrote a treatise on conic sections called *On Conics*, where the term ellipse is mentioned for the first time.

The greatest Greek astronomer was clearly Hipparchus of Nicaea (around 190–120 BC). He compiled an extensive star catalog in which he classified stars according to magnitude. According to the parallax, he calculated the distance of the Moon and simultaneously and independently of Kiddinnu, the chief astrologer in Babylon, the precession of the equinoxes, comparing his observations with those of the astronomer Timocharis 150 years before him. He extended the work of Apollonius of Pergamum on the epicycles and eccentric spheres surrounding the Earth to explain the different durations of the seasons. Hipparchus's model was mathematical, not mechanical. His model is simpler than Eudoxus's hippopede.

Greek astronomy spread to the centers of Hellenistic culture, especially in Alexandria. In the third century, Aristarchus proposed a heliocentric model of which only a few fragments remain. Eratosthenes used the difference in shadow angle at distant places to estimate the Earth's circumference with great accuracy.

Plato and Aristotle were less interested in predicting celestial events than in explaining the rational causes of the movement of the universe. In the *Timaeus*, Plato describes the cosmos as a round body divided into circles that bear the planets and are ruled by the soul of the world. Aristotle's idea of the universe based on Eudoxus's mathematical model of concentric spheres that carry the planets around the Earth remained the basic model until the sixteenth century.

Alexandria

Alexander the Great founded Alexandria in 331 BC and from then on, the Greco-Roman period in Egyptian history begins. Alexandria became one of the most respected Hellenistic cities. The inhabitants of that city kept some of their Egyptian culture, but mixed with Persians, Syrians, Macedonians, Greeks, Romans, and Jews.

In this dynamic scene, philosophical speculations and reflections have an equally important place as observations based on experimental science. The Babylonian (Chaldean) astronomers Kidinnu, Berosus, and his students with the apparently Greek names Antipatrus and Ahinapolis create their own image of cosmology and related world history. Their influence on the Western world is enormous.

Since the first times, Alexandria has become an attractive center for scientific and intellectual work. As the dissection of the human body was allowed, it became the place where the first known anatomist Herophilus of Chalcedon (ca. 335–ca. 280 BC) and his student Erasistratus of Chios (ca. 304–ca. 250 BC) worked. There lived the erudite Eratosthenes of Cyrene (ca. 276–ca. 194 BC) who was the second best in all scientific fields, which earned him the nickname Beta. Here Heron of Alexandria (ca. AD 62) was solving mathematic problems, mainly in practical mechanics and engineering. Numerous scientists in various fields spread through the centuries, until Pappus of Alexandria (ca. AD 290–ca. 350), the last great mathematician of the old world, an encyclopedist who collected the entire knowledge of the Greek mathematics in the work *Mathematical Collection*, translated to Latin and published in 1588.

In the first and second centuries the scientific revolution ended and astrology was generally accepted. At that time, Ptolemy lived and wrote in Alexandria. Almost nothing is known about him. He was not Greek nor probably from the Egyptian Ptolemaic family. He was an Egyptian philosopher, mathematician, and geographer who lived near Alexandria. It is only from his writings and the writings of his contemporaries that one can guess that he was born in Upper Egypt and that he may have been the chief librarian or librarian of the library in Alexandria.

Ptolemy collected information from ancient astronomers about more than a thousand stars and compiled a list of forty-eight constellations and published it in the book *Almagest*. He believed that earth was at the center of the universe. Explaining the retrograde movement of the planets, he claimed that the planets move in smaller and larger circles, epicycles. In the *Almagest* and *Tetrabiblos*, he describes how the planets influence life on earth. The books mention benevolent and malignant influences and relate more to persons than to regions.

Ptolemy also tried his hand at other scientific fields. He wrote *Geography* and drew maps with longitudes and latitudes. In *Optica* he discussed the refraction of light. He also dealt with harmonics and wrote another book describing his observations in *A Mathematical Treatise in Four Books*, called *Prognoses Addressed to Sirus*, which may be considered the basis of modern astrology as practiced in the West. Today, the common name for that book is *Tetrabiblos*. It is not known how Ptolemy collected data for his works, and it is most acceptable to think that he had free access to the library. Today, there is no original version of the *Tetrabiblos* and those that exist are translations and copies, the oldest of which is an Arabic translation dating from around AD 900. The book consists of four parts, each of which deals with a different aspect of astrology.

In the first book, Ptolemy's position on astrology and astronomy is explained, because at that time many were opposed to astrology. Ptolemy emphasizes this by saying that astrology should not be rejected just because a few do not accept it. In that book various influences of the planets, the Moon, and the Sun are discussed. Ptolemy explains in detail which aspects are favorable and which are not. He explains the signs in the same way.

In the second book of the *Tetrabiblos*, he describes astrology according to the regions. Ptolemy emphasizes that the influence of astrology on regions and peoples goes beyond the influence on individuals. It explains which planets relate to certain regions. He states that the influences of constellations that have an animal form refer to animals, and the influence of those that have a human form to people. The planets affect the earth according to their characteristics: Saturn causes cold, flood, poverty, and death. Mars ignites and causes wars, comets and meteors affect the weather.

The third book is about persons. *Tetrabiblos* investigates conception and birth, arguing that it is better to make predictions by date of conception than birth. It introduces the key elements for forecasting: you need to pay attention to which sign is coming out at that moment, what Moon phase is taking place, and how the planets are moving. The father's heritage is seen through the influence of the Sun and Saturn, and the mother's through the influence of the Moon and Venus.

The fourth book deals with occupation, marriage, children, travel and houses in astrology. These concepts were calculated according to certain angles between different planets.

Tetrabiblos gathered almost all the knowledge up to that time. Only a few modifications were made later and what is considered astrology today mainly comes from that book. Critics say that it is laborious and dry and that there are certain contradictions in Ptolemy's ideas. He did not consider the precession of the equinoxes, although he undoubtedly knew about the phenomenon. The fact that he did not investigate or explain this phenomenon is the biggest omission in his work. In addition to this, there are a number of errors in the book, mostly common to his time, which were caused by a lack of understanding of astronomy.

Ptolemy was a great compiler who is thought to have never dealt with astronomy or compiled a single horoscope, and for sure he was more of a reporter than a scientist. Ptolemy is accused of deliberately presenting wrong information and adapting it to his own hypotheses, which preserved his ideas for centuries. [2]

Although Ptolemy was followed by many astrologers—Paul of Alexandria, Hephaestion of Thebes, and others of whom only names remain—the decline of this scientific discipline began with him. Ptolemy's work continued through the Alexandrian mathematician Papa, Theon of Alexandria, and the Greek mathematician Proclus, who wrote a paraphrase of Ptolemy's *Tetrabiblos*.

With the development of Christianity, sometime after the year AD 500, astrology disappeared for a while and was maintained mainly thanks to the *Sefir Yatzira* and the *Zohar*, the books from which the Kabbalah developed. Together with the decline of the influence and knowledge of the Greek language in the West, the extensive Greek literature was reduced to only a few small summaries and practical texts. The most important Latin authors were Macrobius, Pliny, Marcian Capella, and Chalcidius. In the sixth century, Bishop Gregory of Tours says that he learned astronomy from Marcian Capella.

In the Arab world around AD 800, interest in this forgotten knowledge arose again. An intensive search and translation of old lost books began. Many important Greek and Indian books were translated into Arabic.

---

2. Newton, *Crime of Claudius Ptolemy*.

This new era in the development of both astronomy and astrology began with Abu Ma'shar al-Balkhi (Albumasar), through whom astrology spread throughout Europe. He developed the heliocentric model, believing that the movement of the planets can be better explained by the heliocentric rather than the geocentric system. His work is preserved only in the statements of al-Hashimi and al-Biruni. At the end of the ninth century, al-Fargani wrote about the movement of the planets and his books were translated into Latin in the twelfth century.

The great theme of the creation of the world has not been ignored by any culture. In the Bible, although there is little mention of cosmology, at the very beginning there is mention of heavenly lights that were created to be signs of holidays, days, and years (Gen 1:14). Divination by the stars was forbidden, but there are descriptions in the Bible that correspond to constellations, such as the four beasts from Ezekiel, which correspond to the four Jewish tribes and solid zodiac signs.[3] Orion is mentioned in the book of Job.

The Jews interpreted the universe differently. One time they thought it was expanding, the other time it was a solid body. The foundations are located in the middle of the waters and separated the upper from the lower waters.

The stars are called the "heavenly army" that surrounds God. This phrase refers to angels and other creatures (the stars symbolize angels in 2 Enoch), similar to the Assyrians.

Only a few stars and two planets (Saturn and Venus) are mentioned in the Old Testament. A particularly bad sign was the red moon.

In the Talmud, knowledge related only to matters of religion has been preserved. There were reservations about the study of the stars and they were practiced mainly to determine feast dates. Fragments mentioning the stars were accumulated over the centuries by various authors of the Jerusalem and Babylonian Talmuds, many of whom were inclined to mysticism.

A high level of astronomical knowledge is demonstrated in the Book of Enoch, as are the sayings of Eleazar Hisma, a skilled mathematician "who could calculate the number of drops in the ocean" and who declared that the ability to calculate solstices and calendars was a delicacy of wisdom. The ability to calculate the path of the Sun and the Moon was highly valued: the one who can calculate the paths of the Sun and the Moon and prove it belongs to the title of prophet.

Despite the general importance and religious significance of astronomy in Israel, no important contribution to astronomy took place there. The

3. Martin, "Temple Symbolism in Genesis."

starry sky was of interest to the Jews as God's creation, in order to calculate the feast days, but for a deeper knowledge of the stars, the Jews should thank their Greek and Babylonian neighbors, as can be seen from the foreign term *gematria*, which refers to the calculation of the calendar. In the Bible as in the Talmud, heaven and earth are defined by two boundaries. One Tanaiste author estimates the diameter of the Earth to be one-sixth of the daily path of the Sun, and another one, from Babylon, at one thousand parasangs. According to others, the diameter of the foundation is fifty or five hundred years of travel. The diameter of the foundation and its distance from the Earth are equal, and this is the path that the Sun must travel to become visible. According to some, the foundation is made of fire and water, and according to others, only of water. Heaven and earth kiss, and the horizon or line separating the upper and lower waters is barely a few fingers wide. The Earth lies on water and it surrounds it. According to others, the Earth is supported by one, seven or twelve foundations. They stand under the water, the water is under the mountains, the mountains lay under the wind and the wind is under the storm (the ancient peoples generally considered the Earth to be a disk floating on water). A globe, *kaddur*, is mentioned, although the word can be interpreted as a disk. When Alexander decided to climb to the sky, he climbed higher and higher, until the Earth appeared as a globe, and the sea as a plane. The Earth is divided into three parts: the inhabited world, the desert, and the sea.

Until now, there have been many worlds created by God, and that is why he is often called the "Lord of the Worlds." The ocean is mentioned in the Talmud and the whole world is said to drink from it. According to mystical speculations there are seven heavens, the first is called "velum" (curtain); another, "foundation," etc. The Talmud lists the twelve signs of the zodiac.

The first three signs are in the east, the second three in the south, the third three in the west, and the fourth three in the north, and they are all in the service of the Sun. The first three months (spring) the Sun passes south to melt the snow, the second three (summer) in the middle of the Earth so that crops can ripen, the third three (autumn) over the sea to absorb moisture, and the fourth three (winter) over the desert to keep it from drying out and withering vegetation.

The four points in the eclipse, two solstices and two equinoxes, are often mentioned as determining the seasons. And that obviously refers to the place where the sun rises. Sometimes six seasons are mentioned. The Moon is also part of the calendar, and it begins to shine on the first of the month and its light increases until the fifteenth when the disk is full and decreases until the thirtieth when it is invisible.

There are two different cosmologies in the Talmud. One believes that the Earth is a flat plate, which refers to the mythologies of the Middle East. The second, which is based on Greek astronomy, is the geocentric model, according to which the stars move around the Earth. According to Greek philosophers, the stars do not have their own movement, but are firmly connected to the spheres on which they move. The merits of the Jews for the restoration of the old mystical teachings are invaluable. The Arab renaissance spread towards Europe and Jews appeared in all the key stages of the transfer of this knowledge, primarily as translators, and as creators of astronomical tables. In the Renaissance, Jewish astrology lost its importance.

John's Observations

Images of celestial events are mixed with terrestrial events. Political relations between Rome and Parthia drag Armenia in a dangerous war adventure. With the approval of Rome, Armenia accepts Tigranes VI, who was brought up in Rome, as its ruler, and who, immediately after assuming his new position, undertakes limited military operations in the neighboring area of Media. The dream of Greater Armenia, which reached its zenith under Tigranes the Great 150 years ago, was still alive and motivated the new ruler, but he had neither the strength nor the ability for such a goal. The political circumstances, especially the issues in the opposing states with which Tigranes the Great fought to the death, were in his favor and he knew how to take advantage of them, while the new ruler had fully consolidated superpowers against him. Tigraness's military operations in Media were readily welcomed by Vologases I. He saw in them an opportunity to solve the dynastic problem that he had to solve. His brother Pacorus ruled Media and he intended to place his second, younger brother Tiridates on the Armenian throne. Tigraness's trust in Rome, which readily reacted and came to his aid, eventually backfired. For the sake of higher political interests, Rome agreed to a compromise and, having received the territories, placed its enemy at their head. Tigranes was tricked, as were all those who represented his policy. John sees a new opportunity in the Jewish–Roman War in which he campaigns for an Armenian–Israeli alliance, but apparently without success. Armenia remained a loyal Roman ally during the Jewish-Roman War. Elements that may have been taken from Agrippa's speech set the date of John's Revelation to AD 67–68. However, another great event was inserted into the chronicle between the end of the war and the Treaty in Rhandeia, and that is the fire in Rome in AD 64, mentioned by John when speaking of the revenge of the people who would hate Rome, leave her naked, and burn her with fire.

In Revelation, therefore, John writes about four events:

1. Plague of locusts during the time of Claudius
2. Celestial signs of the coming Savior
3. Rome sitting on Armenia, probably in AD 63 after the Treaty of Rhandeia
4. Fire in Rome in AD 64

These historical events are followed by heavenly signs—John himself says that he saw the Revelation in signs. These historical events are accompanied by conjunctions—eclipses of celestial bodies: the Sun, which represents Parthia, the Moon, which represents Armenia, and Venus, which represents Rome. These heavenly events are not only a casual and unreliable sign of future events, but "they have been created, as Moses tells us, not only that they might send light upon the earth, but also that they might display signs of future events. For either by their risings, or their settings, or their eclipses, or again by their appearances and occultations, or by the other variations observable in their motions, men oftentimes conjecture what is about to happen," says Philo at the beginning of the first century.[4]

Eclipses of the Sun, Moon and Venus can occur in five possible ways:

1. The Moon can cover Venus
2. The Moon can cover the Sun
3. Venus can cover the Sun
4. The Sun can cover Venus
5. Lunar eclipse

According to the descriptions given by John, the date of the event can be accurately determined, because John intentionally and consciously gives the elements of the date.

The events took place under a certain condition that astronomical interpretations must also satisfy:

1. The first event is directly dated.
2. The elements of the second event are located throughout the text and should be gathered in one place. If read in group they provide a date.

---

4. Philo, "Works of Philo," §19.

3. The third event occurred exactly 1,260 days after the woman went into the wilderness and is dated according to the second event.
4. The fourth event is the first lunar eclipse after the third event.

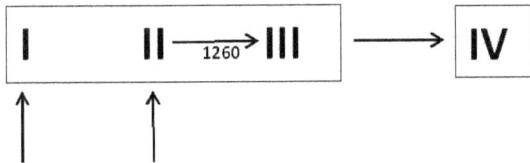

John's schedule of events

The reconstruction of John's visions and real events enable a precise interpretation of hitherto incomprehensible parts of the text. The Revelation of John is a fully dated, exact, and reliable account of astronomical events.

FIRST EVENT

When the fifth trumpet sounded during the reign of Claudius (AD 41–54), the star with the keys of the abyss fell. The star opened the shaft of the abyss, smoke came out and the Sun was darkened. The star with the keys to the shaft of the abyss is the same as the Son of Man who holds the key of David and the keys of death and the underworld, like Armenia and the Moon as her heavenly pair. The Moon, truly, due to its proximity to Earth and therefore the relatively largest surface in the firmament, is the one that causes the most occultations in the sky and symbolically holds the key to the abyss (eclipse). It does not take much to conclude that John here referred to an eclipse of the Sun that opened the "abyss" from which obscure creatures similar to armies of locusts emerged.

Even if John mentions a specific eclipse here, it is not of much use because up to seven or eight solar and lunar eclipses occur during one year, i.e., during the first century, when the Revelation was certainly written, exactly 242 eclipses occurred, of which John could see about half of them, i.e., those that happened above the horizon. On average, there is more than one eclipse per year, and from this John's statement it is not possible to distinguish which one. In order to determine the exact year based on this data, he would have to indicate the place in the sky (in the proximity of which star the eclipse occurred) or, which is the same, the date of the year. The Sun is in the same place on the same date every year, giving sense to the calendar, and if John had indicated the exact place where the eclipse occurred, the exact date could also be calculated. John is an excellent astronomer, and if he had wanted to mark the time of the event, he would not have missed the opportunity and made such a mistake. And, indeed, John places this event which took place in Claudius's time, between the announcement of the first "woe," which he closes with a sign off, and the announcement of the second event with a formula that he continues to use for other events (The first woe is past; two other woes are yet to come.). In this way, he enclosed this short fragment and separated it from the rest of the text as a separate whole. That short part (Rev 9:1–12) refers to only one fully described event and ends with a vague sentence that was added at the end of the description: "They had as king over them the angel of the Abyss, whose name in Hebrew is Abaddon, and in Greek, Apollyon—the Destroyer." The king of the abyss, who is above the eclipse, is the star that determines the exact location of the event and thus the date. The name of the star Castor, Alpha Geminorum, is Apollo in Greek. As solar eclipses are nonperiodic events, John uses the simplest and most precise method of dating a nonperiodic event using celestial topography.

CASTOR; Apollo	Date RA: 5h27m19.23s DE:+33° 20'42.6"
R 2891 HD 60179	Tel Aviv 48-5-31 108h32m (TU + 2h00m)
Flamsteed: 66	Sidereal time: 1h21m
Bayer designation: Alpha	Hour Angle: -4h06m
Constellation: Gemini	Azimuth: +70°35'
Visual magnitude: 1.98	Altitude:+38°49'
Color index: 0.03	Rising: 5h00m Azimuth: +49°18'
Spectral class: A1V	Climax: 12h40m
Annual Proper Motion: -0.171 -0.098	Setting: 20h19m Azimuth: +310°42'
J2000 RA: 7h34m36.00s DE:+31°53'18.0"	

Table 2. Position of the star Castor (Apollo) on 31 May AD 48

Castor is the first star of Gemini and is located at the top of the line outlined in the sky by the stars of that constellation, the line has a shape similar to the Greek letter lambda and crosses the ecliptic in two places.

The line follows the stars Alzir, Alhena, Mekbuda, and Wasat to Hercules (Pollux) and further to Apollo (Castor) and through Mebsuta, Tejat Posterior, Tejat Prior to Propus, and the boundary line of the constellations of Gemini and Taurus.

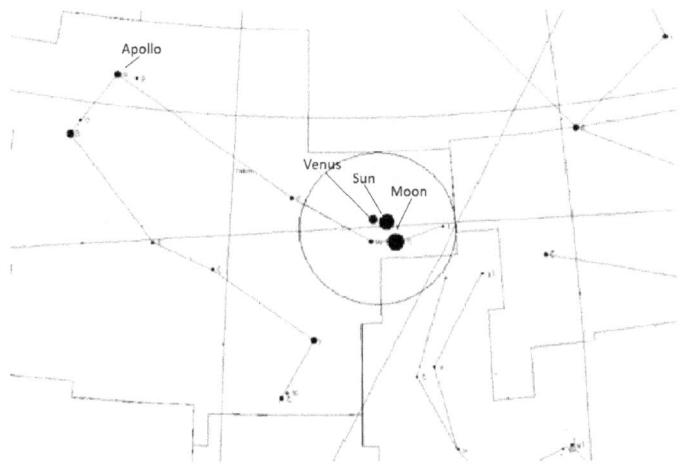

Apollo (Castor) above the eclipse on 31 May AD 48

Above one arm of the constellation is the star Pollux (Hercules), and above the other is Castor (Apollo). Metaphorically, these two stars are rulers over the points where the constellation line crosses the ecliptic and with which they are in conjunction at that point. The assumed time of the event can be narrowed down, but it does not present any obstacle to see in which years the eclipse occurred on those dates.

Solar eclipses also occurred in the same place in the sky during the first and first half of the second century:

Date	Major eclipse	Duration	
30 May AD 2	07:45:43 PM	01m00s	too early
30 May AD 21	08:07:52 AM	-	too early
1 June AD 29	12:33:40 AM	-	below the horizon
31 May AD 48	10:32:07 AM	06m33s	visible
31 May AD 67	05:42:22 PM	04m08s	visible
31 May AD 86	06:33:47 AM	00m08s	visible

Date	Major eclipse	Duration	
1 June AD 94	08:51:32 PM	-	below the horizon
1 June AD 113	12:24:30 PM	02m29s	too late
1 June AD 132	10:57:16 AM	07m14s	too late

Table 3. Solar eclipses near the star Castor (Apollo) from the beginning of the first century till the middle second century

The eclipses of AD 29 and 94 were not visible from Patmos or from the whole of Anterior Asia, the years AD 2 and 21 had taken place early for the Revelation to refer to them, just as AD 113 and 132 are too late. Only three remain during the entire first and first half of the second century and one is a certain date of the locust invasion.[5] The eclipse of AD 86 happened at dawn and was short-lived.

There are several criteria for choosing the right date:

1. Revelation lists the events in chronological order and the second event is the event after which this one did not happen (*terminus post quem non*).
2. The event must be significant in order for John to use it for his construction.
3. It must correspond to the description of the event.
4. Three stars (planets) take part in the event, as John himself says: "As I watched, I heard an eagle that was flying in midair call out in a loud voice: Woe! Woe! Woe to the inhabitants of the earth, because of the trumpet blasts about to be sounded by the other three angels!" (Rev 8:13)

In the account of the event, there is an entirely meaningless statement of the locusts coming out of the abyss: "They were told not to harm the grass of the earth or any plant or tree, but only those people who did not have the seal of God on their foreheads." The sentence is completely out of context, unless John is arguing with some other opinion that interprets this astronomical event as damage that will be done to the crops (drought) and will cause famine, which is a possible reason why he mentions locusts, which equipped like this may serve as an army or pests.

Of the three given dates, the dating of the second event will later clearly determine which date it is, but once again the event of 31 May AD 48 is special. While the usual solar eclipses occurred on the other two dates, one of which was unremarkable and short-lived, the eclipse of 48 AD is an extraordinary astronomical event, because on that day the Moon covered

5. Espenak and Meeus, "Five Millennium Catalog."

both the Sun and Venus, which was behind it (double eclipse)[6] or as John himself says, "Woe! Woe! Woe to the inhabitants of the earth, because of the trumpet blasts about to be sounded by the other three angels!" (Rev 8:13).

Three angels/stars take part in the event. The discrepancy between the number of events of John's Revelation (4) and the possible variants of mutual occultations of the Moon, Venus and the Sun (5) is hereby resolved, because two possibilities occurred in the first date.

Moon 48-5-31 10h33m	Sun 48-5-31 10h33m	Venus 48-5-31 10h33m
Magnitude: 0.00		Magnitude: -3.9
Diameter: 29.8 '	Diameter: 31.4 '	Diameter: 9.7 "
Illuminated part: 0.000		Illuminated part: 1.000
Phase: 179 °		Phase: 1°
Distance: 401156.7 km	Distance: 1.0175 ua	Distance: 1.7359 ua
Position angle: 3.6	Position angle: -16.5	Position angle: 349.6
llat: -0.34	PoleIncl: 2.3	PoleIncl: -1.0
llon: 25.76		
SunIncl: -0.12		SunIncl: -1.3
J2000 RA: 6h21m31.28s DE:+23°04'17.5"	J2000 RA: 6h19m08.73s DE:+23°37'23.2"	J2000 RA: 6h22m46.07s DE:+23°50'06.9"
Date RA: 4h24m18.72s DE:+21°18'48.9"	Date RA: 4h21m32.38s DE:+21°44'41.4"	Date RA: 4h24m51.48s DE:+22°07'09.0"
Sidereal time: 3h22m	Sidereal time: 3h22m	Sidereal time: 3h22m
Hour Angle: -1h03m	Hour Angle: -1h00m	Hour Angle: -1h03m
Azimuth: +122°47'	Azimuth: +123°04'	Azimuth: +120°24'
Altitude: +72°35'	Altitude: +73°22'	Altitude: +73°00'
Rising: 4h25m Azimuth:+66°14'	Rising: 4h32m Azimuth:+63°37'	Rising: 4h36m Azimuth:+63°20'
Climax: 11h30m	Climax: 11h34m	Climax: 11h37m
Setting: 18h40m Azimuth:+295°14'	Setting: 18h35m Azimuth:+296°23'	Setting: 18h38m Azimuth:+296°40'

Table 4. Relative positions of the Moon, the Sun, and Venus in the sky on 31 May AD 48 at 10h33m

---

6. Sun, Geneva 48-5-31, Rising: 4h32m Azimuth:+63°37', Climax: 11h34m, Setting: 18h35m Azimuth:+296°23', HR 2891 HD 60179, Flamsteed: 66, Bayerov designation: Alpha, Constellation: Gemini, Visual magnitude: 1.98, Color index: 0.03, Spectral class: Name: Castor, Apollo, Geneva 48-5-31, Rising: 5h00m Azimuht:+49°18', Climax: 12h40m, Setting: 20h19m.

Famine

The astrological interpretation of this event is clear: the Moon and Venus are the only female planets (in addition to Mercury, which can be both), they both have similar influences on the earth, moistening and giving fertility. Venus gives fertile winds, fertility and moisture, and what is important for the further reading of Revelation, rules the flowing waters and springs. The Moon rules the seas (the angel who stands with one foot on the sea and the other on land), provides humidity due to its proximity to the earth, and governs the seasons. The old astrologers thought that the Sun will burn the powers of the planets that are in its heart. Mazdaeans would interpret this event as the time of birth that emerges from the conjunction of two planets on which it depends and whose influence is enhanced by the connection with the Sun. Ancient astrologers would have interpreted this double eclipse in this way, but for John, who writes about it from a distance in time, it is not as important as another interpretation that fits his story. For him, the Sun represents Parthia, Venus is Rome, and the Moon is Armenia, and this event is a picture of the occultation of their relations on earth. For John, the planet that in conjunction covers another also takes over its power, and in this case, he says that power passed from Rome to Parthia and from it to Armenia and that Parthia ruled Armenia again at the time that John dates this occultation.

Somewhere around that time, there really was a worldwide drought that was prophesied by the prophet Agabus and which was of such proportions that it is mentioned in the Acts of the Apostles, and Josephus Flavius writes about it somewhat more extensively in the *Antiquities*.

In the Acts of the Apostles, there is an explicit statement that mentions a certain prophet Agabus who predicted these events: "Now at this time some prophets came down from Jerusalem to Antioch. One of them named Agabus stood up and began to indicate by the Spirit that there would certainly be a great famine all over the world. And this took place in the reign of Claudius. And in the proportion that any of the disciples had means, each of them determined to send a contribution for the relief of the brethren living in Judea" (Acts 11:27–29).

Eusebius narrates the same event from the Acts of the Apostles: "Agabus, one of the prophets who was with them, prophesied that there would be a famine. So Paul and Barnabas, making themselves available, were sent to serve the brothers." In the *Church History*, there is another reference to the same event: "Caius had held the power not quite four years, when he was succeeded by the emperor Claudius. Under him the world was visited with a famine, which writers that are entire strangers to our religion have recorded in their histories." And he adds: "Then one of them, named Agabus, stood up and showed by the Spirit that there was going to be a great famine throughout all the world."[7]

Such prophecies may have been very common at the time, and Eusebius feels the need to distinguish between Agabus and others who prophesied with motives not as clear and pure as his. Agabus prophesied by the spirit, according to Eusebius, unlike other saviors who, in an almost ecstasy, accompanied by audacity and fearlessness, began with voluntary ignorance only to fall into involuntary mental frenzy. The need to separate in the context of the story of Agabus, who is one of those who prophesied in the New Testament, from those who did not, suggests that the same event was seen by different prophets and that the Revelation was conveyed in visible signs that could be seen by many, so and Apollonius of Tyana who also prophesied famine all over the world.[8]

Apollonius of Tyana (Cappadocia in Asia Minor) was one of the most prominent neo-Pythagoreans in the first century. His life is known from the novelized biography written by Philostratus on the order of Empress Julia Domna in the first half of the third century.[9] He possessed unusual abilities; so on his way to India he refused the services of a translator claiming that he understood all languages and what was said and what was not said; in Asia Minor he witnessed the assassination of Domitian at the moment it happened in Rome. In his polemic with the Christians, Hierocles referred to him as a miracle worker who excels above Christ by his works, which provoked an energetic reaction from Eusebius and Lactantius, who asserted that Christ is not a god because he performed miracles or revealed divine mysteries, but all prophesied is about him, and that Apollonius's gift is coming not from the Spirit but from demons, after which Apollonius became the incarnation of Satan more than two hundred years after his death. The previously stated position of Eusebius is an echo of the same polemic with Hierocles and brings Agabus's prophecy into connection with Apollonius's. If both prophesied the same event, then that event was foretold in signs that both could see.

Although famine was common at that time, this event has a distinct reflection in literature. There are certain issues in the chronology of determining the date of this event, and the sources cannot be exactly reconciled, so the famine is dated from AD 44 to the beginning of Nero's reign.

---

7. Eusebius, *Church History*, bk. 3, ch. 4.
8. Mead, *Apollonius of Tyana*.
9. Philostratus, *Life of Apollonius of Tyana*.

Josephus Flavius mentions the queen of Adiabene Helena, who accepted Jewish customs and helped the Jews during the great famines from which many died.[10] This happened during Claudius's reign and the high priest Ishmael. The only high priest with that name is Ishmael ben Phiabi,[11] who is assumed to have been appointed by Marcus Julius Agrippa (Herod II Agrippa) when he became a tetrarch with the right to appoint a high priest in AD 48. Ishmael ben Phiabi became famous because of the expensive suit that his mother bought him, and after the Jewish war he was caught and his head was cut off.

Marcus Julius Agrippa is the seventh and last king from the Herodian dynasty, the son of Herod I Agrippa. After his father's death in AD 44, he was too young to inherit the throne and remained in Rome where he completed his education. After the death of his uncle Herod in AD 48, Claudius (the same year Messalina was killed) appointed him king of Judea with the obligation to take care of the temple and appoint a high priest. Claudius added to his state the Golan Heights and some neighboring areas, and Nero later on added Tiberias and the areas on the east bank of the Jordan. His palaces were in Caesarea and Jerusalem, where the Roman governor lived, with whom he apparently cooperated well. He rebuilt the city, which he named Neronia in honor of Nero.

The temple was rebuilt in AD 63 and Jewish workers lost their jobs and wages en masse, and high Roman taxes further impoverished the population. During Agrippa's stay in Alexandria, a mutiny broke out due to high taxes and the governor Gesius Florus had some of the rebels crucified. Agrippa tried to distract the population from the war but failed and left Israel. After Nero's death, Agrippa and his sister Berenice accompanied Vespasian's son Titus to Rome to support Galba and continued to live in Rome after that. He returned to Israel in AD 70 exactly when Titus attacked Jerusalem. So he watched the very temple he rebuilt being destroyed.

Not much is left of his kingdom. The temple was destroyed, foreigners lived in the cities, and the number of Jews was reduced. He continued to rule from AD 75 until he died around AD 100 in the third year of Trajan's rule.

Next, Josephus Flavius directly states that Tiberius Julius Alexander succeeded Cuspius Phadus as procurator and that then a great famine reigned in Judea. Phadus was the procurator of Judea from AD 44–46, and Alexander from AD 46–48, when he was succeeded by Ventidius Cumanus.

---

10. Josephus, *Antiquities*, bk. 20, ch. 2.
11. This is the second priest with that name. The first was appointed in AD 15.

Tiberius Julius Alexander was the son of Alexander, the chief tax collector in Alexandria and one of the most influential men of his time, both by origin and wealth. The father was respected for his piety more than the son, who did not pursue the faith of his people. "Under these procurators that great famine happened in Judea, in which queen Helena bought corn in Egypt at a great expense, and distributed it to those that were in want, as I have related already. And besides this, the sons of Judas of Galilee were now slain; I mean of that Judas who caused the people to revolt, when Cyrenius came to take an account of the estates of the Jews, as we have showed in a foregoing book. The names of those sons were James and Simon, whom Alexander commanded to be crucified."[12] These discrepancies in the timing between Ishmael's ministry and Alexander's regency have given rise to various theories and explanations that the famine occurred between AD 44 and the beginning of Nero's reign. There are attempts to solve the problem by assuming that there were two famines, one in the time of Alexander and the other in the time of Ishmael ben Phiabi.

Helena's role is unusual because Rome often responded by sending aid in the event of a crisis. Thus, in AD 19 Germanicus returned to Egypt the food that had been taken to Rome and stored there, and so did Trajan in AD 99/100.[13] In this case, Rome did nothing and left the care to the queen of Adiabene.

The year of John's occultation is the last year of Tiberius Julius Alexander and the first year of Marcus Julius Agrippa, who during Claudius's reign received power in Israel and the right to elect the high priest and could have chosen Ishmael ben Phiabi in his inaugural year.[14]

It is possible that John was following this story about Agrippa's rule, which began with a great famine and leaving the old cities to foreigners, which led the entire nation into poverty, caused a rebellion, and ended at the beginning of a fateful war with cowardly flight and betrayal.

12. Josephus, *Antiquities*, bk. 20, ch. 5.
13. Pastor, *Land and Economy*.
14. The timing of ben Phiabi's appointment is a key point in the chronology of first-century Israel. Flavius dates the famine to the time of ben Phiabi and Claudius. Most authors associate ben Phiabi with Felix, whose accession year is 52, when he succeeded Fadus, or, more likely, ruled together with him, as stated by Tacitus. On this: Schwartz, *Studies in the Jewish Background*, 218. Schwartz dates his inaugural year to 49. The question of whether his ministry can be connected with Alexander, Cumanus, Felix, Claudius, and Agrippa is subject to further discussion.

Invasion

The famine announced by this occultation happened a long time ago and its consequences were not so important for John. He interprets the event, which was remembered by astrologers of that time in a different way. For him, it was a sign that would not harm plants and crops, but a sign that announced a great invasion of the army from the East into Armenia. The image of the army, in form of hairy locusts, is taken from Jeremiah, but its description also corresponds to the army from Vohuman: "The locusts looked like horses prepared for battle. On their heads they wore something like crowns of gold, and their faces resembled human faces. Their hair was like women's hair, and their teeth were like lions' teeth. They had breastplates like breastplates of iron, and the sound of their wings was like the thundering of many horses and chariots rushing into battle. They had tails and stings like scorpions, and in their tails they had power to torment people for five months" (Rev 9:7–8).

It is evident from John's story that he is writing about the events in Armenia and that it is in his focus, but from such a general picture it is difficult to make a connection with the historical data related to AD 48 in Armenia. The succession of Armenian kings from Vonones in AD 15/16 and the Roman interregnum ensured the power of Rome in Armenia until AD 34/35 when it became a Parthian protectorate. Mithridates reigned from AD 35–37. As a Roman vassal even after Orodes, who had been a Parthian vassal in AD 37–42, he returned again with the help of the Idumean army and remained in power from AD 42–51, which means that John's invasion took place in Mithridates's time.

Mithridates was Iberian claiming his Arsacid origin. He seized the Armenian throne with the help of his brother, the Idumean king Parasman I, and expelled the Parthians, causing great devastation in the country. The Roman authorities recalled him and imprisoned him in Rome, and Armenia was left to the Parthians. Orodes, a son of Artabanus, was placed on the throne. After Artabanus's death (in AD 38), a civil war broke out in Parthia. Mithridates was again restored to the throne with the help of Pharasmanes. Civil war continued in Parthia for several years until Gotarzes came to the Parthian throne.

Then Pharasmanes promised his ambitious son Rhadamistus the Armenian throne, on which he had already placed Mithridates, and he broke into Armenia with a strong Iberian army and killed Mithridates, his uncle and the father of his wife Zenobia. In that year (AD 51), the grain crops failed in Italy and there was a famine; buildings were collapsing in frequent earthquakes.[15] Vologases I saw an opportunity in these perturbations and expelled the Iberians, who returned after the winter. After returning to power, according to Tacitus, the cruelty of Rhadamistus was so great that it caused a rebellion and enabled Vologases to place his brother Tiridates on the throne (AD 55). During his flee, Rhadamistus tried to kill his pregnant wife Zenobia, who could not move fast enough. Zenobia was found abandoned by the river and miraculously survived.

The time around this event is very turbulent both in Rome and in Parthia, as well as in Israel and Armenia. Mithridates's rule was anything but stable, and it is possible that some historical episodes occurred during that time that correspond exactly to John's description, but it is also possible that he introduces Agrippa's rule as a fateful fact that will cause dire consequences and lead to a terrible war. What can be determined for sure is that John's prediction refers to the current AD 48 and to the events between the solar eclipse on May 31 and the lunar occultation of Venus on October 28, when the danger passed and when the two fertility-giving planets were again in conjunction. Between the first sign and its opposition in heaven, exactly five months or exactly 150 days passed, as he himself states: "They were told not to harm the grass of the earth or any plant or tree, but only those people who did not have the seal of God on their foreheads. They were not given power to kill them, but only to torture them for five months. And the agony they suffered was like that of the sting of a scorpion when it strikes a man" (Rev 9:4–5).

SECOND EVENT

As in the previous case, John attributes the same formula to another event. "The first woe is past; two other woes are yet to come" (Rev 9:12) and concludes, "The second woe has passed; behold, the third woe is soon to come" (Rev 11:14). In the passages from Rev 9:13 to 11:14, one event lasting in the sixth time is described (the beginning of the Roman-Parthian war—the second woe), along with events marking the beginning of the seventh time.

In the first passage, Rev 9:13 to 9:21, the sixth angel sounds his trumpet, initiating the reign of the new emperor Nero (54–68 AD) succeeding Claudius. The altar before God instructs the sixth planet Saturn/time to release four angels bound at the Euphrates River. Here, John is referring literally to the Euphrates, Mesopotamia, the Parthian state, and the army led by four kings: Vologases I, the king of Parthia; Pacorus, the king of Media; Monobazus, the king of Adiabene; and Tiridates, Vologases's younger

15. Tacitus, *Annals*, bk. 12, ch. 43–5.

brother and a claimant to the Armenian throne. These massive armies were ready to kill a third of humanity within an hour, a day, a month, and a year (compare to "no earthquake like it has ever occurred since man has been on earth," Rev 16:18). The description of the army resembles Vohuman, the eastern army that comes at the end of time. The time of the final resolution has not yet arrived. It will only occur at the beginning of the seventh time when the seventh angel sounds his trumpet. The armies from the Euphrates began to move in AD 58.

The war with Parthia is the only event that took place during Nero's reign in the sixth trumpet, while the other events occur at a single moment at the transition from the sixth to the seventh time. The beginning of the new time, which signifies the birth of the Savior, is announced by the image of an angel descending from the clouds. The angel has feet like the Son of Man (fiery pillars, "his feet were like bronze glowing in a furnace, refined in a furnace," Rev 1:15; "whose feet are like burnished bronze," Rev 2:18). As the Son of Man, he gives the little scroll and cries out like a lion: "There will be no more delay! But in the days when the seventh angel is about to sound his trumpet, the mystery of God will be accomplished, just as he announced to his servants the prophets" (Rev 6:7). John takes the scroll/revelation that he wants to transmit further.

The seventh trumpet is the announcement of the time of the Moon. The following passage (Rev 11:1–14) is a synchronized event. John is given a reed like a measuring rod, just as the Muses gave the eloquent-speaking Hesiod a laurel staff to celebrate gods and heroes in his poems:

> So spoke the daughters of great Zeus, mincing their words.
> And they gave me a staff, a branch of good sappy laurel,
> Plucking it off, spectacular. And they breathed into me
> A voice divine, so I might celebrate past and future.
> And they told me to hymn the generation of the eternal gods,
> But always to sing of themselves, the Muses, first and last.[16]

In ancient times, reed divination[17] was widespread, but here John refers to a measurement used in the astronomy of the ancient world to locate celestial events. He must have detailed knowledge of astrological books, of which there are four: one about the fixed visible stars, another about the positions of the planets, the Sun and the Moon, a third about conjunctions and phases of the Sun and the Moon, and a fourth about their rising. Such an astronomical instrument can be envisioned as a hollow reed attached to a handle through which the positions of visible stars could be determined.

---

16. Hesiod, "Theogony," 29–34.
17. Rhadamanthus, rod diviner.

John measures the temple of God in heaven. The two witnesses dressed in sackcloth God will send to prophesy for 1260 days. These two witnesses are two olives and two lampstands, which draw on metaphors taken from Homer's hymns:

> But the wide-pathed earth yawned there in the plain of Nysa, and the lord, Host of Many, with his immortal horses sprang out upon her—the Son of Cronos, He who has many names. He caught her up reluctant on his golden car and bare her away lamenting. Then she cried out shrilly with her voice, calling upon her father, the Son of Cronos, who is most high and excellent. But no one, either of the deathless gods or of mortal men, heard her voice, nor yet the olive-trees bearing rich fruit.[18]

And no one came to Demeter's rescue, neither gods nor mortals nor demigods. The olives and lampstands are demigods, neither mortal nor immortal. They are also two stars (cf. "the seven stars are the angels of the seven churches, and the seven lampstands are the seven churches" (Rev 1:20), implying a series: seven planets/stars—seven angels of the seven churches/powers of the planets that transmit the revelation to the churches—seven lampstands/faith inherited and preserved by the churches—seven churches/stars on earth).

"If anyone tries to harm them, fire comes from their mouths and devours their enemies. This is how anyone who wants to harm them must die" (Rev 11:5). "These men have power to shut up the sky so that it will not rain during the time they are prophesying; and they have power to turn the waters into blood and to strike the earth with every kind of plague as often as they want" (Rev 11:6).

Pollux and Castor are twins, alike in every way, except that one is mortal and the other immortal. Clinging to each other, they did not want to be separated even after death, so they divided their own mortality and immortality, thus becoming both mortal and immortal at the same time (olives and lampstands), and one day they stayed together on Olympus with the gods as immortals, and the next in the Underworld along with other mortals. They took part in the search for the Golden Fleece, saved the ship *Argo* from the storm, and became the protectors of the sailors who invoked them in stormy weather, because they were credited with the power to stop the rain. Static electricity known as St. Elmo's fire was considered to be their fire.

Here is what Hesiod writes about them:

---

18. Hesiod and Homer, *Homeric Hymns*, II, lines 16–24.

> (II. 1–17) Bright-eyed Muses, tell of the Tyndaridae, the Sons of Zeus, glorious children of neat-ankled Leda, Castor the tamer of horses, and blameless Polydeuces. When Leda had lain with the dark-clouded Son of Cronos, she bare them beneath the peak of the great hill Taygetus,—children who are delivers of men on earth and of swift-going ships when stormy gales rage over the ruthless sea. Then the shipmen call upon the sons of great Zeus with vows of white lambs, going to the forepart of the prow; but the strong wind and the waves of the sea lay the ship under water, until suddenly these two are seen darting through the air on tawny wings. Forthwith they allay the blasts of the cruel winds and still the waves upon the surface of the white sea: fair signs are they and deliverance from toil. And when the shipmen see them they are glad and have rest from their pain and labour.
>
> (II. 18–19) Hail, Tyndaridae, riders upon swift horses! Now I will remember you and another song also. [19]

He also writes this:

> (II. 1-4) Sing, clear-voiced Muse, of Castor and Polydeuces, the Tyndaridae, who sprang from Olympian Zeus. Beneath the heights of Taygetus stately Leda bare them, when the dark-clouded Son of Cronos had privily bent her to his will.
>
> (I. 5) Hail, children of Tyndareus, riders upon swift horses! [20]

Two prophets are the zodiac sign of Gemini. In four places John provides time limits:

1. "But exclude the outer court; do not measure it, because it has been given to the Gentiles. They will trample on the holy city for 42 months" (Rev 11:2).
2. "And I will give power to my two witnesses, and they will prophesy for 1,260 days, clothed in sackcloth" (Rev 11:3).
3. "The woman fled into the desert to a place prepared for her by God, where she might be taken care of for 1,260 days" (Rev 12:6).
4. "The woman was given the two wings of a great eagle, so that she might fly to the place prepared for her in the desert, where she would be taken care of for a time, times and half a time, out of the serpent's reach" (Rev 12:14).

19. Hesiod and Homer, *Homeric Hymns*, §33.
20. Hesiod and Homer, *Homeric Hymns*, §17.

In all four cases, the same time period is in question, which obviously indicates the time that will pass from these events to a new real event, but it also shows that two events, the arrival of the prophet and the appearance of the woman clothed with the Sun, are simultaneous events. This introduces the central part of Revelation (the woman clothed with the Sun) and establishes an element for calculating time with that event. The Woman clothed with the Sun appeared sometime between May 21 and June 20. The seventh trumpet signifies the time of the Savior's arrival, and the Woman giving birth is the sign. The Savior brings hope and the word. He proclaims a new time, the renewal of faith, and the world and his mission are in the litte book he gives to John. This happens at the transition from the time of Saturn's rule to the time of the last ruler, the Moon, whose rule is the worst but also a time of hope. It is precisely in the passages that refer to these rulers that John mentions the revelation of the little book. He mentions the time until the third event, which is equally distant from the time of the arrival of the two prophets and the appearance of the woman clothed with the Sun, clearly indicating that both events are simultaneous, and he mentions the two prophets for no other reason than to date the event. Additionally, it should be noted that he states seeing the events on the Lord's Day in Patmos. The mention of place and the day of the week is crucial. All these elements are deliberately and skillfully interpolated throughout the text, while leaving enough traces to be followed.

When all the references mentioning the little book/revelation are gathered, all the elements of the date are obtained:

1. "On the Lord's Day I was in the Spirit, and I heard behind me a loud voice like a trumpet" (Rev 1:10).
2. "Then I saw in the right hand of him who sat on the throne a scroll with writing on both sides and sealed with seven seals" (Rev 5:1).
3. "Then one of the elders said to me, 'Do not weep! See, the Lion of the tribe of Judah, the Root of David, has triumphed. He is able to open the scroll and its seven seals" (Rev 5:5).
4. "The sky receded like a scroll, rolling up, and every mountain and island was removed from its place" (Rev 6:14).
5. "Mighty angel coming down from heaven. He was robed in a cloud, with a rainbow above his head" (Rev 10:1) and "Then the voice that I had heard from heaven spoke to me once more: 'Go, take the scroll that lies open in the hand of the angel who is standing on the sea and on the land'" (Rev 10:8).

6. "I took the little scroll from the angel's hand and ate it. It tasted as sweet as honey in my mouth, but when I had eaten it, my stomach turned sour" (Rev 10:10).

7. "I was given a reed like a measuring rod and was told, 'Go and measure the temple of God and the altar, and count the worshipers there'" (Rev 11:1).

8. "And I will give power to my two witnesses, and they will prophesy for 1,260 days, clothed in sackcloth. They are two olive threes and two lampstands that stand before the Lord of the earth" (Rev 11:3–4).

The sentence numbered 5 repeats the second sentence, and 6 is not an element of the date but only a symbolic figure. The first element is in two sentences:

- (4) "The sky receded like a scroll" (Rev 6:14),
- (8) "And I will give power to my two witnesses, and they will prophesy for 1,260 days, clothed in sackcloth. They are two olive trees and two lampstands that stand before the Lord of the earth" (Rev 11:3–4).

The planets are arranged as follows: (Moon), Sun, Mars, Mercury, Venus, Jupiter, Saturn, and Moon. The mentioned fragment is found in the sixth seal and is associated with Saturn—it means that Saturn announces. Finally, the times of Saturn and the Moon border, at the same moment the time of Saturn ends and the time of the Moon begins.

The second fragment says that the announcement will be witnessed by Gemini. If Gemini[21] witness Saturn's revelation, then they are in the same place—Saturn is in Gemini. That's the first part of the date.

The second element is simple: "I was given a reed like a measuring rod and was told, 'Go and measure the temple of God and the altar, and count the worshipers there.'" (Rev 11:1). It is found in the part that describes Gemini and means that is the time of the zodiac sign of Gemini.

The third part: "Then I saw in the right hand of him who sat on the throne a scroll *with writing on both sides* and *sealed* with seven seals" (Rev 5:1) and "Then one of the elders said to me, 'Do not weep! See, the Lion of the tribe of Judah, the Root of David, has triumphed. He is able to open the scroll and its seven seals.'" (Rev 5:5). This means that the Moon is in the constellation of Leo.

---

21. According to Talmud, a certified contract is a sealed contract between two parties with the presence of two witnesses—this indicates that Gemini is a witness to the seal of Saturn, during which time the sky turned into a book—revelation.

The fourth part: "On the Lord's Day I was in the Spirit, and I heard behind me a loud voice like a trumpet" (Rev 1:10) could be a later intervention and it is unlikely that John would have left one of the key date elements in such a general formula. It is possible that he meant Sunday, but even without this information, a series of dates can be calculated, which can be compared with the description in Revelation. John combines the positions of the planets of the longest and shortest revolutions with two fixed terms: Saturn in Gemini, the Moon in Leo, the time of Gemini (May 21–June 20) and probably the exact day of the week. As in the first case when he dated an aperiodic event using celestial topography, this time he uses the most rational method for dating an atypical event using two dynamic and two static elements. John's chronometer is similar to a clock with four hands, one of which shows the longest period of time and the other the shortest in combination with two static ones, thus reducing the time by 7×12^3 per unit in four steps. So if 36,500 days in a century are divided by 12,096 (7×12^3), we obtain 3.1 possible dates. It is neither his intention nor his need to calculate the exact date for the entire century. A formula was previously set, from which it can be seen that the earliest possible date is AD 48, which cuts the century in half and thereby increases the accuracy of the formula twice or to 1.55 possible dates.

Saturn's revolution lasts thirty years and during that time he passes through all the zodiac signs staying one twelfth of the time, assuming that all the zodiac signs have the same arc lengths of the ecliptic, i.e., $30 / 12 = 2.5$ years. From the beginning of our era to the mid-second century AD, Saturn was in Gemini as follows:

1. from mid-June 29 till mid-July 31,
2. from end of July 58 till beginning of September 60,
3. from beginning of June 88 till end of June 90, and
4. from mid-July 117 till end of April 120.

Where the first passing through Gemini is earlier than the previous event on May 31, 48, wherefore it should not be taken into consideration, same as the fourth is just around fifteen years earlier than Justin's dialogue in the *Dialogue with Trypho* and absolutely too late.

In the second and third passage, Saturn enters Gemini after June 20 and leaves Gemini before May 21. This reduces the transit time to two calendar years, which can again be reduced to one month per year, i.e., two months per transit in which Saturn is in Gemini during Gemini:

1. 21 May–20 June 59

2. 21 May–20 June 60
3. 21 May–20 June 89
4. 21 May–20 June 90

The Moon crosses the ecliptic in 29.5 days, and stays in Gemini for 2.5 days per revolution. This reduces the time per transit from thirty years per one Saturn revolution to two years, two years to two months, and two months to five days. The total number of dates for the period from AD 32 to AD 117 was thus reduced to 9–10 days.

The exact information about the day of the week would reduce the choice by seven times and show infallibly one or at most two days on which John's main event and the birth of the Savior took place. John probably means Sunday, which would reduce the entire calculation to one to two days.

The days when Saturn is in Gemini, Gemini time, and the Moon is in Leo are as follows:

1. (Tuesday) 3 June 59
2. (Wednesday) 4 June 59
3. (Thursday) 5 June 59
4. (Sunday) 23 May 60
5. (Monday) 24 May 60
6. (Wednesday) 1 June 89
7. (Thursday) 2 June 89
8. (Monday) 19 June 90
9. (Tuesday) 20 June 90

It should be taken into account that John dated these events for his contemporaries and for a much shorter time, and those who were supposed to count the time knew what was behind the expression "day of the Lord."

All the listed dates passed without significant astronomical events, except for one that completely matches John's description, which is the most important proof of the accuracy of the previous method and interpretations of John's metaphors. That date is 23 May 60.

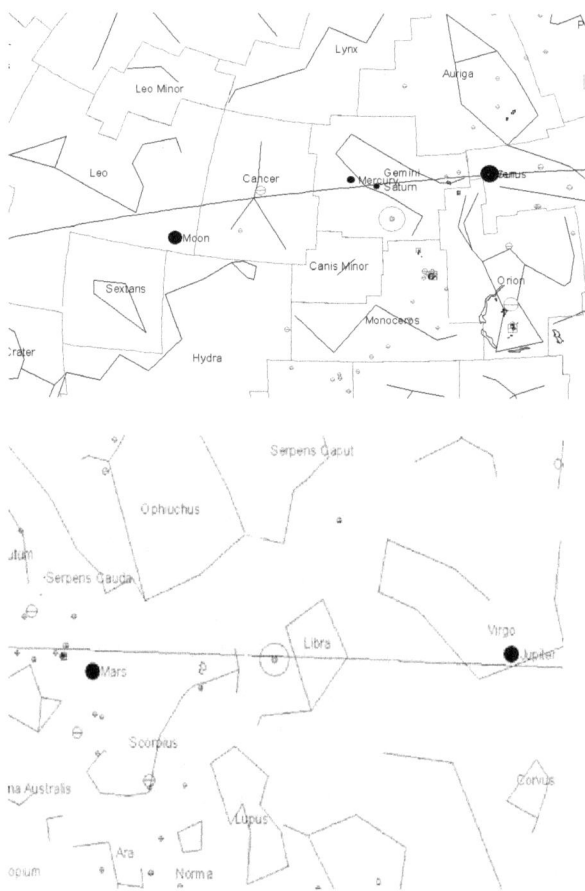

Position of the planets on the ecliptic on 23 May AD 60 (from Cartes du Ciel)[22]

According to heavenly signs, that day meant the birth of the Savior ("A great and wondrous sign appeared in heaven: a woman clothed with the sun, with the moon under her feet and a crown of twelve stars on her head. She was pregnant and cried out in pain as she was about to give birth" [Rev 12:1–2]), as well as Nero's death and the appearance of a new ruler. The second event did not come true, but a little later John says that "he who has an ear, let him hear. If anyone is to go into captivity, into captivity he will go. If anyone is to be killed with the sword, with the sword he will be killed. This calls for patient endurance and faithfulness on the part of the saints" (Rev 13:9–10). The prophecy failed and the beast wounded by the double-edged sword (prophecy) was healed. But not for long, the prophecy would be fulfilled later. Suetonius mentions the comet that in AD 60 appeared during

22. See https://www.ap-i.net/skychart/en/start.

several nights and was believed to foretell the death of the great ruler,[23] and Tacitus mentions two: one, probably the same as Suetonius in AD 60[24] and another in AD 64.[25] It is stated in the Talmud that Halley's comet in 66 caused ship captains to make errors in navigation.[26] The elements of that event,[27] dangerous for Nero, of which he was spared by spilling the blood of the innocent, can be read from the Revelation.

The passage in which the woman gives birth in heaven clothed in the Sun (Rev 12:1) should be decomposed so that interpretations are not mixed and repeated. There is no dramatic fiction here, but the entire text is a literally translated vision. John's intervention and addition is negligible and refers only to the composition of the whole, but does not manipulate any element of the story. As in the rest of the book, John should divide the image into two levels, the celestial/astronomical and the terrestrial/historical. John himself made a demarcation here when he states that the dragon descended to earth. Up to that place the event is in heaven, and further on earth. The war begins in heaven and the devil descends to earth after defeat.

The temporal determinant of the departure of the woman into the desert is the exact data that dates the next event, but also the link that fixes the simultaneity of the prophet's arrival and this event.

"A great and wondrous sign appeared in heaven: a woman clothed with the sun, with the moon under her feet and a crown of twelve stars on her head" (Rev 12:1).

The sign in the sky is an extraordinary astronomical event that has not been seen in Europe since 1155 BC. On the specified date 23 May AD 60 at dawn, the Sun appeared at 5:07 AM, in the Taurus constellation, with Venus at its maximum transit, in the best conditions for observation without optical aids. The transit lasted up to nine hours and ten minutes. The moon was under the feet of the woman, in Leo, below the horizon, and it rose at nine hours and twenty-nine minutes, exactly as John states: "When he opened the seventh seal, there was silence in heaven for about half an hour"[28] (Rev 8:1). The twelve stars represent the horoscope.

---

23. Suetonius, *Caesars*, Volume II, 36.

24. "Inter quae sidus cometes effulsit, de quo vulgi opinio est, tamquam mutationem regis ortendat" (Tacitus, *Annals*, bk. 14, ch. 22).

25. "Fine anni vulgantur prodigia imminentium malorum nuntia: vis fulgurum non alias crebrior, et sidus cometes, sanguine inlustri semper [Neroni] expiatum" (Tacitus, *Annals*, bk. 14, ch. 22).

26. Rodkinson, *Babylonian Talmud*, 9:21.

27. Ptolemy asserts that Mars opposite Algol, or the Sun or Moon opposite or square Algol, means decapitation and violent death. Moon square Algol.

28. From the opening of the seventh seal to the appearance of the Moon.

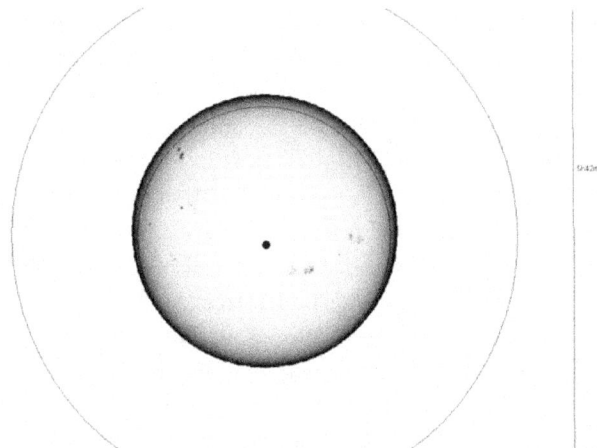

Transit of Venus at its maximum at dawn on 23 May AD 60 (from Cartes du Ciel)

In good weather, the transit of Venus over the Sun's disk can be seen from Earth. This transit is one of the rare periodic astronomical events and last occurred in 1882 and in a pair in 2004 and 2012. Transits are observed in pairs of eight years and with a mutual distance of 105.5 or 121.5 years according to the model 8 + 105.5 + 8 + 121.5 years. Since 1631, four transits distributed this way have been regular in the 243-year cycle, although a few centuries before that, one of the double transits in a row was missing, so that in the same period of 243 years there were only three of them. Transits were missing in AD 1388, 1145, 902, 659, 416, etc. In an even earlier period, one transit from each pair was missing, so at that time the transit was regular every 121.5 years, on 24 May AD 303,[29] 22 November AD 181 (it was not visible from the old world), and on 23 May AD 60. The transit of Venus is the event that John describes and it happened on 23 May AD 60.

Transit of Venus 23 May 60, series: 3^{30}				
I phase	II phase	max	IV phase	V phase
1:05	1:19	5:07	8:55	9:10

Table 5. Phases of the transit of Venus on 23 May AD 60

---

29. The transit on 24 May AD 303 happened at the very beginning of Diocletian's tenth persecutions.

30. 23 May 60, 3, 23:05, 23:19, 3:07, 6:55, 7:10, 87, 43, 817, 20, 25, 15, 938, -31, -30 (Espenak and Meeus, "Six Millennium Catalog").

Cartes du Ciel 23 May 60: Sunrise: 4h37m, Azimuth: +65°40', Climax: 11h32m, Sunset 18h28m, Azimuth: +294°20.

The first phase is the time of external contact between Venus and the Sun, the second is the time when Venus leaves the Sun's rim and moves to the center, the transit maximum is the moment when Venus is in the center of the Sun's disc, and analogous to the second is the fourth phase and to the first is the fifth.

Because of the position in the sky in relation to the position of the observer, transits are even more rare because they can only be seen if they are in the visible part of the sky and at dawn, because otherwise they would not be visible without optical aids due to the strong sunlight in the background. The previous transit was in the visible part of the sky observed from Patmos only on 22 May 426 BC at dawn, and only for the last two-fifths, and the next one in all phases, therefore of a weaker intensity than the one described by John, when it was at its maximum at the moment of best visibility on the rising Sun disk, 24 May AD 303. It has not been as noticeable since 21 May 1155 BC.

John's description completely agrees with the previous calculation and corresponds in detail to the following text, which can be fully interpreted.

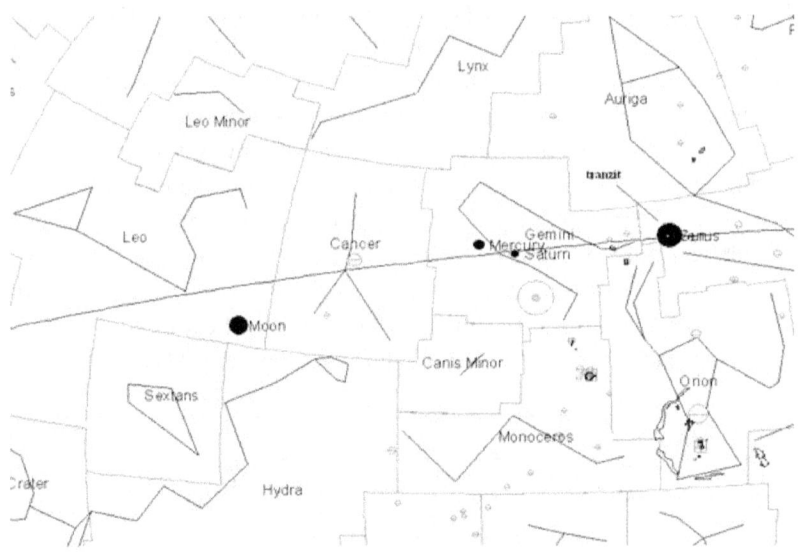

Planet position on the ecliptic on 23 May AD 60

"She was pregnant and cried out in pain as she was about to give birth. . . . She gave birth to a son, a male child, who will 'rule all the nations with an iron scepter.' And her child was snatched up to God and to his throne. . . . The woman was given the two wings of a great eagle, so that she might fly to the place prepared for her in the desert, where she would be taken care of for a time, times and half a time, out of the serpent's reach" (Rev 12:2, 5, 14).

A woman seizes power from the Sun in labor (of war). The child she gave birth to was announced by the prophets, he is the king of the kings of the earth and will rule with an iron scepter. After giving birth, the woman goes to the desert (heaven) where she will stay for 1,260 days until a new appearance and a new event. Jews consider a woman clean after giving birth because she brings life, while among Mazdaeans a cleansing ritual is prescribed. Purity is the basis of their religious life. Nothing impure must be in contact with the elements of water, fire, and earth. A dead body that has been defiled by death must not be buried or burned, but only exposed. Mazdaeans expose their dead on mountain slopes and leave them completely exposed to the birds and beasts of the earth. In the event that a group of Mazdaeans settles in a foreign city where different laws rule and where it is not possible to apply this ritual, the Mazdaeans build a wall higher than human height around a circular space with only one entrance. In such a space, which they call *dakhma*, on a floor paved with brick or stone, they place the bodies of the deceased: "And I saw an angel standing in the sun, who cried in a loud voice to all the birds flying in midair, 'Come, gather together for the great supper of God, so that you may eat the flesh of kings, generals, and mighty men, of horses and their riders, and the flesh of all people, free and slave, small and great'" (Rev 19:17–18). A menstruating woman is also considered impure during her cycle, and as after giving birth, she leaves the house for the desert, where her family members bring her food and clothes. After the prescribed time and ritual washing, she returns home. John's interpolation of the woman going into the desert speaks of his cultural contamination.

An astronomer like John could not have remained indifferent to the transit of Venus, and the detailed investigation of this event continues. The Moon that rises four minutes after the transit stops is in Leo, right next to Regulus, the first star of Leo, and at the same celestial longitude (conjunction) with it. There are several old astrological interpretations that say that a woman will give birth to a male child if the star Regulus is in Moon's aura. The prophecies of Nergal-etir and Borsippa say that a woman will give birth to a male child when a large halo surrounds the Moon and the star Regulus is located on it.[31]

---

31. Thompson, "Reports of the Magicians."

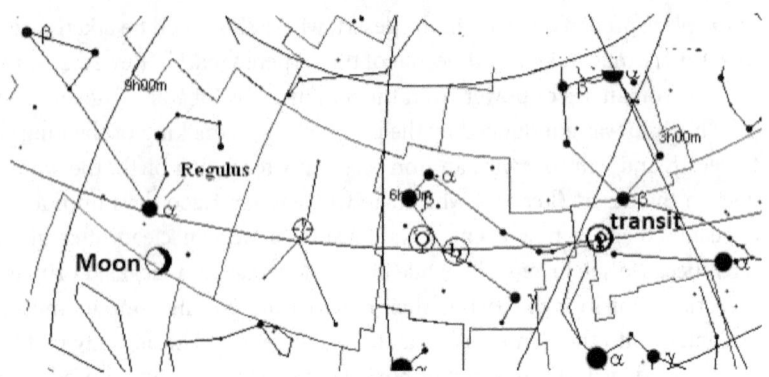

Planets arrangement on the ecliptic on 23 May AD 60

"Then another sign appeared in heaven: an enormous red dragon with seven heads and ten horns and seven crowns on his heads. His tail swept a third of the stars out of the sky and flung them to the earth.... And there was war in heaven: Michael and his angels fought against the dragon, and the dragon and his angels fought back. But he was not strong enough, and they lost their place in heaven.... The great dragon was hurled down—that ancient serpent called the devil, or Satan, who leads the whole world astray" (Rev 12:3-4, 7, 9). "The dragon stood in front of the woman who was about to give birth, so that he might devour her child the moment it was born" (Rev 12:4).

There are various myths that describe the falling of the stars, the sky shaking and the war in heaven. These understandings are based on not inexplicable events in the sky, especially in the movement of the planets, which, due to the mutual inclination of the ecliptic, seem to move backwards or stop on the sky background. From a geocentric point of view, this cannot be explained, except by existence of some higher force that governs their movement. The observations that eclipses in longer cycles are periodic in particular, as well as Hipparchus's discovery of precession, must have suggested the idea of only one law and only one higher power governing everything. Retrograde motion is an important element in astrological divination. Planets that move in this way have less influence, depending on other planets they lose power or it changes. On this date, all the planets, except the Sun and the Moon, move retrograde. It is a clear sign of rebellion and war in heaven.

It should be noted here that the dragon has seven heads and ten horns. The seven heads are the kings who ruled Rome, but in the beginning only seven crowns have ten horns. The historical picture refers to the time before the Roman victory in Armenia and before the treaty in Rhandeia. Armenia is not yet a Roman protectorate and Rome does not yet have its crown. Rome's transformation from the woman clothed in the Sun to the red dragon refers to events on the battlefield in AD 60, perhaps Corbulus's assumption of command, which later led to the betrayal at Rhandeia and the surrender of Armenia to the Parthian enemy.

For astrological forecasts in general, as well as for making a natal horoscope, one of the key elements is noticing which star is in the zenith above the place of birth. This information can be of double use: if John has in the foreground the place where the event took place on earth (the birth of a certain child in a certain place), he needs to determine what was in the zenith at that moment, but he can determine the place on earth where the event will take place. The birth of a divine child is an event of universal importance, and it can happen anywhere. John states it was on Patmos, which as part of Asia Minor is connected to the Taurus constellation, as is Parthia. The most important celestial events, again according to Ptolemy, are solar and lunar eclipses.

Planets have male and female aspects, according to their position relative to the zenith. If they are located in the eastern half of the sky, if they rise, they have a male aspect, and on the contrary, if they are located in the western half and towards the sunset, they have a female aspect. All planets have astrological characteristics except for the Sun and Mercury, whose presence increases the influence of other planets or zodiac signs with which they are in conjunction. There are a number of fragments and shorter texts about the astronomy of John's time and the methods used to compile astrological forecasts, as well as two more comprehensive books, the *Astronomicon*[32] by Manilius and the *Tetrabiblos* of Ptolemy. The *Tetrabiblos* is a treatise on astrology which, as Ptolemy himself says, includes the astrological experience of older astrologers and is a relevant text for John's forecast, even though he is about half a century younger. *Tetrabiblos* can serve as a manual, although due to its character it keeps some topics closed. The *Astronomicon* is a poem in which Manilius describes the sky and is particularly interesting because it introduces trines, squares, and oppositions into astrological forecasting (which is also found in the Tetrabiblos), which is important for the reconstruction of John's method. John's Revelation and the *Astronomicon* are temporally synchronous, the *Tetrabiblos* is somewhat more recent.

---

32. Manilius, *Five Books of Mr. Manilius*, 109–14.

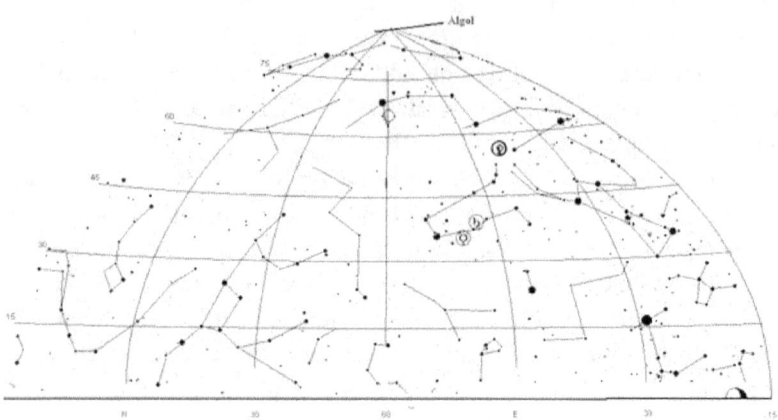

Algol at the zenith at moonrise (from Cartes du Ciel)

The stars of the Perseus constellation are above Aries, which is again related to Israel (lamb).[33] At the moment when the transit stopped and the Moon appeared with Regulus on the horizon in a relative zenith above Patmos, there was the constellation Perseus, i.e., its second largest star Algol. John calls that star the Great Dragon, the Old Serpent—by the name of the devil, Satan, the seducer of the whole world, and which the Jews also call Rosh ha Satan, Satan's Head, Rosch hassatan, and Lilith, and is known as the Gorgon, Gorgonea Prima, the Demon Star, El Ghoul.

Algol is a star from the Perseus constellation, or, according to some, from the special constellation called Gorgon. Algol is the eye of the Gorgon. The reason why demonic properties were attributed to this yellow star, listed as red in all old catalogs to emphasize its ominous character, lies in the fact that Algol is an eclipsing star visible to the naked eye. Due to the overlapping of the ecliptic, the passage of its twin star with a much larger mass (almost a K-class giant), but with a much weaker brightness (about three times that of the Sun), covers Algol every 2.9 days exactly like a celestial clock, and it disappears in the sky. The celestial star that appears and disappears at regular intervals in the sky became associated with the myth of the Gorgon, a beauty who, after being raped, became so disfigured that anyone who looked at her would turn to stone. The Gorgon was killed by Perseus, equipped with

---

33. "Each of the fixed stars has familiarity with the countries with which the parts of the zodiac, which have the same inclinations as the fixed stars upon the circle drawn through its poles, appear to exert sympathy." (Ptolemy, *Tetrabiblos*, 160–1).

winged sandals, looking at her reflection on his shield. Snakes formed from the blood dripping from the Gorgon's severed head as he carried it over the Sahara. Perseus used Gorgon's head to save his beloved Andromeda from the giant Cetus,[34] turning him into stone. Zeus placed the Gorgon's head on a shield made of Amalthea's skin, which would turn anyone who opposed him to stone. Athena also carried Gorgon's head on her shield. From this story comes the expression "under the aegis," under protection. The savior who redeems the sins of the world metaphorically holds the Gorgon's head on his shield—the sky. He is the one who will subdue the sky and all the stars in the sky to his will. His word is an order that will make the stars benevolent. As the Gospel of Philip says, he will put seventy-two colors (constellations) in one vessel and they will become white.

Sun 23 May 60 8h56m	Venus 23 May 60 8h56m
Betlehem 23 May 60 8h56m (TU + 2h00m)	Betlehem 23 May 60 8h56m (TU + 2h00m)
Sidereal time: 0h40m	Sidereal time: 0h40m
Arc hour: -3h10m	Arc hour: -3h09m
Azimuth: +100°00'	Azimuth: +100°19'
Altitude: +45°31'	Altitude: +45°38'
Sunrise: 4h54m Azimut:+63°02'	Rising: 4h55m Azimut:+63°26'
Climax: 12h07m	Climax: 12h06m
Sunset: 19h20m Azimut: +296°58'	Setting: 19h17m Azimut: +296°34'

Table 6. Relative positions of the Sun and Venus in the sky on 23 May AD 60

The table shows the time of sunrise 4h54/4h55, climax and sunset, common sidereal time, arc hour, azimuth, and altitude. The same parameters apply to the comparison of the Moon and Regulus in the table below. The time of Moonrise is at the same time as Algol's climax.

34. "Cepheusque et Cassiepia
in poenas signata suas iuxtaque relictam
Andromedam vastos metuentem pristis hiatus,
expositam ponto deflet scopulisque revinctam,
ni veterem Perseus caelo quoque servet amorem
auxilioque iuvet fugiendaque Gorgonis ora
sustineat spoliumque sibi pestemque videnti." (Manilius, "Astronomicon Liber Primus.")

Moon 23 May 60 8h56m	Regulus; Cor Leonis; Rex; Al Kalb al Asad; Kabeleced	Algol; Gorgona; Gorgonea Prima; Demon Star; El Ghoul
Betlehem 23 May 60 8h56m (TU + 2h00m)	Betlehem 23 May 60 8h56m (TU + 2h00m)	Betlehem 23 May 60 8h56m (TU +2h00m)
Sidereal time: 0h40m	Sidereal time: 0h40m	Sidereal time: 0h40m
Arc hour: -7h30m	Arc hour: -7h41m	Arc hour: -0h32m
Azimuth: +64°26'	Azimuth: +58°39'	Azimuth: +132°20'
Altitude: -07°08'	Altitude: -05°12'	Altitude: +80°50'
Moonrise: 9h29m Azimuth:+69°47'	Rising: 9h28m Azimuth:+63°3	Rising: 1h28m Azimuth:+47°06'
Climax: 16h32m	Climax: 16h39m	Climax: 9h29m
Moonset: 23h30m Azimuth:+289°04'	Setting: 23h49m Azimuth:+296°25'	Setting: 17h31m Azimuth:+312°54'

Table 7. Relative positions of the Moon, Regulus, and Algol on 23 May AD 60

From these tables, the conjunction of the Sun and Venus and the conjunction of the Moon and Regulus are visible. A woman in the Sun gives birth because that's what Regulus near the Moon means. At the moment of the rising of the Moon and Regulus (from 9:10 a.m. to 9:29 a.m.), and about half an hour after the woman gave birth and left for the desert, above Betlehem was the star Algol, the devil who wanted to defeat and devour the child.

Moon	Regulus	Algol
Rise: 9h29m	Rise: 9h28m	Climax: 9h29m

Table 8. Moon and Regulus rising time and Algol climax on 23 May AD 60 at 9h29m

"He was hurled to the earth, and his angels with him. Then I heard a loud voice in heaven say: 'Now have come the salvation and the power and the kingdom of our God, and the authority of his Christ. For the accuser of our brothers, who accuses them before our God day and night, has been hurled down. They overcame him by the blood of the Lamb and by the word of their testimony; they did not love their lives so much as to shrink from death. Therefore rejoice, you heavens and you who dwell in them! But woe to the earth and the sea, because the devil has gone down to you! He is filled with fury, because he knows that his time is short!' . . . Then from his mouth the serpent spewed water like a river, to overtake the woman and sweep her away with the torrent. But the earth helped the woman by opening its mouth and swallowing the river that the dragon had spewed out of his mouth. Then the dragon was enraged at the woman and went off to make war against the rest of her offspring—those who obey God's commandments and hold to the testimony of Jesus. . . . And the dragon stood on the shore of the sea." (Rev 12:9–12, 15–18; 13:1).

The devil failed to conquer heaven and the heavenly angels hurled him down to earth. The scene is transferred to the ground and the events are sequenced through an already existing matrix. Rome is unsuccessful in their battle against Parthia. The entire war campaign, which aimed to return Armenia under its own control and repel Vologases's invasion, was brought into question. The Roman army was pushed back behind the Euphrates; the defeat of Paetus's III Scythian and XII Fulminata legions almost turned the entire war campaign into an unprecedented tragedy. Nero's intervention and dismissal of the commander turned the events in a favorable direction for Rome, but in a most unfavorable direction for Armenia. At the time of these astronomical events, John had hope, because the coming of the Savior was prophesied and seen in signs. He is the one who will free Armenia from the enemy and turn the fortunes of war in the opposite direction. Long before in the confrontations with the Parthians, Caligula's expedition found itself in a crisis when unusual signs appeared; the level of the Euphrates rose during drought and eddies appeared on its surface. This represented a bad sign for the Roman army, but also a real danger that the army could find itself surrounded by water. In this campaign, Paetus's army was defeated on the banks of the Arax and retreated across the Euphrates. The grief of the sea divides land and water. It is a thin line that protects the world from a flood, just as the rainbow over Mount Massis is a sign of covenant and a guarantee that there will be no flood. The clash of the heavenly armies and the attack of Ahriman on heaven in the Zend Creation is described as follows:

> In the month Frawardin and the day Ohrmazd he rushed in at noon, and thereby the sky was as shattered and frightened by him, as a sheep by a wolf. He came on to the water which was arranged below the earth, and then the middle of this earth was pierced and entered by him. Afterwards, he came to the vegetation, then to the ox, then to Gayomard, and then he came to fire; so, just like a fly, he rushed out upon the whole creation; and he made the world quite as injured and dark at midday as though it were in dark night. And noxious creatures were diffused by him over the earth, biting and venomous, such as the snake, scorpion, frog (kalvak), and lizard (vazak), so that not so much as the point of a needle remained free from noxious creatures. And blight was diffused by him over the vegetation, and

it withered away immediately. And avarice, want, pain, hunger, disease, lust, and lethargy were diffused by him abroad upon the ox and Gayomard.... And, afterwards, he (the evil spirit) came to fire, and he mingled smoke and darkness with it. The planets, with many demons, dashed against the celestial sphere, and they mixed the constellations; and the whole creation was as disfigured as though fire disfigured every place and smoke arose over it. And ninety days and nights the heavenly angels were contending in the world with the confederate demons of the evil spirit, and hurled them confounded to hell; and the rampart of the sky was formed so that the adversary should not be able to mingle with it. Hell is in the middle of the earth; there where the evil spirit pierced the earth and rushed in upon it, as all the possessions of the world were changing into duality, and persecution, contention, and mingling of high and low became manifest.[35]

On the conflict of the creations of the world with the antagonism of the evil spirit it is said in revelation, that the evil spirit, even as he rushed in and looked upon the pure bravery of the angels and his own violence, wished to rush back. The spirit of the sky is himself like one of the warriors who has put on armor; he arrayed the sky against the evil spirit, and led on in the contest, until Ohrmazd had completed a rampart around, stronger than the sky and in front of the sky. And his guardian spirits (farohar) of warriors and the righteous, on war horses and spear in hand, were around the sky; such-like as the hair on the head is the similitude (anguni-aitak) of those who hold the watch of the rampart. And no passage was found by the evil spirit, who rushed back; and he beheld the annihilation of the demons and his own impotence, as Ohrmazd did his own final triumph, producing the renovation of universe for ever and everlasting.[36]

After Corbulo's conquest of Artaxata, balance is restored. The Roman army withdraws from Parthia, Parthia from Armenia. Nero's diplomacy arranges for Tiridates to come to Rome to collect the royal diadem, which he left in front of Nero's statue in Rhandeia.

Peace comes to Rhandeia, concluded by two rulers, the treacherous Rome and the hostile Parthia. Nero's family is associated with Venus who is born from sea foam. Rome is a kingdom made up of Greece (leopard), Gaul (bear), and Italy (lion). Nero was foretold of an early death by the

35. West, *Bundahishu*, ch. 3.
36. West, *Bundahishu*, ch. 6.

appearance of a comet that stood in the sky for several days, but this sign is also unfavorable for the world ruler. Algol finally transfers the power over Armenia to Nero and all nations accept such a decision, because no one can fight Rome. Rome was given authority to attack the saints and to blaspheme God, it was given authority to rule over all nations. The prophecy and destiny foretold by the comet bypassed Nero, but the prophecy would be fulfilled. The second beast is Vologases I, ruler of Parthia, which has two kingdoms: Parthia and Media. His counterpart is the sky constellation of Taurus, which has the same two horns as Aries, related to Israel. Algol is above Aries and shows that the child will be born in Israel (Bethlehem). Vologases raises Nero's statue and asks everyone to bow to him.

John condemns those who worship the beast and says, "Who is like the beast? Who can make war against him?" referring to the defeatists who opposed the war. Agrippa's speech reflects the intonation to which John objects:

> Who are you to have to go to war and who are those against whom you have to fight . . . there are ten thousand peoples who have more reason than us to seek their freedom, and yet they submitted . . . what kind of army do you rely on? What weapons do you rely on? Where is your fleet that can reach the Roman seas? And where is the treasure necessary for such an undertaking? Do you suppose, please, that you are going to war with the Egyptians or the Arabs? Why not think carefully about the Roman Empire? Will you not perceive your own impotence? Isn't your army often defeated even by your neighbors, while the Roman power is invincible in all parts of the inhabited world?[37]

Through Flavius's literary interpretation, Agrippa's speech was designed and conceived in such a way as to glorify Roman power and that Flavius, as one of the generals of the Jewish army, to court the Roman emperors, whose surname he took. But behind Flavius's interpretation is the real political background and the speech with which Agrippa tried to calm the population of Jerusalem and distract them from the war adventure. Agrippa did not succeed and left Jerusalem before the start of the war.

THIRD EVENT

The new people at Mount Zion sing a new song to liberty, which was not sung completely in Armenia. Ezra mentions the peoples and their number:

---

37. Josephus Flavius, *War of Jews*, ch. 16.

"These are the people of the province who came up from the captivity of the exiles, whom Nebuchadnezzar king of Babylon had taken captive to Babylon (they returned to Jerusalem and Judah, each to his own town)" (Ezra 2:1). The new song is sung before Armenia, before four creatures and before twenty-four kingdoms. It is sung by a Lamb which stands before the throne and before the elderly. "These are those who did not defile themselves with women," because the Moon is in Virgo, nothing more. It flies in the middle of heaven with the Everlasting Gospel (the little book). This is the introduction to the third event that John prepares through the succession of angels and their appearances in heaven, which is the key to interpreting the seven trumpets. The second angel announces the fall of Babylon (figurative Rome), the third one threatens those who worship Rome for they are threatened by hell. Again, a moon which reaps (Rev 14:14) in Virgo. The method which dated the first event by stating the solar eclipse with the Apollo star is repeated. This event is related to the Moon, which is in Virgo.

The image of emerging angels is important for John's story as a fulfilment of void or inaccuracy with which the celestial events follow prophecies. The text becomes clearer. Opening the tent of prophecy is a metaphor for the heaven and planets rising one after the other on the horizon, dressed in white linen clothing with a gold sash across their chest, and nobody could rise to heaven, nothing could happen in heaven until the planets had risen. The planets pour bowls of God's wrath, their powers onto Earth, and by the description of their powers, their rising order may be established:

1. "The first angel went and poured out his bowl on the land, and ugly and painful sores broke out on the people who had the mark of the beast and worshiped his image" (Rev 16:2). The attribution is not clear, but the statue of the beast and the beast are connected to Saturn—it is its time.

2. "The second angel poured out his bowl on the sea, and it turned into blood like that of a dead man, and every living thing in the sea died" (Rev 16:3). The attribution is clear: the master of the sea pours his bowl into the sea and that must be the Moon.[38]

3. "The third angel poured out his bowl on the rivers and springs of water, and they became blood" (Rev 16:4). It is Venus which rules the waters and springs of waters. The addition is especially interesting: "Then I heard the angel in charge of the waters say: 'You are just in these judgments, you who are and who were, the Holy One, because you have so judged! for they have shed the blood of your saints and

---

38. Hesiod often uses the epithet "unfruitful sea."

prophets, and you have given them blood to drink as they deserve'" (Rev 16:5-6). The revenge John talks about is revenge against Rome who spilt blood in Armenia and who is represented by Venus in the Revelation.

4. "The fourth angel poured out his bowl on the Sun, and the Sun was given power to scorch people with fire. They were seared by the intense heat, and they cursed the name of God, who had control over these plagues, but they refused to repent and glorify him" (Rev 16:8-9). Mars ignites and under its influence the Sun's heat is stronger.

5. "The fifth angel poured out his bowl on the throne of the beast, and his kingdom was plunged into darkness. Men gnawed their tongues in agony and cursed the God of heaven because of their pains and their sores, but they refused to repent of what they had done" (Rev 16:10-11). The fifth is the Sun which ceases to shine over Rome and Venus—the throne of the beast is Rome, and the event John invokes happened when Venus was in the west just before it set.

6. "The sixth angel poured out his bowl on the great river Euphrates, and its water was dried up to prepare the way for the kings from the East" (Rev 16:12). The pouring of the bowl corresponds to the third trumpet which describes wintertime. The waters of Euphrates shall freeze symbolically which means that the event happens in winter and that its planet is Mercury. There are two interpolations between the appearances of the sixth and the seventh planet.

    a. "Then I saw three evil spirits that looked like frogs; they came out of the mouth of the dragon, out of the mouth of the beast and out of the mouth of the false prophet. They are spirits of demons performing miraculous signs, and they go out to the kings of the whole world, to gather them for the battle on the great day of God Almighty." The demon who performs miracles is another beast, Vologases, who "performed great and miraculous signs, even causing fire to come down from heaven to earth in full view of men" (Rev 13:13-15) and collected armies everywhere for the final battle.

    b. "Behold, I come like a thief! Blessed is he who stays awake and keeps his clothes with him, so that he may not go naked and be shamefully exposed. Then they gathered the kings together to the place that in Hebrew is called Armageddon" (Rev 16:15-17). John repeats the phrase directed at the church in Sardis (Rev 3:3).

7. "The seventh angel poured out his bowl into the air, and out of the temple came a loud voice from the throne, saying, 'It is done!'" (Rev 16:17) This is the answer to seeking the just so the sixth seal (Jupiter) performs justice: "When he opened the fifth seal, I saw under the altar the souls of those who had been slain because of the word of God and the testimony they had maintained. They called out in a loud voice, 'How long, Sovereign Lord, holy and true, until you judge the inhabitants of the earth and avenge our blood?'" (Rev 6:9–10).

The order of the planets is as follows: Saturn rises first in Leo, the second and the third are the Moon and Venus in Virgo, the fourth is Mars in Libra, the fifth and the sixth are the Sun and Mercury in Scorpio, and the seventh is Jupiter in Capricorn.

Glory on earth follows: "Then there came flashes of lightning, rumblings, peals of thunder and a severe earthquake. No earthquake like it has ever occurred since man has been on earth, so tremendous was the quake. The great city split into three parts, and the cities of the nations collapsed. God remembered Babylon the Great and gave her the cup filled with the wine of the fury of his wrath. Every island fled away, and the mountains could not be found. From the sky huge hailstones of about a hundred pounds each fell upon men. And they cursed God on account of the plague of hail because the plague was so terrible" (Rev 16:18–21). The apocalyptic image invokes judgment of Rome.

Planet	Rising	Culmination	Setting
Saturn	23h09m Azimut: +68°09'	5h58m	12h48m Azimuth: +291°51'
Moon	1h48m Azimut: +80°42'	8h20m	14h46m Azimuth: +277°12'
Venus	2h30m Azimut: +85°54'	8h41m	14h51m Azimuth: +274°06'
Mars	4h01m Azimut: +96°10'	9h50m	15h39m Azimuth: +263°50'
Sun	6h02m Azimut: +107°38'	11h27m	16h52m Azimuth: +252°22'
Mercury	7h22m Azimut: +115°27'	12h28m	17h33m Azimuth: +244°33'
Jupiter	10h14m Azimut: +118°17'	15h13m	20h11m Azimuth: +241°43'

Table 9. Sequence of the planets risings, culminations, and settings on 4/5 November AD 63

From the previous analysis, the sequence of planets emerging on the horizon is evident: Saturn, Moon, Venus, Mars, the Sun, Mercury, and Jupiter. The Moon is in Virgo, and Venus is in the west at the moment of the event. The real chronological determinant is in the direct instruction that this event happens after forty-two months of prophets' predictions and that the woman shall return from desert after 1,260 days or one time, two times, and half the time. Time is not a casual piece of information for John, he literally thinks of the time between the second and third event. The time of the third event is precisely 1,260 days from 23 May AD 60 and that day is 4 November AD 63. Nothing interesting happened in the sky, but it did one day later on 5 November AD 63 and those events completely correspond to the description (adulteress sits upon a beast).

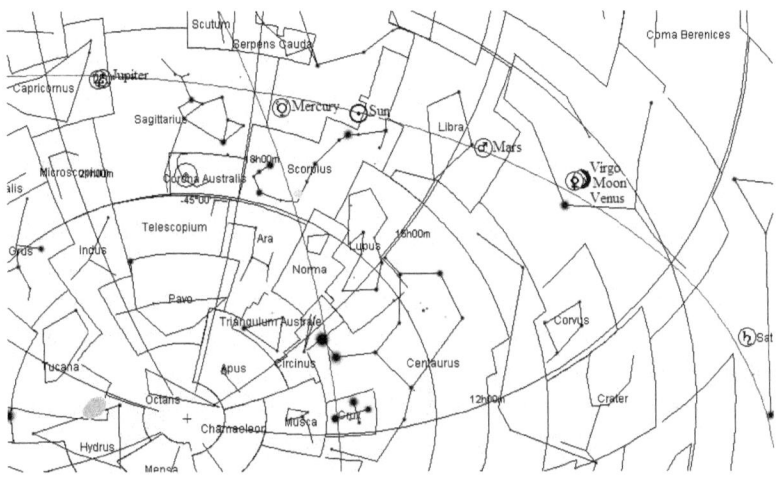

Planet alignment on the ecliptic on 5 November AD 63 (Cartes du Ciel)

The astronomers make ephemerides at midnight, when the sky is the most perceptible and when the transition of the astronomical days happens. Saturn rises a day early, just before midnight and John spreads the event on the previous day to satisfy the prophecy. The main event connected to the rising of the planets satisfies the matrix and thus extended starts exactly 1,260 days after the transit of Venus. In John's writing the positions of planets have an auxiliary role and they serve as an introduction to main events. Main events are the eclipses and the transit: all planets are on the same side of the sky on that day, and they appear in the east one after the other just like John states. It is not difficult to determine the events. Venus has a bad character in the western sky. It is also called Hesperus, the Evening Star, Cloaca, the Protector of Prostitutes, and the one spreading the disease of Venus, or, as John puts it, "then the angel carried me away in the Spirit into a desert. There I saw a woman sitting on a scarlet beast. . . . The woman was dressed in purple and scarlet, and was glittering with gold, precious stones and pearls. She held a golden cup in her hand, filled with abominable things and the filth of her adulteries. This title was written on her forehead: mystery, Babylon the great, the mother of prostitutes and of the abominations of the Earth" (Rev 17:3–5). This is a rightful image of Rome after the great betrayal in Rhandeia. Rome is drunken with deceit and abomination. However, the image of Armenia changes. It is not Armenia from the beginning of times, the country that John put above all other; it is alien and a foreigner reigns in it, but his time shall pass: "The beast, which you saw, once was, now is not, and will come up out of the Abyss and go to his destruction. The inhabitants of the earth whose names have not been written in the Book of Life from the creation of the world will be astonished when they see the beast, because he once was, now is not, and yet will come" (Rev 17:8). In this sentence there is one ominous element which announces the fourth event: the beast was, now is not, and will come up out of the abyss; the Moon shall appear from the eclipse and punishment shall be done unto the adulteress.

The resolution of the drama announced by the second event in which Rome aches from the terrors of war ends with a compromise in Rhandeia in 63 and Rome (Venus) transfers its power to Armenia (the Moon). According to previous events, Venus is below the Moon, and this is about lunar eclipse of Venus, which happened on 5 November 63.

The Moon is setting, it covered Venus around half past one in the afternoon, and shall appear again as a participant in the fourth event.

Moon and Venus Occultation on 5 November AD 63

This is the most important event in John's story. Unlike Agrippa's defeatism, John does not consider Rome a power that cannot be confronted. If all peoples rebelled, with God's help, Roman power would be broken. Finally, every righteous man knows that Rome had previously fought with Parthians who confronted it like Hannibal. Everyone knows that Rome betrayed Armenia and left it to the mercy of its enemies even though Armenia relied on Rome for help. The same happened to Israel. Did Rome not bring foreigners into the country and give them what they did not have, did Rome not impose taxes that could not be paid and to which they were not entitled, did Rome not bring pictures, statues, and idols to Israel that disrespect God, new religions, and new doctrines? Is this not an unprecedented moment in history that one enemy harmed the entire world and caused injustice? Not much wisdom is needed to notice the opportunity to jointly overthrow the oppressor of the world. For this mission to be executed, John needed a good story in order to start mobilization.

Ascension of Isaiah

In order to understand the text better, it is interesting to consider the correlation to Isaiah's revelation, that is the *Ascension of Isaiah*. This short text seems to describe the same events but from a greater time distance. It summarizes a few topics into one and parts of John's story appear to be interpolated into this text. However, the *Ascension of Isaiah* is a simpler and more superficial text, yet it may help form a picture of the actual influence Revelation had in space.

There are similar phrases in both texts: the *Ascension of Isaiah* tells a story about Hezekiah's renegade son Manasseh who refused to follow his father's righteous way, but sided with evil, consorted with the false prophet Beliar, and took too many vices. The king wanted to teach his son about the everlasting judgement and the tortures of Gehenna, the ruler of this world, his angels, his command, and powers, and about Christ whose teaching he had seen himself during his illness. The elements of the Old Testament are evidently connected to the myth of Sophia and the myth of Abgar.

He gave to Manasseh what the scribe Samnas had written together with what Isaiah had given him, which referred to the judgement of angels, the destruction of this world, the clothes of the holy ones and their transformation, and the exile and the entry of the Beloved one. After Hezekiah's death, Manasseh sided with Beliar[39] and magic, ritual killing and persecution of the righteous ones ensued and spread throughout Israel. The crimes were conducted by Manasseh, Belachira, Tobia, John of Anathoth, and Zadok.

When the righteous Isaiah saw that Satan and witches were being worshiped in Israel, he retired together with the righteous ones including Micah, Ananias, and Habakkuk to Bethlehem and then to the mountains. They only wore garments of hair and lived naked. They spent two years living like that and feeding on the herbs.

39. Beliar appears in more apocryphal texts and in the *Sibylline Books*.

Then Alagar Zagar (Vologases Arzakos?), king of Assyria, intruded and took the captured ones to the mountains of the Medes and the river of Tazon. Belchira escaped before Alagar Zagar to Jerusalem and preached lawlessness and accused Isaiah there.

Moses persuades Isaiah that no one can see God, to which Isaiah tells him that he had seen God and calls Jerusalem Sodom. Beliar envied Isaiah on his vision in which he had seen the Beloved One descending on Earth, being crucified before Saturday and his disciples. He saw the descent of the Catholic church from heavens, which shall happen at the end of times. And that the angel Gabriel of the Holy Spirit and Michael the commander of the holy angels shall open the grave on the third day. And that the Beloved One shall exit upon their shoulders and send his twelve disciples. They shall teach all peoples and all languages on the resurrection of the Beloved One, through which those who believe in his cross shall be saved and shall ascend to the seventh heaven from where he comes. And many who believe in him shall speak by the Holy Ghost, and many signs and miracles shall happen at that time. Early Christian polemics, possible related to Docetism, echo here.

After this happened, Beliar, the great ruler, king of this world, shall rise; he shall rise in form of a man, an unjust king, killer of his mother. This is a direct symbolism. Vologases attacks and takes slaves, Nero, the killer of his mother withdrawing before him.[40]

They shall persecute the generation led by the apostles and the Beloved One. One of the twelve shall fall into his hands.

- "And he will set up his image before him in every city."[41]
- "And as above so on the earth also; for the likeness of that which is in the firmament is here on the earth."[42]
- "And there I saw a throne in the midst, and on his right and on his left were angels."[43]
- "And I said to the angel who conducted me: 'What is this which I see, my Lord?' And he said: 'I am not thy lord, but thy fellow servant.'"[44]

The allusions are of the statue of beast, the earth is the reflection of the heaven, the throne in heaven is a direct phrase from the Revelation: "At this I fell at his feet to worship him. But he said to me, 'Do not do it! I am a

---

40. Charles, "Ascension of Isaiah," 4:2.
41. Charles, "Ascension of Isaiah," 4:11.
42. Charles, "Ascension of Isaiah," 7:10.
43. Charles, "Ascension of Isaiah," 7:14.
44. Charles, "Ascension of Isaiah," 8:4–5.

fellow servant with you and with your brothers who hold to the testimony of Jesus. Worship God! For the testimony of Jesus is the spirit of prophecy'" (Rev 19:10).

What follows is Isaiah's way to heaven where he goes in spirit dressed in garments of the righteous ones. Christ descends with him from the seventh heaven, but the rulers of the lower spheres do not recognize him. He was crucified on earth and resurrected. Upon return to heaven, the rulers of the spheres praise him and rejoice his return. The final descent shall happen like lightning flashing from the east to the west. Christ and Isaiah cross spheres in all journeys and they remain intact. The spheres shall change upon final arrival. These are general instances of apocryphal literature.

In 1Q33 from the *Dead Sea Scrolls*, the battle of the judgment day shall be between the sons of darkness and the sons of light, between Beliar's army of demons and the army of angels. The battle will take place on Kittim (Cyprus) upon the realization of the tenth jubilee (490 years). The winning armies of light shall be guided by two messiahs.[45]

FOURTH EVENT

John's prophecy follows the interconnected eclipses of the Sun, Venus, and the Moon. They are heavenly messengers who personify real people, and their interconnected positions personify military and political relations. At the very beginning, it was indicated that the eclipses of these heavenly bodies may happen in five different ways:

1. The Moon with the keys to the abyss may cover the Sun
2. The Moon may cover Venus
3. The Sun may cover Venus
4. Venus may cover the Sun
5. Lunar eclipse

In the first event, two options happened: lunar eclipse of the Sun and the solar eclipse of Venus (double eclipse), the second event is the Venus eclipse of the Sun (Venus's transit), and the third event is the lunar eclipse of Venus. The lunar eclipse is missing for the completion of the versions, which close the cycle and signify a complete prophecy.

Lunar eclipses happen only when the Moon is opposite the Sun and when there is a full moon, like the old Babylonian astronomic observation

---

45. Jassen, "Dead Sea Scrolls."

says: "When the Moon is very big, there shall be an eclipse."[46] John states this clearly: "After this I saw another angel coming down from heaven. He had great authority, and the earth was illuminated by his splendor" (Rev 18:1). Full moon anticipates the fall of Rome: "With a mighty voice he shouted: 'Fallen! Fallen is Babylon the Great! She has become a home for demons and a haunt for every evil spirit, a haunt for every unclean and detestable bird. For all the nations have drunk the maddening wine of her adulteries. The kings of the earth committed adultery with her, and the merchants of the earth grew rich from her excessive luxuries'" (Rev 18:2–3). God's people are summoned to take revenge over Rome.

The peoples shall weep when they see the fire, the helmsmen and the travelers shall watch the smoke of her burning. But the heaven above shall rejoice, as well as the saints and the apostles and the prophets, for God has judged them by judging her. The time of the Moon has already come. It is the ruler of recent times; it judges and shows what shall happen. After the eclipses of the Moon, the Sun, and Venus in the year AD 48, transit of Venus in AD 60, and lunar eclipse of Venus in AD 63, what follows chronologically is a lunar eclipse that happened 17 July AD 64, a night before the great fire in Rome. The fire started on the night of 18 July AD 64.

Rome sits on many waters, which "are peoples, multitudes, nations and languages." It is the ruler of the world. "The beast and the ten horns you saw will hate the prostitute. They will bring her to ruin and leave her naked; they will eat her flesh and burn her with fire" (Rev 17:15–16). But Armenia shall hate and burn with fire Rome and the ten kingdoms that it rules over. Revelation is the oldest source which mentions the fire in Rome and directly says that Rome was burned intentionally by those who it had enslaved.

Mutual accusations of Nero and the Christians for burning Rome resulted in first persecutions. Tacitus, who was a boy at this time and moved to Rome a little later for educational purposes, criticizes Nero's actions in the *Annals*. Tacitus states that Nero helped the citizens after the fire but that his revenge on Christians was a consequence of his cruelty rather than an expression of public opinion. Nero tortured Christians in various ways to hide his responsibility for the fire which he started himself:

> But all human efforts, all the lavish gifts of the emperor, and the propitiations of the gods, did not banish the sinister belief that the conflagration was the result of an order. Consequently, to get rid of the report, Nero fastened the guilt and inflicted the most exquisite tortures on a class hated for their abominations,

---

46. In Elul an eclipse of Elam. From Nergal-etir. Thompson, "Reports of the Magicians."

called Christians by the populace. Christus, from whom the name had its origin, suffered the extreme penalty during the reign of Tiberius at the hands of one of our procurators, Pontius Pilatus, and a most mischievous superstition, thus checked for the moment, again broke out not only in Judaea, the first source of the evil, but even in Rome, where all things hideous and shameful from every part of the world find their center and become popular. Accordingly, an arrest was first made of all who pleaded guilty; then, upon their information, an immense multitude was convicted, not so much of the crime of firing the city, as of hatred against mankind.[47]

Such actions were not unusual for Nero. All sources refer to him as a psychotic tyrant who committed a series of abominable crimes including the murder of his own mother. These crimes indicate that he is essentially an eccentric addict of public opinion completely devoted to art for which he is talentless. Furthermore, he was ridiculed for his behavior. However, Sallust states that he was in possession of Nero's handwriting, which proves that he was very serious in his approach to writing poetry. He lost his father at the age of three, and soon after he lost his estate. He survived an assassination attempt and became the absolute master of the world at the age of barely seventeen. The sources unanimously agree on the amount and the nature of his crimes; however, it is certain that the gods were not fond of him or his tragic reign.

He succeeded Claudius during whose last year of reign there was a catastrophic fire. There were bad omens already on his first, inaugural day.[48] He allegedly caused an epidemic with his behavior, which took thirty thousand lives in only one spring.[49] In Britain a military defeat and robbery happened, which led to slaughter of a large number of citizens. In the East he suffered a shameful defeat because of which almost the entirety of Syria was lost.

Nero surrounded himself with astrologers who predicted an art career, rule of the East once he is overthrown in Rome, and especially rule of Jerusalem, and a new happiness. In Delphi he was prophesied to live to be seventy-three. Ultimately, he did not even believe the news of the rebellion in Gaul.[50] Nero decided to redeem his own life and satisfy the gods by sacrificing all respectable people in the Empire when a comet appeared

47. Tacitus, *Annals*, bk. 15, ch. 15.
48. Suetonius, *Caesars, Volume II*, 8.
49. In Camulodunum and Verulamium, according to Xiphilinus (Dio, *Roman History*, bk. 61, ch. 1.), eighty thousand died.
50. Suetonius, *Caesars, Volume II*, 39–40.

in the sky and remained there for a few days, because this was considered a bad omen foretelling death of a great ruler.[51] His grave was graced with flowers long after his death, because it was said that Nero shall return and take revenge upon his enemies (Neron Redivivus).

This legend rose after Nero's suicide and it is mentioned by Tacitus and Suetonius, but Dio Chrysostom's comments are interesting. He was a Greek orator, philosopher, and historian (around AD 40 to 120). His name means "golden-mouthed" in Greek. Eighty *Discourses* have been preserved of his writing.

Chrysostom arrived in Rome during Vespasian rule and became one of the sharpest critics of Domitian, who banished him from Rome and later also from Bithynia because he was consulting a conspirator. The Oracle of Delphi instructed him to dress as a beggar and travel the world with one of Plato's and one of Demosthenes's book. His wandering ended once Domitian was murdered. He was highly esteemed by Nerva and Trajan. He was a friend of Apollonius of Tyana. In the *Discourse on Beauty* Chrysostom mentions Nero and his inappropriate behavior several times, starting with the claim that unlimited power is inappropriate for man. Nero served as an example. Chrysostom shares a bizarre story about Nero's affection for a young man whom he castrated and married publicly.

That young man was called Sporus. He resembled Nero's wife Poppaea Sabina, therefore after her death Nero called him Sabina. Sporus was present when Nero committed suicide. After that, he was intimate with Otho, who was previously married to Poppaea Sabina. Sporus committed suicide during the Vitellius era because he refused to perform in theater under conditions that he did not conform with.[52] Furthermore, Chrysostom describes Nero's scandalous behavior: "But that youth of Nero's actually wore his hair parted, young women attended him whenever he went for a walk, he wore women's clothes, and was forced to do everything else a woman does in the same way. And, to cap the climax, great honors and boundless sums of money were actually offered to anyone who should make him his wife."[53]

Chrysostom claims that to be the truth about Nero. Nobody confronted him or warned him that something he ordered was impossible to do. Even if he told someone to fly, he would remain convinced that they would fly in a while. Nero was the only man who was not concerned about the money, neither when giving nor when taking which was the consequence of his lack of constraint because of which he lost his life.

51. Suetonius, *Caesars, Volume II*, 36.
52. Suetonius, *Caesars, Volume II*, 28.
53. Chrysostom, "On Beauty," 281.

His friends turned against him because of such actions and made him escape. "Indeed, the truth about this has not come out even yet; for so far as the rest of his subjects were concerned, there was nothing to prevent his continuing to be Emperor for all time, seeing that even now everybody wishes he were still alive. And the great majority do believe that he is, although in a certain sense he has died not once but often along with those who had been firmly convinced that he was still alive."[54]

A few years after Nero's death many appeared and claimed to be Nero. First of those was a slave from Pontus or a freedman from Italy who appeared in the year 69. Tacitus mentioned a pretender called Terentius Maximus from Asia who appeared during Titus's first rule (AD 79–81) and had the support of Parthians. Suetonius talks about a man who claimed to be Nero twenty years after Nero's death and again had the support of Parthians in the *Life of Nero*. It is possible that it is the same man mentioned by Tacitus.[55]

Discerning the real portrait from a legend and fictionalized history is difficult. However, when Tacitus describes Nero's last hours, his psychological state, and obstructive fear in a moment he deserved more than anyone ever before, there is a high level of imagination and expression that helps him write about his end as if he had witnessed it. Nero was alone at that time and there were no witnesses to confirm the way he dealt with his destiny. Nero is a caricatured character who served various ideologies precisely in the way he has been depicted and his biography is partly a product of other interests. For instance, Nero was criticized for giving Armenia to the Parthians thus betraying Roman interest no matter the fact that it was an actual victory of the Roman politics and political pragmatism built on realistic foundation that ensured peace to continue for so long.

The Roman state reached the zenith of its power during Nero's rule. All external problems were resolved in Britain, Gaul, and in the East. The borders of the Empire were secured so Rome entered a peaceful time and the gates at the Temple of Janus were closed. The peace in the East with the Parthians lasted for fifty years until Trajan intervened. Credit for this peace belong to Corbulo certainly and his destiny demonstrates Nero's character. Despite all credit, Nero demanded his suicide during his tour of Greece. Corbulo struck himself with a mortal blow saying, "Your due."[56] Tiridates's open admiration of Corbulo's loyalty to a ruler who did not deserve respect resulted in an expected epilogue. Afterwards, Armenia became a destabilizing factor and subject of seizing for both sides.

54. Chrysostom, "On Beauty," 281.
55. Tacitus, *History of Tacitus*, bk. 2, ch. 8–9.
56. Dio, *Roman History*, bk. 63, ch. 17.

Fire of Rome

The reasons for the mutual accusations of Nero and the Christians for burning Rome are partly not based on realistic grounds. Rome is known to have burned many times in its history and the conditions on the hot summer night in the year AD 64 suggested that if there was a fire it would be a major one.

Sources may confirm how often fires with very serious consequences were in Rome, especially when large areas, houses, markets, storehouses, and public buildings were on fire. The assumption that nothing could burn in the city of marble is wrong. Rome was overpopulated, cramped with multistoried buildings, and with no gardens or free space among the houses; it was a city of narrow crooked streets and houses made of poor quality and easily flammable materials often build with reed, soil, and mortar. Without the appropriate prevention and prompt extinguishing equipment, there was a constant risk. Fires occurred repeatedly and they were caused by negligence and carelessness not seen in many other cities in history. An additional element that increased the risks was the fact that half of the entire population were slaves and that only a small number had ownership. Rome was a city of proletarian masses by large and people did not consider it a home, or they simply hated it.

At the time of the Republic in 391 BC there was a catastrophic fire of the year, which was recorded in literature with as much attention as was the fire in Nero's time. Both had such horrendous consequences that the city had to be built anew. However, neither fire destroyed the city completely. In the fire of 391 BC the houses, which were small and built of mud and wood with thatched roofs, were an easy target for a fire. Therefore, the fire did not cause much damage since everything that was burned could easily be replaced. The real pity was that the Forum was devastated, and the surrounding porticos and stores were burned and destroyed together with the documents written on bronze or stone.

The Gallic fire was caused by an uncontrolled fire in a sanctuary made during the Numa's rule of woven wattle and guarded by Vestals. The temple was rebuilt, and the new Temple of Vesta burned in 241 BC. The event is remembered because the great priest Caecillius Metellus risked his life to save the Trojan Palladium brought by Aeneas and, consequently, lost his sight.[57]

A catastrophic fire occurred again in 213 BC in the area between Tiber and Capitoline and to the end of the Forum. Three years later, in 210 BC, a

---

57. Pliny the Elder, *Natural History*, bk. 7, ch. 43.

great fire ravaged the north and south part of the Forum. Stores and many private houses turned to dust and then again in 203 BC when the street going from Circus Maximus to Aventine burned.

In 192 BC many lives were lost in a fire that lasted day and night. Houses with storage along Tiber were destroyed. The Temple of Venus near Forum was completely destroyed in the fire of 178 BC. There was another fire in 148 BC. The Temple of Magna Mater, whose cult was introduced to Rome from Asia Minor, burned down in 111 BC. The Temple of Jupiter Capitolinus was burned to the ground during the civil war in 83 BC when the body of the notorious Clodius was burned on a fire ignited using chairs and benches used by senators and judges. The fire spread to the Senate, which burned down completely with the Basilica Porcia. There were two more fires in Rome's ancient history, one in 49 BC caused by thunder and one in the year 36 BC.

There were fifteen fires during imperial Rome, eight of which were major, and at least one important building burned down in the others. It is hard to estimate the number of smaller fires that did not damage important buildings or did not happen along Tiber or in the center of the city, meaning they were not mentioned in the annals.

Fire continued in imperial Rome and the same parts of the city were affected: Circus Maximus, Forum, and the Campus Martius mainly because these were the liveliest parts and thus were in the greatest risk of a fire. From the beginning and till the end of the Empire, fires were becoming more frequent than in the first part especially because of the sudden increase of the population followed by the infrastructure, an increase of the number of storage storehouses for various goods, increased dynamic in construction, and the density of houses, which were often made of wooden, flammable structures. Buildings were built in all possible places, obstructed free space, and caused roads to become narrower. The construction quality was not improving—just the opposite, buildings rose with additional floors whether the conditions allowed it or not.

During Augustus's rule there were nine fires. At the very beginning of his rule a great part of the Circus Maximus, the Temple of Ceres, and many houses were burned during tax protests. In the year 14 BC the Basilica Aemilia was burned in a fire which spread to the Temple of Vesta. In the years 12 and 7 BC there were fires that burned many houses around the Forum. A year later a large part of the city was burned. Augustus organized a night guard that had to maintain public order and promptly respond in case of fire.

During Tiberius's rule, five fires were recorded out of which two were major. The fire in the year AD 27 devastated houses and tall buildings. There were not many temples in the fire area and there is no mention of their destruction. However, the damage was so severe that Tiberius compensated the owners for the damage from the sales of stone materials that remained. The second, in the year AD 36 started along the Circus Maximus towards Aventine and then spread to Aventine itself. The greatness of this fire is evident in the fact that Tiberius willingly donated six million sesterces to help those who were affected.

In the last year of Claudius's rule, AD 54, there was a great fire which lasted one day and two nights. When the firefighters could not stop the fire, Claudius gathered people from different parts of the city and paid them to help extinguish the fire.

It was written extensively about the fire of AD 64 in Nero's time. This fire is considered one of the greatest in history and it lasted at least six days and nights. It started in the eastern part of the Circus Maximus, devastating the surrounding area, then spread to Aventine, Capitolium, and Palatine, and then stopped at Esquiline where a large number of multistoried houses burned. The only area that was spared in this fire was the area around the Forum, although some public buildings were damaged. Three parts of the city were entirely destroyed, and six others were severely damaged. Around four thousand insulae were burned, all art pieces disappeared, which were missed later even though a new city rose after this fire, much brighter than the old one.

During Tito's rule there was a fire in the year 80 that was somewhat less catastrophic than the previous one. It ravaged for three days and nights. The fire devastated the Capitolium. The Temple of Jupiter Capitolinus with surrounding temples were burned. Cassius Dio mentions the eleven buildings that burned and adds, "For anyone can estimate, from the list of buildings that I have given, how many others must have been destroyed."[58] At least five buildings of the greatest importance were listed as well as a large number of public and private houses.

During Commodus's rule in the year AD 189, thunder set fire to the Temple of Jupiter Capitolinus and the library that was inside. Then in AD 191 the Temple of Vesta was destroyed. The Temple of Apollo, which was built by Augustus and had a library, was burned along with part of the imperial palace and state archives.

During Carus's rule there were two fires. One in 283 when the Theater of Pompey was burned which had burned three times already, and the other in 283, which was more severe and damaged at least seven city monuments.

---

58. Dio, *Roman History*, bk. 66, ch. 24.

This is not nearly the complete picture because many smaller fires were not recorded. However, it is evident what kind of destruction this catastrophe caused Rome. The Temple of Vesta burned five times, the Theater of Pompey at least four, the Temple of Jupiter and the Basilica Julia three times, the Theater of Marcellus, the Pantheon, and the Colosseum two times.[59] The fires in Rome enabled the development and advancement of the urban organization both from a public health and aesthetic viewpoint. The irregular layout of Rome with narrow and crooked streets slowly changed into straight lines with empty areas among buildings. New grandiose buildings were being built after the fire in 210 BC. The second opportunity for reconstruction was during Sulla's reign after the fire in the year 83 BC. Rome became a marble city during Augustus's reign. After Nero's fire (he is criticized for setting the fire because of ambitious construction plans) the streets were broadened and aligned, and the construction of wooden buildings was limited. From Nero to Diocletian the city was devastated four times and new buildings were being built in different styles, sizes, and orientations.

The causes of fires were usually accidental or due to negligence in households or during work. Gauls burned Rome after the conquest just like Alaric in 410. Fires were set during civil unrest in the year 52 BC by the supporters of Clodius or in the year 69 when Vitellius burned the Temple of Jupiter. It is considered that ten larger or smaller fires were set and the most popular of these is Nero's fire in 64.[60] Thunder struck a significant building thirty times.

Nero introduced a number of regulations to control the construction in Rome with the intention to reduce the risk of fire, including the firefighters, who were led by *tresviri nocturne*[61] since the Republic. John writes about this fire long before Tacitus, Suetonius, and Chrysostom (who writes about Nero and does not mention the fire or name the perpetrator), who wrote after Domitian's era, and especially before Dio Cassius who wrote much later. He says directly that the Moon, that is Armenia, or a wider area of enslaved peoples from the East shall set a fire. Nero perhaps wanted a reconstructed city to show the greatness and splendor of the new empire which was stronger and wealthier than ever before. His extravagance reveals a tendency for such actions. However, these are the rational reasons: Rome was in constant danger and in Nero's era fires were actually less frequent than during the reign of not just his predecessors but also his successors.

59. Platner, *Topographical Dictionary of Ancient Rome*.

60. "A disaster followed, whether accidental or treacherously contrived by the emperor, is uncertain, as authors have given both accounts" (Tacitus, *Annals*, bk. 15, ch. 38).

61. Canter, "Conflagrations in Ancient Rome."

A MESSAGE TO THE CHURCHES

Revelation is primarily a politically engaged text and John coveys accurately the intention and will, which shall be realized in the immediate future. His optimism is based on a succession of catastrophes that must occur and the completion of which is a prerequisite for a final, good solution and the completion of the objective. Dividing the text into two, heavenly and historic level, assumes extraordinary coincidence which may objectively in every segment entirely replicate the events simultaneously on both levels and transmit the message from one to the other. John's visions of conjunctions and eclipses of the visible heavenly bodies is a real correlation between John's theology and historic events to which he refers thus converting his text partly into an extraordinary hymn to liberty with a strong political attitude and vision of a beneficial outcome of the drama, which was about to end at the time he was writing the text. He divides time into eons, into periods ruled by planets, personifying them and giving them identity corresponding to the living substance.

He considers the Moon as a throne in the sky set in accordance with the appearance of the Son of Man before whom there is a lake. This image integrates the display of the Son of Man and Sophia. It is a display of Jesus Christ, her fiancé, who comes at the end of times. In Revelation she is Jesus' syzygy just like in apocryphal and gnostic texts, the idea of which is reflected in the Christian canonical teaching. John describes the fallen Sophia and her marriage to Jesus; she is the new Jerusalem at the end of times, she is the eon of eons in which various divided elements shall unite. Christ's light shall guide Sophia in the right direction, and she shall rise from the materialistic world to the principle and unity of time.

In the foreground of John's theology is the fact that he builds the story on syzygies, what seals and trumpets are like, and the planets and their characteristic, but also the relationship between the Son of Man and the churches in the Asia Minor, Jesus and his fiancé (the new Jerusalem), the equestrian and his name, and the Sun and the man with its name.

He sends a message to the churches in Asia Minor. On the one hand it is a message which invites to mobilize against the common enemy and puts a difficult task before them. The objective of the task is freedom and life in an independent common state which shall be achieved with the help of God, the help John believes in more than the weaponry and military discipline. However, it is obvious that John's objective is far from naive romanticism. He is pragmatic and the work of God may serve as powerful motivation and argument in making the decision. He supports and proves his initiative with authoritative texts and proclamations which have ultimate power. Did God not send hunger and war to punish those who do not have the seal of God? Did God not show signs that he had sent his Son, for whom it was known that he shall arrive at the end of times, and was his arrival not a sign that a new righteous order shall be established by God's will? Did he not show that the oppressed people shall detest the oppressor of the world, and did he not punish and burn him?

These arguments had to be extraordinarily significant because they were followed in real time by heavenly signs and revelations. This is John's message and the broader context of what he tells the churches.

A Message to the Churches

The book is a series of arguments which represent John's cosmology to which he integrated planetary and historic events, linking them into units with a theological background. However, he partially relies on purely theological postulates that have a clear analogy in religious texts from John's time.

In prologue he only announces, "The Revelation of Jesus Christ: which God gave him to show his servants what must soon take place. He made it known by sending his angel to his servant John, who testifies to everything he saw—that is, the word of God and the testimony of Jesus Christ. Blessed is the one who reads the words of this prophecy, and blessed are those who hear it and take to heart what is written in it, because the time is near!" (Rev 1:1–3)

John just indicates that what he had seen and heard comes from God (and that this had been shown via angels/planets) and that it should be declared to his servants with the emphasis that the time of fulfillment is near. This is a key position where John expresses his intent. Complete clarification is in the modification that John conveys his own, God's, and Jesus' revelation. Those are three separate stories that refer to the model that God uses to create (cosmology), Jesus uses to create (eschatology), and the model John uses to record (history). All three stories happen according to the mutual matrix.

In the following text he speaks to churches (Rev 2:1–3:22). He encourages them, supports them, but also makes observations:

a. He praises them:

> "I know your deeds, your hard work and your perseverance. I know that you cannot tolerate wicked men, that you have tested those who claim to be apostles but are not, and have found them

false. You have persevered and have endured hardships for my name, and have not grown weary" (Rev 2:2-3).

"But you have this in your favor: You hate the practices of the Nicolaites, which I also hate" (Rev 2:6).

I know your afflictions and your poverty—yet you are rich! I know the slander of those who say they are Jews and are not but are a synagogue of Satan" (Rev 2:9).

"I know where you live—where Satan has his throne. Yet you remain true to my name. You did not renounce your faith in me, even in the days of Antipas, my faithful witness, who was put to death in your city—where Satan lives" (Rev 2:13).

"I know your deeds, your love and faith, your service and perseverance, and that you are now doing more than you did at first" (Rev 2:19).

"Yet you have a few people in Sardis who have not soiled their clothes. They will walk with me, dressed in white, for they are worthy" (Rev 3:4).

"I know your deeds. See, I have placed before you an open door that no one can shut. I know that you have little strength, yet you have kept my word and have not denied my name. I will make those who are of the synagogue of Satan, who claim to be Jews though they are not, but are liars—I will make them come and fall at your feet and acknowledge that I have loved you. Since you have kept my command to endure patiently, I will also keep you from the hour of trial that is going to come upon the whole world to test those who live on the earth" (Rev 3:8–10).

He praises churches for loyalty and endurance. He praises them for resistance and not accepting false teachers—Nicolaites, whether they are heretics, which would make Revelation the first text to treat heresy with negativity and criticism over a hundred years before Justin and Irenaeus, or he negatively treats the participant of political parties who had an unacceptable relationship with Armenia and the Roman-Parthian War or towards Israel.

b. The Son of Man criticizes churches for missed obligations and inconsistency. The previous sequence is continued but with a negative indication:

"Yet I hold this against you: You have forsaken your first love" (Rev 2:4).

"Nevertheless, I have a few things against you: You have people there who hold to the teaching of Balaam, who taught Balak to entice the Israelites to sin by eating food sacrificed to idols and by committing sexual immorality. Likewise, you also have those who hold to the teaching of the Nicolaites" (Rev 2:14–15).

"Nevertheless, I have this against you: You tolerate that woman Jezebel, who calls herself a prophetess. By her teaching she misleads my servants into sexual immorality and the eating of food sacrificed to idols. I have given her time to repent of her immorality, but she is unwilling. I will cast her on a bed of suffering, and I will make those who commit adultery with her suffer intensely, unless they repent of her ways. I will strike her children dead. Then all the churches will know that I am he who searches hearts and minds, and I will repay each of you according to your deeds" (Rev 2:20–23).

"I know your deeds; you have a reputation of being alive, but you are dead. Wake up! Strengthen what remains and is about to die, for I have not found your deeds complete in the sight of my God" (Rev 3:1–2.)

"I know your deeds, that you are neither cold nor hot. I wish you were either one or the other! So, because you are lukewarm—neither hot nor cold—I am about to spit you out of my mouth. You say, 'I am rich; I have acquired wealth and do not need a thing.' But you do not realize that you are wretched, pitiful, poor, blind and naked" (Rev 3:15–17).

c. John recommends and encourages:

"Remember the height from which you have fallen! Repent and do the things you did at first. If you do not repent, I will come to you and remove your lampstand from its place.... Do not be afraid of what you are about to suffer. I tell you, the devil will put some of you in prison to test you, and you will suffer persecution for ten days" (Rev 2:5, 10).

"Repent therefore! Otherwise, I will soon come to you and will fight against them with the sword of my mouth" (Rev 2:16).

"Now I say to the rest of you in Thyatira, to you who do not hold to her teaching and have not learned Satan's so-called deep secrets (I will not impose any other burden on you): Only hold on to what you have until I come" (Rev 2:24–25).

"Remember, therefore, what you have received and heard; obey it, and repent. But if you do not wake up, I will come like a thief, and you will not know at what time I will come to you" (Rev 3:3).

"I am coming soon. Hold on to what you have, so that no one will take your crown.

I counsel you to buy from me gold refined in the fire, so you can become rich; and white clothes to wear, so you can cover your shameful nakedness; and salve to put on your eyes, so you can see. Those whom I love I rebuke and discipline. So be earnest, and repent. Here I am! I stand at the door and knock. If anyone hears my voice and opens the door, I will come in and eat with him, and he with me" (Rev 3:11, 18–20).

Encouragement is the word, the teaching that John advocates for. John urges caution because time is near. He uses biblical phrases:

"Now learn this lesson from the fig-tree: As soon as its twigs get tender and its leaves come out, you know that summer is near. Even so, when you see all these things, you know that it is near, right at the door.

Truly I tell you, this generation will certainly not pass away until all these things have happened. Heaven and earth will pass away, but my words will never pass away.

But about that day or hour no one knows, not even the angels in heaven, nor the Son, but only the Father. As it was in the days of Noah, so it will be at the coming of the Son of Man. For in the days before the flood, people were eating and drinking, marrying and giving in marriage, up to the day Noah entered the ark; and they knew nothing about what would happen until the flood came and took them all away. That is how it will be at the coming of the Son of Man. Two men will be in the field; one will be taken and the other left. Two women will be grinding with a hand mill; one will be taken and the other left.

Therefore, keep watch, because you do not know on what day your Lord will come. But understand this: If the owner of the house had known at what time of night the thief was coming, he would have kept watch and would not have let his house be broken into. So, you also must be ready, because the Son of

Man will come at an hour when you do not expect him." (Matt 24:32–43)

"Now learn this lesson from the fig tree: As soon as its twigs get tender and its leaves come out, you know that summer is near. Even so, when you see these things happening, you know that it is near, right at the door. Truly I tell you, this generation will certainly not pass away until all these things have happened. Heaven and earth will pass away, but my words will never pass away.

But about that day or hour no one knows, not even the angels in heaven, nor the Son, but only the Father.

Be on guard! Be alert!" (Mark 13:28–31)

"Be on guard! Be alert! For you do not know when the moment shall come. When a man going on a journey leaves home, he commands rule to the servants, to each his affair, and the doorman is told to stay alert. Therefore, stay alert for you do not know when the owner shall return." He told them this parable: "Look at the fig tree and all the trees. When they sprout leaves, you can see for yourselves and know that summer is near. Even so, when you see these things happening, you know that the kingdom of God is near. Truly I tell you, this generation will certainly not pass away until all these things have happened. Heaven and earth will pass away, but my words will never pass away." (Luke 21:29–33)

John's message to the churches builds on a fragment which refers to the sixth seal, Saturn's domination, which is the last period before the arrival and which leads to dramatic events of the last of times: "And the stars in the sky fell to earth, as late figs drop from a fig tree when shaken by a strong wind" (Rev 6:13).

Interpretation of this parabola is given here:

And I, Peter, answered and said unto him: Interpret unto me concerning the fig-tree, whereby we shall perceive it; for throughout all its days doth the fig-tree send forth shoots, and every year it bringeth forth its fruit for its master. What then meaneth the parable of the fig-tree? We know it not. And the Lord answered and said unto me: Understand thou not that the fig-tree is the house of Israel? Even as a man that planted a fig-tree in his garden, and it brought forth no fruit. And he sought fruit thereof many years, and when he found it not, he said to the keeper of his garden: Root up this fig-tree that it make not our ground to be unfruitful. And the gardener said unto God: rid it of weeds and dig the ground round about it and water it. If then it bear no fruit, we will straightway remove its roots out of the garden and plant another in place of it. Hast thou not understood that the fig-tree is the house of Israel? Verily I say unto thee, when the twigs thereof have sprouted forth in the last days, then shall feigned Christs come and awake expectation, saying: I am the Christ, that am now come into the world. And when Israel shall perceive the wickedness of their deeds they shall turn away after them and deny him (whom our fathers did praise), even the first Christ whom they crucified and therein sinned a great sin. But the deceiver is not the Christ. And when they reject him he shall slay with the sword, and there shall be many martyrs. Then shall the twigs of the fig-tree, that is, the house of Israel, shoot forth: many shall become martyrs at his hand. Enoch and Elias shall be sent to teach them that this is the deceiver which must come into the world and do signs and wonders to deceive. And therefore shall they that die by his hand be martyrs who have pleased God in their life.[62]

Earth shall be judged together with heaven. Macarius Magnes, of whom very little is known other than he lived in the fourth century, wrote a book about the attack on Christianity, particularly naming Porphyry and Hierocles as his coauthors. In one instance he states that Peter claimed in the Apocalypse that the heaven shall be judged together with the earth, which surrounds it. "And all the might of heaven shall be dissolved, and the heaven shall be rolled together as a scroll, and all the stars shall fall as leaves from a vine, and as leaves fall from a fig tree."[63]

This is an old phrase that belongs to Isaiah:

> "Come near, you nations, and listen; pay attention, you peoples! Let the earth hear, and all that is in it, the world, and all that comes out of it! The Lord is angry with all nations; his wrath is on all their armies. He will totally destroy them, he will give them over to slaughter. Their slain will be thrown out, their dead bodies will stink; the mountains will be soaked with their blood. All the stars in the sky will be dissolved and the heavens rolled up like a scroll; all the starry host will fall like withered leaves from the vine, like shriveled figs from the fig tree. My sword has drunk its fill in the heavens; see, it descends in judgment on Edom, the people I have totally destroyed." (Isa 34:1–5)

62. "Apocalypse of Peter."
63. Crafer, *Apocriticus*, bk. 4, chs. 6, 7.

The invitation to repent is the acceptance of the word, and the word is the clothes that hides the nudity, the animalistic, hylic aspect of human nature. The word is gnosis, interpreted in various texts as clothes of glory, light, or clothes made of pure white linen. One who obeys and does not sully their clothes shall be dressed in white clothes and shall not sully their name in the Book of Life. He wears his clothes with his name on them. His name is his word, his teaching is his Sophia: "He who overcomes will, like them, be dressed in white. I will never blot out his name from the book of life but will acknowledge his name before my Father and his angels" (Rev 3:5).

The Son of Man is a common character especially in gnostic texts and their attributes are similar. Enoch is called the son of man on his way to the heaven, but the Son of Man also appears with the one who is from the beginning of times. He is beside the one who is from the beginning of times, who has hair white as wool, and looks like a man. This depiction of Enoch is the image of a Man who was in the beginning and who has angelic origin (Adam) and the image of the Son of Man who arrives at the end of times to announce hidden mysteries. The first world, which started with Adam and ended with the great flood, shall be repeated at the end of times in the world that started with Noah as per Messianic expectations (Matt 24:37 and Luke 17:26). The ark (*tebah*) saved Noah from a flood just like repentance (*shubah, tubah*) shall save the sons of Israel from the flood of corruption and decay. Religion is the ear of the soul and the acceptance and life in faith lead to salvation ("Who has an ear let them hear what the Ghost tells the churches!" [Rev 2:7]). Those who lost the ear for religion have lost the foundations: faith, hope, and love. They have become deaf and fallen on the ground.[64] "I came not to send peace, but a sword." They also maintain that John indicated the same thing when he said, "The fan is in His hand, and He will thoroughly purge the floor, and will gather the wheat into His garner; but the chaff He will burn with fire unquenchable."[65]

Balaam

There are numerous inputs about Balaam in the Old Testament, and his role in John's story may be interpreted. Nehemiah states all necessary reasons:

> The Book of Moses was read aloud in the hearing of the people and there it was found written that no Ammonite or Moabite should ever be admitted into the assembly of God, because

---

64. Clement of Alexandria, *Stromata*, bk. 5, ch. 2.
65. Irenaeus. "Against Heresies: Book 1," ch. 3.

they had not met the Israelites with food and water but had hired Balaam to call a curse down on them. Our God, however, turned the curse into a blessing. When the people heard this law, they excluded from Israel all who were of foreign descent. (Neh 13:1–3)

Moab was on the east side of the Dead Sea. Amon was north of it, and Edom was on the south. In the past, the three religions shared culturological and religious connection, and they were in close contact with Israel, yet they preserved a specific form of polytheism. The first traces of Moabite culture go back to the fourteenth century BC. They were conquered by David in the eleventh century but maintained autonomy by paying large taxes. In the sixth century they were conquered by the Babylonians. Their culture was completely assimilated. Nabateans inhabited their area in the fourth century BC. Ammonites shared a similar history along with the mention that they were a numerous people by Justin Martyr.

The episode about the Moabite and Ammonite resistance towards Jewish passage over the land east of the Dead Sea when the Moabite king Balaam pleads to the Ammonite sorcerer to call a curse down on the Jews (Num 22:1–41) to ensure a military victory fits completely to John's story. Although the Balaam's donkey saw an angel that got in its way, Balaam himself did not see it.

The episode about Balaam, the prophet who did not see the obvious, is common in the earliest Christian texts.

Jude the apostle attacks him furiously:

> In the very same way, on the strength of their dreams these ungodly people pollute their own bodies, reject authority and heap abuse on celestial beings. But even the archangel Michael, when he was disputing with the devil about the body of Moses, did not himself dare to condemn him for slander but said, "The Lord rebuke you!" Yet these people slander whatever they do not understand, and the very things they do understand by instinct—as irrational animals do—will destroy them. Woe to them! They have taken the way of Cain; they have rushed for profit into Balaam's error; they have been destroyed in Korah's rebellion. These people are blemishes at your love feasts, eating with you without the slightest qualm—shepherds who feed only themselves. They are clouds without rain, blown along by the wind; autumn trees, without fruit and uprooted—twice dead. They are wild waves of the sea, foaming up their shame; wandering stars, for whom blackest darkness has been reserved forever. (Jude 1:8–19)

The Second Epistle of Peter is in accordance with the Epistle of Jude:

> They are blots and blemishes, reveling in their pleasures while they feast with you. With eyes full of adultery, they never stop sinning; they seduce the unstable; they are experts in greed—an accursed brood! They have left the straight way and wandered off to follow the way of Balaam son of Bezer, who loved the wages of wickedness. But he was rebuked for his wrongdoing by a donkey—an animal without speech—who spoke with a human voice and restrained the prophet's madness. (2 Pet 2:13–16)

Peter says the same as John, Balaam received a wage for irrational and hostile doings towards Israel.

Egypt is a body in the mythological terminology, an empty clay dish that shall be broken by the Son of Man with an Iron scepter. The exodus of Moses out of Egypt describes the path of the soul and its climb through the heavenly spheres. The crossing of the Red Sea is a crossing of pneumatic over the material world in which Pharaoh's armies drown. On the way, Israel/the soul crosses the materialistic world on their way to heaven/the promised land. On this way, the Jews encounter Balaam and Balak who stop them and try to seduce them and return them to the materialistic world/Egypt. Balaam and Balak do the same as Nicolaus, who did the same as the devil, the seducer, Algol. He discourages the righteous ones away from the kingdom of God. This must be the image in John's head when he writes about the Nicolaites and Jezebel who are the same as Balaam and Balak. They all forget the obvious truth that God and his word are on John's side and that they must win.

Jezebel

Jezebel was the daughter of a Phoenician king Ithobaal, and much was written about her in 1 and 2 Kings. She became the synonym of an immoral woman, prone to promiscuity and dishonesty. When the king of Israel Ahab married her, she imposed her religion and customs. She built temples of Baal in Israel, and the Phoenician religion became state religion under the protection of the king. Jewish turned to worshiping idols under her influence and this ultimately led them to tyranny. This is described in 1 Kings in the following way: "Ahab son of Omri did more evil in the eyes of the Lord than any of those before him. He not only considered it trivial to commit the sins of Jeroboam son of Nebat, but he also married Jezebel daughter of Ithobaal king of the Sidonians and began to serve Baal and worship him.

He set up an altar for Baal in the temple of Baal that he built in Samaria. Ahab also made an Asherah[66] pole and did more to arouse the anger of the Lord, the God of Israel, than did all the kings of Israel before him" (1 Kgs 16:30–33). Jezebel murdered all Israeli prophets, and her prophets were challenged to a competition by Elijah, who murdered them, thus provoking Jezebel's hostility: "Now Ahab told Jezebel everything Elijah had done and how he had killed all the prophets with the sword. So Jezebel sent a messenger to Elijah to say, 'May the gods deal with me, be it ever so severely, if by this time tomorrow I do not make your life like that of one of them.'" (1 Kgs 19:1–2). After Ahab's death Jezebel continued to reign through her sons Ahaziah and Jehoram.

Her husband wished for another person's vineyard, so she persuaded servants to falsely accuse the owner, so the public killed him.

Angered by their behavior, God the Father used prophets to select Jehu as king and he destroyed Ahab's house. He said to the prophet:

> "Tuck your cloak into your belt, take this flask of olive oil with you and go to Ramoth Gilead. When you get there, look for Jehu son of Jehoshaphat, the son of Nimshi. Go to him, get him away from his companions and take him into an inner room. Then take the flask and pour the oil on his head and declare, 'This is what the Lord says: I anoint you king over Israel.' Then open the door and run; don't delay!" So the young prophet went to Ramoth Gilead. When he arrived, he found the army officers sitting together. "I have a message for you, commander," he said. "For which of us?" asked Jehu. "For you, commander," he replied. Jehu got up and went into the house. Then the prophet poured the oil on Jehu's head and declared, "This is what the Lord, the God of Israel, says: 'I anoint you king over the Lord's people Israel. You are to destroy the house of Ahab your master, and I will avenge the blood of my servants the prophets and the blood of all the Lord's servants shed by Jezebel. The whole house of Ahab will perish. I will cut off from Ahab every last male in Israel—slave or free. I will make the house of Ahab like the house of Jeroboam son of Nebat and like the house of Baasha son of Ahijah. As for Jezebel, dogs will devour her on the plot of ground at Jezreel, and no one will bury her.'" (2 Kgs 9:1–10)

Jehu did as God instructed him through prophets and his servants threw Jezebel through the window (who put on makeup preparing for the

---

66. Asherah is originally a sacred tree, garden, but also a cane used to maintain fire at the altar when bulls were sacrificed. Here the reference is to Phoenician goddess.

worst which is especially scandalous) and her body was eaten by dogs. Only her head, hands and feet remained:

> Then Jehu went to Jezreel. When Jezebel heard about it, she put on eye makeup, arranged her hair and looked out of a window. As Jehu entered the gate, she asked, "Have you come in peace, you Zimri, you murderer of your master?" He looked up at the window and called out, "Who is on my side? Who?" Two or three eunuchs looked down at him. "Throw her down!" Jehu said. So they threw her down, and some of her blood spattered the wall and the horses as they trampled her underfoot. Jehu went in and ate and drank. "Take care of that cursed woman," he said, "and bury her, for she was a king's daughter." But when they went out to bury her, they found nothing except her skull, her feet and her hands. They went back and told Jehu, who said, "This is the word of the Lord that he spoke through his servant Elijah the Tishbite: On the plot of ground at Jezreel dogs will devour Jezebel's flesh. Jezebel's body will be like dung on the ground in the plot at Jezreel, so that no one will be able to say, 'This is Jezebel.'" (2 Kgs 9:29–37)

Ahab was wounded too, he bled in a chariot, which was washed, and his blood was licked by dogs.

The history of Jezebel corresponds to Balaam in all elements. They both seduce Jews, introduce false prophets and foreign beliefs, and, interestingly, probably erect the statue of a foreign goddess (the statue of beast).

Nicolaites

John found Nicolaus and the Nicolaites in Ephesus and Pergamum the strongest Roman centers, and Jezebel in Thyatira, but he criticizes other churches that they have few righteous ones (Sardis), while false Jews settles in Philadelphia and Smyrna. Nicolaites are considered a large group when mentioned in the two strongest cities. False Jews are the indecisive ones, those who assumed their safety and well-being to a greater national or religious interest and who do not accept John's ideas and do not respond to his mobilization.

Jezebel teaches Jews to eat meat dedicated to idols, thus metaphorically accepting wage and benefits offered by the Roman authorities. Everything John criticizes about churches is singular: they have to renounce defeatism and not be half-hearted, but wholeheartedly accept the undertaking which must finally be fruitful, just like Micah laments. "My people, remember:

What Balak king of Moab plotted? And what Balaam son of Beor answered?" (Mic 6:1)

Nicolaites are a group recorded only in Revelation and commentaries on the Revelation. Eusebius says about them that at that time, for a very short time indeed, there was a Nicolaite heresy. He says that John's Revelation mentions it. Nicolaites assumed Nicolaus as one of the deacons, Stephen's associate, whom the apostles selected to care for the poor.[67]

Furthermore, in the same text Eusebius mentions Clement of Alexandria who says the following in the third book *Stromata* about Nicolaus: "They say that he had a beautiful wife, and after the ascension of the Savior, being accused by the apostles of jealousy, he led her into their midst and gave permission to any one that wished to marry her. For they say that this was in accord with that saying of his, that one ought to abuse the flesh. And those that have followed his heresy, imitating blindly and foolishly that which was done and said, commit fornication without shame."[68] Eusebius takes this quote from Clement's *Stromata*, which is already tendentious because it mentions Nicolaites and Nicolaus right after sworn hedonist Aristippus, the most famous follower of the Cyrenaic school of philosophy, thus putting him in the same order of value. Clement says, "He who fought with pleasure by pleasure, advances on pleasure in feigned combat . . . it was no great thing for a man that had abstained from it, but for him not to be overcome by pleasure, as is manifested in Aristippus, the Cyrenaic who continued his relationship with a Corinthian courtesan claiming that he possessed her, and that he was not possessed by her!" This is Clement's way of using Aristippus to introduce a short review of Nicolaus and the Nicolaites exposing his attitude. His followers distorted his attitude and committed all sorts of adultery justifying their actions by a rational reason that body ought to be abused.[69] These are all references to Nicolaites, and it is not certain whether Clement puts Nicolaites under the same name of gnostics who in his opinion preach our truths with hypocrisy because of self-interest.

From the context of Revelation, it ensues that Nicolaus and Nicolaites might have been a respectable group considering that John records their significant influence in two cities. However, it is not certain that he would condemn them for heresy or avoiding the truth.

Antipas has already been mentioned, and his visit to the city with the strongest Roman influence and a powerful administrative center of Roman

---

67. Eusebius, *Church History*, bk. 3, ch. 29.
68. Eusebius, *Church History*, bk. 3, ch. 29.
69. Clement of Alexandria, "Stromata," bk. 2, ch. 20.

reign is an evident reflection of John's anti-Rome opinion. John calls this city Satan's center where those who falsely declare themselves as Jewish are settled.

In John's story Balaam is the one who speaks against John's idea; he is against an independent Armenia and against Israel, and he advocates cohabitation, coexistence, and compromise with global superpowers. This is the attitude of Marcus Julius Agrippa when he confronted Jews in the early 67 and tried to dissuade them from going to war with Rome. This was primarily a political initiative which could be well represented during time of crisis and which many could have supported, especially the ethnically and politically divergent Asia Minor. Balaam supports the political option which does not admit Jewish supremacy that is manifested in God's protection. He is a political realist who understands the dangerous adventure upon which the Jewish people embarked as well as the entire religion. Balaam says the same as Nicolaus and his party. Nicolaus is not a heretic teacher, but a political pragmatic, someone who cooperates with Roman authorities or writes biographies of Roman emperors and participates in delegations to Rome. This is someone who does not necessarily have to be alive at that time, nor be an active participant of events. This is a man of good reputation, whose name is connected to Roman authorities and who advocates for diplomatic solutions and political agreements with Rome, someone whose example is followed by many because they consider his path to be good even in the later case when the political conditions repeated themselves to which he had responded. Perhaps someone like Nicolaus of Damascus.

Nicolaus (born in the year 64 BC) was a historian and philosopher, a friend of King Herod the Great, born in Damascus. He came from a wealthy family, and he had a good education. He studied and followed Aristotle's philosophy, not accepting Judaism even though he supported Saturday as a holy day in Asia Minor. Herod supported him in writing a comprehensive history of Assyria, Media, Lydia, and Persia, which has been completely lost except for the parts conveyed by Josephus Flavius. He wrote the history of Roman emperors and only two have been preserved, on Octavian's youth and on the death of Caesar. He lived in Asia Minor around 14 BC, and later in Rome. In Rome, he defended Archelaus from his brothers and Jews persuading him to give up on Greek cities who had opposed Jewish domination and to preserve half of the state in his power. Nicolaus's philosophical beliefs and the rejection of the Jewish faith, and especially his political activity that defied the interests of Jewish politics, shaped a profile which suited John's thesis well.[70]

70. Gottheil and Krauss, "Nicholas of Damascus."

The rebellion in the year AD 66/67 occurred because of the issue of Greek cities who wanted independence. This reactivated the issue that Archelaus was supposed to resolve, yet Nicolaus consulted him to make territorial concessions. Territorial or other concessions were the opinion of the Nicolaites in John's time, which was unacceptable for him.

All these groups can be put under the umbrella—Jezebel and her followers, Balaam and his followers, and Nicolaus and his followers, who are the same, soft, indecisive ones who do not want war. This is not about a heretic group, but about political differences among the Jews in Asia Minor.

With this the first of the events described by John, which correlates to a double Moon, Sun, and Venus eclipse from 48, extends beyond the frame. John's description is not in accordance with the events during Mithridates's reign or possibly the events related to Radamistus's burglaries or the Tiridates's first rule (AD 53–58) in a way that the events in Israel do: the inaugural year of Marcus Julius Agrippa and of the high priest Ishmael ben Phiabi, the last year of Tiberius Julius Alexander, and the hunger foretold by Apollonius of Tyana at the same time as Agabus, as well as the conflicts with the Greeks, brought to the focus the old questions discussed already by Nicolaus of Damascus with Augustus while defending the interests of the first Jewish kings.

John's Theology

EXEGESIS

In these events the destiny of the world and the destiny of Israel and Armenia are parallel to each and every individual soul, because John's word, same as Jesus', relates to both the universal and the individual levels. The destiny of the world makes the destiny of a nation and the destiny of an individual. They will go through the same process until the fulfillment of the history and the life.

This is introducing the problem of the exegesis, described analogously with cosmological and terrestrial events. John calls the churches to vigilance because the time of the fulfillment is near. His message is clear: the flood that destroyed the world will be repeated. The world is going to its end. But this time it will not be flooded but incinerated, whereafter the earth incinerated with fire will reconnect and a new cycle will be started.[1] The fire will destroy the sinners and only the righteous will survive, who will feel the heat pleasant like warm milk. Time will return to the beginning and a new historical cycle will begin. Adam, the first man, or Noah, who saved the world and from whom everything originated, are warning the churches. He is now the Son of Man, one in being with the Father, who was in the beginning of the time, who was the first Adam or the first Man. In the end he comes as his own Son, the self-begotten Man Son of Man. The Man and the Man Son of Man are the same. They are Alpha and Omega, the beginning and the end of the entire creation; they are the Moon that is the first among the planets, and from whom everything is created, and Omega, the last, coming at the end of the succession and with whose rule the time is fulfilled.

Irenaeus states briefly the Ophite tradition[2] that Theodoret connects with the Sethians, according to which (Ophites/Sethians) speak prophetically that there is the original light that is in the power of Bithos, blessed,

1. Guthrie, *Kasni Platon i Akademija*, 285.
2. Irenaeus, "Against Heresies: Book I," ch. 30.

indestructible, endless, that is the father to everything and is called the First Man. They claim that Mind was created from it, which is his Son whom he sent; and that Mind is the Son of Man, the Second Man. Above them is the Holy Spirit, whereas below these highest spirits are the primary elements, called water, darkness, abyss, and chaos; and from them created is the spirit, by them called the First Woman.

According to them, the physical man is just a temporary dwelling of the soul, the first time the dwelling of the very soul, and the second time of the soul and the demonic forces (the essence of the elements) or the soul and the word that came from above, from pleroma into this world, where it dwells in the body made from clay, together with the soul, once the demons left it.

This body is Egypt or the hylic world or the material universe. John says, "Now when they have finished their testimony, the Beast that comes up from the Abyss will attack them, and overpower and kill them. Their bodies will lie in the great city, which is figuratively called Sodom and Egypt, where also their Lord was crucified" (Rev 11:7–8).

The place of the mythic confrontation is the place of the crucifixion of Jesus. The polemics with Abgar and the tradition about the center of the world where demons hide under the Kissaneh's sanctuary have already been mentioned. In this text John compares the city where two prophets will be assassinated to Sodom and Egypt. Obviously, Sodom is a city, but Egypt is a state. Furthermore, John states enormous dimensions of Jerusalem, shaped as a square of the sides of two thousand four hundred kilometers in length, the dimensions of a region rather than a city. Here, too, John means the world. Square is the center of a city, in this case the world. This is obviously Rome where two prophets will be assassinated.

The John's cosmology opens to four levels. The lowest level is hebdomad, the space that encloses the earth and the air space up to the Moon. Above this level rule planets and the zodiac. This world is divided into sky (the first seal), the sea (the second seal), the earth (the third seal), and the underground (the fourth seal). In this world, time circles, seasons come in turns, year after year passes, until the time is fulfilled (the sixth seal). Over this cycle rules the fifth seal, Jupiter. This is the world of perpetual births and deaths: "They were given power over a fourth of the earth to kill by sword, famine and plague, and by the wild beasts of the earth" (Rev 6:8). This is the world that advances in no other direction but to its own inevitable end. In this world the ruler is the Man the Son of Man, who appears with his syzygy, the church. It makes his pair and his wife. He is seated above the air space, on the throne with his wife Sophia. The Man, the one who is from the beginning, but also the same as his own Son. Around him there are myriads of myriads of souls coming from the earth and gathering on the Moon, while waiting for the last judgment. The passage into the heaven is closed and no one can open the books held in his hand by the Man. No one can open the book but the lamb lying as slaughtered before the throne. It knows the secrets of the word and the formulas, the gnoses that are to be said at the door of the higher spheres. In the books written is the model by which the world is created, the model as written in the Plato's *Timaeus*. The god (demiurge) created from the matter and in accord with the forms that were in his mind. The matter is the soil, the dirt from which everything is made. The form is his idea, the paradigm of things that he conceived. The world that is made of impure matter and pure divine idea is neither good nor bad. It is a mixed world. The form conceived by God is the general principle. It exists in all things and is hidden. It is the Holy Spirit, the principle contained in everything, it is the same with the Man and the Man the Son of Man. They are three, but also one.

Above the Moon is the lower area of ethereal space in which there are the spheres of the planets. This area contains hebdomad, and above it is the celestial ethereal space (universe) extending to the end of the space and time. This space is divided into powers, hierarchies, areas, and domains (constellations). The planetary spheres of the lower ethereal space can be passed only by a soul that knows its secrets, mysteries, and gnoses. At the door it is to say the key gnosis as a password and pass to the next sphere. The mysteries and the secret formulas are the robes in which the soul hides to pass unnoticed by the keeper of the planetary spaces. In his coming, Christ will pass through these worlds unnoticed (same as the soul hidden by his name, without the Word there is no salvation, because the soul will be discovered and returned to a new body), hidden by mysteries that make him invisible, but in his ascension he will pass through them and the sphere will celebrate and rejoice him.

No one knows the mysteries of the spheres. They are written in the Adam's book given to him by the God at the beginning of the time. The Man holds it in his hand all the time, because he is the one who keeps in his hand the key to the death and the underground. But no one can open the book and break its seals. No one except the lamb that is before the throne. Obviously, the lamb is Christ that will return Sophia from her delusion and will become one with her. This is how he understands his mission:

> Now, therefore, for the sake of sinners have I torn myself asunder and come into the world, to save them, and also because it is necessary that the righteous, who have never done evil, and have never committed sin, should find the mysteries which

are in the Books of Ieou, which I made Enoch write down in Paradise, when I spoke to him from the Tree of Knowledge, and from the Tree of Life, and which I made him deposit in the rock of Ararad; and I set Kalapatauroth, the Ruler that is over Skemmut, on whose head is the foot of Ieou—the latter surrounded all the Eons and the Fate-Sphere—I set [then] this Ruler to preserve the Books of Ieou from the flood, and [also] lest any of the Rulers out of enmity should destroy them. These [books] will I give unto you, when I have finished telling you the emanation of the pleroma.[3]

These are the mysteries of the mysteries, and only a few will understand the highest secrets. "I am telling you, thee will be one in a thousand and two in ten thousand who will fulfill the secrets of the First Mystery."

"Before the coming of the First Mystery no soul of this humanity had fully entered into the Light; none of the prophets or patriarchs had as yet entered into the Light, but they will be sent back into righteous bodies and so find the mysteries and inherit the Kingdom."[4]

The souls of the righteous pass the lower ethereal spheres ruled by the planets (seals) and come to the sphere of destiny (zodiac). Here they halt because the door to the pleroma, that is above them, is closed. No one ever before them passed this door. The righteous who by their lives earned the kingdom cannot enter it. They will be given righteous bodies and will be returned to the life, where they will explore the mysteries and study the gnoses with which they will save themselves from the endless succession of births and deaths. The souls of the righteous are standing before the door to the pleroma, dressed in white robes washed in the Lamb's blood, waiting for the door to the pleroma to open, when they will enter the kingdom of light. Passing from the ethereal world of the visible universe requires secret knowledge that has not been revealed yet. The pupils are promised these by the Savior: "I will also reveal unto you all the grandeurs of the height, from the interior of the interiors to the exterior of the exteriors, that ye may be perfect in every gnosis, and in every pleroma, and in every height of the heights, and every deep of the depths."[5] This is the book that contains secrets, names, and numbers of the eons that a soul is to pass through to rise to the heaven. It contains the mysteries of the light of the world (pleroma) and the mysteries and secret names required to pass through lower spheres.

---

3. Mead, *Pistis Sophia*, 292.
4. Mead, *Pistis Sophia*, 292–3.
5. Mead, *Fragments of a Faith*, 506.

This is the book written inside and outside and held in his hand and given to the Lamb by the Man.

He "is the one who holds the Keys of the Mysteries." And Mary answered and said to the Savior: "Now we know, O Master, freely, surely, plainly, that Thou hast brought the keys of the mysteries of the Kingdom of Light, which remit the sins of souls, that they may be cleansed, and be transformed into pure light, and be brought into the Light."[6]

Mystic rituals were performed by a strictly defined procedure as the preparation and invocation of the ruler of the spheres that are to be propitiated in order to pass the spheres safely and risk free. In the *Books of the Savior* described is the ceremony of invocation of the pleroma: Jesus is standing on the ocean, surrounded by the pupils, male and female, saying the solemn prayer: Hear me, oh Father, the Father of all fatherhood.[7] The prayer consists of mystic vowels and formulas mixed with "authentic" names. The pupils are around him and women standing before him are dressed in white cloaks. Jesus is standing at the altar turning to the four sides of the world, every time invoking three times the name Iao, meaning I, the pleroma will come; A, they will return with it; O, there will be the end of the ends.

Follows is the mystic formula that is interpreted as "O Father of every fatherhood of the boundless [light-spaces], hear Me because of My disciples, whom I have brought into Thy presence, that they may believe in all the words of Thy truth; grant unto them all things for which I have cried unto Thee, for I know the Name of the Father of the Treasure of Light."[8]

The souls are still waiting in the sphere of destiny, before the door to the pleroma. Before it there is a closed curtain and they still do not see clearly what is above them. Their mind reflects from it like from a mirror, same as when they tried understanding it on the earth. They need Sophia, who can help them partly, because she had known the secrets before she fell into the material world.[9] She saw the light of the pleroma (the kingdom of light) and desired to reach it. She knew the secrets and the opposites of all the spheres,[10] they're written in the book held by the Man in his hand. But

---

6. Mead, *Pistis Sophia*, 294.

7. The father of everything is time—Saturn. Jesus invocates the Father whose father (time) is in his own idea. The phrase means that he is invocating the Eternal, the one before all the times.

8. Mead, *Fragments of a Faith*, 509.

9. The soul knows the secrets of the pleroma before it materializes. This knowledge disappears at the birth and the cycle of cognition starts from the beginning.

10. Opposites of all the spheres—this often appears as the symbol of syzygy, relationship in the unity divided from inside.

she did not know the last secret—the secret of the kingdom of light, that she so desired but was unable to reach.

Looking at the Sophia's endeavors and how she kept moving away from them, the rulers of the lower spheres tricked her in envy. They collected all the light of the lower, material world of neither light nor darkness, and when Sophia looked down, she followed that light and fell into the material world. She was overcome by the light of the lower eons and she was weakened and lost the strength to return to her kingdom. In the material world she intuitively feels (*pistis* = faith) that Christ will come, who has the light in him and who radiates the light, and that she will absorb it and become his fiancée in a mystic wedding. She understands the spheres and the eons up to the thirteenth, she understands the visible world (the cognitive mind), she suspects (intuitive mind), but she does not know the world above her, the one that cannot be understood because it is not revealed but is hidden behind a curtain that the mind cannot penetrate. These, the highest mysteries, are still to be revealed by Christ, this is a new covenant and announcement after which the highest mysteries of the universe will emerge. The souls are waiting before the door to the pleroma, Sophia and the Man's book could have helped them but the Last Mystery is not revealed yet. Only the Savior can solve this adverse situation. His is Christ, the only begotten. He is the son of the pleroma, virgin—the world of not materialized ideas—who will come and carry his experience and knowledge of the world that no one knows and that no one can enter without his knowledge. He is the light and he is carrying the light in him. The light that Sophia can see and the light that she can receive. It will direct her in the right direction, she will reject delusions and surrender to Christ completely, and with his help she will ascend again to the spheres from which she fell into the material world. The coming of Christ is hope and salvation. He will reveal to the righteous the last secrets that they are to know, the formulas and the secret names. The curtains will rise and the pleroma will appear.[11]

And the pleroma showed itself.

The transit of Venus is the image of the pleroma, dressed in light, same as her kingdom is. The Moon in conjunction with Regulus is announcing the birth of the child, the only begotten (the one born to one parent only, a pure pleroma's child). He will reveal the mysteries known only to him. He will enable the door to the pleroma to open and the souls of the righteous to enter its kingdom. But before the door, at the highest point of the sky,

---

11. Sophia's two aspects, the affective and the cognitive aspect (faith and knowledge), are coordinated by the mediator that is the Word—Christ (Logos), thus making a triad. Sophia is a Greek word of feminine gender, Logos is masculine, and this etymology puzzles Philo.

the deceiver stops the passage. The souls of the righteous are confused, they cannot pass into the kingdom of light. They are waiting for the revelation in the sphere of destiny. If none happens, they are risking again to fall into the material world (*metensomatosis*). The star Algol is an ecliptic star, it appears and disappears in the sky. It is a symbol of the material world of Osiris, dying and born again, and a symbol of *metensomatosis*.[12]

Algol confronts Christ and his Sophia. He does not allow the souls to enter the Kingdom but returns them to the earth, and with him Michael will fight in the sky, where there will be no survival for him.[13] Then he passed the authority on the earth to Nero and Vologases. They do not permit a new kingdom, Armenia, to be created. They are serving the deceiver. And those who could not resist, but demonstrated they were not Jews and did not respect John's word, will perish, because it is explained that many who received the mysteries perished and did not repent; that is worse than the many unenlightened who never knew them. To those indifferent, who thought they had many more births in front of them and did not hurry, the Teacher gave time to convert.

John prophesizes to the entire world; he wants his word to be spread, the mysteries to be announced. "Do not seal up the words of the prophecy of this book, because the time is near!" (Rev 22:10), so that those who hear can be saved in the new kingdom.

> Preach ye unto the whole world, saying unto men: "Strive together that ye may receive the mysteries of light in this time of stress, and enter into the kingdom of light. Put not off from day to day, and from cycle to cycle, in the belief that ye will succeed in obtaining the mysteries when ye return to the world in another cycle."
>
> For at a Certain Time the Gates of the Light will be shut. Such men know not when the number of perfect souls [shall be filled up]; for when the number of perfect souls shall be completed, I will then shut the Gates of the Light, and from that time none will be able to come in thereby, nor will any go forth thereafter, for the number of perfect souls shall be [completed], and

---

12. Plutarch, *Isis and Osiris*, bk. 5, ch. 54.

13. Michael is placed to the position of God's army archstrategist, instead of the fallen Lucifer. A clear alusion to the seventy-two constellations is in the Luke's Gospel: "The seventy-two returned with joy and said, 'Lord, even the demons submit to us in your name.' He replied, 'I saw Satan fall like lightning from heaven. I have given you authority to trample on snakes and scorpions and to overcome all the power of the enemy; nothing will harm you. However, do not rejoice that the spirits submit to you, but rejoice that your names are written in heaven'" (Luke 10:17–20).

the mystery of the First Mystery be perfected—[the mystery] whereby all hath come into existence, and I am that mystery.

From that hour no one shall any more enter into the Light, and none shall come forth, in that the time of the number of perfect souls shall be fulfilled, before I set fire to the world, that it may purify theœons, and veils, the firmaments and the whole world, and also all the matters that are still in it, the race of human kind being still upon it.

At that time, then, the faith shall show itself forth more and more, and also the mysteries in those days. And many souls shall pass through the cycles of transmigrations of body and come back into the world in those days; and among them shall be some who are now alive and hear Me teach concerning the consummation of the number of perfect souls, [and in those days] they shall find the mysteries of light, and shall receive them. They shall mount up to the Gates of Light, and shall find that the number of perfect souls is complete, which is the Consummation of the First Mystery and the Gnosis of the Pleroma; they will find that I have shut the Gates of Light, and that from that hour no one can come in or go forth thereby.

Those souls then will cry within through the Gates of Light, saying: "Master, open unto us." And "I know not whence ye are." I will answer unto them, saying, "I know not whence ye are." And they will say unto Me, "We have received the mysteries, and we have fulfilled all Thy doctrine; Thou didst teach us on the high ways." And I will answer unto them, saying, "I know not who ye are, ye who have practiced iniquity and evil even unto this day. Wherefore go [hence] into the Outer Darkness." Forthwith they will depart to the Outer Darkness, where there is weeping and gnashing of teeth.[14]

What more than this did John wish to say?

The kingdom can be announced only to the worthy ones. In the *Book of the Great Logos*, Jesus is addressing the pupils with the words standing in the very title: "I have loved you. I have wanted to give you life!" followed by the statement "this is the book of the gnoses of the invisible God!" This is the book of the gnoses of the living Jesus, meaning that all the secrets have been revealed to the Chosen One. Jesus is the savior of the souls, the logos of the life, sent to the men by the Father from the kingdom of light, who taught the pupils the one and only teaching, saying: "This is the teaching where the gnoses are."[15]

14. Mead, *Fragments of a Faith*, 502–3.
15. Mead, *Fragments of a Faith*, 518.

The New Jerusalem

The John's cosmology consists of four levels:

1. Air space where the Son of Man and the church appear
2. Ethereal space above the Moon
3. Space of the pleroma announced by Christ
4. The kingdom of God where the God is

The last vent of this drama is the coming of the new Jerusalem to the earth. The old sky, sea, and earth disappear and "I saw the Holy City, the new Jerusalem, coming down out of haven from God, prepared as a bride beautifully dressed for her husband" (Rev 21:2). She is a dove (*peristera*), alpha and omega (the number of her name is alpha and omega, 800 + 1 = 801). *Peristera* is 801. She has the same name number as the Son of Man. Here the entire story turns towards the Plato's *Timaeus*. Plato presumes the creator (demiurge) who from matter creates forms (*paradigmes*). From the forms existing before the creation, same as every craftsman who has the idea of what he is doing, demiurge creates the entire creation. Bythos is the basic, the first, uncreated idea from which all the ideas are created. It is the idea of the idea. Christ is born by the pleroma, the world of ideas, and he has the idea of it. He teaches about it and announces it. He is, thus, the idea of the idea, consubstantial with the father, but uncreated, from the beginning of the time. Idea is the form that in the Revelation, same as in almost all religious texts, appears metaphorically like clothing. In these clothes, worn by Christ in accordance with the eons—the emanations of the pleroma—he sees mysteries. Clean linen white clothing is a spiritual being, a pneumatic that left its hylic aspect and exists only as an immaterial being. In the gnostic and Indian texts appears the idea on transferring of the soul into the world of light, carried by angel by one hair only (Indian *nadi*). If the soul is burdened with sins, the hair will break and the soul will fall into the material world and the cycle of new births. According to the only preserved description of Jesus, he was of markedly dark complexion, bold and of a thick, long, curly beard. The description figuratively means that the Christ's soul is so pure, with no sin and light that it levitates by itself, requiring no hair to reach the heavenly kingdom.

Then John goes to a mountain great and high, meaning the philosophical sphere, and sees the fiancée, Jesus' wife, all "shining with the glory of God, and its/her brilliance was like that of a very precious jewel, like a jasper, clear as crystal" (Rev 21:11). The sphere of destiny in the new Jerusalem is made of jewels and stars and planets and lower rulers have power no more and cannot deceive, because the lantern will be the Jesus' teaching. Of course, this is an image of the earthly state spreading from the Upper Egypt to Caucasus and from Bosporus to the mouth of the Euphrates. This is the land where the God's people will dwell after the fateful battle and outside of which will remain "the dogs, those who practice magic arts, the sexually immoral, the murderers, the idolaters and everyone who loves and practices falsehood" (Rev 22:15).

A really extraordinary description of the Sophia's wedding is in the apocryphal *Acts of Thomas*:

> The damsel is the daughter of light, in whom consisteth and dwelleth the proud brightness of kings, and the sight of her is delightful, she shineth with beauty and cheer. Her garments are like the flowers of spring, and from them a waft of fragrance is borne; and in the crown of her head the king is established which with his immortal food (ambrosia) nourisheth them that are founded upon him; and in her head is set truth, and with her feet she showeth forth joy. And her mouth is opened, and it becometh her well: thirty and two are they that sing praises to her. Her tongue is like the curtain of the door, which waveth to and fro for them that enter in: her neck is set in the fashion of steps which the first maker hath wrought, and her two hands signify and show, proclaiming the dance of the happy ages, and her fingers point out the Gates of the City.[16] Her chamber is bright with light and breatheth forth the odour of balsam and all spices, and giveth out a sweet smell of myrrh and Indian leaf, and within are myrtles strown on the floor, and garlands of all manner of odorous flowers, and the door-posts are adorned with freedst.
>
> And surrounding her her groomsmen keep her, the number of whom is seven, whom she herself hath chosen. And her bridesmaids are seven, and they dance before her. And twelve in number are they that serve before her and are subject unto her, which have their aim and their look toward the bridegroom, that by the sight of him they may be enlightened; and for ever shall they be with her in that eternal joy, and shall be at that marriage whereto the princes are gathered together and shall attend at that banquet whereof the eternal ones are accounted worthy, and shall put on royal raiment and be clad in bright robes; and in joy and exultation shall they both be and shall glorify the Father of all, whose proud light they have received, and

---

16. The hands show the divided world, the world of contrasts, and the gate to New Jerusalem.

are enlightened by the sight of their lord; whose immortal food they have received, that hath no failing, and have drunk of the wine that giveth then neither thirst nor desire. And they have glorified and praised with the living spirit, the Father of truth and the Mother of Wisdom.[17]

This hymn in an exceptionally beautiful way describes the marriage of Sophia and Christ. This is a common motif found in a large number of gnostic texts. In this marriage the cosmic Sophia returns to the world of light and unites with it. This happened in the great fulfillment but, mystically, this happens to anyone who unites with their own higher self. Same as when in the fulfillment of the universe, the soul of the world unites with the mind of the world, so in perfection a single soul unites with itself.

The bride is the daughter of the pleroma of light—she represents the majesty of the kings, the masters of the world of light. Above her, in the kingdom of light, sited is the King of Glory, Christ, giving the food of immortality to the souls (pneumatics) worth invitation to the marriage ceremony.

In this high initiation the entire pleroma (thirty-two eons) sings songs, celebrating the victory. These are only the perfect souls that can put the language of wisdom into motion in the glory of the God, only they can create the substance making these heights vibrate in the song of glory. The city is the pleroma, the bridal chamber is Pastos, shrine, sacred place, where the heavenly Jerusalem is initiated.

A cleaned soul is refreshed with seven pairs of powers or syzygies. While ascending, it takes with it twelve of them, its servants, its masters in the previous life, of which it liberated itself because no more it is bound with chains of desire. Now the twelve are her purified powers reflecting the Christ's light. In the phrase "both will enjoy pleasure and happiness," "both" relates to the soul reunited with its angel, the angel permanently looking at the Lord's face.

Astronomical motives are in the *Books of the Savior*, too: "It cometh to pass after these years, when the sphere of the Little Sabaōth (that is to say, Zeus) revolveth so as to come into the first æon of the Sphere, which is called in the world the Ram of Bubastis (that is to say, Aphroditē); when, then, she [Aphroditē] shall have come into the seventh house of the Sphere, which is the Balance, [it cometh to pass that] the veils between them of the Right and them of the Left are drawn aside, and there glanceth forth from the height, among them of the Right, the Great Sabaōth, the Good, [Lord] of the whole world and of all the Sphere. But before he glanceth forth, he gazeth down

---

17. *Acts of Thomas*

on the regions of Paraplēx [the ruler of the first daemonian hierarchy], that they may be dissolved and perish, and that, all the souls which are in her torments may be brought forth and again led into the Sphere, for they are perishing in the torments of Paraplēx."[18]

The extract ends with the pupils asking Jesus to be merciful to them: "Three by three, they went to the four sides of the heaven, announcing the good news of the Kingdom to the entire world. Jesus participates with them in the confirmation in signs and miracles with which he unites with them. So the God's Kingdom was announced on the entire earth and the entire world of Israel, and this is a testimony for all the peoples from the east towards the west."[19] The seven planetary rulers and their seven emanations, the spheres of destiny (the twelve signs of the zodiac) so far were Sophia's master, and now she has the power over destiny; the thirty-two powers are astrological powers serving her, then all the lower regions moved toward the west, left of the Sun's and the Moon's circles.

The Sun's circle is presented symbolically as a large dragon with its tail in its mouth, with seven powers, driven by four horse-like creatures. The Moon's wagon is presented as a ship, whose rudder or steering oar are two dragons, male and female, pulled by two oxen and steered by a child at the stern, at the bow there being a face of cat.

Then in the *Books of the Savior* Jesus, whose secret name is Aberamentho, calls the name of the Father of the first curtain, saying, "Let all the mysteries of the rulers, authorities, archangels, and all the powers and all the works of the Invisible Gods [their three mystery-names being given] withdraw themselves and roll themselves on to the right."[20]

And Jesus with his pupils rose from the face of the earth into the air space, the middle path, and came to the first order of the middle path. Here the pupils are taught on the nature of this area and its rulers. They are told that above them there are twelve eons, six of them ruled by Iabraoth and six by Adam. The six eons under Iabraoth repented and practice the mysteries of light, wherefore he took them to Ieou, "the father of my father," to the clean atmosphere near the Sun's light. The six under Adam rejected the secret of the light and lived in sexual intercourse, creating rulers and archangels, angels and demons. Therefore Ieou placed them in the sphere of destiny (zodiac). In each eon there are 360 and 1,800 (1,800 = 360 x 5) of them. Above them Ieou placed five great rulers: Cronus, Ares, Hermes, Aphrodite, and Zeus.

18. Mead, *Fragments of a Faith*, 512–3.
19. Mead, *Fragments of a Faith*, 510.
20. Mead, *Fragments of a Faith*, 509–10.

Their sinless names are given. Zeus is the ruler of four, because Ieou says, "They are to rule the world and the eons of spheres." Zeus is good, and the revolution of the other four ruling forces lasts three months (seasons) each to avoid injustice. Zeus himself rules two eons.

This relates to the order of the sphere of destiny, but Mary, appearing in this summary as the main questioner, wants to know more about the Middle Path, at which they are, and that lies below the sphere of destiny, placed above the world of passion. She prays the Savior to be merciful to them and to allow the receivers to take the soul to the judges of the middle path.

The teacher, in his reply, promises to give them all the knowledge on the secret of the twelve. All the mysteries promised to them by the source of light, on the eons and the rulers, their seals, their numbers, and the ways of invoking to enter their regions; also the secret of the thirteenth eon (left); the secret of baptizing those in the middle; and the great secret of the source of light.

"I will give unto you all the mysteries and every gnosis, that ye may be called the Sons of the Plērōma, perfect in every gnosis and every mystery. Blessed indeed are ye beyond all men who are on the earth, for the Sons of Light have come in your time."[21]

These mysteries are kept in the greatest secrecy and are revealed to no one unworthy. They could be revealed only to the worthy alone, neither to father nor to mother, neither to sister nor to brother, to no relative, neither for food nor for drink, neither for woman nor for gold or silver, to no one in the world. Above them there are no magicians, those practicing various false rites, like those whose God is the son of the great ruler, Sabaoth Adamas—the enemy of the kingdom of the heaven, the master of six rulers who did not repent. Stated are their secret name and their monstrous shape.

The way to the heaven is not achieved only by deeds, but also by knowledge. The souls ascend by the spheres and before each of them they say the words allowing them passage to the next level. This is a motif similar to the Egyptian exegesis as stated in the Egyptian *Book of the Dead*.[22] The souls pass through seven doors and by twenty or twenty-one columns, where their past life is examined. This teaching is attributed to Cerinthus, who is also mentioned as a possible author of the Revelation. The time when he lived is somewhat after the time of John, and his activities were most probably at their peak at the end of the first century. There are certain stories about the contacts between John and Cerinthus, that is, a claim

21. Mead, *Fragments of a Faith*, 511.
22. Budge, *Book of the Dead*.

that John was appalled when he heard that Cerinthus was baptizing in the baths where he himself had been and from where he had escaped to prevent heaven from falling on him. Cerinthus is said to have taught an Egyptian teaching that, given the time, could mean therapeutic teaching and teaching connected with Philo. This would mean that he above everything placed the one and only God, above the world created in matter. Jesus is a man, the son to Joseph and Mary, and at his baptizing the Father came down to him in the form of a dove. Only after that Jesus began teaching. Before Jesus died on the cross, Christ had left him, whereafter to have resurrected, joined the pupils, and continued teaching. Before Cerinthus, and his predecessor Simon the Sorcerer, lived one Dositheus, about whom little is known and whose teaching is connected with the Essenes, and who around him gathered twenty-nine pupils and one woman, according to the number of days of one Moon's orbit (twenty-nine and a half, a trace that may have remained from the Valentinus's division to thirty eons including Sophia), as an obvious sign of worshiping the Moon. The Moon is the throne in the heaven on which someone is seated, the seated one being the Man, is one in being with the Man the Son of Man who gives John the book. The color of the Man is the color of jasper and sard, the minerals of the reddish-yellow color of the Moon. The emerald-colored rainbow around the throne, which is the Moon, is the aura that is important in astrological interpretations. The twenty-four thrones are the twenty-four emanations of the pleroma or the twenty-four eons, of which Sophia is the thirteenth. The elders seated around the throne on their thrones are dressed in white robes, same as the Son of Man who appeared to John at Patmos. This comparison means that every one of the twenty-four emanations of the pleroma, eons, looks like the Son of Man and that he in his hand holds a book that hides his secrets. Around the throne and in the center of the elders are four creatures with six wings each, or four sides of the world that are given six emanations each. In the prayer performed before the pupils, Jesus turns to the four sides of the world saying the mystic initials of the hidden god. Tetragrammaton is the symbolic translation of the savior's secret name, that according to the Semitic and the Caldean traditions consists of four letters. In the *Book of the Great Logos* he firstly shows them Ieou in his own nature, as a simple emanation from an indescribable Source that is the Father. The unusual combination of letters and signs is the "name" of that God according to the exterior signs that are outside his area—or in the twelve lowest, visible eons.[23] The lake before the throne is reflection of the pleroma. The John's fabulation is complete. The book held by the Man in his hand is the book

---

23. Mead, *Fragments of a Faith*, 518–46.

hiding the secrets of the eons, the seven spheres, the pleroma, and God. It contains secrets and prayers of all the levels required for a safe travel of the soul into the kingdom of light. Of course, this is also an image of the earthly Armenia and its throne on which seated is an Armenian, like Hayk in the ancient times, with twenty-four kingdoms at the four sides of the world, bowing down to the king of the kings and the master of the masters. The elders and the creatures are singing the song of the heavenly harmony in honor of the God.

Pistis Sophia

The holy dove is again Sophia or the soul of the world. According to Bardaesan, she had two daughters. Ephraim, a bitter enemy of the Bardaesans, says that they were called Shame of Waterless Dryness and Image of Water. Regardless of whether these are their real names or not, this is obviously about material water and creative water, certainly about terrestrial and sublunar areas. The name Pistis Sophia literally translates as Faith and Wisdom. This translation, however, is inadequate because Pistis is not faith but rather an intuitive knowledge helping Sophia to remain convinced that she will be saved and returned to the place from which she came. Jesus resurrected and taught the pupils for eleven years speaking about the First Mystery that is behind the curtain and before all other mysteries, Father in the form of dove: "I am come from that First Mystery, which also is the Last, the Four-and-Twentieth Mystery."[24]

The old wise men gave soul a female name. It is of female nature indeed. It even has the womb.

While she was together with the Father, she was a virgin and a male form. But when she fell into the body and descended into this world, she came to the hands of numerous outlaws. Fornicators were giving her to one another. Some raped her, some seduced her with gifts. She prostituted her body and gave herself to everyone, thinking someone would become her husband. When she prostituted herself, giving herself to unfaithful seducers who took advantage of her, she looked deeper and regretted. But even when she turned away from these seducers, she ran to others who talked her into living with them and serving them in the bed as her masters. With no shame, she did not dare leaving them, because they had been cheating her too long, pretending to be true, faithful husbands and respecting her, eventually to abandon her and go away.

24. Blavatsky, *Collected Writings*.

At that moment she became a poor, abandoned, helpless widow. Not a scoop of food did she have from the time when she had been in love. From them she received nothing but the dirt they had given her when she had sexual intercourses with them. Her giving birth with the seducers was stupid, blind, sick, and feebleminded.

But when she was visited by the Father who is in the height and having looked at her he saw her sighs and her suffering and misery, and that she regretted about the prostitution that she got into, and when she called his name to help her, saying with all her heart, "Save me, Father, I shall do everything for you. I shall leave the home and go away from my women's quarters. Take me with you." Then he saw her in that condition, and saw that she was worth the mercy, because after leaving her home she was exposed to numerous misfortunes.[25]

John's prostitute (Rome) did not repent, she still did not understand the transience of her glory, believing that the kings of the world will remain faithful to her. She says, "On the throne I sit a queen, and am no widow, and will never mourn!" (Rev 18:7).

The entire corpus of early Christian texts is full of images of the lost son, lost sheep, or souls gone astray repenting and asking for forgiveness. A solution must be found for such, because every soul is such, it wanders and seeks and when it finally finds, that is fulfillment. That is the soul of a pneumatic exploring the truth and not stopping until it is found, same as the soul went astray that does not stop until it finds its husband. Opposite of this is the soul that does not engage in searching but remains in the body, and this is the soul of the hylics. Their soul will avoid the traps of delusion, but will never feel the happiness of the truth, because the truth is the way that is to be searched for. The soul of the hylics is doomed to repetition.

Eusebius reports about John an almost biographical detail: that in his later age, upon returning from Patmos, in mountains he chased on horseback an escaped Christian who went rogue. Actually this is yet another version of the myth of Sophia, emphasizing the care and acting of priests, and John was a priest, for a soul that lost the faith. Certainly, opening the pleroma and promising the entering of light and souls into its kingdom of light, Michael's victory over the seducer, means lowering the stage down to the earth. The time of the consumption is close and the world is going to the final solution through a combat and more and more radical division. The pleroma is coming down to the earth, its flame, the fire coming out of the revelation, from the Word and the idea reflecting the Idea of idea, suffices to turn the world into ashes and a new world to be created on them, just

---

25. Robinson, *Exegesis of the Soul*.

because it exists in the Idea of idea and only from that idea, meaning that the world is created and is to be announced.

Many felt the call to spread the faith, since the apostolic times. The apostle Thomas Judas, or the Jesus' twin brother, says that he got India for his apostolic sphere of work. Initially Thomas did not want to go, but Jesus sold him as a slave to a merchant from the East, saying he was a fine carpenter, but there the money Judas received for royal projects he spent for food for the poor, building a live church (the apocryphal *Acts of Thomas*). John himself carries his understanding and his revelation to the churches in Asia Minor.

SYNTHESIS

The very beginning, "This is the revelation of Jesus Christ, which God gave Him to show His servants what must soon come to pass. He made it known by sending His angel to His servant John, who testifies to everything he saw. This is the word of God and the testimony of Jesus Christ. Blessed is the one who reads aloud the words of this prophecy, and blessed are those who hear and obey what is written in it, because the time is near" (Rev 1:1–3), is the announcement of an event soon to come, but the things are not that simple. In attempting to identify the author of this message (God, Jesus, or John) authors get mixed. At one moment one of them takes the dominant role, at another moment another one. The reply to the question of the author is clear: all the three are authors and all the three are telling their authorial stories simultaneously. The narrator, it can be said this is John, is telling all the three stories at the same time in symbols, and this is the main reason why the Revelation has remained an unsolved riddle for so long time. The Revelation is a story about cosmology, told by God, about eschatology told by Jesus, and about the earthly, human history in the focus of which is fighting for liberation from a stranger's rule and creation of a free state, and all three stories are told and compressed as a unique story told in symbols that are neutral, to reflect all the levels.

The applied aspect of the Revelation, related to the political history and events connected with the drama of the war in Armenia, is shaped in accordance with the above higher model that relates to cosmological and the soteriological levels as well. The theological and eschatological complex is legible as well and obviously, contrary to the previous statement that John's Christian education is superficial, it can be stated now that he is extremely resourceful and inventive, that he uses interpolations, but that not for a moment he abandons the matrix well-known to him.

The Revelation is a sequence of images that can be read at all the three levels:

	Cosmology	Eschatology	History
Rev 1:1–3	God	Jesus	John
Rev 1:4–3:22	Moon (omega)	Son of Man / Churches	John / John's community
Rev 4:1–5:14	Moon (alpha)	Man / Sophia	Armenia before Rome
Rev 6:1–17	Planets	Planetary spheres	Seven Roman emperors
Rev 7:1–17	Zodiac	Sphere of destiny	Jewish tribes
Rev 8:1	Moon (omega)	Son of Man	Future free Armenia
Rev 8:2–13	Seasons	Influence of planets	Powers of emperors
Rev 9:1–12	Sun and Venus eclipse on 31 May 48	Little Sabaoth	Great famine
Rev 9:13–21, 11:1–13	Gemini	Book given by angel	Army from Euphrates
Rev 11:1, 4–19	Moon	Son of Man	Armenia free at the end of the time
Rev 12:1–18	Transit of Venus on 23 May 60	Birth of the Savior	Armenia of Tigranes
Rev 13:1–18	Sun and Venus in Taurus	Nicolaites	Nero and Vologases
Rev 14:1–5	Moon in Virgo on 5 November 63	Pneumatics	John's army
Rev 14:1, 4–20	Moon in Virgo on 5 November 63	Word of Jesus	Treaty of Rhandeia
Rev 15:1–16, 20	Planets dawn on 5 November 63		Extended event
Rev 17:1–18	Moon and Venus on 6 November 63		Extended event
Rev 18:1–24	Moon eclipse on 17 July 64		Fire of Rome 18 July 64
Rev 19:1–20, 21	New cosmic cycle	Marriage of Christ and Sophia	New Jerusalem

Table 10. Comparison of meanings of the same events in the Revelation by the levels

Each of these three stories can be told independently, as the story told by the God, the story told by Jesus, and the story told by John. In these three levels evident is the basic idea of the Revelation: The universalism that appeared in the earliest development of the Christianity is a necessarily deducted philosophical conclusion on the unity of the spirit, the soul, and the mater, and that the world (universe) as a live composite resulting from the Idea of idea has the same destiny as the man and his soul.

The first level announced by God: God is the Idea of idea, archetypal idea, that in itself contains all ideas, and that creates ideas that create their own emanations. This is the image of the unknowable God standing at the top of the universe, encompassing everything as both spatially and timely, the largest principle from whose ideas created is the pleroma—the world of ideas. This world is totally unreachable and unknowable, every idea reflects from it like from a mirror, and it will reveal itself only in the end through the Christ's word. The next is the ethereal world, created by division of the upper and the lower waters by killing or dividing the primordial fish, Tehom or the Moon, of which made are the heavenly spheres, the planets, and the celestial sphere. Below and in it is the area of the aerial world, made of air, abyss, darkness and water. It is the reflection of the upper world, its image and itself are not alive but half-alive. In it dwell the immortal divine spirit and the death. For John this is a surprisingly convenient platform for connecting and building the second and the third levels. Astronomical events took place so that with no intervention they documentarily confirm all the levels, and on these the entire story can be exactly positioned.

The second level is the level of the Savior. John, the narrator, begins the Revelation from Jesus, introducing the exegesis that begins with the Son of Man and his syzygy, the church, through the First Man and his announcement given by the God at the beginning of the time. Both images show the starting point of the soul that is moving towards the kingdom of light (pleroma). The soul comes to the beginning, provided with the Adam's or the Noah's announcement and passes the spheres of the planets where it must know the secret passwords that will enable it to hide and pass unnoticed over the spheres of the heavenly archons, to come to the zodiac sphere (sphere of destiny). Here its deeds will be judged and it will return to the earth into the body it has deserved. No one entered this kingdom before Christ, because he is the first one to announce his mysteries and secure passage for the souls. The image of Algol, the ecliptic star that appears and disappears in the sky, is the image of the material world that is repeated and the connection with the Nero's and the Vologases's political confrontations that are not allowing the Armenian independence.

THE WAY OF THE SOUL

The Greeks expressed the real world by anthropocentric terms, for them the architecture of the universe being similar to the human anatomy. Such organized, live principle of the universe is denoted by the word Logos. It denotes the inner, intuitive understanding, but also the outer, oral expression of thinking. In the Hebrew literature, especially the Septuagint, Logos denotes the God's influence on the world through the words of prophets, through which the God communicates. For Plato and everyone who followed his teaching, body is an evil and dead thing, opposed to the idea. Philosophers are requested to neglect body and bodily desires and to focus on studying the phenomena, aimed to knowing the true and real God: learning this is the highest philosophical happiness. Philo follows Plato and interprets Logos as the divine mind which is the form of the forms, the idea of idea, or the final sum of forms and ideas. Logos is the indestructible form of wisdom: "But the seal is an Idea of Ideas, according to which God fashioned the world, being an incorporeal Idea, comprehensible only by the intellect."[26]

Philo transfers the experiences of the Greek philosophy to the Jewish mythology. The Greek philosophy synthesizes the Greek mythology at the philosophical level, which Philo is trying to apply to the Jewish biblical tradition. He contemplates that the visible world must be created in accordance with the image of the archetype existing in the divine mind and that it is created the same way as the man is created after the God's image in the biblical creation. Both the world and the man are reflections of the same, archetypal, highest idea: "The archetypal seal, which we call that world which is perceptible only to the intellect, must itself be the archetypal model, the idea of ideas, the Reason of God," thinks Philo. The invisible and incomprehensible world that logos took as the model of creation or shaping of the visible world from the existing unshaped matter existed always in God's mind: "The incorporeal world then was already completed, having its seat in the Divine Reason; and the world, perceptible by the external senses, was made on the model of it."[27] God cannot be in contact with the matter, he cannot take and work clay and from it shape a sculpture that he will later on breathe life into. God creates the world without an actual intervention, without touching the chaotic matter. He only introduced its shaping. This thinking brings Philo to contradiction. The question is whether the matter existed before God, which he, as a dedicated monist, cannot accept, or the matter too is created from idea, which cannot be, because idea is the agent

---

26. Yonge, *Works of Philo*, 493.
27. Yonge, *Works of Philo*, 10, 12.

of creation and everything bad that exists in the matter, its imperfection, would have come from the divine mind, which contradicts the divine nature, or has its own causation that is not God, which would mean that it is created ex nihilo, which contradicts his statement that "nothing comes from nonexistence and nothing returns to nonexistence." Philo as a dedicated monist cannot accept that anything had existed before and outside God.

Philo believes that Logos is "God's man" or "God's shadow." His model of the creation comes from Plato's *Timaeus*, but with changes and adaptations. For Philo, the direct agent of the creation is not God (Plato's Demiurge, the Creator) but Logos. Logos shapes the primary unshaped mater, turning it from the four primordial elements into shapes. Philo negates Aristotle's idea that comes, according to him, from a superstitious thinking that the world existed from the beginning: "For some men, admiring the world itself rather than the Creator of the world, have represented it as existing without any maker, and eternal, and as impiously and falsely have represented God as existing in a state of complete inactivity."[28] He introduces the theory of perpetual creation that was later on elaborated by Proclus in a single sentence: "The world is constantly created . . . it constantly begins existing"; the world is constantly beginning, but never actually to exist.[29]

But God is also the creator of the time and the father of the world. Even his son is older than time because he is the idea one in being with the Father. Time is God's younger son, given power over the material world, whereas Logos, exercising the right of the first born, remained with the Father. The Father and Logos are above the time, whereas the rest of the world is subordinated to his power.

The God acts and thinks at the same time; he creates while talking to the world, but the other way around as well, he talks about the creation in symbols and through the prophets. His thought is not older than the creation and there has never been any time when he has not been creating. On the first day he created the heavens, earth, air (darkness), empty space (abyss), water, soul (mind), light, the Sun, and stars. Here is a difference between Plato and Philo. Plato thinks that the space is not provided with intelligence, but that it has a special status. In God there are two primary powers: the power to rule and the power to create, mutually connected by Logos. The biblical cherubs are symbols of the two divine powers, whereas the burning sword is Logos. According to John this is a double-edged sword (two sided), two sides of the world are the two edges put together to make a sword—the sword is the metaphor of the united world that will be made by

---

28. Yonge, *Works of Philo*, 6.
29. "Philo of Alexandria," para. 9.

repression. In the Revelation the Lamb standing before the throne is reading the book that is in God's hand. The book is sealed inside and outside, the secrets in it are related to both the ontological and the eschatological levels. The Lamb opens the seals of the planets standing round it. The seals are the ideas by which they are created and in which their purpose is. The Lamb knows its mysteries and provides phrases and formulas that open the door either on the way of the soul through the planetary spheres or on the way of the pneumatic through seven cognitive levels of the inner universe. But angels call by sounding seven trumpets. They are the archons, rulers of living planets calling their emanations and their actions on the earth. They are the syzygies of the planets and the planetary pairs. Summer is the season when effect of the Sun is most intense, astrologically autumn is in harmony with Mars, winter with Mercury, spring with Venus. The fifth seal is the seal of the Little Sabaoth (who is good) and his emanation is the invasion of the locusts. The sixth is Saturn, and his emanation is the old world. When John speaks about the man whose name is 666, he says he is the emanation of the Sun and his syzygy. Perhaps the problems of the connection between the name of Vologases and the number of his name do not have to be solved in a literary gematric translation. The number of his name does not have to be deduced from a mathematical operation because it itself is, literally, the number of the Sun's name. Vologases is the master of the material, the hylic world, and the Moon on which the man and Sophia and her emanations reflect his false glow, same as the lower eons reflected and with which they seduced Sophia.

JOHN

The comparison of the language and the style of the Revelation, the Gospel According to John and the John's Epistles, show beyond doubt that the author of the Revelation is not the author of the other two texts. Evidently, John's theology in the Revelation is not the theology of John's Gospel, by neither the idea, the style, or the contents. John's Gospel treats Jesus as a historic person, same as all other gospels do, whereas in the Revelation he is a heavenly person appearing only in the function of a supernatural, higher creature, who carries a message from the heaven, but does not teach like Christ the teacher, living among the pupils and telling them the parables. The Revelation mentions neither the apostles nor Jesus' surroundings and does not quote him. In the Revelation Christ is an abstract supernatural creature who has only one divine message.

Comparison of the languages of the Revelation and of other texts signed by the name John (Gospel and Epistles) shows differences that could not have resulted from a possible additional learning and mastering the language, that would mean that the Revelation was written before the Gospel, and that in the meantime the author advanced in his knowledge of the Greek language. This assumption is not realistic because the Revelation is written by an exceptionally educated person who was not only familiar with, but was an exceptional expert in, numerous skills and scientific fields of the time. He had to be advanced in years to have had the authority listened to in distant lands, far from his homeland. He was a man that must have been heard of to be accepted and listened to and must have had undisputed reputation in a circle much wider than the one where the people of his time usually ran. John knew the history and the politics of the time half a century before the time in which he wrote and which he testified when connecting the Nicolaites and the events repeated in his time. He was educated in the spirit of the Greek philosophy, close to the Platonism, knew Hesiod, Plato, and Philo. He used excellently the texts of Zend Avesta, knew what Berosus had spoken, and accepted the ideas of Antipatrus. He knew the Egyptian mythology. He was a master in astronomy, able precisely to measure positions of planets and stars, and to foretell by these. He probably wrote and used the ephemerides. His knowledge and skills were fascinating and it was obvious that he could not have acquired all that reputation and intellectual capital right away, in his youth, but it is certain that the author of the Revelation at the time when this text was written was in his mature years. It is hard to believe that he learned and overcame the imperfections in his Greek language, vocabulary, and style to the level used by the author of the Gospel only later on. On the other hand, John's energy and resoluteness produced in his book and his entire project speak for a man in his full intellectual power, still far from his old age.

John of the Revelation and John the author of the Gospel could have been the same person, perhaps and only if the Revelation was written by someone else after the model that person had heard from John. This person could have spoken Greek less and could have left his personal and not John's trace in the manuscript, causing him to differ from the evangelist. This speculation is totally impossible because the Revelation is an exceptionally complex and integrated text that could have been written only by a person who had witnessed these events, who had sufficient knowledge and inventiveness to interpret them and compose a story so complex in meanings.

By all the elements, John was a freely and independently thinking man who built his story and acted on his own. He was a member of no theological group and was probably not an apostle, because he did not lean on Christ's word, which he would have heard and followed as an apostle. On the contrary, John built an idea of his own. The Revelation is no apology but an author's story, using elements of religious teachings and philosophies as required. From a reconstruction of the Revelation emerges the author's personality. He is a man calling for sacrifice for higher causes, and speaking on the dignity of a nation, on the pneumatics, those dressed in white robes. If he wanted to be reliable, he was to prove that by his own living. John certainly had the reputation of a philosopher who followed high standards brought by philosophic living. By his education he must have come from a wealthy family that had cultural interests and respected education. The family must have had money for his studies. Only such an environment could have offered John enough time for developing his interests. His reputation must have been extraordinary, because it opened doors for him and people listened to him. Otherwise he could not have reached them.

The earlier stated assumptions that he was not a Jew but an Armenian are based on his knowledge of the Armenian mythology and geography and his placing Armenia in the center of the events, while following with great interests the events during the Roman-Parthian War. However, he as an engaged man, probably provided with enough money and time to travel, could have learned all these information even as a Jew. Furthermore, he described the events that had happened in Israel in the year 48, the accession year of Marcus Julius Agrippa and of the great famine. In the beginning of the Jewish war his interests turned again towards Israel and he called for a united politics and a war alliance with Armenia, which never occurred because Armenia in these events remained totally passive. It is therefore perfectly logical to assume that he was a wealthy man, educated at various places and traveling a lot. This profile is absolutely contrary to that of John son of Zebedee.

All in all, John could have been a coeval of Jesus Christ and, as a member of the higher class, must have been in Jerusalem, either permanently or at times, but as a man interested in religion and the destiny of his people, he did not know the physical Jesus Christ. This is obvious when he speaks about the coming of Messiah, which is the common place of the Jewish believing, who is to appear at a moment when the providence so decided.

The basic idea of the John's theology is God's Word, the Logos, or the book held in his hand by the Man who was at the beginning of the time. This is the secret and the mystery of the shape according to which the world is created, and this secret is held in his hand by God himself. The Son of Man is the one who comes at the end of the time, and who knows the first and the twenty-fourth mysteries that are a single mystery, because he is the Savior and the Last Mystery, one in being with the First Mystery that is his Father at the beginning of time and with which he is one in being. This is, strangely, the clear theology of the beginning of the Gospel According to John: "In the beginning was the Word, and the Word was with God, and the Word was God. He was with God in the beginning. Through him all things were made; without him nothing was made that has been made" (John 1:1–3).

John's Revelation does not speak about an embodied Christ but only about the divine one, in all other elements, however, the idea is the same.

Around God there are twenty-four mysteries, they being twenty-four pleroma emanations. From the creation of the world and coming of the Savior in power there have been seven planets and their emanations, seasons, ruled by Little Sabaoth, above him being time and, finally, the Savior, the Son of Man, with his pair—the church, which is responsible about keeping and carrying his word. Above everything is the sphere of destiny with twelve archons (apostles), above all this being the pleroma.

Similar to Plato's spheres and division to the impure matter and the pure idea, this is a theology allegorized in the gospels, and John follows the same matrix. The echoes of the Plato's philosophy are undoubted, and John's theology in the Revelation and the beginning of the Gospel of John appear to be based on the foundations set by Philo in Alexandria.

Philo

Philo came from a respected Alexandrine family. One of his brother's sons was the first husband of the Queen Berenice, another, Tiberius Julius Alexander, was the procurator of Judea in 46–48. In the year 40 Philo led the Jewish delegation from Alexandria to Caligula, where they were to justify the activities of the Jews in the conflicts with the Greeks in Alexandria. Philo defended the Jews energetically, claiming the Greeks to be culpable about the conflicts and opposed the Caligula's intention to erect his sculpture in the temple in Jerusalem, arguing that this would cause a war.[30] The respect that Philo earned by this attitude made an immeasurable political capital that the Jews appreciated, whereas his and his family's reputation must have rose significantly. His brother, Alexander, respected his people's belief and tradition, that his children would abandon. Acting of Tiberius Julius Alexander was completely opposite to that of Philo, and Philo's opinion on this can only be imagined. In the beginning of the Jewish war another conflict occurred with the Greeks. From the assumed John's profile, John was an outstanding member of his community, by birth, education, and repute. These two portraits are mutually similar.

30. Josephus Flavius, *Antiquities*, bk. 28, ch. 8.

An essential difference between the two was the John's poorer knowledge of Greek. He built his own syntax, formed words, and used the Greek language in a particular way. On the other hand, Philo, although defending the Jewish position and habits, knew the Hebrew language very little. Philo's family lived in Alexandria for generations and was completely Hellenized. Philo, allegedly, understood but could not read Hebrew. An equidistance is to be assumed to have existed at both sides: as much as the John's Greek was poor, the Philo's Hebrew was even poorer.

Yet, the word about this wise man spread worldwide and his books were circulated among the literate Jews. John did not study in Alexandria, because his Greek would have been much better if he had, but he was able to read Philo's texts.

The first particularity and innovation of the Philo's philosophy is the assertion that God is not a creator. The world existed always, but God gave it the soul. In the Revelation God appears as the demiurge. He is the Moon from which the world was created and he is the God. They are metaphorically the same: both existed from the very beginning.

Philo adds to the Plato's model the soul that descends to the material world, from which only a philosopher's soul may rise and avoid transmigration and endless repetition, having found pleasure in the sky.[31] In the Revelation these are the souls of the pneumatics standing in the sphere of destiny, seduced by Algol to sin and transmigration, and accusing them before the God.

He divides the soul into three parts. The soul is breathed in as a divine substance, and Philo says, "While we are alive, our soul is dead and buried in our body like in a grave, but when we die, our soul will live its own life, freed from evil and dead body that it is connected to."[32]

Philo believed that the things not available to the senses or the mind could even be comprehended. Such a comprehension is the result of mental exercise, whereas in the theological aspect that is the feeling of unity with God in the sense of the space and time transcendence. The possibility of uniting with God can be achieved up to the level of the Logos. God is incomprehensive.

This is similar to the later teaching on the connection between the human intellect and the transcendental mind developed later on by Alexander of Aphrodisias and Ibn Rushd, differing from the Plotinus's teaching about uniting in an unspeakable One. The idea of transcendence origins from as early as Anaximander and exists in the Plato's idea of good. The

---

31. Yonge, *Works of Philo*, 289–90.
32. "Philo of Alexandria," §4; Yonge, *Works of Philo*, 20–21, 70.

main reason of the Philo's acceptance of the divine transcendence was his concept of the biblical tradition that God or his name is incomprehensible. In the Bible, God is presented as a bodily being. Therefore Philo makes difference between the bodily God, who can show himself, and his nature, which is incomprehensible. God's essence is outside any human experience and comprehension, wherefore it can be described only by stating what the God is not (*via negativa*) or depriving it of any sign of a perceptive object or placing it outside any mark that relates to the perceptive world, because the God's essence is his very existence.[33]

Philo asserts that the God's essence is one and unique, that it belongs to no species and that the God has neither sex nor species. Therefore nothing can be said about his qualities, and he is neither of the human form,[34] he is "free of particular marks."[35] In a strict sense, nothing can be said about God, neither affirmative nor negative: "Who can venture to affirm of him . . . that he is a body, or that he is incorporeal, or that he has such and such distinctive qualities, or that he has no such qualities? . . . But He alone can utter a positive assertion respecting himself, since he alone has an accurate knowledge of his own nature, without the possibility of mistake."[36]

Moreover, the real God's essence is incomprehensible, the only thing that can be said with certainty is that in his nature is that he acts: "Now it is an especial attribute of God to create, and this faculty it is impious to ascribe to any created being."[37] The instrument of his acting is the Logos, that at the same time is his mind. Although the God is hidden, he manifests himself through Logos. In the sensitive world, Logos manifests itself as the image of God, while on the other side it is "the archetypal model, the idea of ideas."[38]

This is why God's existence can be perceived, although his essence cannot be comprehended. Comprehension is possible by degrees and levels up to a certain point. The highest comprehension is that of God's unity, the second one of Logos as the ruling energy, the third understanding the material world.[39] The way into mystic experience is a proof of nothingness of the existing and of relinquishing the perception.[40] The mystic state produces a

33. "Philo of Alexandria," §7.
34. Yonge, *Works of Philo*, 55.
35. Yonge, *Works of Philo*, 58, 307.
36. Yonge, *Works of Philo*, 140–1.
37. Yonge, *Works of Philo*, 168.
38. Yonge, *Works of Philo*, 10.
39. Yonge, *Works of Philo*, 614, 786.
40. Yonge, *Works of Philo*, 368–9, 413–4, 455, 526–7.

sense of tranquility and stability, it happens suddenly and is described as the "sober drunkenness."[41]

God controls matter with his mind. His mind is not older than his creation and there has never been a time when he has not been creating. His mind did not exist before him; he is a permanently creating divine mind.[42]

Philo substantially changed Plato's teaching about shapes by introducing the idea that the God is permanently changing the world of ideas.

Philo compares the world with a town map in its designer's mind. The designer in his head has a model that cannot be shown and that can be explained by the mind only (the new Jerusalem). By this map he is building a town that is perceptive.

Philo says that with God everything is possible. But all the miracles are in line with the natural order and God cannot act outside these.

The most important part of Philo's teaching is the doctrine of Logos. In developing this doctrine Philo connected Greek philosophical concepts with the Hebrew religious thought, thus having set the foundations of the Christianity, firstly through Paul's teaching and in John's Gospel, later on in the teaching about the Hellenistic Christian Logos and the development of gnostic thought in the second century.

The Symbolism of the Revelation

In the Jewish tradition, the Logos is a channel through which God conveys his will to the prophets, which he does in symbols. John's vision is concrete, he sees announcement of the events shown to him by the Son of Man. Philo identifies shapes and the God's powers directly. The powers are his glory, visible and comprehensible only to the purest mind. These are thunders, lightnings, and voices coming from God's throne. God has two powers: the power to create and the power to rule (the throne in the heaven and the book held in his hand). He is the one in whose mind exists the new world—new Jerusalem, he is the king of kings. The God's powers descend by the spheres, becoming weaker and invisible as they pass the lower spheres. At the lowest sphere, the sphere of iron, the Spirit (Logos) descends into the material world, in the last stage to become a mixed world or a world where the Spirit is mixed with iron.

Philo accepts the Plato's forms. Forms are eternal, although their impression can disappear. They are not independently existing beings, they exist only in God's mind. Philo's complete rejection of the earthly and the

41. "Philo of Alexandria," §7.
42. Yonge, *Works of Philo*, 9, 639.

bodily life demands the philosophers to identify themselves with the idea. In the ideal form they are bodiless beings existing in the idea or in God's mind only. They identify themselves with him and together with him become not a great one, but the inhabitants of his kingdom. Philo gives the name the Son of God to the man who has dedicated his intellectual work to God.

The Philo's Logos has many names. He calls it Wisdom of Parable, Principle, Picture, Image of God. His names are secret, comprehensible only through meditation. John shows this image through the horse rider around whose belt is the name "Mystery." The entire earthly wisdom is a copy of the heavenly Logos.[43] Logos, similar to other archangels, is given the duty to protect the borders of the higher world. And Logos cheers, saying, "And I am standing between the God and you" (Num 16:48), because it is neither uncreated like God, nor not yet embodied like the man. For John it is an eagle flying in midair: "As I watched, I heard an eagle that was flying in mid-air call out in loud voice: 'Woe! Woe! Woe to the inhabitants of the earth, because of the trumpet blasts about to be sounded by the other three angels!'" (Rev 9:13).

God sends a ray of his wisdom to the men that changes the men and transforms them in the unchangeable wisdom: "And He who sits on the throne will shelter them with his presence. Never again will they hunger; never again will they thirst. The sun will not beat down on them, nor any scorching heat. For the Lamb at the center of the throne will be their shepherd; he will lead them to springs of living water. And God will wipe away every tear from their eyes" (Rev 7:15–17).

Logos is God's cup bearer remaining in the unmixed state, spreading around himself satisfaction and happiness.

Here John's Revelation can be reduced to a single, simple message. The historic events reopened old political questions, and John deems that he and other Jews, who are that, should act bravely and resolutely. They have to act like this because God in symbols showed his intentions. The theological and historic framework is an argument, whereas the true story is in the relationships between the Jewish fractions. This problem became crucial at the beginning of the Jewish war, when the defenders split into three quarrelling parties. John speaks about the policies backed by Nicolaus of Damascus and Philo of Alexandria, that is, this could be said to be a story of the conflicts between the Nicolaites and the Philoites on one side and John's followers on the other. The Nicolaites and the Philoites cannot see the obvious signs from the God, same as Balaam cannot see the angel in front of him while his donkey can. They are like Jezebel and Balak, those introducing and accepting

---

43. Yonge, *Works of Philo*, 56–57.

foreign customs and beliefs, while forgetting their own origin, faith, and language, the way this was done by the Hellenized Jews. The events will catch them unprepared and off guard.

John is an excellent astronomer, seeing and interpreting things clearly, and his message is perfectly clear. He sees the events that, according to Hierocles and Porphyry Polyhistor, are seen also by Apollonius of Tyana, the black mage whose prophesies are absolutely unacceptable. These events are seen also by Agabus from the Acts of the Apostles. He prophesied the hunger in the year 48, the captivity in the year 60, and the later martyrdom of Peter and Paul in Rome.

There are no additional arguments connecting these three persons and supporting any attribution of authorship of the Revelation to Apollonius of Tyana. The very complexity of this interpretation supports the thesis that this is one and not three different persons who saw the same events that developed through three different narrative channels. In his time Apollonius of Tyana enjoyed respect and authority to call the Jews and their communities to vigilance.

Philostratus in his *Life of Apollonius of Tyana* claims that Apollonius knew all languages, that he had understood them before anyone spoke. Recent scientific analyses of Apollonius's letters come to conclusion that he was not a native Greek speaker and that he did not know the Greek language very well, which would correspond to the language in which the Revelation is written. Also, the Apollonius's usual passing messages corresponds to the Revelation where John writes letters to the churches in Asia Minor.

Over a hundred of Apollonius's letters have been preserved, where the author identified himself as a Tyanean, saying about himself that he is a Neopitagorean and a mage. Most of the letters were written around the mid-second century, but they contain older elements, some of them perhaps actually related to Apollonius. In the time of Severus, Apollonius was raised into an imperial cult.[44]

---

44. Magie, "Severus Alexander: Part 2," 235–36.

Summary

It is needless to mention how important and influential text John's Book of Revelation is. Statements in the secondary literature on the date when the book was written, at the times of Domitian, Nero or, as stated by Epiphanius of Salamis, those of Claudius, are just various authors' subjective opinions that cannot be taken seriously into consideration when solving this enigma. Therefore, in this interpretation a completely different method is applied.

The Revelation is listed as one of the *Antilegomena*. There are two reasons for this, resulting in two different interpretations, from which a third one can be made that will bring us to the preliminary definition of this book.

1. The Book of Revelation is hard to follow because it comprises not one but three fragmentary and mutually interlaced stories told in images. One story is cosmological, the second historical, and the third eschatological. All the three stories are structured in the same way, and each of them contains implicitly or explicitly all the three levels. Thus, the Book of Revelation is introducing the idea of unity of the cosmological, the terrestrial and the eschatological histories.

2. From one image to the next, the characters are completely transformed, following them becoming impossible, but everything that is described in the same way in the book indeed is the same. But the attention is to be paid to the accessories. For instance, at Patmos John sees the Son of Man and describes him in an integral text that may be divided into seven epithets. The epithets are conveyed to the one who dictates to John the letters to the churches in Asia Minor connecting them mutually this way, this meaning that the Son of Man at Patmos is the same person who dictates the letters to John. It is to be noticed here that each of them holds a key, one key that can be used to open or close something by no one except the person holding it, and the other the key of death and Hades. The keys connect them, but the key is also held by the star with the key of abyss and the angel with the keys of

abyss that closes the devil in the abyss for a period of a thousand years. This means that these four characters are identical, that is, that the Son of Man at Patmos is the same as the one dictating the letters to the churches in Asia Minor, that this is the same person as the star with the keys of the abyss, and as the angel with the keys of the abyss, and that all of them are the same person, but at different levels.

3. John wants to communicate and he emphasizes the important points in the text by using the term *mystery* to attract particular attention of the readers. He does this three times. The first time when he says, "This calls for wisdom. Let the person who has insight calculate the number of the beast, for it is the number of a man. That number is 666" (Rev 13:18). The man with the number 666 is at the historical level, a real person of the John's time. He does this for the second time when mentioning the rider on the white horse riding on a cloud, on his thigh being written the name mystery (Rev 19:12,16). Since the thigh is at the middle of the human figure, John wants to tell us that the rider is at the middle, the eschatological level. He does this for the third time when he mentions the woman prostitute with the name mystery written on her forehead (Rev 17:5), meaning that the woman is at the highest, the cosmological level, that is, she is the star. Here John made a transversal by marking one person at each level, but each of them having their counterparts at the other two levels. The man at the terrestrial level has his counterparts at the eschatological and the cosmological levels, the rider on the white horse has his counterparts at the terrestrial and the cosmological levels, whereas the woman-star has her counterparts at the eschatological and the terrestrial levels. Each story has three main characters.

John's Book of Revelation is a story made of three interlaced and interconnected stories: eschatological, cosmological, and terrestrial, told in images. Each image contains, implicitly or explicitly, all the three levels. At each level there are three main characters. The method used in interpreting the story is iconography with particular accent placed at the accessories.

Certainly, the most intriguing part of the Revelation is the sequence of the seven seals. Since everything in the Book is at the same time at the eschatological, cosmological, and terrestrial levels, the sequence of the seven seals are to be interpreted as the cosmological level as seven stars, that is, the seven planets known at the John's time, and they are in this order:

1. The rider on the white horse with a bow is the conqueror, Sol Invictus.
2. The second, with a sword, is Mars.

3. The third, selling wheat and barley at high prices, is the merchant Mercury.
4. The fourth, followed by the death and Hades, is Venus, the mother who together with the life also gives her children the death.
5. The fifth is the god of order and justice, Jupiter.
6. The sixth is Saturn.

Now it remains perfectly unclear why John does not mention the seventh seal that, by elimination, should be the Moon, but only says that when the Lamb opened the seventh seal there was silence in the heaven for about half an hour. However, John does not mention the seventh seal because he mentioned it earlier in the chapter 4. John sees the heaven open and in it a throne with someone sitting on it. This is the description of the Moon Alpha that is identical to the Moon Omega that is at the end of the order, wherefore John cannot describe it. Since Moons Alpha and Omega are identical, only the description of the Moon Alpha in the chapter 4 can be copied and added to the description of the Moon Omega or omitted, which John actually did.

Nicolaus of Damascus says that the Jews worshipped Moon and placed it at the beginning of all things. Berosus claims that at the beginning was Omoroca, Um Uruk, Mother of Uruk, also called Tiamat, Tehom, Thalassa, or Moon. The Seven Tablets of Creation (Enuma Elish) says Bel Marduk split Tiamat in halves and made the upper waters of one half, the lower waters of the other, and of the rests he made seven planets and among the last the very Moon. The most direct connection of the Revelation is that with Zend Avesta and the *Book of the Angel Vohuman*. Vohuman, same as John, divides the history into seven periods, ruled successively by seven rulers. Over the time, the world is getting worse and worse, and in the final, the seventh, period, when the situation becomes unbearable, comes the Zarathustra's third son, with whom the time stops and a new period begins. At that moment the righteous will resurrect and the world will disappear in flames. John states there are 144,000 righteous, because here he made a substitution, replacing the Jewish tribes from which the righteous come, here thinking of the twelve zodiac signs replacing each other over 12,000 years, this totalling to 144,000 months. This is the duration of the Mazdaean era, which shows how much the Revelation leans on the Mazdaean beliefs. The true analogy is the *Book of the Angel Vohuman* with which this book is connected.

However, a real interpretation of the sequence of the seven seals is somewhat more complex. In the description of Moon Alpha there is the image of a throne with someone sitting on it, around whom there are four living creatures in the shapes of an ox, a lion, formerly an eagle now scorpion, and a man, that is, Aquarius. These are the so called four solid zodiac signs, placed one opposite the other and closing a square above the zodiac. Also, they are the signs that do not touch the solstice and the equinox points, having the most pronounced seasonal characteristics.

The first creature, the lion, is calling the Sun—"Come!"—and when the Sun enters Leo, this is the true summer and this sequence now is linked to the first trumpet—which is when plants die from heat and drought.

The second creature, formerly eagle now scorpion, is calling Mars, and when Mars is together with the Sun in the Scorpio, which is the true autumn, the weather is turbulent and, of course, we link it to the second trumpet. Those at seas perish because in autumn, at the *dies navalis navigationis*, sea navigation is stopped because the weather conditions are unstable and the sea is rough. Extraordinary is the description of Mercury selling wheat and barley at high prices, because if Mercury is in Aquarius, the winter will be unusually harsh and famine will occur. Knowing that, Mercury buys wheat and barley at the time of the harvest, stores these, and waits for the famine to occur to be able to sell them dearly. But cold makes harm to neither oil nor wine but conserves them. At that time, water springs turn bitter, that is, they freeze. The fourth—Venus in Taurus followed by death and Hades—is exceptionally fertile and fruitful, and at that time the life drizzles to the earth like rain.

So, this is about the four horsemen of the Apocalypse, and they are actually the four seasons, each of them given power over one fourth of the earth to kill with sword, hunger, plague, and earthly beasts.

The connection between the cosmological and the terrestrial levels is hard to notice. John only says that at the end there will be the judgment day battle and that this battle will be at the end of the time, which at the cosmological level corresponds to the time of the Moon Omega, that certainly does not provide sufficient arguments to understand the context, unless the previous scheme is followed up. So, the judgment day battle takes place at the end of the time, at the time of the Moon Omega, and the Moon Omega is identical to the Moon Alpha. The story says that Armageddon was at the beginning and at the end of the time. Already in the chapter 4 John mentions the throne with someone sitting on it, and the someone is the Moon. John sees the Moon's throne or the Aramaic Athor Anahta, which is the hypocoristic of Armenia. John is saying that at the beginning was Armenia and at the end will be Armenia. The word "Harmagedon" origins from the Aramaic *har, hara*, meaning "mountain," and the name of the mountain Massis or, according to Strabo, Massius. The present day name of the mountain Ararat at that time denoted the area around Massis, and not the very mountain ("let the horsemen attack like hairy locusts from the kingdoms of Minni, Ashkenaz and Ararat"). The two highest peaks of Mount Ararat are still called Greater Massis and Little Massis. Armasis is the name of the mountain and Harmagedon of the area around the mountain, that is, Armenia (Mithridates is mentioned as the king of Armadoeiron). Now the chronological order can be clearly established. In the beginning, at the time of the Moon Alpha, there was powerful Armenia. At the time of the First Triumvirate it fell under the rule of Rome (Pompeius). The first king is Caesar, the second Augustus, the third Tiberius, the fourth Caligula, the fifth Claudius, and this is the sequence of five fallen kings. The time when the Book of Revelation was created was the time of the sixth king, Nero, after who the seventh will come to stay shortly, when the Armenian Kingdom (New Jerusalem) will be established once again.

The Book of Revelation mentions four events that can be reconstructed and dated to a minute. The first event took place when the star appeared with the keys of Abyss (the Moon) and when appeared smoke like from a large furnace—the solar eclipse, that took place near the star Abaddon or Apollyon (the star Castor—Castor and Pollux are the Greek Apollo and Heracles), which happened on 31 May 48 (double eclipse, the Moon covered the Sun, and the Sun covered Venus at the same time). Astrologically this means that the Sun will burn the powers of both the Moon and the Venus, two female planets of similar astrological characteristics—they give fertility and humidity, this meaning that at this time they will not be able to act, that will again result in draught and hunger.

The second event took place when the Moon entered Leo, Saturn entered Gemini, and at the period of time of Gemini.

1. The Moon roars like lion.

2. Two prophets: two olives and two lampstands. The olives symbolise the mortals, the lampstands the immortals. The two prophets are mortals and immortals at the same time, that clearly refers to Pollux and Castor. This indicates that the temple in the heavens is the zodiac sign of Gemini.

3. At one moment the prophets become witnesses. They saw something that they can testify about or they are witnesses in some legal matter, as the case is here. In the Jewish legal practice there are several legal contract forms, the most important being the so called sealed contract made in the presence of two witnesses. This means that Gemini are witnesses to a contract between the Heaven and the Earth, and that this contract is in the sixth seal, and this is Saturn (the sky rolled up

like a scroll). This shows that all of them gathered at the same place, that is, that Saturn entered the constellation of Gemini. Based on this the date of event described by John can be calculated:

a. Saturn revolves once in around 30 years. It remains in Gemini for around 2.5 years (30 years / 12 zodiac signs). Every time in the first century AD when Saturn entered Gemini this was after the period of Gemini, and left it before the period of Gemini. During the first century AD it was in Gemini three times, remaining there two years, which reduces the number of possible dates from one hundred years down to six. John's Book of Revelation is a chronicle, and the events are stated in their chronological order. Since the event that preceded this one is dated 31 May 48, only two pairs of years remain as possible: 59/60 and 89/90.

b. If it is the period of Gemini, the possible date can be reduced to four months: from 21 May till 20 June 59, from 21 May till 20 June 60, from 21 May till 20 June 89, from 21 May till 20 June 90.

c. If the Moon is in Leo, each month can be reduced to two and a half days, or the total of ten days during the entire first century. If it is the Lord's Day (Sunday), only one possible day remains, and this is 23 May 60.

On this day the transit of Venus took place, at the moment when Venus was in its sign, meaning that she was the queen of the zodiac—the crown of stars. The Moon is under her feet—the Moon is in Leo. According to the prophesies from Nergal-etir and Borsippa, the woman will give birth to a male child if the star Regulus is in the aura of the Moon. That was the case here. At exactly ten minutes past nine, when the Moon appears on the horizon, in the zenith appears red dragon, as John says, the devil, the prosecutor before the God, and the ancient serpent. And really, at ten minutes passed nine, exactly in the zenith is the star Algol, also known as Algul, Satan or Rash ha Satan (the Satan's head), and the ancient serpent Gorgon or Gorgonea Prima. Algol is the only ecliptic star known at the John's time.

The third event is when the woman goes to the desert for 1,260 days. Exactly 1,260 days after this event, that took place on 23 May AD 60, was 3 November AD 63, when in the afternoon an eclipse of the Moon and Venus took place in its bad aspect. Venus when setting is the protectrix of prostitutes and spreader of the venereal diseases.

The first event, the lunar eclipse of the Sun and Venus near the star Castor (31 May AD 48), can be interpreted, both iconographically and astrologically, to mean famine and war. This event happened in the inaugural year of Marcus Julius Agrippa and the great priest Ishmael ben Phiabi, when famine, riot, and military intervention in Syria did occur. In the Acts of the Apostles this event is mentioned as the famine prophesied by Agabus, which makes this a firm basis for establishing the chronology of the events described in the Acts of the Apostles, where it is stated, among others, that in that time St. Paul still persecuted the Christians, not having converted yet.

The second event relates to the mutual positions of the Sun, the Moon, and Venus. Here the Moon represents Armenia, the Sun Parthia, and Venus Rome. In the year AD 60 Rome intervened to protect Armenia against Parthia. At the same time Agabus prophesied captivity of the apostles in Rome.

The third event, where Rome covered Armenia (Moon and Venera Cloaca), spilling blood of the saint, relates to the Treaty of Rhandeia. By this treaty Rome took Armenia, and to its throne inaugurated the Parthian prince Tiridates. Peace was made against the interests of Armenia, although it did provide peace over the next fifty years, until the Trajan's first expedition of AD 115.

The fourth event took place on the day of the great fire of Rome, preceded that morning by the lunar eclipse, on 17 July AD 64.

John's Revelation story follows mutual eclipses of the Sun, the Moon, and Venus, which took place at that time in dramatic circumstances, and that could have happened in five possible ways:

- In the first event, of 31 May 48, there was a double eclipse. The Moon covered the Sun, and the Sun covered Venus (two ways).
- In the event of 23 May 60, Venus covered the Sun.
- On 3 November 63, the Moon covered Venus.
- The final event took place on 17 July 64, when in the morning there was a lunar eclipse, and on that day Rome was destroyed in a devastating fire, as God's punishment on Rome for betraying Armenia, which was given in the hands of the Parthian prince Tiridates.

The Book of Revelation was written at the very beginning of the Jewish war, before the Nero's death (the sixth king was still alive), and after Marcus Julius Agrippa had left Caesarea, between the spring of the year AD 67 and the summer of the year AD 68.

The Revelation is among the most interesting and the most influential texts of all times. Since the very beginning, the believers were resented to have prized this book over the Gospels, which are the only true revelations of faith. In all the contemporary mentions, the book is covered with a nontransparent veil, raising doubts about its orthodoxy since the very beginning, but the very book left certain trails in other literatures and other religious systems, at least at their superficial, iconographic levels.

John's visions were seen by many, they happened in the sky, but only a few were able to measure and interpret them exactly. These events are mentioned in the Acts of the Apostles by Agabus who, like John, could have been an expert and learned astronomer and astrologist. Lactantius and Eusebius on one side, and Hierocles and Porphyry on the other, quote Apollonius of Tyana who saw the same that is described by Agabus in the Acts of the Apostles. This may lead to the conclusion that this is one and the same person, that is, that the person who saw and interpreted these events and wrote the book on them could have been Apollonius of Tyana, mentioned in the Acts of the Apostles by the nickname Agabus, and who took the name John and left numerous letters behind. The Jews considered the members of the Herodian dynasty to be foreigners. Archelaus, whose advisor was Nicolaus of Damascus, was overthrown from the position of ethnarch due to cruelty and allegedly exiled to Lyon. Tiberius Julius Alexander, Philo's nephew, suppressed the Jewish uprising in Alexandria and later on commanded the Roman army during the destruction of the temple in Jerusalem. Marcus Julius Agrippa was also present at that event. Tigranes VI of Armenia was the grandson of Herod of Colchis and belonged to the same family. The protagonists of this story are members of the Herodian dinasty. John singles out Herod Antipas in his letter to the church in Pergamum, calling him "my faithful witness." Herod Antipas was the tetrarch who gladly listened to John the Baptist, and later on ordered his head to be cut off. He was also deposed and exiled until he was assassinated in AD 39.

Bibliography

Abu Ma'sar. "The Astrological Metaphors." Italian translation by Giuseppe Bezza. Translated by Daria Dudziak. Cielo e Terra, n.d. http://www.cieloeterra.it/eng/eng.testi.metafore/eng.metafore.html.

"The Acts of Xanthippe and Polyxena." In *The Ante-Nicene Fathers: The Writings of the Fathers down to A.D. 325* 9:203–17, edited by Philip Schaff, translated by W. A. Craigie. Grand Rapids: Christian Classics Ethereal Library, n.d. https://ccel.org/ccel/anonymous/acts_xanthippe/anfo9.

Agrippa von Nettesheim, Heinrich Cornelius. *Three Books of Occult Philosophy*. Philadelphia: University of Pennsylvania, n.d. https://onlinebooks.library.upenn.edu/webbin/book/lookupid?key=olbp10312.

Allen, James P. *Genesis in Egypt: The Philosophy of Ancient Egyptian Creation Accounts*. Yale Egyptological Studies, edited by William Kelly Simpson, vol. 2. New Haven, CT: Yale Egyptological Seminar, 1988.

Allen, Richard Hinckley. *Star Names—Their Lore and Meaning*. New York: Dover Publications, 1963. http://penelope.uchicago.edu/Thayer/E/Gazetteer/Topics/astronomy/_Texts/secondary/ALLSTA/home.html.

Aphrahat. *Demonstrations*. Translated by John Gwynn. Nicene and Post-Nicene Fathers: Second Series, edited by Philip Schaff and Henry Wace, vol. 13. Buffalo, NY: Christian Literature, 1890. Rev. and ed. by Kevin Knight. http://www.newadvent.org/fathers/3701.htm.

"The Apocalypse of Peter." In *The Ante-Nicene Fathers: The Writings of the Fathers down to A.D. 325* 9:141–47, edited by Philip Schaff. Grand Rapids: Christian Classics Ethereal Library, n.d. https://ccel.org/ccel/anonymous/apocalypse_peter/anfo9.

"The Apocalypse of Sedrach." In *The Ante-Nicene Fathers: The Writings of the Fathers down to A.D. 325* 9:175–180, edited by Philip Schaff. Grand Rapids: Christian Classics Ethereal Library, n.d. https://ccel.org/ccel/anonymous/apocalypse_sedrach/anfo9.

"The Apocalypse of the Virgin." In *The Ante-Nicene Fathers: The Writings of the Fathers down to A.D. 325* 9:167–74, edited by Philip Schaff. Grand Rapids: Christian Classics Ethereal Library, n.d. https://ccel.org/ccel/anonymous/apocalypse_virgin/anfo9.

"Apocrypha of the New Testament." In *The Ante-Nicene Fathers: The Writings of the Fathers down to A.D. 325* 8:347–598, edited by Philip Schaff. Grand Rapids: Christian Classics Ethereal Library, n.d. https://ccel.org/ccel/anonymous/apocrypha_nt/anfo8.

"The Apology of Aristides." In *The Ante-Nicene Fathers: The Writings of the Fathers down to A.D. 325* 9:259–79, edited by Allan Menzies, translated by D. M. Kay. New York: Charles Scribner's Sons, 1912. https://archive.org/details/antenicenefather09robe/page/n3/mode/2up.

Armstrong, James. *An Exposition of the Fulfilled Prophecies of the Apocalypse, from the First Seal to the End of Chapter XIX: In Three Parts*. Dublin: James M'Glashan, 1851. https://books.google.hr/books?id=iEFVAAAAcAAJ&printsec=frontcover&hl=hr#v=onepage&q&f=false.

Athanasius. *Select Works and Letters*. Nicene and Post-Nicene Fathers: Second Series, edited by Philip Schaff and Henry Wace, vol. 4. Grand Rapids: Eerdmans, n.d. https://ccel.org/ccel/schaff/npnf204.html.

Augustine, Saint. *The City of God*; *Christian Doctrine*. Nicene and Post-Nicene Fathers: First Series, edited by Philip Schaff, vol. 2. Grand Rapids: Eerdmans, n.d. https://ccel.org/ccel/schaff/npnf102.html.

———. *Homilies on the Gospel of John*; *Homilies on the First Epistle of John*; *Soliloquies*. Nicene and Post-Nicene Fathers: First Series, edited by Philip Schaff, vol. 7. Grand Rapids: Eerdmans, n.d. https://ccel.org/ccel/schaff/npnf107.html.

———. *Sermon on the Mount*: *Harmony of the Gospels*; *Homilies on the Gospels*. Nicene and Post-Nicene Fathers: First Series, edited by Philip Schaff, vol. 6. Grand Rapids: Eerdmans, n.d. https://ccel.org/ccel/schaff/npnf106.html.

Bardesan. "The Book of the Laws of Divers Countries." In *The Ante-Nicene Fathers: The Writings of the Fathers down to A.D. 325* 8:723–34, edited by Philip Schaff, translated by B. P. Pratten. Christian Classics Ethereal Library, n.d. https://ccel.org/ccel/anonymous/memoirs/anf08.ix.xvi.html.

Barr, David L. "Towards an Ethical Reading of the Apocalypse: Reflections on John's Use of Power, Violence, and Misogyny." Wright State University, n.d. http://www.wright.edu/~dbarr/moral.htm

———."Transforming the Imagination: John's Apocalypse as Story." Wright State University, 2000. http://www.wright.edu/~david.barr/Imagination.htm.

———. "Using Plot to Discern Structure in John's Apocalypse." *Proceedings of the Eastern Great Lakes and Mid-West Biblical Societies* 15 (1995) 23–33. http://www.wright.edu/~dbarr/plotrev.htm.

———."Who Says? Who Hears?: The Narrative Rhetoric of John's Apocalypse." Wright State University, 1998. http://www.wright.edu/~david.barr/rhet.htm.

"Berossus: From Abydenus; Of the Chaldaean Kings and Deluge." Internet Sacred Text Archive, n.d. http://www.sacred-texts.com/cla/af/afo4.htm.

"Berossus: From Alexander Polyhistor; Of the Cosmogony and Deluge." Internet Sacred Text Archive, n.d. http://www.sacred-texts.com/cla/af/afo2.htm.

"Berossus: From Appolodorus; Of the Chaldaean Kings." Internet Sacred Text Archive, n.d. http://www.sacred-texts.com/cla/af/afo3.htm.

"Berossus: From Josephus, &c." Internet Sacred Text Archive, n.d. http://www.sacred-texts.com/cla/af/afo5.htm.

Bethge, Hans-Gebhard, and Bentley Layton, translators. "On the Origin of the World." The Gnostic Society Library, n.d. http://www.gnosis.org/naghamm/origin.html.

Biguzzi, G. "A Figurative and Narrative Language Grammar of Revelation." *Novum Testamentum* 45.4 (2003) 382–402.

Blavatsky, H. P. *Collected Writings*. Wheaton, IL: Theosophical, 1991. http://www.katinkahesselink.net/blavatsky/articles/v13/.

Blocker, Wade, translator. "Hegesippus, Translated from Latin into English." Christian Classics Ethereal Library, 2005. http://www.ccel.org/ccel/pearse/morefathers/files/hegesippus_01_book1.htm.

Bloom, Harold, ed. *The Revelation of St. John the Divine*. New York: Chelsea House, 1988.

Boyce, Mary. "Middle Persian Literature." In *Handbuch der Orientalistik*, edited by Bertold Spuler, 1:3–66. Leiden: Brill, 1958. https://archive.org/details/MiddlePersianLiterature1968/page/n1/mode/2up.

Brashler, James, and Roger A. Bullard, translators. "The Apocalypse of Peter." In *The Nag Hammadi Library*, edited by James M. Robinson, 339–45. San Francisco: Harper & Row. 1981.https://archive.org/details/naghammadilibraroojame/page/338/mode/2up.

Buck, Adriaan de, ed. *The Egyptian Coffin Texts 5: Texts of Spells*. Chicago: University of Chicago Press, 1954.

Budge, E. A. Wallis, ed. *The Book of the Dead: The Papyrus of Ani*. Santa Cruz: Internet Sacred Text Archive, 2000. Orig. pub. 1895. https://www.academia.edu/63921957/The_Book_of_the_Dead_or_The_Papyrus_of_Ani_transl_E_A_Wallis_Budge_1895_

Budge, E. A. Wallis, and Sidney Smith, eds. *The Babylonian Legends of the Creation and the Fight between Bel and the Dragon, as Told by Assyrian Tablets from Nineveh*. London: British Museum, 1921. https://onlinebooks.library.upenn.edu/webbin/gutbook/lookup?num=9914.

Canter, H. V. "Conflagrations in Ancient Rome." *The Classical Journal* 27.4 (1932) 270–88.

Charles, R. H., translator. "The Ascension of Isaiah." Early Christian Writings, n.d. https://www.earlychristianwritings.com/text/ascension.html.

———. *A Critical and Exegetical Commentary on the Revelation of St. John*. Vol. 1. Edinburgh: T. & T. Clark, 1920. https://bibletranslation.ws/down/Charles-Revelation-Vol-1.pdf.

———. *A Critical and Exegetical Commentary on the Revelation of St. John*. Vol. 2. New York: Charles Scribner's Sons, 1920. https://bibletranslation.ws/down/Charles-Revelation-Vol-2.pdf.

———, ed. "Enoch, or the Book of the Secrets of Enoch." In *The Apocrypha and Pseudepigrapha of the Old Testament in English*, vol. 2, 425–69. Oxford: Clarendon, 1913. https://archive.org/details/cuaapocryphaandpoochar/page/n13/mode/2up.

"Chronicon Paschale: Olympiads 112 to 187." Attalus, n.d. https://www.attalus.org/translate/paschal.html.

"Chronological Listing of Parthian Rulers." Parthia, Feb 26, 2021. https://www.parthia.com/parthia_chrono.htm.

Chrysostom, Dio. "The Twenty-First Discourse: On Beauty." In *Discourses 12–30*, translated by J. W. Cohoon. Cambridge: Harvard University Press, 1939. https://penelope.uchicago.edu/Thayer/E/Roman/Texts/Dio_Chrysostom/Discourses/21*.html.

Chrysostom, Saint. *Homilies on the Acts of the Apostles and the Epistle to the Romans*. Nicene and Post-Nicene Fathers: First Series, edited by Philip Schaff, vol. 11. Grand Rapids: Eerdmans, n.d. https://www.ccel.org/ccel/schaff/npnf111.html.

———. *Homilies on the Epistles of Paul to the Corinthians*. Nicene and Post-Nicene Fathers: First Series, edited by Philip Schaff, vol. 12. Grand Rapids: Eerdmans, n.d. https://www.ccel.org/ccel/schaff/npnf112.html.

———. *Homilies on the Epistles to the Galatians, Ephesians, Philippians, Colossians, Thessalonians, Timothy, Titus, and Philemon*. Nicene and Post-Nicene Fathers: First Series, edited by Philip Schaff, vol. 13. Grand Rapids: Eerdmans, n.d. https://www.ccel.org/ccel/schaff/npnf113.html.

———. *Homilies on the Gospel of St. John and the Epistle to the Hebrews*. Nicene and Post-Nicene Fathers: First Series, edited by Philip Schaff vol. 14. Grand Rapids: Eerdmans, n.d. https://www.ccel.org/ccel/schaff/npnf114.html.

———. *Homilies on the Gospel of St. Matthew*. Nicene and Post-Nicene Fathers: First Series, edited by Philip Schaff, vol. 10. Grand Rapids: Eerdmans, n.d. https://www.ccel.org/ccel/schaff/npnf110.html.

Church, A. J. *The Story of the Last Days of Jerusalem: From Josephus*. London: Sheeley & Co. Limited, 1903. https://www.heritage-history.com/index.php?c=read&author=church&book=jerusalem&story=_front.

Clement of Alexandria. "Exhortation to the Heathen." In *The Ante-Nicene Fathers: The Writings of the Fathers down to A.D. 325* 2:171–206. Grand Rapids: Christian Classics Ethereal Library, n.d. https://ccel.org/ccel/clement_alex/exhortation/anf02.

———. "Instructor." In *The Ante-Nicene Fathers: The Writings of the Fathers down to A.D. 325* 2:207–98. Grand Rapids: Christian Classics Ethereal Library, n.d. https://ccel.org/ccel/clement_alex/instructor/anf02.

———. "Salvation of the Rich Man." In *The Ante-Nicene Fathers: The Writings of the Fathers down to A.D. 325* 2:589–605. Grand Rapids: Christian Classics Ethereal Library, n.d. https://ccel.org/ccel/clement_alex/salvation/anf02.

———. "Stromata, or Miscellanies." In *The Ante-Nicene Fathers: The Writings of the Fathers down to A.D. 325* 2:299–588. Grand Rapids: Christian Classics Ethereal Library, n.d. https://ccel.org/ccel/clement_alex/stromata/anf02.

Clement of Rome. "The Epistles of Clement." In *The Ante-Nicene Fathers: The Writings of the Fathers down to A.D. 325* 9, edited by Philip Schaff. Grand Rapids: Christian Classics Ethereal Library, n.d. https://archive.org/details/antenicenefather09robe/page/n3/mode/2up.

———. "The First Epistle of Clement to the Corinthians." In *The Ante-Nicene Fathers: The Writings of the Fathers down to A.D. 325* 1, edited by Allan Menzies. Grand Rapids: Christian Classics Ethereal Library, n.d. https://www.ccel.org/ccel/schaff/anf01.html.

Crafer, T. W., ed. *The Apocriticus of Macarius Magnes*. Translations of Christian Literature. London: Society for Promoting Christian Knowledge, 1919. Edited by Roger Pearse. https://www.tertullian.org/fathers/macarius_apocriticus.htm.

Cureton, William, ed. *Spicilegium Syriacum: Containing Remains of Bardesan, Meliton, Ambrose and Mara Bar Serapion*. London: Francis and John Rivington, 1855.

Darmesteter, James, translator. *The Zend Avesta, Part I: The Vendidad*. Oxford: Oxford University Press, 1880. https://www.academia.edu/49251092/The_Zend_Avesta_Part_I_tr_James_Darmesteter_1880_.

———, translator. "Hordad Yasht." In *The Zend Avesta, Part II: The Sîrôzahs, Yasts, and Nyâyis*, edited by F. Max Muller. Oxford: Clarendon Press, 1883. http://www.avesta.org/ka/yt4sbe.htm.

———, translator. "Vishtasp Yasht." In *The Zend Avesta, Part II: The Sîrôzahs, Yasts, and Nyâyis*, edited by F. Max Muller. Oxford: Clarendon Press, 1883. http://www.avesta.org/fragment/vytsbe.htm.

De Jong, Albert. *Traditions of the Magi: Zoroastrianism in Greek and Latin Literature*. Religions in the Greco-Roman World, vol. 133. Leiden: Brill, 1997. https://archive.org/details/TraditionsOfTheMagiZoroastrianismInGreekAndLatinLiterature/page/n1/mode/2up.

Dio, Cassius. *Roman History*. Vol. 1. Translated by Earnest Cary and Herbert B. Foster. Cambridge: Harvard University Press, 1914. https://penelope.uchicago.edu/Thayer/E/Roman/Texts/Cassius_Dio/62*.html.

Dionysius. "Against the Sabellians." In *Ante-Nicene Fathers: The Writings of the Fathers down to A.D. 325* 7:363–8. Grand Rapids: Christian Classics Ethereal Library, n.d. https://ccel.org/ccel/dionysius/sabellians/anf07.

———. "Extant Fragments of Dionysius." In *Ante-Nicene Fathers: The Writings of the Fathers down to A.D. 325* 6: 81–110. Grand Rapids: Christian Classics Ethereal Library, n.d. https://ccel.org/ccel/dionysius/extant_fragments/anf06.

Draper, John William. *History of the Conflict Between Religion and Science*. Urbana, IL: Project Gutenberg, 1998. https://www.gutenberg.org/files/1185/1185-h/1185-h.htm

Drower, E. S. *Ginza Rba: The Canonical Prayerbook of the Mandaeans*. Leiden: Brill, 1959. http://www.gnosis.org/library/ginzarba.htm.

———. *The Haran Gawaita and the Baptism of Hibil-Ziwa*. Vatican City: Bilioteca Apostolica Vaticana, 1953. http://gnosis.org/library/The_Haran_Gawaita_and_The_Baptism_of_Hibil_Ziwa_Drower.pdf.

———. *The Mandaeans of Iraq and Iran: Their Cults, Customs, Magic Legends, and Folklore*. 1937. Reprint: Leiden: Brill, 1962.

Droz, J. P., ed. *A Literary Journal*. Vol. 3. Dublin: S. Powell, 1745. https://www.google.hr/books/edition/A_Literary_journal_ed_by_J_P_Droz/H8IPAAAAQAAJ?hl=hr&gbpv=0.

Elliott, Edward B. *Horae Apocalypticae: Or, A Commentary on the Apocalypse, Critical and Historical; Including Also an Examination of the Chief Prophecies of Daniel*. Vol. 1. London: Seeley, Jackson, and Halliday, 1862. https://archive.org/details/HoraeApocalypticaeVol.1EdwardBishopElliott1862/page/n11/mode/2up.

———. *Horae Apocalypticae: Or, A Commentary on the Apocalypse, Critical and Historical; Including Also an Examination of the Chief Prophecies of Daniel*. Vol. 2. London: Seeley, Jackson, and Halliday, 1862. https://archive.org/details/HoraeApocalypticaeVol.2EdwardBishopElliott1862/page/n7/mode/2up.

Elliot, J. K., ed. *The Apocryphal New Testament*. Oxford: Oxford University Press, 2005.

Ephraim, Saint. *Prose Refutations against Mani, Marcion, and Bardaisan*. Vol. 2. London: Williams & Norgate, 1921. Edited by Roger Pearse. https://www.tertullian.org/fathers/ephraim2_0_intro.htm.

Epiphanius. *The Panarion of Epiphanius of Salamis*. Vol 1. Translated by Frank Williams. Leiden: Brill, 2009.

Espenak, Fred, and Jean Meeus. "Five Millennium Catalog of Solar Eclipses: -1999 to +3000 (2000 BCE to 3000 CE)." NASA Eclipse Web Site, 2007. https://eclipse.gsfc.nasa.gov/SEcat5/SEcatalog.html.

———. "Six Millennium Catalog of Venus Transits: 2000 BCE to 4000 CE." NASA Eclipse Web Site, 2007. https://eclipse.gsfc.nasa.gov/transit/catalog/VenusCatalog.html.

Eusebius of Caesarea. *Church History from A.D. 1-324*. Nicene and Post-Nicene Fathers: Second Series, edited by Philip Schaff and Henry Wace, vol. 1. Grand Rapids: Eerdsmans, n.d. https://www.ccel.org/ccel/schaff/npnf201.html.

———. *Praeparatio Evangelica (Preparation for the Gospel)*. Translated by E. H. Gifford. Oxford: Oxford University Press, 1903. https://www.tertullian.org/fathers/eusebius_pe_00_eintro.htm.

———. *The Proof of the Gospel: Being the Demonstratio Evangelica of Eusebius of Caesarea*. Vol. 1. Translated by W. J. Ferrar. London: Society for Promoting Christian Knowledge, 1920. https://ia802705.us.archive.org/15/items/proofofgospelbe01euse/proofofgospelbe01euse.pdf.

Farina, Luca. "The Greek Fragments of the Works of Māšā'allāh ibn Aṯarī." In *Mediterranea: International Journal on the Transfer of Knowledge* 7 (2022) 225–79. https://journals.uco.es/mediterranea/article/view/13659.

Firth, Florence M., ed. *The Golden Verses of Pythagoras and Other Pythagorean Fragments*. Hollywood: Theosophical, 1904. https://www.sacred-texts.com/cla/gvp/index.htm.

Flint, Valerie I. J. "Honorius Augustodunensis." In *Authors of the Middle Ages* 2, edited by Patrick J. Geary. Aldershot, UK: Variorum, 1995.

Ford, J. Massyngberde. *Revelation*. Garden City, NY: Doubleday, 1975.

Foxe, John. *Fox's Book of Martyrs, or A History of the Lives, Sufferings, and Triumphant Deaths of the Primitive Protestant Martyrs*. Urbana, IL: Project Gutenberg, 2007. http://www.gutenberg.org/files/22400/22400-h/22400-h.htm.

Gibbon, Edward. *The History of the Decline and Fall of the Roman Empire*. Vols. 1–6. New York: Harper & Brothers, 1836. https://www.gutenberg.org/ebooks/25717.

"The Gospel of Peter." In *Ante-Nicene Fathers: The Writings of the Fathers down to A.D. 325* 9, edited by Philip Schaff. Grand Rapids: Christian Classics Ethereal Library, n.d. https://ccel.org/ccel/anonymous/gospel_peter/anf09.

"The Gospel of Philip." Translated by Wesley W. Isenberg. The Gnostic Society Library, n.d. http://gnosis.org/naghamm/gop.html.

Gottheil, Richard, and Samuel Krauss. "Nicholas of Damascus (Nicolaus Damascenus)." Jewish Encyclopedia, 1906. http://www.jewishencyclopedia.com/view.jsp?letter=N&artid=271.

Grant, Robert M. *A Historical Introduction to the New Testament*. New York: Harper & Row, 1963. https://www.religion-online.org/book/a-historical-introduction-to-the-new-testament/.

Gregory of Nyssa. *Dogmatic Treatises, etc. (Select Writings and Letters)*. Nicene and Post-Nicene Fathers: Second Series, edited by Philip Schaff and Henry Wace, vol. 5. Grand Rapids: Christian Classics Ethereal Library, n.d. https://www.ccel.org/ccel/schaff/npnf205.html

———. *Sermones Volume 1: De vita Gregorii Thaumaturgi; De sancto Theodoro; In sanctum Stephanum I et II; In Basilium fratrum; In XL Martyres Ia, Ib et II*. Gregorii Nysseni Opera, edited by G. Heil et al., vol. 10.1. Leiden: Brill, 1990.

Guthrie, W. K. C. *Kasni Platon i Akademija*. Povijest grčke filozofije, knjiga 5, translated by Dražen Pehar. Zagreb: Naklada Jurčić, 2007.

Hanson, K. C. "Blood and Purity in Leviticus and Revelation." *Listening: Journal of Religion and Culture* 28 (1993) 215-30.

Haug, Martin, translator. "The Book of Arda Viraf." In *The Sacred Books and Early Literature of the East, Volume VII: Ancient Persia*, edited by Charles F. Horne. New York: Parke, Austin, and Lipscomb, 1917. Transcribed by Cris Weimer. http://www.avesta.org/mp/viraf.html.

Herodotus. *The History of Herodotus*. Translated by G. C. Macaulay. London: McMillan & Co., 1890. https://www.gutenberg.org/files/2707/2707-h/2707-h.htm.

Hesiod. "Hesiod: Works and Days." Translated by Hugh G. Evelyn-White. Internet Sacred Text Archive, 1914. https://sacred-texts.com/cla/hesiod/works.htm.

―――. "The Teogony of Hesiod." Translated by Hugh G. Evelyn-White. Internet Sacred Text Archive, 1914. https://sacred-texts.com/cla/hesiod/theogony.htm.

Hesiod, and Homer. *Hesiod, the Homeric Hymns, and Homerica*. Edited by Hugh G. Evelyn-White. Urbana, IL: Project Gutenberg, 2008. https://www.gutenberg.org/files/348/348-h/348-h.htm#chap27.

Hippolytus. "On Christ and Antichrist." In *Ante-Nicene Fathers: The Writings of the Fathers down to A.D. 325* 5, edited by Alexander Roberts et al., translated by J. H. MacMahon. Buffalo, NY: Christian Literature, 1886. Rev. and ed. by Kevin Knight. https://www.newadvent.org/fathers/0516.htm.

―――. "The Refutation of All Heresies." In *Ante-Nicene Fathers: The Writings of the Fathers down to A.D. 325* 5, edited by Alexander Roberts et al., translated by J. H. MacMahon. Grand Rapids: Christian Classics Ethereal Library, n.d. https://ccel.org/ccel/hippolytus/refutation/anf05.

Housman, A. E. "Manilius, Augustus, Tiberius, Capricornus, and Libra." *The Classical Quarterly* 7.2 (1913) 109-14. https://penelope.uchicago.edu/Thayer/E/Journals/CQ/7/2/Manilius_Augustus_et_al*.html.

Idatius Aquae Flaviensis. *Chronicon*. Patrologia latina, vol. 51. Edited by J. P. Migne. Paris: Excudebat Migne, 1846. https://artflsrv04.uchicago.edu/philologic4.7/PLD/navigate/5984/table-of-contents

―――. *Descriptio consulum*. Patrologia latina, vol. 51. Edited by J. P. Migne. Paris: Excudebat Migne, 1846.

Ignatius of Antioche. "Epistles of Ignatius." In *Ante-Nicene Fathers: The Writings of the Fathers down to A.D. 325* 1. Grand Rapids: Christian Classics Ethereal Library, n.d. https://ccel.org/ccel/ignatius_antioch/epistles_of_ignatius/anf01.

―――. "Martyrdom of Ignatius." In *Ante-Nicene Fathers: The Writings of the Fathers down to A.D. 325* 1. Grand Rapids: Christian Classics Ethereal Library, n.d. https://ccel.org/ccel/ignatius_antioch/martyrdom_of_ignatius/anf01.

Irenaeus, Saint. "Against Heresies: Book I." In *Ante-Nicene Fathers: The Writings of the Fathers down to A.D. 325* 1. Grand Rapids: Christian Classics Ethereal Library, n.d. https://ccel.org/ccel/irenaeus/against_heresies_i/anf01.

―――. "Against Heresies: Book V." In *Ante-Nicene Fathers: The Writings of the Fathers down to A.D. 325* 1. Grand Rapids: Christian Classics Ethereal Library, n.d. https://ccel.org/ccel/schaff/anf01/anf01.ix.vii.html.

―――. "Fragments from the Lost Writings of Irenaeus." In *Ante-Nicene Fathers: The Writings of the Fathers down to A.D. 325* 1. Grand Rapids: Christian Classics Ethereal Library, n.d. https://ccel.org/ccel/irenaeus/fragments_of_the_lost_writings_of_irenaeus/anf01.

Irwin, Lee. "Omens of the Millennium: The Gnosis of Angels, Dreams, and Resurrection by Harold Bloom." Esoterica, 2021. https://esoteric.msu.edu/VolumeII/BloomReview.html.

Iunilli. "Instituta regularia divinae legis." Georgetown University, n.d. http://www9.georgetown.edu/faculty/jod/texts/junillus.trans.html.

Jahn, John. *History of the Hebrew Commonwealth from the Earliest Times to the Destruction of Jerusalem A. D. 72*. London: Hurst, Chance, & Co., 1829. http://www.archive.org/stream/historyofhebrewco1jahnuoft#page/n2/mode/1up.

James, M. R., translator. "Acts of Andrew." Early Christian Writings, n.d. https://www.earlychristianwritings.com/text/actsandrew.html.

———. "Acts of Peter." Early Christian Writings, n.d. https://www.earlychristianwritings.com/text/actspeter.html.

Jassen, Alex P. "Religion in the Dead Sea Scrolls." *Religion Compass* 1 (2007) 1–25.

Jerome, Saint. *De Viris Illustribus (On Illustrious Men)*. Translated by Ernest Cushing Richardson. Nicene and Post-Nicene Fathers: Second Series, edited by Philip Schaff and Henry Wace, vol. 3. Buffalo, NY: Christian Literature, 1892. Rev. and ed. by Kevin Knight. http://www.newadvent.org/fathers/2708.htm.

———. *Letters and Selected Works*. Nicene and Post-Nicene Fathers: Second Series, edited by Philip Schaff and Henry Wace, vol. 6. Grand Rapids: Eerdmans, n.d. https://ccel.org/ccel/schaff/npnf206/npnf206.i.html.

Johns, Loren L. "Conceiving Violence: The Apocalypse of John and the Left Behind Series." *Direction* 34 (Fall 2005) 194–214. http://www.directionjournal.org/article/?1400.

Josephus, Flavius. *Against Apion*. Translated by William Whiston. Urbana, IL: Project Gutenberg, 2001. http://www.gutenberg.org/etext/2849.

———. *Antiquities of the Jews*. Translated by William Whiston. Urbana, IL: Project Gutenberg, 2001. https://www.gutenberg.org/ebooks/2848.

———. *An Extract out of Josephus's Discourse to The Greeks Concerning Hades*. Translated by William Whiston. Urbana, IL: Project Gutenberg, 2001. https://www.gutenberg.org/ebooks/2847.

———. *The Wars of the Jews; Or, The History of the Destruction of Jerusalem*. Translated by William Whiston. Urbana, IL: Project Gutenberg, 2001. https://www.gutenberg.org/ebooks/2850.

Justin Martyr. "Dialogue of Justin, Philosopher and Martyr, with Trypho, a Jew." In *Ante-Nicene Fathers: The Writings of the Fathers down to A.D. 325* 1:194–270. Grand Rapids: Christian Classics Ethereal Library, n.d. https://ccel.org/ccel/justin_martyr/dialog_with_trypho/anf01.

———. "The First Apology of Justin." In *Ante-Nicene Fathers: The Writings of the Fathers down to A.D. 325* 1:163–87. Grand Rapids: Christian Classics Ethereal Library, n.d. https://ccel.org/ccel/justin_martyr/first_apology/anf01.

———. "The Second Apology of Justin." In *Ante-Nicene Fathers: The Writings of the Fathers down to A.D. 325* 1:188–93. Grand Rapids: Christian Classics Ethereal Library, n.d. https://ccel.org/ccel/justin_martyr/second_apology/anf01.

Khorenats'i, Moses. *History of the Armenians*. Translated by Robert W. Thomson. Cambridge: Harvard University Press, 1978.

King, Karen L. *The Secret Revelation of John*. Cambridge: Harvard University Press, 2006.

King, L. W., translator. "The Code of Hammurabi." The Avalon Project: Documents in Law, History and Diplomacy, 2008. https://avalon.law.yale.edu/ancient/hamframe.asp.

———. *The Seven Tablets of Creation*. London: Luzac & Co., 1902. http://www.sacred-texts.com/ane/stc/index.htm.

Kurkjian, Vahan M. *A History of Armenia*. New York: Armenian General Benevolent Union, 1958. http://penelope.uchicago.edu/Thayer/e/gazetteer/places/asia/armenia/_texts/kurarm/home.html.

Lactantius. "The Divine Institutes." In *Ante-Nicene Fathers, The Writings of the Fathers down to A.D. 325* 7:9–223. Grand Rapids: Christian Classics Ethereal Library, n.d. https://ccel.org/ccel/lactantius/institutes/anf07.

———. "Of the Manner in Which the Persecutors Died." In *Ante-Nicene Fathers, The Writings of the Fathers down to A.D. 325* 7:301–22. Grand Rapids: Christian Classics Ethereal Library, n.d. https://ccel.org/ccel/lactantius/persecutors/anf07.

Lambrecht, John. "The Opening of the Seals (Rev 6,1–8,6)." *Biblica* 79 (1998) 198–221.

Lanciani, Rodolfo. *Pagan and Christian Rome*. Boston: Houghton, Mifflin & Company, 1892. http://penelope.uchicago.edu/Thayer/E/Gazetteer/Places/Europe/Italy/Lazio/Roma/Rome/_Texts/Lanciani/LANPAC/home.html.

Lawrence, D. Herbert. *Apocalypse and the Writings on the Revelation*. New York: Cambridge University Press, 1980.

Layton, Bentley, translator. *The Gnostic Scriptures*. 2nd ed. New Heaven: Yale University Press, 2021.

———. "The Hypostasis of the Archons (The Reality of the Rulers)." The Gnostic Society Library, n.d. http://gnosis.org/naghamm/hypostas.html.

Lee, Francis Nigel. *John's Revelation Unveiled*. Brisbane: Queensland Presbyterian Theological College, 2000. http://www.williamcareybi.com/uploads/1/0/4/1/104153586/johns_revelation_unveiled_dr_francis_nigel_lee.pdf.

"The Legend of Sargon of Akkadê, c. 2300 BCE." In *Archaeology and the Bible*, 3rd ed., by George A. Barton, 310. Philadelphia: American Sunday-School Union, 1920. http://www.fordham.edu/halsall/ancient/2300sargon1.html

Lightfood, J. B., ed. "The Didache or Teaching of the Apostles." Early Christian Writings, n.d. http://www.earlychristianwritings.com/text/didache-lightfoot.html.

Lupieri, Edmondo F., et al. "Mandaeans." Encyclopaedia Iranica Online, 2020. https://referenceworks.brillonline.com/entries/encyclopaedia-iranica-online/mandaeans-COM_392.

Lynche, Richard. *An Historical Treatise of the Travels of Noah into Europe: Containing the First Inhabitation and Peopling Thereof*. London: Adam Islip, 1601. http://www.annomundi.com/history/travels_of_noah.htm.

Magie, David, translator. "The Life of Severus Alexander: Part 1." In *Histora Augusta*, 179–229. Cambridge: Loeb Classical Library, 1924. https://penelope.uchicago.edu/Thayer/E/Roman/Texts/Historia_Augusta/Severus_Alexander/1*.html.

———. "The Life of Severus Alexander: Part 2." In *Histora Augusta*, 235–83. Cambridge: Loeb Classical Library, 1924. https://penelope.uchicago.edu/Thayer/E/Roman/Texts/Historia_Augusta/Severus_Alexander/2*.html.

Manilius, Marcus. *The Five Books of Mr. Manilius Containing a System of the Ancient Astronomy and Astrology: Together with the Philosophy of the Stoicks Done into English Verse with Notes by Mr. Tho. Creech*. Ann Arbor, Michigan: Early English Books Online, n.d. http://name.umdl.umich.edu/A51767.0001.001.

———. "M. Manilii Astronomicon Liber Primus." The Latin Library, n.d. https://www.thelatinlibrary.com/manilius1.html.

Marcellinus, Ammianus. *History, Volume I: Books 14–19*. Translated by J. C. Rolfe. Cambridge: Harvard University Press, 1950. https://www.loebclassics.com/view/LCL300/1950/volume.xml.

———. *History, Volume II: Books 20–26*. Translated by J. C. Rolfe. Cambridge: Harvard University Press, 1940. https://www.loebclassics.com/view/LCL315/1940/volume.xml.

———. *History, Volume III: Books 27–31; Excerpta Valesiana*. Translated by J. C. Rolfe. Cambridge: Harvard University Press, 1939. https://www.loebclassics.com/view/LCL331/1939/volume.xml.

Marcion. "The Gospel of the Lord." The Gnostic Society Library, n.d. http://www.gnosis.org/library/marcion.htm.

Martin, Ernest L. "The Temple Symbolism in Genesis." Edited by David Sielaff. Associates for Scriptural Knowledge, Mar 1, 2004. https://www.askelm.com/temple/t040301.htm.

Maspero, Gaston. *History of Egypt, Chaldaea, Syria, Babylonia, and Assyria*. Urbana, IL: Project Gutenberg, 2009. https://www.gutenberg.org/ebooks/28876.

Maurice, Frederick Denison. *Lectures on the Apocalypse: Or, Book of Revelation of St. John the Divine*. Cambridge: Macmillan & Co., 1861. https://books.google.com.na/books?id=Z-0EAAAAQAAJ&printsec=frontcover#v=onepage&q&f=false.

Mead, G. R. S. *Apollonius of Tyana: the Philosopher-Reformer of the First Century A.D.* London: Theosophical Publishing Society, 1901. https://www.gutenberg.org/files/35460/35460-h/35460-h.htm.

———. "As Above, So Below." *The Theosophical Review* 34 (1904) 456–64. http://www.gnosis.org/library/grs-mead/grsm_asabove.htm.

———. *The Caldaean Oracles: Vol. 1*. Echoes from the Gnosis, vol. 8. London: Theosophical Publishing Society, 1908. http://www.gnosis.org/library/grs-mead/grsm_chaldean.htm.

———. "The Fourth-Gospel Problem." *The Theosophical Review* 28 (1901) 405–15. http://www.gnosis.org/library/grs-mead/grsm_fourth_gospel.htm.

———. *Fragments of a Faith Forgotten*. London: Theosophical Publishing Society, 1906. Edited by John Bruno Hare. http://www.gnosis.org/library/grs-mead/fragments_faith_forgotten/fff00.htm.

———. *The Gnosis of the Mind*. Echoes from the Gnosis, vol. 1. 1906. http://www.gnosis.org/library/grs-mead/grsm_gnosismind.htm.

———. *The Hymn of the Robe of Glory*. Echoes from the Gnosis, vol. 10. 1908. http://www.gnosis.org/library/grs-mead/grsm_robeofglory.htm.

———. *The Hymns of Hermes*. Echoes from the Gnosis. London: Theosophical Publishing House, 1906. http://www.gnosis.org/library/grs-mead/grms_hymn_hermes.htm.

———, translator. *The Mandaean Book of John the Baptizer*. N.p.: The Nazarenes of Mount Carmel, n.d. http://www.essene.com/B'nai-Amen/vjohnIndex.htm.

———. *The Misteries of Mithra*. Echoes from the Gnosis, vol. 5. 1907. http://www.gnosis.org/library/grs-mead/grsm_mythra.htm.

———. "The Outer Evidence as to the Authorship and Authority of the Gospels." *The Theosophical Review* 28 (1901) 237–48. http://www.gnosis.org/library/grs-mead/grsm_outer_evidence_as_to_the_authors.htm.

———, translator. *Pistis Sophia.* London: J. M. Watkins, 1921. http://gnosis.org/library/pistis-sophia/index.htm.

———. "The Present Position of the Synoptical Problem." *The Theosophical Review* 28 (1901) 324–35. http://www.gnosis.org/library/grs-mead/grsm_synoptic_problem.htm.

———. *Simon Magus: An Essay on the Founder of Simonianism Based on the Ancient Sources with a Re-Evaluation of His Philosophy and Teaching.* London: The Theosophical Society, 1892. http://www.gnosis.org/library/grs-mead/mead_index.htm.

———. *The Vision of Aridaeus.* Echoes from the Gnosis, vol. 3. 1907. http://www.gnosis.org/library/grs-mead/grsm_aridaeus.htm.

Memnon. "History of Heracleia: Chapters 1 to 21." Attalus, n.d. http://www.attalus.org/translate/memnon1.html.

———. "History of Heracleia: Chapters 22 to 40." Attalus, n.d. http://www.attalus.org/translate/memnon2.html.

"Memoirs of Edessa and Other Ancient Syriac Documents." In *Ante-Nicene Fathers: The Writings of the Fathers down to A.D. 325* 8, edited by Philip Schaff. Grand Rapids: Christian Classics Ethereal Library, n.d. https://ccel.org/ccel/anonymous/memoirs/anf08.

Miller, Andrew. *Miller's Church History.* London: Pickering & Inglis, 1967. http://www.stempublishing.com/history/.

Modi, Jivanji Jamshedji, translator. "Jamasp Namak ('The Book of Jamaspi')." Avesta, n.d. http://www.avesta.org/mp/jamaspi.htm.

Moyise, Steve. *The Old Testament in the Book of Revelation.* Sheffield, England: Sheffield Academic, 1995.

———. "The Use of Scripture in Revelation 1–3." In *The Old Testament in the Book of Revelation,* 24–44. Sheffield, UK: Sheffield Academic, 1995.

Nabaraz, Payam. "Mithras and Mithraism." The Circle of Ancient Iranian Studies, 1999. https://www.cais-soas.com/CAIS/Religions/iranian/Mithraism/mithras_mithraism.htm

Nagy, Gregory, ed. "Description of Greece: A Pausanias Reader, Scrolls 1–10." Translated by W. H. S. Jones. Harvard University's Center for Hellenic Studies, Nov 2, 2020. https://chs.harvard.edu/description-of-greece-a-pausanias-reader/.

Newton, Isaac. *Observations upon the Prophecies of Daniel, and the Apocalypse of St. John: In Two Parts.* Urbana, IL: Project Gutenberg, 2005. https://www.gutenberg.org/ebooks/16878.

Newton, Robert R. *The Crime of Claudius Ptolemy.* Baltimore: Johns Hopkins University Press, 1977.

Nicolaus of Damascus. *Life of Augustus.* Translated by Clayton M. Hall. California State University Northridge, Jan 29, 2016. http://www.csun.edu/~hcfll004/nicolaus.html.

Nordgreen, Otto. "The Problems of a Pre-70 Date of the Apocalypse." The Preterist Archive, 2000. https://web.archive.org/web/20171021070814/http://www.preteristarchive.com/CriticalArticles/2000_nordgreen_late-dating.html.

Origen. "Epistle to Gregory and Origen's Commentary on the Gospel of John: Books I–X." In *Ante-Nicene Fathers: The Writings of the Fathers down to A.D. 325* 9:289–408, edited by Philip Schaff and Allan Menzies. Grand Rapids: Christian Classics Ethereal Library, n.d. https://ccel.org/ccel/origen/epistle_john/anf09.

———. "Origen Against Celsus." In *Ante-Nicene Fathers: The Writings of the Fathers down to A.D. 325* 4:395–670, edited by Philip Schaff. Grand Rapids: Christian Classics Ethereal Library, n.d. https://ccel.org/ccel/origen/against_celsus/anf04.

———. "Origen's Commentary on the Gospel of Matthew: Books I, II, and X-XIV." In *Ante-Nicene Fathers: The Writings of the Fathers down to A.D. 325* 9:411–512, edited by Philip Schaff and Jofn Patrick. Grand Rapids: Christian Classics Ethereal Library, n.d. https://ccel.org/ccel/origen/commentary_matt/anf09.

———. "Works of Origen." In *Ante-Nicene Fathers: The Writings of the Fathers down to A.D. 325* 4:221–386, edited by Philip Schaff, translated by Frederick Crombie. Grand Rapids: Christian Classics Ethereal Library, n.d. https://ccel.org/ccel/origen/works/anf04.

Ovid. *Metamorphoses*. Translated by Sir Samuel Garth et al. Cambridge: The Internet Classics Archive, n.d. http://classics.mit.edu//Ovid/metam.html.

Papias. "Fragments of Papias." In *Ante-Nicene Fathers: The Writings of the Fathers down to A.D. 325* 1:151–5. Grand Rapids: Christian Classics Ethereal Library, n.d. https://ccel.org/ccel/ignatius_antioch/fragments_of_papias/anf01.

Pastor, Jack. *Land and Economy in Ancient Palestine*. London: Routledge, 1997.

Peters, O. K. *Politics of Violence in the Apocalypse of John: Moral Dilemma and Justification, John's Apocalypse and Cultural Contexts*. San Antonio: Society of Biblical Literature, 2004.

Philo of Alexandria. *About the Contemplative Life, or the Fourth Book of the Treatise Concerning Virtues*. Edited by Frederick C. Conybeare. Oxford: Clarendon, 1895. https://archive.org/details/aboutcontemplatioophiluoft/aboutcontemplatioo philuoft/page/n7/mode/2up.

———. "The Works of Philo." Early Christian Writings, n.d. https://www.earlychristianwritings.com/yonge/book1.html.

"Philo of Alexandria (c. 20 B.C.E.—40 C.E.)." Internet Encyclopedia of Philosophy, n.d. https://iep.utm.edu/philo/.

Philostratus. *The Life of Apollonius of Tyana*. Edited and translated by Christopher P. Jones. Cambridge: Harvard University Press, 2005.

Platner, Samuel Ball. *A Topographical Dictionary of Ancient Rome*. Completed and revised by Thomas Ashby. London: Oxford University Press, 1929. https://www.lib.uchicago.edu/cgi-bin/eos/eos_title.pl?callnum=DG16.P72.

Plato. *Timaeus*. Translated by Benjamin Jowett. Cambridge: The Internet Classics Archive, n.d. http://classics.mit.edu/Plato/timaeus.html.

"Pliny and Trajan: Correspondence, c. 112 CE." In *Internet Ancient History Sourcebook*, edited by Paul Halsall. New York: Fordham University, 1998. https://sourcebooks.fordham.edu/ancient/pliny-trajan1.asp.

Pliny the Elder. *The Natural History*. Edited by John Bostock and H.T. Riley. London: Taylor & Francis, 1855. https://www.perseus.tufts.edu/hopper/text?doc=Plin.+Nat.+toc.

Pliny the Younger. *Letters, Volume I: Books 1–7*. Translated by Betty Radice. Cambridge, MA: Harvard University Press, 1969. https://www.loebclassics.com/view/LCL055/1969/volume.xml.

Plutarch. *Concerning the Face Which Appears in the Orb of the Moon*. Cambridge: Loeb Classical Library, 1957. http://penelope.uchicago.edu/Thayer/E/Roman/Texts/Plutarch/Moralia/The_Face_in_the_Moon*/A.html.

———. *Isis and Osiris*. Cambridge: Loeb Classical Library, 1936. https://penelope.uchicago.edu/Thayer/E/Roman/Texts/Plutarch/Moralia/Isis_and_Osiris*/D.html.
———. *Lives of the Noble Grecians and Romans by Plutarch*. Edited by A. H. Clough. Urbana, IL: Project Gutenberg, 1996. https://www.gutenberg.org/ebooks/674.
———. *Plutarch's Lives*. Vol. 1. Translated by Aubrey Stewart and George Long. London: George Bell & Sons, 1894. https://www.gutenberg.org/files/14033/14033-h/14033-h.htm.
———. *Plutarch's Lives*. Vol. 2. Translated by Aubrey Stewart and George Long. London: George Bell & Sons, 1899. https://www.gutenberg.org/files/14114/14114-h/14114-h.htm.
———. *Plutarch's Lives*. Vol. 3. Translated by Aubrey Stewart and George Long. London: George Bell & Sons, 1892. https://www.gutenberg.org/files/14140/14140-h/14140-h.htm.
———. *Plutarch's Lives*. Vol. 4. Translated by Aubrey Stewart and George Long. London: George Bell & Sons, 1892. https://www.gutenberg.org/files/44315/44315-h/44315-h.htm.
Polybius. *The Histories of Polybius*. Vol. 1. Translated by Evelyn S. Shuckburgh. London: Macmillan & Co., 1889. https://www.gutenberg.org/files/44125/44125-h/44125-h.htm.
Polycarp. "The Epistle of Polycarp to the Philippians." In *Ante-Nicene Fathers: The Writings of the Fathers down to A.D. 325* 1:33–36, edited by Alexander Roberts and James Donaldson. Grand Rapids: Christian Classics Ethereal Library, n.d. https://ccel.org/ccel/polycarp/epistle_to_the_philippians/anf01.
———. "Fragments from Victor of Capua." Translated by Stephen C. Carlson. The Tertullian Project, 2015. https://www.tertullian.org/fathers/polycarp_fragments_01_text.htm.
Porphyry. "On Images." Translated by Edwin Hamilton Gifford. The Internet Classics Archive, n.d. http://classics.mit.edu//Porphyry/images.html.
Ptolemy. *Tetrabiblos*. Translated by F. E. Robbins. Cambridge: Harvard University Press, 1940. https://www.loebclassics.com/view/LCL435/1940/volume.xml.
Pythagoras. *The Golden Verses of Pythagoras and Pythagorean Fragments*. London: Forgotten Books, 2007. https://people.math.harvard.edu/~knill/various/eterosego/pythagoras_verses.pdf.
Riesner, Rainer. *Paul's Early Period: Cronology, Mission Strategy, Theology*. Grand Rapids: Eerdmans, 1997.
Robinson, William C., Jr., translator. *The Exegesis on the Soul*. The Gnostic Society Library, n.d. http://gnosis.org/naghamm/exe.html.
Rodkinson, Michael R., translator. *Babylonian Talmud*. Boston: The Talmud Society, 1918. Edited by John Bruno Hare. https://sacred-texts.com/jud/index.htm#talmud.
Royalty, Robert M. "Don't Touch This Book: Rev 22:18–19 and the Rhetoric of Reading (in) the Apocalypse of John." Biblical Interpretation 12.3 (2004) 282–300.
Russell, James Robert. *Zoroastrianism in Armenia*. Cambridge: Harvard University Press, 1982. https://archive.org/details/JamesRussellZoroastrianismInArmenia.
Sayce, A. H. *The Early History of the Hebrews*. London: Rivingtons, 1897. https://babel.hathitrust.org/cgi/pt?id=mdp.39015063908068&view=1up&seq=1.

Schaff, Philip and Henry Wace, eds. *Gregory the Great (II), Ephraim Syrus, Aphrahat.* Nicene and Post-Nicene Fathers: Second Series, vol. 13. Grand Rapids: Eerdsmans, n.d. https://www.ccel.org/ccel/schaff/npnf213.html.

———, eds. *Theodoret, Jerome, Gennadius, and Rufinus: Historical Writings.* Nicene and Post-Nicene Fathers: Second Series, vol. 3. Grand Rapids: Eerdmans, n.d. https://www.ccel.org/ccel/schaff/npnf203.html.

Schüssler Fiorenza, Elisabeth. *In Memory of Her: A Feminist Theological Reconstruction of Christian Origins.* New York: Crossroad, 1994.

Schwartz, Daniel R. *Studies in the Jewish background of Christianity.* Tübingen, Germany: Mohr, 1992.

Smith, Frederick George. *The Revelation Explained: An Exposition, Text by Text, of the Apocalypse of St. John.* Urbana, IL: Project Gutenberg, 2004. https://www.gutenberg.org/ebooks/13229.

Smith, William, et al., eds. *A Dictionary of Greek and Roman Antiquities.* London: John Murray, 1890. https://www.perseus.tufts.edu/hopper/text?doc=Perseus%3atext%3a1999.04.0063.

Steele, David. *Notes on the Apocalypse.* Philadelphia: Young & Ferguson, 1870. http://www.gutenberg.org/files/14485/14485-h/14485-h.htm.

Stocker, Charles William. *The History of the Persian Wars, from Herodotus.* London: Longman, 1843. https://www.google.hr/books/edition/The_history_of_the_Persian_wars_from_Her/Jd8DAAAAQAAJ?hl=hr&gbpv=1&dq=Stocker,+Charles+William.+The+History+of+the+Persian+Wars,+from+Herodotus&printsec=frontcover.

"St. Irenaeus." Catholic Encyclopedia, n.d. https://www.newadvent.org/cathen/08130b.htm.

"St. Papias." Catholic Encyclopedia, n.d. https://www.newadvent.org/cathen/11457c.htm.

Strabo. *Geography.* Edited by H. C. Hamilton and W. Falconer. Medford, MA: Perseus Digital Library, n.d. http://www.perseus.tufts.edu/hopper/text?doc=Perseus%3Atext%3A1999.01.0239%3Abook%3D1&force=y.

Suetonius. *Lives of the Caesars, Volume I: Julius. Augustus. Tiberius. Gaius. Caligula.* Translated by J. C. Rolfe. Cambridge: Harvard University Press, 1914. https://www.loebclassics.com/view/LCL031/1914/volume.xml.

———. *Lives of the Caesars, Volume II: Claudius. Nero. Galba, Otho, and Vitellius. Vespasian. Titus, Domitian. Lives of Illustrious Men: Grammarians and Rhetoricians. Poets (Terence. Virgil. Horace. Tibullus. Persius. Lucan). Lives of Pliny the Elder and Passienus Crispus.* Translated by J. C. Rolfe. Cambridge: Harvard University Press, 1914. https://www.loebclassics.com/view/LCL038/1914/volume.xml.

Tacitus, Cornelius. *Annals of Tacitus.* Translated by A. J. Church and W. J. Brodribb. London: Macmillan & Co, 1876. https://www.perseus.tufts.edu/hopper/text?doc=Perseus%3atext%3A1999.02.0078.

———. *The Germania and Agricola of Caius Cornelius Tacitus: With Notes for Colleges.* Translated by W. S. Tyler. New York: D. Appleton & Co., 1864. http://name.umdl.umich.edu/AHT6987.0001.001.

———. *The History of Tacitus.* Translated by Alfred John Church and William Jackson Brodribb. New York: Random House, 1942. www.perseus.tufts.edu/hopper/text?doc=Perseus%3Atext%3A1999.02.0080.

———. *The Life of Cnaeus Julius Agricola*. Translated from the Latin of Cornelius Tacitus, etc. New York: Random House, 1942. https://www.perseus.tufts.edu/hopper/text?doc=Perseus%3Atext%3A1999.02.0081.

Tatian. "The Diatessaron of Tatian." In *Ante-Nicene Fathers: The Writings of the Fathers down to A.D. 325* 9:33–130, edited by Philip Schaff. Christian Classics Ethereal Library, n.d. https://ccel.org/ccel/tatian/diatessaron/anf09.

———. "Tatian's Address to the Greeks." Translated by J. E. Ryland. In *The Ante-Nicene Fathers: The Writings of the Fathers down to A.D. 325* 2:59-84. Christian Classics Ethereal Library, n.d. https://ccel.org/ccel/tatian/greeks/anf02.

Tavo, Felise. "The Structure of the Apocalypse: Re-examining a Perennial Problem." *Novum Testamentum* 47.1 (2005) 47–68.

Tertullian. "Latin Christianity: Its Founder, Tertullian." In *Ante-Nicene Fathers: The Writings of the Fathers down to A.D. 325* 3:1–718, edited by Allan Menzies. Christian Classics Ethereal Library, n.d. https://ccel.org/ccel/schaff/anf03.html.

———. "Prescription against Heretics." In *Ante-Nicene Fathers: The Writings of the Fathers down to A.D. 325* 3:237-67, edited by Allan Menzies. Christian Classics Ethereal Library, n.d. https://ccel.org/ccel/tertullian/heretics/anf03.

———. "Tertullian, Part Fourth." In *Ante-Nicene Fathers: The Writings of the Fathers down to A.D. 325* 4:3–126, edited by A. Cleveland Coxe. Christian Classics Ethereal Library, n.d. https://ccel.org/ccel/schaff/anf04.html

Thimmes, Pamela L. "Women Reading Women in the Apocalypse: Reading Scenario 1, the Letter to Thyatira (Rev. 2.18–29)." *Currents in Biblical Research* 2 (2003): 128–144.

Thomas, Robert L. "The Kingdom of Christ in the Apocalypse." *The Master's Seminary Journal* 3.2 (1992) 117–40.

Thompson, R. Campbell, ed. "The Reports of the Magicians and Astrologers of Nineveh and Babylon, c. 2500–670 BCE." In *Assyrian and Babylonian Literature: Selected Transactions, with a Critical Introduction by Robert Francis Harper*, 451–60. New York: D. Appleton & Company, 1904. https://sourcebooks.fordham.edu/ancient/bablylonian-astrology.asp.

Timmer, Daniel C. *Creation, Tabernacle, and Sabbath: The Sabbath Frame of Exodus 31:12–17; 35:1–3 in Exegetical and Theological Perspective*. Göttingen, Germany: Vandenhoeck & Ruprecht, 2009.

"Topical Index of the Dead Sea Scrolls." Bible Query, Jan 9, 2003. http://www.biblequery.org/History/Archaeology/DeadSeaScrollsIndex.htm.

Turner, Robert, translator. *Arbatel of Magic: Or, The Spiritual Wisdom of the Ancients, as Well Wise-Men of the People of God, as MAGI of the Gentiles; For the Illustration of the Glory of God, and His Love to Mankinde*. N.p.: Converted to Acrobat format by Benjamin Rowe, 1999. http://www.akor.cc/More%20Books/Arbatel.PDF.

Ulansey, David. *The Origin of the Mithraic Mysteries: Cosmology and Salvation in the Ancient World*. Oxford: Oxford University Press, 1991.

Victorinus. "Commentary on the Apocalypse of the Blessed John." In *Ante-Nicene Fathers: The Writings of the Fathers down to A.D. 325* 7. Grand Rapids: Christian Classics Ethereal Library, n.d. https://ccel.org/ccel/victorinus/apocalypse/anf07.

"The Vision of Paul." In *Ante-Nicene Fathers: The Writings of the Fathers down to A.D. 325* 9:149–66, edited by Philip Schaff. Grand Rapids: Christian Classics Ethereal Library, n.d. https://ccel.org/ccel/anonymous/vision_paul/anf09.

Vitruvius. *The Ten Books On Architecture*. Translated by Morris Hicky Morgan. Cambridge: Harvard University Press, 1914. https://www.gutenberg.org/files/20239/20239-h/20239-h.htm.

West, E. W., translator. "Bundahishn ('Creation'), or Knowledge from the Zand." In *Sacred Books of the East* 5. Oxford: Oxford University Press, 1897. http://www.avesta.org/mp/bundahis.html.

———. "Denkard." In *Sacred Books of the East* 5. Oxford: Oxford University Press, 1897. http://www.avesta.org/denkard/dk5.html.

———. "Zand-i Vohuman Yasht." In *Sacred Books of the East* 5. Oxford: Oxford University Press, 1897. Digital ed. edited by Joseph H. Peterson. http://www.avesta.org/mp/vohuman.html.

Wisse, Frederik, translator. *The Apocryphon of John (The Secret Book of John—The Secret Revelation of John)*. The Gnostic Society Library, n.d. http://gnosis.org/naghamm/apocjn.html.

Yonge, Charles Duke, translator. *The Works of Philo Judaeus the Contemporary of Josephus*. London: H. G. Bohn, 1890. Christian Classics Ethereal Library, n. d. https://www.ccel.org/ccel/p/philo/works/cache/works.pdf.

Zosimus. "The Narrative of Zosimus." Translated by W. A. Craigie. In *Ante-Nicene Fathers: The Writings of the Fathers down to A.D. 325* 9:219–24, edited by Philip Schaff. Christian Classics Ethereal Library, n.d. https://ccel.org/ccel/zosimus/narrative/anf09.

———. "The Testament of Abraham." Translated by W. A. Craigie. In *Ante-Nicene Fathers: The Writings of the Fathers down to A.D. 325* 9:183–201, edited by Philip Schaff. Christian Classics Ethereal Library, n.d. https://ccel.org/ccel/zosimus/testament_abraham/anf09.

Index

Abaddon, 100, 146, 241
Abbasids, 52
Abel, 39
Abgar Ouchama, king of Edessa, 45, 127–29, 181, 208
Abraham, 52, 80–81
Abu Ma'shar, 141
Abydenus, 82–83
Abyss, 42, 74, 78, 100, 103, 112, 146, 180, 208, 241
Acts of Andrew, 47
Acts of John, 46–47
Acts of the Apostles, 9, 17, 33, 150, 236, 243–44
Acts of Thomas, 46, 216–17, 223
Adam, 37, 40, 51, 54–56, 58, 77, 120, 126, 199, 207, 209, 218, 225
Adiabene, 113, 123–24, 152–53, 155
Aelia Capitolina, 35
Agabus, 150–51, 206, 236, 243–44
Against Heresies, 2, 5–7, 36, 199, 207
Agathangelos, 121
Agrippa, Castor, 35
Agrippa von Nettesheim, Heinrich Cornelius, 67–68
Ahab, 201–203
Ahinapolis, 138
Ahura-Mazda, 91
Akkad, 134
Alagar Zagar, 182
Albania, 124
al-Biruni, 141
Alcazar, Ludovico, 22
Alexander of Aphrodisias, 232

Alexander the Great, 26–27, 82, 114, 121, 138, 142
Alexander Polyhistor, 82–83, 85
Alexander (the tax collector), 153
Alexander, Tiberius Julius, 152–53, 206, 231, 244
Alexandria, 15, 27–30, 32, 39, 41, 137–40, 152–53, 227, 231–35
al-Fargani, 141
Algol, 164, 170–72, 175, 201, 213, 225, 232, 242
al-Hashimi, 141
Almagest, 139
amillenarianism, 13
Anahita, 123
Anaxagoras of Clasomena, 135
Anaximander, 30, 136, 232
Anaximenes, 136
Andrew, 7, 47
Andrew of Cappadocia, 10
anti-heresiarchs, 35–36, 50
Antilegomena, 1, 237
Antiochus I Soter, 82–83
Antipas, 85, 194, 204, 244
Antipatrus, 85, 138, 229
Antiquities of Jews, 126, 150, 152–53, 231
Apocalipsyn, 22
Apocalypse, 1–2, 10–12, 16, 18, 24, 26, 51, 198, 240
apocrypha, 4, 9, 40, 46–47, 181, 183, 192, 216, 223
Apollo, 105, 146–49, 176, 190, 241
Apollodorus, 82–83
Apollonius of Pergamum, 137

261

INDEX

Apollonius of Tyana, 151, 186, 206, 236, 244
Apollyon, 100, 146, 241
Apology, 2
apostles, 4–7, 9, 15, 21, 26, 33, 36, 77, 182, 184, 193, 204, 228, 231, 243
Aquarius, 99, 105, 132, 240
Ararat, 121–22, 125, 240–41
Arbatel of Magic, 80–81, 90
Archimedes, 28, 137
Arethas of Caesarea, 11
Aries, 54, 170, 175
Ariobarzanes, 123
Aristobulus, 29
Aristophanes, 28
Aristotle, 28, 31, 133, 136–38, 205, 227
Armageddon, 1, 88, 93, 113, 120, 122, 177, 240
Armenia, 8, 113–16, 118, 120–27, 129–30, 143–45, 150, 154–56, 169, 173–77, 180, 184, 187, 191, 194, 205, 207, 213, 221, 223–25, 230, 240–41, 243
Armstrong, James, 23
Artabanus, 114, 154
Artaxata, 114–16, 123–25, 174
Arthaban, 114
Ascension of Isaiah, 181–82
Ashekenaz, 122, 241
Asia Minor, 4–6, 16, 21, 23, 25–26, 30, 32, 40, 62, 72, 78, 84, 117, 121, 123–24, 127, 151, 169, 189, 192, 205–6
Askew Codex, 48
Assyria, 81–82, 121, 134, 141, 182, 205
astrology, 38, 44, 54, 61, 80–82, 87, 96–97, 133, 135, 138–41, 143, 169
Astronomicon, 169, 171
astronomy, 8, 22, 44, 54, 60, 80, 82, 84–85, 87, 96, 110, 131, 133–37, 139–41, 143, 156, 169, 229
Athens, 82, 136
Athor Anahta, 123, 240
Atropatene, 124
Augustine, 22

Augustus Octavian, 113, 118, 189–91, 205–6, 241

Baal, 201–2
Babylon, 6, 52–53, 81–83, 86, 90, 111, 121–22, 134, 137–38, 141–42, 164, 176, 178, 180, 183–84
Babylonia, 34, 53, 82
Babyloniaca (*Chaldaica*), 82
Bacchus, 27, 130
Bagdad, 52–53
Balaam, 26, 195, 199–201, 203–6, 235
Balak, 195, 201, 204, 235
Bar Kokhba, 5
Bar Salib, 12
Bardaesan, 45–46, 221
Barnabas, 2, 17, 150
Barr, David L., 23, 70
Basilides, 35, 38, 41, 119
Basra, 52
beast, 6, 10, 65, 117, 208
Bede, 12
Bel, 56, 82–83, 86, 122
Bel Marduk, 81, 86, 239
Beliar, 181–83
ben Phiabi, Ishmael, 152–53, 206, 243
Berosus, 82–87, 103, 126, 138, 229, 239
Bhagavad Gita, 27
Bible, 10, 121, 141–42, 233
Biguzzi, G., 24
Book of the Angel Vohuman, 239
Book of the Dead, 219
Book of the Great Logos, 48, 50, 214, 220
Book of the Zodiac, 54
Books of the Savior, 50, 217–18
Borsippa, 167, 242
Buddha, 30
Buddhism, 27
Bythos, 42, 215

Caesarea, 4, 152, 243
Cain, 38–39, 200
Cainites, 37, 38, 39
Caligula, 118, 173, 231, 241
Callimachus, 28
Cappadocia, 123, 125, 151
Capricorn, 178

Carpocrates, 39
Carpocratians, 39
Castor, 146-49, 157-58, 241-42
Celsus, 36
Cerdon, 40
Cerinthus, 15, 40, 219-20
Ceylon, 55
Chalcidius, 140
Chaldea, 29-32, 34, 52-53, 55, 80, 85, 121, 126, 138
Chaldeans, 45, 52-53, 85, 133
Charles, R. H., 21-22, 63, 77, 182
chiliasm, 32
Christianity, 4, 21, 29-30, 32-33, 45-46, 50-51, 53, 77, 92, 127, 129-30, 140, 198, 225, 234
Chronicle, 4, 10
Chronicon Paschale, 4
church, 5-6, 8-9, 12-14, 25-26, 29, 32-33, 37, 40, 43, 46, 51, 53, 73, 88, 177, 182, 208, 215, 223, 225, 231
Church History, 1-2, 4, 7, 10-11, 15-16, 19, 21, 35-36, 127-28, 150-51, 204
Cilicia, 114, 125
Claudius, 3-4, 11, 80, 118, 140, 144-46, 150, 152-53, 155, 185, 190, 237, 241
Clement of Alexandria, 3, 11, 29, 32, 36, 38, 43, 46, 50, 82, 199, 204
Colarbasus, 34
Collins, Yambro, 24, 88
Cologne Manichean Codex, 54
Colossae, 25
Comments on the Revelation, 4
Commodus, 190
Confucius, 30
Constantinople, 11
constellation, 54, 98, 117, 147, 160, 164, 169-70, 175, 242
Copts, 35, 50
Corbulo, 112, 114-15, 174, 187
Corinth, 5
Cos, 82, 85
cosmology, 40, 42, 44, 108, 138, 141, 193, 208, 215, 223
Crassus, 121
Cratylus, 119

Cyprus, 41, 53, 183
Cyrenius, 153

Damascius, 86
Damascus, 205
Dana Nuk, 56-59, 104
Daniel, 6, 56, 76-77, 87, 94, 104
Darius, 27, 114
David, 23, 25, 70-71, 73-74, 78, 145, 159-60, 200
De fide catholica, 14
Dead Sea, 33, 183, 200
Dead Sea Scrolls, 34, 51, 183
demiurge, 42, 79-80, 136, 209, 215, 232
Democritus of Abdera, 135
Demosthenes, 186
Dialogue with Trypho, a Jew, 2, 5, 161
Diatessaron, 129
Dio Cassius, 117, 190-91
Dio Chrysostom, 186
Dionysius, 2-3, 6, 15-16, 19, 21, 31
Discourse on Beauty, 186
Discourses, 186
Docets, 38
Domitian, 2-4, 6, 10, 12, 15, 21, 23, 113, 151, 186, 191, 237
Drower, E. S., 54, 57, 59

Ebion, 34
Ebionites, 34-35, 40
eclipses, 2, 6, 8, 10, 12, 14, 16, 18, 20, 22, 24, 26, 28, 30, 32, 34, 36, 38, 40, 42, 44, 46, 48, 50, 52, 54, 56, 58, 60, 64, 66, 68, 70, 72, 74, 76, 78, 80, 82, 84, 86, 88, 90, 92, 94, 96, 98, 100, 102, 104, 106, 108, 110, 112, 114, 116, 118, 120, 122, 124, 126, 128, 130, 132, 134-36, 138, 140, 142, 144-50, 152, 154-56, 158, 160, 162, 164, 166, 168-70, 172, 174, 176, 178-80, 182-84, 186, 188, 190, 192, 194, 196, 198, 200, 202, 204, 206, 208, 210, 212, 214, 216, 218, 220, 222, 224, 226, 228, 230, 232, 234, 236, 238, 240-44
Eden, 37
Edessa, 127-29

Egypt, 27, 29–32, 40–41, 43, 48, 55, 60, 80–81, 103, 111, 126, 135, 138–39, 153, 201, 208, 216, 219–20, 229
Eleusinian mysteries, 27, 31
Elijah, 202–3
Elisabeth, 55, 59–60
Elkesai, 34
Enoch, 76–77, 88, 141, 198–99, 210
eon, 24, 38, 39, 41–43, 49, 57–58, 61, 93, 95, 101, 107, 192, 210, 212, 215, 217–21, 228
Ephesus, 2, 5, 6, 9, 11, 17, 25, 71, 73, 88, 203
Ephraim, 46, 221
Ephrem of Nisibis, 10
Epicureanism, 28
Epiphanius, 3–4, 11, 35–36, 50, 237
Epiphanus, 34, 39
epiphany, 39
Epistles, 2–3, 6, 16, 21, 32–33, 41, 228–29
equinox, 131–32, 137, 140, 142, 240
Erasistratus of Chios, 138
Eratosthenes, 137–38
eschatology, 22, 77, 193, 223
Essenes, 27, 33–34, 220
Euanthas, 6, 65, 119
Euclid, 137
Euclides, 28
Eudoxus of Cnidus, 136
Euphrates, 92, 96, 101, 103, 109, 111, 113, 115, 123, 155–56, 173, 177, 216, 224
Eusebius, 1–4, 7, 10–11, 15–16, 19, 21, 35–36, 38, 41, 50, 80, 83, 127–28, 150–51, 204, 222, 244
Eve, 40, 55
Ezekiel, 76, 141

famine, 95–96, 148, 150–54, 208, 224, 230, 240, 242–43
Farrer, Austin, 24, 88
Faustus, 121, 130
flood, 27, 46, 55, 83, 104, 125–26, 139, 173, 196, 199, 207, 210
Focius, 8
Ford, J. Massyngberde, 3

Fragments, 8–9, 14, 46, 63, 141, 210–11, 214, 218–20
Futurism, 12

Galba, 10, 152
Gallia, 5, 35, 36
gematria, 66–67, 120, 142
Gemini, 146–47, 149, 158, 160–62, 224, 241–42
Germanicus, 114, 153
Ginza Rabba, 53–56
Glaucus, 41
Gnosticism, 29, 35, 37, 41
Gnostics, 5, 26–27, 30, 35–39, 41–46, 48–49, 60–61, 119, 192, 199, 204, 215, 217, 234
God, 1–3, 5–6, 8, 10–11, 13–14, 16–18, 20, 22–25, 30, 32–33, 37–40, 42–46, 52, 56–60, 62–64, 70–81, 84–87, 89–91, 98–104, 106–11, 126, 128, 136, 141–42, 148, 155–58, 160, 166–67, 172–73, 175–78, 180–84, 192–93, 195, 197–202, 205, 209, 213–21, 223–28, 230–35, 242–43
Golan, 152
Gorgon, 170–71, 242
Gospel, 2–4, 6, 11, 15–18, 20–21, 32–35, 37, 40–41, 44, 51–52, 77, 79–80, 92, 106–7, 129, 171, 176, 213, 228–29, 231, 234, 243
Gotarzes, 154
Greece, 5, 12, 19, 21–22, 26–31, 44, 48, 50, 66–67, 79, 82, 85, 100, 117, 119–21, 124, 127, 130, 132–33, 135, 137–38, 140, 142–43, 146–47, 174, 186–87, 205–6, 212, 226, 229, 231–32, 234, 236, 241
Gregory of Nyssa, 2, 21
Gregory of Tours, 140
Gregory the Illuminator, 129
Günther, Anton, 14

Hadrian, 32
Hammurabi, 83
Hannibal, 180
Harran Gawaitha, 55

Hayk, 122, 221
heaven, 37, 39, 44, 47, 50, 57–59, 63, 65, 68, 71–72, 74–79, 81, 84, 86–87, 89–91, 96, 98, 102–5, 107, 110–11, 117, 122–23, 125, 128, 135, 142, 155, 157, 159, 163–64, 167–68, 172–73, 176–77, 182–84, 196–99, 201, 209–10, 213, 218–20, 228, 234, 239
hebdomad, 42, 208–9
Hebrew, 5, 21, 28, 34–35, 37, 67, 100, 106, 119–20, 122, 146, 177, 226, 232, 234
Helena, 152–53
Hellenism, 26, 137–38, 234
Heracleon, 42, 44
Herod Agrippa I, 152, 155
Herod Agrippa II (Marcus Julius Agrippa), 117, 143, 152–53, 175, 180, 205–6, 230, 243–44, 244
Hercules, 37
Herod, 152, 205
Herodotus, 27, 37, 91, 121
Heron of Alexandria, 138
Herophilus of Chalcedon, 138
Hesiod, 31, 106, 136, 156–58, 176, 229
Hezekiah, 181
Hierapolis, 25
Hierocles, 151, 198, 236, 244
Hipparchus, 137, 168
Hippolytus, 4, 8, 32, 36–38, 42–43, 50
Hiwel Ziwa, 55–56, 58–60
Holy Spirit, 18, 36, 44, 182, 208–9
Homer, 31, 106, 136, 157–58
Hormuz, 52
Horos, 42–43
Hyksos, 30
hyle, 40, 42, 49
Hymn of the Robe of Glory, 46
Hymn of Wisdom, 46

Iberia, 114, 124
Ibn Rushd, 232
India, 27, 53, 91, 151, 223
Inoshwey, 55
Irenaeus, 2–10, 15, 22, 29, 32, 35–36, 38, 40, 43, 65, 67–69, 113, 119, 194, 199, 207

Isaiah, 14, 76, 181–83, 198
Isis, 27, 29, 43, 80, 213
Islam, 53, 91
Israel, 5, 6, 29, 72, 76, 106, 112, 116, 126–27, 129, 141, 152–53, 155, 170, 175, 181, 194, 197–202, 205–7, 218, 230
Ithobaal, 201

Jacob, 39
Jehu, 202–3
Jerome, 3, 4, 8, 12, 21–22, 35–36
Jerusalem, 5, 8, 11, 16–17, 21, 29, 35, 55, 59–60, 62–64, 74, 76, 88, 93, 105, 111, 128, 150, 152, 175–76, 182, 185, 192, 208, 215–17, 224, 230–31, 234, 241
Jesus Christ, 1, 2, 5–6, 8, 11–13, 15–17, 19, 22–23, 29, 32–35, 37–38, 40, 43, 46–49, 51, 62, 70–72, 74–77, 79, 86, 92, 105, 107–8, 110, 117–18, 127–29, 151, 172–73, 181, 183, 192–93, 198, 207–9, 211–18, 220–21, 223–25, 228, 230–31
Jews, 11, 22, 24–26, 28–29, 32–33, 35, 40, 42, 55, 57, 77, 90, 96, 106–7, 117, 128–29, 133, 138, 141–43, 152–53, 167, 170, 175, 194, 200–201, 203, 205–6, 213, 224, 226, 230–32, 234–36, 239, 241, 243
Jezebel, 195, 201–3, 206, 235
Joachim, 12
Job, 141
John, 1–7, 9–19, 21–26, 32, 40, 44, 46–47, 51–53, 55, 59–60, 62–65, 67–76, 78, 83–91, 93, 95–97, 99, 101–3, 105–13, 116–20, 122, 125–27, 129, 143–46, 148–50, 153–59, 161–67, 169–70, 173, 175–77, 179–81, 183–84, 191–93, 195–97, 199–201, 203–8, 213–15, 219–20, 222–25, 227–32, 234–40, 242–44
John the Baptist, 3, 52–53, 55, 59
John the Presbyter, 7, 21
Jonah, 17, 33, 111

INDEX

Jordan, 152
Joseph, 35, 40, 106, 220
Josephus Flavius, 80, 82–83, 126, 150, 152, 175, 205, 231
Judas of Galilee, 153
Jude, 2, 38–39, 200–201
Judea, 150, 152, 153, 231
Julius Caesar, 10, 12, 117–18, 205, 241
Jupiter, 8, 56, 67, 81, 86, 92, 97–100, 103, 105, 108, 118, 133, 160, 178, 189–91, 208, 239
Justin Martyr, 2–5, 22, 36, 50, 161, 194, 200

Kabala, 26
kenoma, 42
Khuzestan, 52
Kissaneh, 129–30, 208
Kiwan, 57

Lactantius, 3, 8, 151, 244
lamb, 6, 14, 72, 74, 84–87, 95, 99, 101, 103–8, 116, 170, 172, 176, 209–11, 228, 235, 239
Lambrecht, John, 24, 88
Lamentabili, 14
Lao Tse, 30
Laodicea, 2, 23, 25, 71, 73
Lateinos, 6, 65, 119
Lawrence, D. H., 26
Leo, 98, 105, 160–62, 164, 167, 178, 240–42
Leucippus of Miletus, 135
Libra, 178
Life of Appolonius of Tyana, 236
Life of Nero, 187
Lion, 35, 71–72, 159–60
Logos, 30, 32, 38, 44, 48, 212, 214, 220, 226–27, 230, 232–35
Lucullus, 121, 124–25
Luke, 12–13, 197, 199, 213
Luther, Martin, 2
Lydia, 205
Lyon, 5

Macarius Magnes, 50, 198
Macrobius, 140
Magnesia, 25

Manasseh, 106, 181
Mandaeans, 34, 52–57, 59–61, 104
Manilius, 169, 171
Mar Apas Catina, 121
Marcellina, 39
Marcian Capella, 140
Marcion, 36, 40
Marcionites, 40
Marcosians, 41, 67
Marcossius, 50
Marcus, 41, 44
Marcus Aurelius, 5, 12
Mark, 12, 17, 197
Mars, 56, 67, 96–99, 103, 105, 118, 133, 139, 160, 164, 177–78, 228, 238, 240
Mary, 30, 35, 37, 40, 46, 48, 211, 219–20
Massis, 122–23, 125–26, 173, 240–41
Mathematical Collection, 138
Mathematical Treatise in Four Books, 139
Matthew, 7, 12–13, 41, 248, 256
Mazdaism, 107, 115, 129, 150, 167, 239
Mead, G. R. S., 43
Media, 72, 113, 115–17, 121, 143, 155, 175, 205
Mediterranean, 26, 28, 96
Melito, 12
Mercury, 55, 68, 81, 92, 96–99, 103, 105, 118, 133, 150, 160, 169, 177–78, 228, 239–40
Mesopotamia, 34, 53, 82, 116, 121–23, 125, 155
Messalina, 152
Messiah, 33, 40, 76, 230
Metaphysics, 136
metensomatosis, 38, 213
Methodius, 3
Micah, 181, 203
Michael, 49, 168, 182, 200, 213, 222
Michaelis, 50
Middle Ages, 67
millenarianism, 8, 13, 19, 22, 32
Millennium, 26, 57, 148, 165
Mind, 38, 44, 51, 208
Minni, 122, 241

Mirbarzanes, 124
Mithraism, 27
Mithridates, 112, 114, 121, 123–25, 154–55, 206, 241
Mitra, 116
Mongols, 52
Monobazus, 113, 155
Monoimus, 38
Montanism, 2
Montecroce, Ricoldo da, 52
Moon, 8, 12, 38–39, 41, 44, 49, 55–59, 68, 79, 81–82, 85, 92, 97–98, 103–6, 108–9, 117–18, 122–23, 125, 132–35, 137, 139–42, 144–45, 148–50, 156, 159–62, 164, 167–68, 170–72, 176, 178, 180, 183–84, 191–92, 206–9, 212, 215, 218, 220, 224–25, 228, 232, 239–43
Moscow, 9
Moses, 29, 39, 55, 144, 182, 199–201
Moses Chorenensis, 121, 126
Moyise, Steve, 24–25
Murena, 124

Naassenes, 37
Nabonassar, 83
Nag Hammadi, 50–51
Nazarenes, 34–35
Nazareth, 35
Nebuchadnezzar, 176
Nergal-etir, 167, 184, 242
Nero, 3, 4, 9–12, 21–23, 80, 113–18, 151–53, 155–56, 163–64, 173–75, 182, 184–88, 190–91, 213, 224–25, 237, 241, 243
Nerva, 2, 6, 10, 186
New Testament, 1–3, 10, 32, 91, 151
Newton, Isaac, 22
Nicene, 12
Nicolaites, 26, 40, 194–95, 201, 203–4, 206, 224, 229, 235
Nicolaus of Damascus, 80, 126, 201, 203–6, 235, 239, 244
Noah, 25, 55–56, 81, 120–21, 125–26, 196, 199, 207, 225
Nochaites, 37
Noreitha, 55

Nua, 55–56
Nuraitha, 55–56

Of Occult Philosophy, 67–68
ogdoad, 60–61, 79
Ohrmazd, 91–94, 173–74
Old Testament, 24–25, 39, 75, 127, 141, 181, 199
Omoroca, 85–86, 239
On Conics, 137
On First Principles, 86
On Illustrious Men, 4, 8, 12, 21
On Monarchy, 5
On Ogdoad, 5
On Promises, 19
On the City of God, 22
On the Heavens, 136–37
On the Revelation, 12
Ophites, 37–38, 207
Oracula Chaldaica sive Magica, 91
Origen, 3, 15, 29, 36, 44, 50
Orodes, 154
Orphism, 27, 31
Osiris, 30, 79–80, 213
Otho, 10, 186
Oxford, 9, 48

Pacorus, 113, 115, 143, 155
Pamphylia, 16–17
Panarion, 4, 35
Papias, 6–8, 13–14, 21
Pappus of Alexandria, 138
paradise, 37, 40, 58–60, 62
parousia, 1
Parthia, 72, 112–18, 120, 123–25, 127, 143–44, 150, 154–56, 169, 173–75, 180, 187, 194, 230, 243
Patmos, 2, 4, 6, 8–10, 17, 70–71, 73, 75, 85, 148, 159, 166, 169–70, 220, 222, 237–38
Paul, 2, 4, 9, 11, 16–18, 25, 32–33, 35, 40–41, 43, 51, 77, 127, 140, 150, 234, 236, 243
Pennini, *See* Montecroce, Ricoldo da
Peratae, 37–38
Pergamum, 2, 16, 25, 71, 73, 85, 137, 203
Peripatetics, 28

Perseus, 170–71
Persia, 27, 30, 53, 82, 91–92, 123, 128, 205
Peter, 2, 4, 7, 9, 11–13, 17, 33, 47–48, 51, 63, 197–98, 201, 236
Peters, Oluola K., 25
Pharasmanes, 154
Pharisaism, 33
Pharisees, 33
Philadelphia, 2, 25, 71, 73, 203
Philastrius, 36
Philo, 27, 30, 33–34, 80, 144, 212, 220, 226–27, 229, 231–35, 244
Philostratus, 151, 236
Phraates, 114, 125
Physics, 136
Pisces, 54, 132
Pistis Sophia, 37, 42–43, 48–51, 181, 192, 199, 208–13, 216–18, 220–22, 224, 228
Pistis Sophia Treatise, 48, 50
planets, 8, 38–39, 44, 48, 55–57, 59, 61, 67, 69, 80–81, 86–87, 96–99, 103, 105–10, 118, 120, 127, 133, 135–41, 148, 150, 155–57, 160–61, 163, 168–69, 174, 176–79, 192–93, 207–10, 215, 218, 224–25, 228–29, 231, 238–39, 241
Plataea, 27
Plato, 27–28, 31–32, 42, 51, 80, 136, 138, 186, 209, 215, 226–27, 229, 231–32, 234
Platonism, 39, 229
pleroma, 38–39, 41–44, 59, 208, 210–12, 215, 217, 220–22, 225, 231
Pliny, 82, 140, 188
Plotinus, 232
Plutarch, 29, 43, 124, 137, 213
Pollux, 147, 157, 241
Polycarp, 5, 6, 7, 9, 14
Pompey, 125, 129, 190–91
Porphyry Polyhistor, 98, 105, 117, 198, 236, 244
Preparation for the Gospel, 80
Preterism, 12
Primas, 12

Proclus, 140, 227
Proof of the Gospel, 4, 11
Proofs of Apostolic Preaching, 5
prophecy, 1, 3, 12–13, 15–17, 19, 23, 62, 64, 70, 91, 93, 109–11, 117, 151, 163, 175–76, 179, 183, 193, 213, 223
prophet, 12, 20, 26, 35, 49, 55, 58, 75, 89, 91, 102–3, 109–10, 129, 150–51, 156, 158–59, 167, 177, 179, 184, 202–3, 208, 210, 226–27, 234, 241
Ptolemy, 27–28, 42, 44, 97–99, 101, 111, 126, 133, 138–40, 164, 169–70
Punjab, 27
Pythagoras, 27–28, 30–31, 35, 42, 66
Pythagoreans, 27, 31, 67, 78, 80, 151

Qumran, 34
Qur'an, 92

Ram, 55, 217
Ramsey, 24–25
Refutation of All Heresies, 8, 37, 251
Refutation of the Allegorists, 15
Regulus, 167, 170–72, 212, 242
Renaissance, 50, 67, 133, 143
Revelation, 1–4, 6, 8, 10–16, 19, 21–24, 26, 40, 51–52, 55–57, 59–65, 67–70, 74–76, 80, 85, 87–88, 93–94, 104, 108–9, 111–13, 117–18, 126, 143–45, 148–51, 159, 161, 164, 169, 177, 181–82, 184, 192–94, 204, 215, 219, 223–25, 228–32, 234–39, 241–43
Rhadamistus, 114, 154–55
Rhandeia, 113, 116, 127, 143–44, 169, 174, 180, 224, 243
Rome, 4, 6, 8–12, 25–28, 32, 39–41, 53, 65, 69, 74–76, 105, 112–18, 121, 123–25, 127, 135, 138, 143–44, 150–55, 168–69, 173–78, 180–81, 184–91, 194, 203–5, 208, 222, 224, 230, 236, 241, 243
Royalty, Robert M., 26

Ruha, 55, 58–60

Salamis, 36
Sam, 55
Samnas, 181
Sandaramet, 130
Sardis, 2, 25, 71, 73, 89, 177, 194, 203
Satan, 1, 74, 81, 151, 168, 170, 181, 194–95, 205, 213, 242
Saturn, 8, 55, 57, 59, 67, 81, 98–101, 103, 107–8, 118, 133, 139–41, 155, 159–62, 176, 178–79, 197, 211, 228, 239, 241–42
Savior, 8, 30, 38, 43, 51, 91, 93, 101, 109, 111, 129, 144, 156, 159, 162–63, 173, 204, 210, 211–12, 217–19, 224–25, 230–31
Severus Alexander, 236
Schüssler Fiorenza, Elisabeth, 24, 88
Scorpio, 99, 105, 178, 240
Scylax, 27
Scythians, 37
Secundus, 41
Sefir Yatzira, 140
Septuagint, 41, 76, 226
Set, 30
Sethians, 37, 207
Seven Tablets of Creation (*Enuma Elish*), 81, 85, 239
Severus Alexander, 236
Sextilius (Publius Sextilius), 124
Shat-al-Arab, 53
Shoorbai, 55
Shurbey, 55
Shurhabiel, 55
Siricius, 50
Sirius, 30, 105
skepticism, 28
Smyrna, 2, 25, 71, 73, 203
Socrates, 28, 136
Sodom, 103, 111, 182, 208
Solomon, 33
solstice, 141–42
Son of Man, 1, 23, 37, 61, 63, 71–73, 75–79, 86, 88, 106–7, 110, 125, 145, 156, 192, 194, 196, 199, 201, 207–9, 215, 220, 224–25, 230–31, 234, 237–38

Sophene, 123
Sophists, 28
Sotis, 30
spheres, 37, 39, 41–42, 44, 59–60, 80, 97, 99, 108, 110, 135–38, 143, 174, 183, 201, 209–13, 215, 217–19, 221, 223–25, 228, 231–32, 234
Stoics, 28
Stromata, 199, 204
Subject of Knowledge, 5
Suetonius, 117–18, 163–64, 185–87, 191
Sufism, 26
Sulla, 123–24, 191
Sumer, 134
Sun, 12, 28, 32–33, 38, 44, 48–49, 55, 56, 58–61, 65, 67–69, 74–82, 92, 96–99, 101, 103, 105–7, 109, 117–18, 120, 131–35, 137, 139–42, 144–45, 149–50, 156, 159–60, 164–72, 177–78, 183–84, 192, 206, 218, 224, 227–28, 240–43
Syncellus, 83
Syria, 10, 34, 114, 121, 123, 185, 243
syzygy, 42–43, 49, 61, 120, 192, 208, 211, 217, 225, 228

Tacitus, 153, 155, 164, 184–87, 191
Talmud, 53, 81, 90, 92, 141–43, 160, 164
Tatian, 82, 129
Taurus, 68, 98, 105, 117, 124, 132, 147, 164, 169, 175, 224, 240
Teitan, 6, 65, 119
Tertullian, 2, 3, 4, 9, 11, 15, 32, 36, 50
Tetrabiblos, 97–99, 101, 111, 139–40, 169–70
Tetragrammaton, 33, 220
Thaddeus, 128–29
Thales, 136
Theocritus, 28
Theodoret, 38, 40, 50, 207
Theogony, 31, 156
Theon of Alexandria, 140
Therapeuts, 27, 30, 33–34
Theudas, 43

Thimmes, Pamela L., 26
Thyatira, 2, 24–25, 71, 73, 88, 195, 203
Tiamat, 81, 86, 108, 239
Tiberias, 152
Tiberius, 114, 118, 152–53, 185, 189–90, 206, 231, 241
Tigranes, 113, 121–27, 143, 224, 244
Tigranocerta, 115, 122–24, 127
Timaeus, 31, 80, 138, 209, 215, 227
Tiridates, 113–16, 129, 143, 155, 174, 187, 206, 243
Titus, 10, 152, 187
Trajan, 112, 116, 152–53, 186–87, 243
Trismegistus, 27, 29, 34, 81, 135
Troy, 25
Tyconius, 22
Typhon, 30

Upanishads, 27
Ur, 54–55, 59
Urartu, 121–23, 126

Valentinianism, 43, 61
Valentinus, 6, 38, 41–44, 220
Vardanes, 123
Vatican, 14, 53, 249
Vecchietti, Gerolamo, 52
Venus, 8, 55, 58–59, 67, 82, 92, 96–98, 103, 105, 117–18, 133–34, 140–41, 144, 149–50, 155, 160, 164–67, 171–72, 174, 176–80, 183–84, 189, 206, 212, 224, 228, 239–43

Vespasian, 10–11, 116, 152, 186
Victorinus of Poetovio, 4, 10, 12, 22, 65–68
Virgo, 176, 178, 224
Vitellius, 10, 186, 191
Vitruvius, 82, 84–85
Vohuman, 91–95, 110, 154, 156, 239
Vologases, 112–15, 117–20, 129, 143, 155, 173, 175, 177, 182, 213, 224–25, 228
Vonones, 114, 154

Xerxes, 27, 31

Yaldabaoth, 37, 39

Zand-î Vohûman Yasht, 91–92
Zarathustra, 30, 34, 91–93, 96, 107, 239
Zebedee, 9, 16, 230
Zend Avesta, 92, 104, 129, 229, 239
Zeno of Elea, 135
Zenobia, 154–55
Zenobios, 121, 130
Zenon, 114
zodiac, 37, 44, 54–55, 68, 80, 98, 103, 105–7, 131–35, 141–42, 158, 160–61, 169–70, 208, 210, 218, 225, 239–42
Zohar, 140
Zoroastrianism, 91, 123

www.ingramcontent.com/pod-product-compliance
Lightning Source LLC
Chambersburg PA
CBHW062006220426
43662CB00010B/1245